Bulala

A True Story of South Africa

Bulala Tagati !

(Kill the wizard!)

Cuan Elgin

[Three maps appear at the end of this book, to help the reader understand the geography of the narrative.]

Published by
Cuan Elgin
P.O. Box 156
Ladismith
Western Cape
South Africa
6655
Email: bulala1@post.com

ISBN-10: 1-58840-294-0
ISBN-13: 978-1-58840-294-3

AUTHOR'S PREFACE TO THE READER

My motivation for writing this novel history came as a result of my *initial* writing of a *political* novel about the disturbing current affairs in the "new South Africa." In researching that political novel, I travelled over 25,000 km. [15,500 miles] throughout South Africa and interviewed many Afrikaner farmers (Boers) and ordinary citizens, recording the shocking events as told to me by numerous first-hand witnesses. The material I gathered I wove into a story, which will, as it now turns out, be the *sequel* ("Book 2") to this book which you now hold in your hands. While writing Book 2, I became acutely aware of a need, equally as great, for a "prequel" ("Book 1")—a *historical* novel (which is likewise, based on factual events but woven into a story), which you now read, which covers the *origins* of our great nation. I realized the need for this Book 1 as a result of two important things which caught my attention in my travels and interviews:

Firstly, I noticed that the history of the "old South Africa" was rapidly being "air-brushed" out of our history books and being hid from, or distorted in the minds of our people. The names of towns established by our Trekker forefathers were being changed, and many significant monuments to our past were being vandalized or even removed altogether.

Secondly, I also noticed that an entire generation of young South Africans is now being taught a significantly different version of our history than the one which was taught to me as I was growing up, and that as a result young Afrikaners are largely ignorant of their own, proud history as a distinct people—a *Volk.*

Recognizing that *all peoples* consider the preservation of their history, religion, and culture to be important, I thus decided to write this *historical* novel, to preserve the memory of *our* people and all they endured to establish this, our great nation. I believed that this historical book was important, not only to preserve the heritage and history of our people, but also to "set the stage" for understanding the events which will be revealed in "Book 2." I chose to present these two factual works in the most popular literary form—the novel—to make it interesting and easy to read: entertaining as well as informative.

Confucius said,

"Study the past if you would divine the future."

Thought provokingly, American clergyman H. F. Hedge (1805-1890) said,

"Every man is his own ancestor, and every man is his own heir. He devises his own future, and inherits his own past."

Robert Alan Balaicius [my editor] has also written,

"If one does not know whence he came, he cannot possibly see where to go and guide his children safely there."

However, God Himself first instructed us in His Word:

"...look unto the rock *whence* ye are hewn, and to the hole of the pit *whence* ye are digged." (Isaiah 51:1)

Thus, recognizing the importance of this historical foundation, I threw myself into the researching and writing of Book 1 (which entailed more traveling and interviews), to preserve in our peoples memories those original names and historical events, and to tell therein the story of the old South Africa from a robustly honest perspective, before our heritage is lost altogether and supplanted entirely by a "new" revisionist history.

The history of the Afrikaner stretches back over 350 years; yet we are now, due to the political developments of the past few decades, mistakenly regarded by much of the rest of the world as "newcomers" or even as "foreigners" in this, *the land of our birth* (and the land of the birth of our fathers and our fathers' fathers). People whose parents have settled in any other country of the world, are considered "natives" and "citizens" of those foreign lands in which they are born, after *only one* generation; yet this right has seemingly been "withheld" from the Afrikaners of South Africa—though we have been here for *at least 10 generations*.

Although my mother-tongue is English, I consider myself an *Afrikaner,* a man of Africa, born and bred. However, in my own estimation (based upon my half-century of life-experience), Afrikaners have *rarely* been portrayed in an altogether-honest light; even by many of our cousins abroad. Some in our kindred nations may have been motivated to present this *inaccurate* image, out of genuine concern for the welfare of other, *ethnic* Africans. However, many have also been motivated by less-altruistic reasons: such as the modern, liberal notion of "political correctness" (which is *ever* changing).

This true story of the history of South Africa will also reveal to the reader other, *sinister* motivations behind the desire of some people to "demonize" the Afrikaner. The current rulers of this land that we love, have *also* tampered with our proud Afrikaner history—removing from modern books and periodicals a long list of *our* achievements (or even falsely claiming these accomplishments as their own). They have painted a new, rather distorted picture of our history to serve a sometimes disingenuous (and often hostile) agenda. Some journalists within the liberal (or perhaps misinformed) media of other nations, have believed—without themselves doing any factual research of their own—much of the negative propaganda that has been churned out against the Afrikaner. Thus, many journalists are themselves guilty of unscholarly (or even sometimes dishonest) journalism which has resulted from their unwarranted prejudice against us. *Prejudice* means to "pre-judge" or "judge before considering the evidence" (or to form a judgment after considering the "evidence" from *one* side alone). The unwarranted prejudice against the Afrikaner people is the result of not considering the *historical facts* before drawing such biased opinions and conclusions. The old motto of the scholarly Welsh druidic priests has as much relevance today as it had centuries ago:

Y Gwir yn erbyn Y Byd! ("The Truth Against the World!")

Jesus Christ Himself declared,

"...ye shall know the truth, and the truth shall make you free." (John 8:32)

The early attempts of the Afrikaner people to carve out their own place in the African sun, and the subsequent attempts of their descendents to retain that place—in a land which is often (behind its unrivaled natural beauty) harsh and unforgiving—are often viewed negatively by the rest of the world; even though the methods employed by the Afrikaner people were not unique to world events. At times the Afrikaners felt it necessary to employ *seemingly* heavy-handed methods to preserve what they had given their lives to establish; methods which may be modernly perceived as "politically incorrect." Yet, again, these methods were not unique to world history and have been practiced by many peoples in most nations to preserve their own distinct national identity.

The detailing in this book of such practices in no way is meant to condone or justify what some may consider oppressive measures. However, such practices will be detailed because they are *historical* events. Though the *reasons* behind such actions will be explained, it will be up to the readers to draw their own conclusions. However, the methods employed by the early Afrikaner pioneers were seldom as harsh as those used by the many other African tribes against *each other* (and against the Afrikaners themselves). It also needs to be realized that Africa is *not* a civilized land—and it never has been (though I sincerely pray that it does one day become so). The old adage "drastic times call for drastic measures," has never been more true than when applied to our current topic: the history of South Africa. However, an objective observer would have to admit that the "harsh measures" employed by the Afrikaners at times, pale in comparison to the barbaric measures more frequently and casually employed *against* them—even sometimes by their own, kindred nations. Again, the facts will be presented and it will be up to the readers to draw their own conclusions. Further, the nations of Europe themselves employed many of those same methods against the *other* peoples of Africa, whenever it suited their political or economic agendas; yet the Afrikaner people have been unforgivably vilified for it—in reality, often for only defending themselves (a basic human right).

Although this book is written in novel form, most of the characters are *actual historical figures*, and the vast majority of the events described *actually happened, as depicted.* A few of the main characters and their family members are fictional; although closely based upon, or inspired by real people and real events. Those persons who were factual historical figures will (whenever possible) have their birth and death dates listed (within parentheses) after the first mention of their names.

Having personally visited every town, district, and battlefield described in the following narrative, I can thus also assure the reader that the physical descriptions contained herein are likewise authentic. No part of this narrative is mere *fantasy;* I have done my research with due diligence and integrity. As far as humanly possible, I have tried to present an *accurate* and hopefully objective picture of the past history of our spectacular and beloved country.

I have many friends and associates who are Africans of diverse hues, alongside whom I have lived peacefully and worked harmoniously in my field of management in wildlife and tourism. I now take my hand to being an author and in advance extend my heartfelt apologies to any who may be offended by some of the historical interpretations or the use of terms which may now be considered "politically incorrect." Certain words or descriptions which are used, are placed in *historical context,* to accurately portray what was said in the *common language of the day,* during the time period which those specific chapters cover. I certainly do not use those words carelessly, and it should be noted that I also use historical terms (and expose events and actions) that are sometimes *uncomplimentary to my own, Afrikaner people.* It was not my intention to *re-write* or *romanticize* our Afrikaner history: my purpose was to paint a *true* and *accurate* picture.

I also urge all readers to pursue further study of their own, by reading reliable books which cover the *actual* history of the old South Africa (rather than merely accepting the *repeatedly-revised,* "official," "politically correct" versions presented modernly)—unless one prefers fantasy over reality. Even the godless Friedrich Nietzsche noted,

> "The majority of men prefer delusion to truth. It soothes. It is easy to grasp. Above all, it fits more snugly than the truth into a universe of false appearances..."

Similarly, Leo Tolstoy astutely recognized,

> "Shallow ideas can be assimilated. Ideas that require people to reorganize their picture of the world provoke hostility. I know that most men, including those at ease with problems of the greatest complexity, can seldom accept even the simplest and most obvious truth if it be such as would oblige them to admit the falsity of conclusion which they have delighted in explaining to colleagues, which they proudly taught to others, and which they have woven, thread by thread, into the fabric of their lives."

Only by doing *objective* study from the traditional view, and then *comparing* it to the modern "version" can anyone truly understand the *factual* history of our nation, as well as the *real* reasons behind modern ethnic tensions and stereotypes.

The historian or journalist who deals with issues which may modernly be perceived to be contentious has the choice of stating facts as he found them (sometimes at the risk of offending certain individuals, institutions, or indeed entire classes of people or nations)—or of caving in and taking the "safe" (though inaccurate) "politically correct" route to avoid that risk. In Bulala, the author has placed the facts on the table, in most cases without personal comment, and has thus left it to the reader to draw his or her own moral conclusions. Questionable or even barbaric acts by certain individuals, groups of people, or nations have been recounted to give a truthful picture of history (not a rose-colored, "feel-good" reconstruction). The re-telling of such acts herein should *not* be construed as the author's attempt to denigrate any particular culture or people. Incidents as recorded in this sometimes traumatic historical narrative of South Africa are included purely as observations of historical fact, and can often be seen to be the actions of *isolated individuals* commiting *personal* acts of their own accord and not acting in concert with any official (or unofficial) policy. These individuals' clearly deplorable actions were thus not necessarily representative of the policies of their governments, or indeed of any institutions they purported to represent—and certainly, such actions were not representative of their people as a whole, nor their nation. The mention of such actions, incidents, and facts in this narrative should thus be seen as the author's attempt to provide real insight into the actual causes behind such historical events.

All peoples have representatives who bring disgrace and shame to their very nation or people as a whole; however, there are also others, among all peoples, who behave with laudable honor and integrity, worthy of our respect. It behooves us, then, as honest, God-fearing, law-abiding people, rather than trying to erase the less-admirable aspects of our individual histories, to study our history "as it was." Only by studying and accepting the reality of the past are we able to recognize any questionable actions of our ancestors—and then use that knowledge to rise above their mistakes, and thus not follow in their sometimes faulty footsteps.

Sadly, Winston Churchill keenly observed,

"The history of mankind is the history of war."

Further, the famous Irishman and British statesman, Edmund Burke (1729-1797) declared,

"Those who fail to learn from history are destined to repeat it."

May we all, by looking in the mirror of history, see reality, so that we can consciously choose a *better* reality for ourselves and our children.

Cuan Elgin,

Klein Karoo,

South Africa.

[A list of recommended titles appears at the end of this book.]

Acknowledgments & Dedication:

First and foremost, I wish to dedicate this book to my beloved wife, for her forbearance, as well as for her inspirational enthusiasm, and for her many, colorful contributions to this work (including her original artwork for the cover). I also dedicate it to our children, who are born-and-bred children of Africa, and to our families, many of whom are themselves descended from those hardy Christian pioneers who built this land from a wilderness, into the dynamic country that it is today. I also dedicate this book to the memory of my late father, who instilled in me a love of nature and travel, and to my mother, whose tragic passing left us all sadly bereft of her faith, love and compassion.

I also wish to thank Robert Alan Balaicius, for his boundless patience, dedication and unerring direction in his tenacious editing of this book, for his many valuable contributions to the substance and style of the narrative, and for his technical knowledge and sharp research. Without his involvement (which was essentially a labor of love for the Afrikaner people), this book would not have become what now we believe it to be: an accurate and insightful—and *grippingly interesting*— story of a nation.

To David Taylor of New Zealand, with whom I shared many an African adventure, and to that legendary guide Jimmy Rea, I also extend my deepest appreciation for their friendship, and for being there when it really mattered.

To those innumerable, helpful and supportive people of South Africa who have selflessly contributed of their own valuable time, knowledge and research to the writing of this book, and to those patriots who will hopefully recognize some of their own insights in this narrative, I extend my heartfelt thanks and appreciation. May God bless our beloved land, and all our people.

Cuan Elgin.

Bulala Tagati !

Chapter One

It was the *second* body which the great white shark had eaten that day. Like the first body, it had been wrapped in canvas and splashed into the water just above the shark as it cruised alongside the *caravel* rounding the Cape of Africa. The big shark followed the canvas bag as it sank rapidly in the deep blue water, weighted down by a cannonball wedged between the feet of the dead man. The shark first nudged the shroud with its sensitive snout and then, satisfied that it was edible, bit into the corpse. Blood clouded the clear, cold water as the shark shook the bag, its serrated, arrowhead-shaped teeth tearing off the upper third of the body wrapped inside. Above the waves, the ship continued on its way. The young *padre* closed his Bible, made the sign of the cross, and then returned to the tiny cabin which now served as a sick-bay. In the larger cabin alongside, the captain of the caravel sat down heavily at his desk, dipped his writing-quill in a small pot of black ink, sighed deeply, and carefully drew a line through each of two names on the list of his small crew. Captain Bartolomeu Dias (c.1450-1500) then inscribed the date of death alongside the names: 11 April, *Anno Domini* 1488.

A *Khoi-Khoi* boy named Tipa was crouched expectantly over a fish trap formed by an arrangement of stones in the shallows by the shore. He was poised to lunge with his spear at a fish, when he first spotted a distant, strange object with his keen eyes. It appeared to him like a small white cloud on the blue horizon, but as it steadily grew larger, he saw that this was no cloud, and that it was heading straight towards the bay. He put down his spear, and clambered onto the large rock that formed the furthest point of the stone corral jutting out into the waves. Shading his eyes from the setting sun, he squinted, intrigued by the white speck.

It had been a warm, cloudless day on the southwestern Cape of Africa, and the fishing had been good. The high tide had brought many fish into the bay and now, as the waters receded, numerous fishes were trapped in the shallows, behind Tipa's wall of stones. His ancestors had built that fish-trap long ago—long before even his ancient grandmother could remember—and every year after the winter storms, Tipa's clan repaired it; piling back up any stones the waves may have battered down.

Tipa picked up the looped rawhide cord that he had threaded through the gills of seven silver fish; each one bearing the mark of his slender fishing spear. He had tipped his spear with a smaller fossilized tooth from a massive creature now called *Megalodon;* a possible ancestor of the great white shark that now cruised the outer limits of the bay. Tipa waded through the shallows towards the beach, using the blunt end of the spear to steady himself over the slippery black rocks. Spotting two long feelers protruding from under a crevice, he swiftly plunged his hand into the water, and dragged out a large, spiny red crayfish, to add to his catch.

His old grandmother would be pleased with his haul—as times had been hard since his father was killed by a leopard while hunting the nimble *rock hyraxes* on the slopes of the flat-topped mountain that past winter. Tipa could already visualize the old crone's toothless grin as the watery eyes in her crinkled face focused on the string of fish that he would proudly present to her when he got back to their cave above the beach. She would let him have the juicy crayfish all to himself, no doubt, after she had baked it for him in the hot coals of the small fire smoldering at the entrance to their cave.

She never allowed that fire to go out, and it had been Tipa's task, ever since he was a very small boy, to collect the piles of dry sticks that kept it burning through the long, wet winters. His own grandfather had started that fire by striking sparks from a stone when his clan had first found, and then inhabited the warm, dry cave—after driving out the brown hyena that had lurked there in the shadows. Tipa had seen the pile of cracked seal bones, which the hyena left behind, and he shuddered as he thought of the shambling, shaggy beast that often followed him at a distance, when he walked alone towards their cave at sunset with the day's catch. But there was no sign of the hyena that day and Tipa climbed steadily up the rocky cliff-path, glancing back towards the western horizon each time he came to a good lookout point. The mysterious white speck in the far distance had now grown to the size of his hand, and he could just make out some long, dark shape beneath it.

That night, Tipa sat at the entrance of the sandstone shelter, and watched the waves in the bay as they shimmered in the moonlight, chasing each other towards the silvery wet sands of the shore. The strange, white shape that he had seen that day was now much closer, and appeared to have stopped at the entrance to the bay. To his amazement, fiery lights were now twinkling within its hulking dark form. Amazingly, the white shape itself had *disappeared* and in its place were what Tipa thought were three or four tall, straight trees, growing out of the dark mass and towering into the moonlit night sky. One of the trees appeared to be broken, and thick, tangled cords hung loosely below it. Tipa imagined, but could not be sure, that he saw movements in the dark hulk, briefly blotting out the lights, and then revealing them again. His two adult sisters, mother and grandmother peered fearfully over his slim shoulders at the strange sight. How could fire float on the water, they wondered? If only his uncles had been there, they would surely have known the meaning of this odd apparition. But they were away hunting on the far slopes of the flat-topped mountain and would probably not return for another day or two. Tipa, tired from the day's fishing, eventually curled up near to the smoldering fire, and pulled the sealskin *kaross* [rug] up over his naked, apricot-colored body. He kept his spear close alongside him, and slept fitfully that night.

At sunrise, Tipa bolted awake, and immediately hurried to the entrance of the cave. The strange hulking form was still in the bay, and to his amazement, a smaller part of it had detached itself and was moving steadily away from the greater mass and was drifting across the bay, towards the shore. Now, astonished, he could clearly see that there were two rows of some kind of men sitting—but moving rhythmically—in the small, hollow object which was cutting across the waters. The men were thrashing the water with long, thick, straight sticks which jutted out over the sides, splashing the calm surface of the bay. At the front stood a large man with dark hair all over his face below his bright red hat. The man was much bigger than even Tipa's uncles. He held upright and in front of him a large, wooden pole, with another shorter pole crossed near the top. From this man's waist hung something long and silvery, which glimmered in the sun. Tipa grabbed his spear, and ran swiftly down the rocky path that led to the shore. He glanced back to see the females of his clan huddled together at the entrance to their cave, peering down the slope towards the beach. When he reached the foot of the cliffs, the strange men were already ashore.

Bartolomeu Dias stepped out of the long-boat and watched as two of his men dragged up the beach a large, heavy wooden cross; similar to the smaller one the man in the red hat carried with outstretched arms. The Portuguese sea-captain had not yet noticed the naked boy watching them from the outcrop above, and Dias surveyed the rocky shoreline from where he stood. Above the beach towered a cone-shaped peak, and behind it loomed the vast, flat-topped mountain, with its table-cloth of swirling clouds, which their lookout had spotted at sunset the previous day. Now he knew for sure that they had found the *legendary* table-shaped mountain alluded to in Greek mythology as being at the foot of Africa: the dungeon of the rebellious *Adamaster,* who was imprisoned there by the Titans. Of course, Dias believed not a jot of the pagan legend that attributed the frequent storms at the Cape to Adamaster's frustration at his confinement. Dias named the forested bay *Porto Fragoso* (Portuguese for "Craggy Port"). It would much later, become known as *t'Houten Baiejtjien* or *Houtbaai* (the Dutch, and then the Afrikaans for "Wood Bay").

The hardy Portuguese mariners had been determinedly seeking a sea-route to the East. Dias, a cavalier of the Royal Court and superintendent of the Royal Warehouses had originally been master of the man-of-war, *o São Cristóvão* (the "St. Christopher"). Commissioned by King João II., he and his crew had set sail from Portugal's capital, Lisboa, in August of 1487 with two 50-ton *caravels* and a small supply ship. Bartolomeu captained one caravel; his brother Pêro Dias was in charge of the supply ship; and the captain of the other caravel was João Infante. The supply ship was strategically left *en route* in a bay off the coast of Angola, to safeguard much-needed provisions for their return journey.

After spending many trying months navigating their way cautiously down the west coast of Africa, they had sailed bravely on after being driven far south and out to sea by a storm wind. Dias noted, with some surprise, that his ship's compass was now pointing due north—and straight at an unknown headland. He soon realized that they had indeed already successfully rounded the feared and fabled *Cabo das Tormentas* ("the Cape of Storms"), at the south-western tip of the vast African continent, and were thus now heading up the *east* coast of southern Africa. He named the next, more southerly but less-prominent headland *Cabo Agulhas* ("Cape Compass"). Dias consulted a chart which was redrawn by the Jewish mapmakers on the island of Majorca, from one made 50 years earlier by Chinese admiral Zheng He (1371-1433). The chart indicated that if they continued on that same course north-east, they would eventually reach India. In doing so, they would finally prove to the western world that there was indeed a sea-route from Europe to the unimaginable riches of the "Spice Islands" of the East Indies—and to the Far East and China itself.

The lookout had then sighted a band of cattle herders[1] near the mouth of a river, the first human inhabitants of this new land they had seen. Dias would have liked to have taken the opportunity to trade for fresh meat, but his tired, scurvy-stricken crew were longing for home after many months at sea, and the rumblings of discontent below deck were growing ever louder and more ominous. He had also been ordered by his king to follow the advice of his senior crewmen, if uncertain. So Dias landed only briefly for fresh water on a beach he called *Aguada de São Brás* ("Waters of St. Blaise"); it was later, renamed,

---

[1] For this reason, it was also called *Baía dos Vaqueiros* ("Cattle-herder Bay").

Mosselbaai, by the Dutch (*Baía dos Mexilhões*, in Portuguese), due to the great abundance of mollusks there. While at *Aguada de São Brás* a group of naked locals, called *Khoi-Khoi,*[2] suddenly appeared, and unprovoked, began hurling spears and rocks at the landing party. This assault ended when one of the natives was shot dead by a bolt from a Portuguese crossbowman; after which the Khoi-Khoi fled. Dias then decided to turn back and head home to Portugal, to avoid a possible mutiny. Dias had, in any case, proved that the feared *Cape of Storms* could indeed be successfully rounded and the long-imagined sea-route to the East now lay open to further exploration. Dias dubbed the area, *Cabo das Tormentas* ("Cape of Storms"); but King João II. of Portugal himself later renamed it *Cabo da Boa Esperança* ("Cape of Good Hope"); which was later called the same in Dutch: *Kaap de Goede Hoop.*

On his passage back around the rugged south-western Cape peninsula, two of his crew had died of scurvy, and were sewn within spare pieces of canvas sail and buried at sea. Then a sudden, gusting head-wind had damaged one of his caravel's masts. Bartolomeu Dias thus decided to drop anchor in a deep bay lined with many tall trees growing on the lower slopes of the shore. He landed there to fell a suitable tree to repair the mast, and judiciously add to his precious supply of fresh water, while waiting for the second caravel to catch up with his own ship. Then they would begin the long haul up the west coast of Africa, back home to Portugal. This was the reason that the Portuguese had landed on the shore which Tipa knew as home.

Tipa crouched behind a large boulder, fearfully watching the strange men on the beach below. They began digging a deep hole in the dry sand, and soon, they had erected the large, wooden "crossed pole" and packed stones around it to hold it upright. Then

---

[2] —or simply as *Khoi*. The Dutch called them *Hottentots* (or *Hotnots*) in imitation of their clicking speech. *Khoi-Khoi,* the name by which they called themselves, means, "men of men;" a name they chose to distinguish themselves from a similar tribe (to whom they considered themselves superior): the *Khoi-San,* "men who have nothing." The Dutch called the *Khoi-San, Boesmans* ("Bushmen")—and many still refer to themselves by this name.

the men did another *strange* thing. They all removed their head-gear, and knelt in the sand at the foot of this "cross," with their heads bowed. The boy could clearly hear the large man—who looked to be their leader—speaking some solemn words in a strange tongue. Just then, Tipa's bare foot dislodged a few stones, which tumbled down the cliff-face, alerting the Portuguese to his presence. They immediately sprang to their feet, and two of them ran towards his hidden position, holding their strange weapons at the ready. Tipa stepped cautiously out from behind the boulder, and raised his right hand in greeting. The two pale, hairy-faced men stopped transfixed, staring back at him; their bushy black eyebrows raised in astonishment. Then, they both burst out laughing, and in their deep voices, shouted to their companions, obviously urging them to come forward and see what they had found. Their leader drew the long, sharp, shiny object from his waist, and advanced towards Tipa, pointing it menacingly at him, and indicating that he should put down his spear. The naked boy let the shaft fall from his left hand, and stood uncertainly, with his right arm still raised. The big man with the red hat then approached the boy, and held out his hand to him. Shyly, Tipa placed his small, copper-colored hand in that of the big, pale stranger from the sea.

The hunting-party of six adult male *Khoi-Khoi* were making their way back down the slopes of the cone-shaped mountain, scouting for game as they went, when they first spotted the strange object anchored in the bay. From the heights, they also noticed a second, similar strange apparition in full sail on the horizon, heading for the bay. They broke into a steady trot, the carcasses of the fat, rabbit-like *dassie hyraxes* swinging rhythmically from the long wooden sticks to which they were tied (each stick being carried upon the shoulders of two men). Their fragile, primitive bows were slung on their backs by their rawhide strings, along with the tiny bone-tipped arrows which rattled in their wooden quivers. The men, though full grown, stood less than 5-feet tall, and their smooth, apricot-hued bodies carried little excess fat, other than on their naked, protruding buttocks. Their small, heart-shaped faces, crinkled and leathery, made them appear much older than they actually were, their eyes appeared almost Oriental, and their hair, which consisted of peppercorn-like curls, widely dispersed on their scalps, was virtually the only hair on their slim bodies (other than a few, twisted wisps on the chins of two of the older men).

Soon, they were approaching the bay, and saw the long-boat pulled up on the beach, with about a dozen strangely, colorfully clothed, pale-skinned, hairy-faced men standing with the tiny figure of Tipa. These big men appeared to be carrying weapons, but their obvious leader, wearing a soft red hat trimmed with gold, was holding the boy by the hand. In his other hand, the leader was carrying a long, sharply pointed silver object, which glinted in the bright sunlight. It was the Cape peninsula Khoi-Khoi's very first sight of both a European and his steel sword. The small band of Stone-age hunter-gatherers carefully placed the carcasses of their kill on some rocks, and then warily approached the group of mariners. Two of the hunters carried wooden spears, the points of which had been blackened and hardened by fire. They chattered excitedly among themselves; their *sing-song* language full of sharp click-exclamations, and bird-like whistles. It was an expressive tongue born of the primeval wilderness, and it imitated many of the natural sounds the natives heard all around them. Realizing that these strangers from the sea intended no harm, they put down their spears.

The Portuguese explorers gazed at the small band of semi-naked hunters before them and noticed that these Khoi-Khoi were even more primitive-looking than the herders they had encountered on the east coast. They noted with some amusement that the males of this peculiar tribe tied their long, thin penises upright by a rawhide cord, then fastening the cord around their waists like a belt. Although the Portuguese mariners themselves were not a tall people, the stockiest of them still stood more than a head above the tallest of the tiny beach-combers. The Khoi-Khoi noted that these strange men were broad and muscular, and that their arms and faces, though pale, bore luxuriant amounts of wavy, dark hair. One of the marines went back to the long-boat, and brought forth a sack of trinkets which Dias proceeded to hand out to the hunters. Among the various shiny metal items were a few small, steel knives with bone handles. The little Stone-age hunters were initially shocked, but then delighted to find that the keen edges easily drew blood through the calloused skin on their hands upon which they tested the blades.

Dias selected one small, odd particular item which he pressed into Tipa's palm. It was a tiny, black crucifix with a silver image of Christ affixed to it. The mariner could not, of course, explain the true meaning of the emblem to the boy; but he did his best by pointing to the sky with an enraptured expression on his face. He then spread his arms wide, and dropped to his knees in the sand with his head bowed, and his hands clasped in supplication. Tipa seemed to understand, and immediately recognized that it was a miniature version of the large, wooden cross which Dias' men had erected on the beach, and that there was some spiritual significance to the gift; as it obviously had no practical function. As an after-thought, the leader of these pale men motioned to one of the older hunters to cut a short length of rawhide from the thong proudly holding up his appendage. Dias then threaded the crucifix onto it, knotted the ends, and slipped it over Tipa's neck. The significance of that act may well have been lost on the primitive hunters, but it was certainly not lost on the devout Catholic mariners.

Eventually, Dias noticed the second caravel sailing into the bay to anchor alongside his own ship. He immediately dispensed with the pleasantries, and brusquely ordered his men to climb the dunes with some axes and the wooden barrels that they had brought ashore. Soon, they were joined by about another dozen men who had rowed their long-boat ashore from the newly arrived ship, and after a round of greetings and handshakes, they also set off after the first group towards the cliffs. The metallic sound of iron axes chopping down a tall, straight hardwood tree rang out across the bay, and the mariners then skillfully stripped the bark and branches off the trunk, before attaching it to one of the boats with a rope and then towing it out to the first caravel, to repair the damaged mast. Other sailors filled the barrels with fresh water from one of the little streams tumbling down the face of the cliff, and transported the barrels back to the anchored ships. The *Khoi* sat transfixed, watching these odd, but industrious mariners for most of that day. They grilled a few of the rock-rabbits, and then offered some of the cooked meat to Bartolomeu Dias. He tasted it, and proclaimed it good, rather like mutton, and soon the party had been joined by Tipa's equally naked female relatives; who brought fresh crayfish, and unashamedly sat cross-legged in front of these pale, hairy strangers from the sea. One of the sailors pointed out to Dias that the *genitalia* of the women protruded and hung in a curious, elongated fashion. The sailors also noted that both the women and the men had very pronounced, protruding buttocks— a form of *steatopygia*—and that was where, apparently, their bodies naturally stored most of their body-fat.

As the sun began to set over the western ocean the Portuguese mariners indicated that they were about to row back to their ships and set sail. Tipa, on a sudden impulse, ran up to his cave in the cliffs, and then hurried back down to the beach and handed Bartolomeu Dias a rawhide thong from which dangled a tiny carved seal. Tipa's father had fashioned the ornament from a whale-tooth, while sitting in their rock shelter during a long, wet winter. It had taken him several days to crudely fashion. He had carefully rubbed the hard tooth on the edge of a rock, until it had taken on the streamlined shape of a Cape fur-seal. Then, he painstakingly drilled a hole through the "tail-end" of the figurine, by spinning a thin, stone-tipped stick between the palms of his hands. This necklace had been recovered from the remains of his body after he was killed by one of the leopards which lurked in the ravines of the flat-topped mountain. These leopards competed with the natives for the tasty *dassies*. The hunter who found the necklace presented it to Tipa, who treasured it as a memento of his late father. However, now Tipa considered his prized necklace as an appropriate exchange for the crucifix which Dias had given him. The explorer smiled and slid the thong over his own neck, before climbing into the long-boat, and then waved farewell to the little band of Stone-age hunter-gatherers. The Khoi-Khoi stood watching the mysterious strangers depart. The black silhouette of the wooden cross the mariners had erected on the beach contrasted starkly against the white dunes above. Soon, the great white sails were unfurled, and the two caravels slipped gracefully over the distant horizon whence they had come.

Nine years later, Tipa had grown into a fine young hunter, had a wife of his own, and was already the leader of his small clan; but he never forgot that visit by those pale strangers from the sea. In all, Bartolomeu Dias erected 3 stone *padrões* ("monuments") along the southern African coast: all proclaiming in chiseled letters that the land thereabouts was now part of the Christian domain of the Portuguese king, João II. But he planted only two *wooden crosses*, including the one at the unscheduled landing in Tipa's bay; where they made an emergency stop to cut wood to repair the damaged mast.

Years later that rugged wooden cross still stood below the dune on the beach beneath the cliffs. Tipa had actually made a habit of kneeling in front of it at sunset, with his arms outstretched towards the western horizon; as he had seen the Portuguese mariner do when he was yet a boy. The miniature crucifix still hung around his neck, where it had been since the day it was placed there by Bartolomeu Dias. Tipa longed for the big, pale men to return, and would often sit on top of the cliffs above the cave, looking out to sea, sometimes imagining that a small cloud on the horizon was the sail of a ship. But they never landed on his beach again. Once, many long summers after those pale men had visited his bay, Tipa saw in the distance a small group of sailing ships which looked similar to (but larger than) the caravels that had visited his shore almost a decade earlier—but those far away ships had sailed on by, heading south; seeming not to see the smoky signal-fire, which Tipa had hurriedly lit, in hopes of attracting their attention.

That later flotilla of caravels, which Tipa saw, was commanded by the uncompromising Portuguese explorer Vasco da Gama (c.1460-1524), who in the summer of 1497 himself had rounded the *Cabo da Boa Esperança*. A "no-nonsense" disciplinarian, he had informed his hand-picked crew that they would open the sea-route to the East—or *die* in the attempt. His navigator was Bartolomeu Dias. Da Gama also made a landing—erecting a *stone* cross—at what he named *St. Helena* on the west coast. Da Gama then sailed on around the Cape up to *Mossel Bay* on the east coast, where they landed for fresh water. Fortunately, this time, there were no altercations between the Portuguese and the local Khoi-Khoi herders. On Christmas day of that year, the little fleet was positioned somewhat further north up the verdant east coast, and in honor of the commemoration of Jesus Christ's birth, da Gama named that lush land *NATAL* (meaning, "Christmas"). Da Gama's flotilla finally made it all the way to India; assisted by a chance meeting with Arab pilot Ibn Majid (an expert in celestial navigation), and guidance from Jewish navigators at Malindi on the east Africa coast. Da Gama and his crew returned home to a *hero's welcome;* their ships laden with precious spices.

Sadly, on yet another voyage around the Cape, Dias' caravel was sunk by a fierce storm. The great white shark which habitually followed the sailing ships was no doubt in attendance on that occasion too; but it is not truly known what happened to that kindly explorer's body... lost at sea.

Tipa the cave-dweller soon had a son of his own and would regale the boy with the tale of the mysterious pale, hairy-faced men, with their fine clothes, who had chopped down a tree with iron axes to repair their ship. He would take his little boy to the foot of the cross planted on the beach, and show him how the big, bearded mariner had knelt in the sand with his arms outstretched. Then he would show his son the miniature crucifix around his neck, and promise him that one day, it would be his— and if the mariners ever returned, they would recognize it as having come from one of their own; and they would treat him well. The stump of the felled tree still stood above the beach, another reminder of the visit by those strange men from the sea. Father and son would sit side-by-side on the old stump while Tipa puffed away at his horn tube containing the hemp-like weed, *Wilde dagga* (of the mint family) which served as a mild euphoric—and he would imagine that he could again hear the ringing of iron axes across the bay as they sang against the tree.

Chapter Two

For the next 150 years, life at the southern Cape of Africa remained much as it had over the previous several thousand years. Tipa's clan descendants lived in their cave above the bay, harvested the fish trapped by the tides behind the stone wall, hunted dassies on the slopes of the flat-topped mountain, collected shellfish, and gathered what plants, roots, berries and herbs they could find in the *fynbos* (Cape flowering shrub) veld around the rugged peninsula. For the roots and berries, they had to compete with the fierce baboons, which lived in the ravines; creatures with fangs longer and sharper than those of the leopard, which had killed Tipa's father. Both the baboons and the leopards were occasionally even bold enough to snatch a child from the entrance to their cave. The baboons would curiously examine the infant, usually without harming it; but the leopard would ravenously consume the child at the first opportunity. When a fat fur-seal washed up on the white sands of the bay, dead or mortally wounded by the great white sharks, which cruised the deeper blue waters, the *Khoi* had to hurry down the cliffs to claim their succulent prize, before the shaggy brown hyena—the *strandwolf* ("beach-wolf")—scented it, and claimed it first. Sometimes, the whole clan would rush down to the beach after spotting the dark shape of a dying seal, only to be driven back in terror by the thunderous roars of a solitary, dark-maned Cape lion, whose coloring had enabled him to escape detection until the cave-dwellers were almost upon him.

The weathered wooden cross now stood askew below the cliffs, and the crumbling stump of the tree, which the mariners had felled, remained as the only signs that the pale men from the sea had once, briefly, set foot in Tipa's bay. Occasionally, a sailing ship or two would be seen passing by, rounding the Cape on the long journey from Europe to the Far East, and then back again, heavily laden with exotic spices and luxuries; which the merchants of Portugal, Holland, France and England would then sell to the courts and wealthy households of Europe. Once or twice, the mariners landed in what is now *Tafelbaai* ("Table Bay") itself, on the far side of the flat-topped mountain. They would make such, brief visits in order to obtain water or to trade for fresh meat (having grown weary of the pungent flesh of the penguins or the oily meat of the seals, which they managed to hunt on *Robben Eiland*—"Seal Island"). Mostly, those meetings between the mariners and the *Khoi* were peaceful and profitable to both sides, but occasionally, violence broke out whenever some young Khoi would try to make a name for himself by spearing one of the strangers from the sea, and robbing them of their trade-goods, cloth and hardware.

One such incident occurred in 1503, when Antonio de Saldanha (a Portuguese merchant) anchored in Table Bay, to take on fresh water. He actually climbed what is now *Tafelberg* ("Table Mountain"); becoming the first European to do so. The Khoi-Khoi herded a cow and a sheep towards him, as if desiring to barter with them—but then the Khoi ambushed the sailors, wounding Saldanha. For a while, the whole area was known as *Aguada de Saldanha* (the "watering place of Saldanha"). Subsequently, a smaller bay further up the west coast was named after him, but for many years the Cape itself was known in Europe as *Saldania,* and the Khoi-Khoi as *Saldanhars* or *Saldanhamen.*

Another violent clash took place in 1510, when Dom Francisco de Almeida (Viceroy and Governor of the Portuguese State in India) went ashore in the same general location. He apparently angered the Khoi-Khoi because he approached one of their settlements uninvited. Some of his marines were injured in a skirmish. In retaliation about 100 of his men returned and took some cattle and a few children as hostages. However, the Portuguese found themselves suddenly surrounded by a large herd of cattle, driven by the Khoi—who then threw fire-hardened, wooden spears at them from behind this moving (and mooing) "defensive wall." The marines had neglected to wear armor, and carried only swords, so they could not effectively defend themselves, and de Almeida and 58 of his men were killed by being speared, or trampled by the cattle. Thereafter, the Portuguese largely avoided the Cape.

However, the wild seas and treacherous currents off the southern African coast ensured that there were more than a few "unscheduled landings"—many ships were wrecked there, and tales of the death or survival of their unfortunate crews and passengers are myriad.

The *St. João* (St. John) came to grief in 1552 off the Pondoland coast, and about 100 drowned. The 440 survivors (including several prominent Portuguese citizens), many of whom had been badly injured on the rocks, made their way on foot northwards, hoping to complete the 500-mile trek to a Portuguese enclave on the east coast. This pitiable traveling group left, along their solemn route, a scattered trail of dying people (the old, the weak, and injured) and discarded possessions (which some had valiantly embraced until they grew too weary to carry them any longer). Some of the wealthier passengers persuaded sailors to carry them in hammocks, paying them with jewelry and gold coins. However, after the sailors themselves became more heavily laden with their payment in valuables, while the nobles themselves became "lighter," the unscrupulous sailors (having been paid-in-full) abandoned their wealthy patrons to their own fate! Thus, these outraged well-to-do Portuguese had to walk like everyone else, if they were able, or die a slow and lonely death.

The survivors finally reached the north-east coast, and to their surprise were welcomed by a Tsonga[3] chief, Nyaka (or *Inhaca*). They subsequently used their firearms to help this friendly chief to defeat a band of "rebellious *kaffirs*," as the Portuguese referred to them. However, the only Portuguese vessel in the vicinity had already left, so they plodded on, and were then attacked and overwhelmed by a horde of savage blacks, who robbed them of all their remaining belongings. The captain of the ill-fated *St. João*, a Portuguese nobleman, was forced to watch as his wife and two daughters were stripped naked and violated. The 3 abused females died, and the poor captain subsequently went mad. Eventually, a remnant of just 8 passengers and a few

---

[3] A *Nguni* offshoot who were later known as *Shangaans,* but who have since reverted back to the name *Tsonga*.

slaves was rescued by a Portuguese ship, almost 1000 miles from the scene of their initial disaster!

Just two years later, the *St. Bento* was wrecked, and 150 passengers drowned. Those 99 Portuguese and 224 slaves who *did* reach the shore fashioned shelters from the many silks and carpets that had washed up. Incredibly, one of those survivors, Manuel de Castro, had survived the *previous* shipwreck of the *St. João* and the subsequent, disastrous trek to Mozambique! After his eventual rescue, he had been picked up by the Portuguese merchant ship *en route* to India. He had then, at long last, been safely on his way home to Portugal aboard the *St. Bento*, when it too sank. The survivors suffered greatly during their attempt to reach the Portuguese settlement of Mozambique; fighting among themselves over tiny scraps of food, and even resorting to eating their leather sandals. A total of 56 Portuguese and just 6 slaves finally reached Delagoa Bay, and relative safety.

A full century after Bartolomeu Dias had landed briefly, at Tipa's bay on the west coast, another Portuguese ship, the heavily laden *Santo Alberto* struck rocks near what is now known as "Hole in the Wall"—an unusual outcrop on the eastern "Wild Coast" (a magnificently scenic tract of land which would later become the Xhosa tribal homeland). Although a vast treasure and 28 Portuguese and 35 slaves went to the sea-bottom, 125 passengers (of which 2 were female), 160 slaves and much of the wreckage, including firearms and goods that would be useful for trade, washed up on the shore in good condition. Their captain, (who had managed to salvage an astrolabe) confident in his own abilities and those of his disciplined and competent crew, now made the bold decision to head *inland* to seek a route to Mozambique. Using as interpreters those slaves who could speak both Portuguese and the local Nguni languages which they would encounter as they came into contact with various tribes, this resolute group was able to discourage any attacks against them, by either man or beast. The captain kept a detailed diary of their adventures and their explorations of the midlands of NATAL, and these men were undoubtedly the first Europeans to see the snows on the mighty peaks of what would come to be

called the *Drakensberg* ("Dragon Mountains"). They successfully hunted game, and caught fish in the streams, and thus lived
quite well. Although a few Portuguese and most of the slaves
elected to settle with friendly tribes *en route,* the rest completed
their 1000-mile trek to Mozambique in 88 days, without further
mishap. To their delight, they found a vessel about to set sail, and
thus concluded a remarkable journey home to Portugal.

In 1607, an English ship named *Consent* found itself becalmed
in the same wooded bay where Bartolomeu Dias had landed over
a century earlier. A young officer named Chapman was sent
ashore to explore the slopes around the bay, but when he had not
returned after a few days, the ship unfurled its sails in readiness
to leave, assuming that he had come to grief. However, their
lookout then spotted a tiny figure frantically waving his shirt on the
peak of the cone-shaped mountain. It was Chapman, who subsequently rejoined his ship in the *nick of time*: the bay was thereafter
known to the English as *Chapmans Chance,* this becoming the
first English place-name on the African subcontinent.

Tipa's cave-dwelling clan descendants had little further
contact with the strange, usually friendly, pale visitors, and
seldom even with the other peoples inhabiting the Cape. They
had no real reason for interaction and little to offer in terms of
trade. They lived much as they had for thousands of years;
content in their simplicity. Other Khoi-Khoi tribes, nomadic
cousins to Tipa's own beach-combing race, who possessed long-
horned cattle and fat-tailed sheep and lived in portable hide
"tents," seldom braved the rugged slopes of the peninsula,
preferring to graze their livestock on the well-watered pastures
of the nearby Cape flats.

The tiny *San Bushmen* (or *Khoi-San),* with their deadly poi-
son-tipped arrows, hunted the vast herds of plains-game on the
veld of the drier interior. They painted evocative and inspirational hunting-scenes in their caves, and even contrived some
moving poetry in their sing-song, clicking language. They settled
disputes among themselves with tension-releasing laughter; sharing all their meager possessions. However, they occasionally
clashed with the somewhat taller, more advanced, but similar-

looking Khoi-Khoi herders. The San Bushmen considered the domesticated livestock of the Khoi-Khoi herders as "fair game"— and since it was simply more easily "hunted," they freely helped themselves to it.

Warlike, Nguni-speaking Negroid tribes were slowly migrating southwards: ever southwards from west, central and east Africa. Having learned iron-working from the skillful Arab traders of ivory, gold and slaves, these *Bantu* possessed better weapons than the original inhabitants of southern Africa, the initial *Khoi-San* and subsequent *Khoi-Khoi* tribes. The Bantu were also taller and darker, as well as more muscular and robust than either of those aboriginal tribes. The *Bantu*, like the Khoi, brought cattle, sheep, goats and dogs along with them. However, they had yet to discover the wheel and had no written language. They lived in crude grass-and-mud huts. The Bantu hunted game and gathered veld vegetables and herbs; but they also grew a few crops when they settled long enough at any particular, suitably fertile location.

The Bantu did not remain long in any particular region, but soon again moved on, ever southwards, in their quest for new, and greener pastures. They regularly preyed upon any weaker neighbors, stealing their crops and herds, enslaving their womenfolk, and killing off the men. But unbeknown to these warlike, wandering black herders and unbeknown to the primitive beach-combing *Strandlopers* ("beach-walkers")—the *Khoi-Khoi Hottentots* of the coastal regions, *or* the tiny *Khoi-San Bushmen* of the vast southern African interior—a grand plan for this region was being hatched half-way around the world. The headquarters of the DUTCH EAST INDIA COMPANY in Amsterdam deigned to establish a refreshment and ship re-supply station on the slopes of Table Mountain, as a mid-way point to their operations in Indonesia.

The *Heeren XVII.,*—the "Seventeen Lords" who formed the hierarchy of the prosperous V.O.C. *(Vereenigde Oostindische Compagnie*—the "UNITED EAST-INDIA COMPANY"), determined that Johan Anthoniszoon van Riebeeck (1619-1677) was the right man for the job. Born in Culemborg in the Netherlands, son of a ship's doctor, Jan van Riebeeck had himself qualified, and then worked as a ship's surgeon for the V.O.C. He was later transferred to their eastern realms in Indonesian *Batavia;* where he operated as an administrator, displaying distinct talent. He soon had done rather well for himself; too well, some thought, for a Dutch company man. Van Riebeeck had been aboard a fleet that rescued the crew of the *Haerlem,* which had run aground at the Cape in 1647. The 58 crew of this vessel had established a wood-and-sand fort to protect themselves and their valuable cargo, and while awaiting rescue explored, hunted and traded with the locals. It was on the basis of their report of 1649, that a decision was made to establish a half-way refreshment station in that area.

Van Riebeeck was an intelligent, industrious man with an inquiring mind. He also had an abiding interest in botany. Although he did not relish the difficult prospect of having to establish fresh-produce gardens and orchards from scratch on the then-inhospitable Cape peninsula (and trade for cattle and sheep with the Khoi herders who pastured their livestock nearby), the thought of investigating the incredibly diverse floral kingdom of the Cape, did hold some appeal for him. Aboard the southbound *Dromedaris,* he took with him his wife Maria (*née* De la Quellerie or Quevellerius, of French Huguenot extraction) and their son. This talented man would in time, become known as the "Father of South Africa" and a handsome portrait, reputed to be of him, would one day grace bank notes.

His first *official* task, when he landed in Table Bay in 1652 was to build a jetty and a fort to protect the Company's interests against a perceived threat from the Khoi. Van Riebeeck's first attempt at such a fortification was only moderately successful, to say the least. The earth-walled fort was subject to the ravages of ocean waves driven by the stormy winds of the wet winters, and life within its damp, crumbling embankments was rather miserable. Not one to be easily deterred, van Riebeeck then established a quarrying operation and soon enough a substantial, 5-pointed, star-shaped, stone fort (complete with moat) began to rise where once, only *Strandlopers,* Khoi herders and wild animals had roamed. From the rugged slopes of the flat-topped mountain towering above, the descendants of Tipa the cave-dweller watched the industrious strangers in awe and wonder.

Though the station was established as a mercantile operation for profit, one of the *first things* van Riebeeck did was to establish the *Calvinistic* Dutch Reformed Church in South Africa. Rev. Johannes Van Arckel was the first Dutch Reformed pastor to arrive, 13 years later, in *Kaapstad* (Cape Town). Some of the earliest members of that little congregation were converted and baptized Jews. Van Riebeeck also instituted legislation providing for the welfare of the fauna and flora in the area, issuing a proclamation in 1657 that all birds and game were protected, and may not be shot. A year later, a second *placaat* ("legal notice") was issued to stop the random felling of trees, and yet another proclaiming that legally harvested ivory, horns and feathers may only be sold directly to the Company. Further, no farmer was allowed to shoot more than one *renoster* ("rhinoceros"), *seekoei* ("hippopotamus" or literally "sea-cow"), eland, or hartebeest antelope per year, to feed his family.

On a rainy day in 1659, chosen because the wet weather would make the matchlock muskets of the Dutch even less reliable than usual, a major Khoi-Khoi clan led by its chief Doman, launched a series of raids on the new, outlying farms. Doman had been nurtured by the Dutch, who had even sent him for a time, across the seas to Batavia, to be schooled in the Dutch language, and to learn something of their culture. On his return, Doman held a monopoly on Khoi-Khoi trade with the Dutch, preventing any other clans from even getting close to the settlement. But as the reality of the Dutch enclave and its continued expansion finally dawned on him, Doman decided to try and *drive the whites back into the sea.* He would taunt Eva (originally called *Krotoa),* the loyal Khoi servant of Maria van Riebeeck, saying: "See! There comes Krotoa, the advocate of the Dutch! She will tell her own people stories and lies, and in the end, betray them all!" Eva who was taught the Christian religion, had also become fluent in Dutch, and acted as an interpreter to the locals.

These concerted raids by Doman's clan briefly forced the settlers to move back closer to the protection of the fort, but Dutch military retribution soon restored the peace. A truce between Khoi and European was then established, and a fast-growing almond hedge was planted around the settlement to stop the movement of stolen cattle. Remnants of this spiky hedge survive to this day. Doman eventually died in 1663, and the Company diarist recorded: *"For his death, none of us will have cause to grieve, as he had been, in many respects, a mischievous man towards the Company."*

Thereafter, the various Khoi clans seemed content to raid *each other's* cattle herds; but before long, the natives again began stealing the settlers' crops and livestock. A new series of indecisive battles and numerous skirmishes ensued, until the Dutch imported horses; which then gave them the mobility to thoroughly rout the more aggressive Khoi clans. These Khoi, being repelled, mostly fled to the mountains; eventually giving rise to the term *Bergies* ("mountain-dwelling vagrants"). Those other Khoi clans which had maintained good relations with the settlers now prospered in the absence of Doman's monopoly. They traded meat for cloth and hardware, and copper for iron. Once the peace was again restored, expansion of the settlement accelerated, and white possession of the Cape peninsula became apparently irreversible.

Van Riebeeck stood on the windy battlements of the stone castle, his wife alongside him, looking out over the growing town at the foot of Table Mountain. "What do you think, Maria?" he asked. "Is this God-forsaken place starting to look at least a little bit more civilized to you?" he inquired hopefully.

She frowned, and wrinkled her nose in distaste, surveying the carts of fly-covered hippo-meat being drawn by oxen to the gates of the castle. After 10 years of toil, van Riebeeck and his modest band of Company employees had achieved only moderate success. Vegetable gardens and orchards, irrigated by the streams that tumbled down the mountain, had been laid out and established. A small town, *Kaapstad* ("Cape Town"), of less than 300 inhabitants had sprung up at the foot of the great, flat-topped mountain, the *Tafelberg,* ("Table Mountain"). The settlement consisted mainly of artisans, farmers, soldiers and sailors—all either employed by the Company, or dependent upon it. But they still struggled to meet the growing demand for fresh produce required by the many passing ships.

"The indigenous inhabitants of this Cape are not willing to bend their backs in paid labor, Jan," Maria responded. "The Seventeen Lords sitting in their plush boardroom in Amsterdam are still not satisfied with the progress. You must submit a request for more Eastern slaves to be imported. They are at least *capable of being trained* as artisans." Maria turned and walked away back towards their quarters, followed by her personal Khoi servant Eva. The Company *had forbidden* the Dutch at the Cape to enslave any of the indigenous inhabitants, and the black slaves brought there *by the Portuguese* traders from the African east and west coasts though considered robust, were also considered unintelligent. Maria looked up at the table-cloth of clouds swirling above the mountain, and sighed. Three times had her husband requested a transfer after his initial 5-year posting had expired, but each time it had been refused—progress was still too slow, and Jan van Riebeeck was ordered to stay on for another few years.

So *Javanese* slaves from Batavia, Indians and Malays began to be imported. The recruitment of officials, soldiers, tradesmen and minor Company functionaries in Europe brought Swiss, German, Scandinavian, French and Flemish peoples to the peninsula and the population of *Kaapstad* slowly grew. However, the Dutch authorities had no interest in "colonizing" the Cape; but keeping it their private "plantation." Their employees were obliged to work for the Company—and for them alone. What anyone built, they built *for the Company.* What anyone grew supplied *the Company's* stores and ships—and at prices *set by the Company.* As a means of escaping from the overpowering and all-pervasive economic control of tight-fisted Dutch corporate governance, many white citizens volunteered to work as laborers on the expanding farms. These "indentured servants" after having worked an *undefined* "period of time"—arbitrarily determined by the all-powerful Governor—were granted the privilege of becoming "free-burghers." Thus were the first *free* "white African" citizens born.

{Around this same time in history, in 1664, Pieter Stuyvesant (c.1612-1672) served as the last colonial Dutch Governor/Director General of New Amsterdam (1614-1664) in New Netherlands (1614-1674). This later became New York and the area further north became New England; after the British drove the Dutch out of the Americas.}

By 1660, there were only about 10 dozen such "free" white citizens. By 1745, only about 1000 white Africans had been born, and there was no influx of European settlers for almost another century, until the British encouraged immigration to the embattled eastern Cape frontier between 1820-50. By comparison, during this same period, *a few million* Europeans had been encouraged to settle in the Americas, and just a few decades later, more than *a hundred thousand* had made their way to Australia (some involuntarily, of course, being convicts), and then eventually to New Zealand. Thus, the DUTCH EAST INDIA COMPANY was actually an *impediment* to the "colonization" of Southern Africa; rather than an encouragement. This dearth of any significant early Dutch settlement would later, in hindsight, come back to haunt this slowly growing "white tribe" in a future South Africa.

Some of the very first Dutch settlers—among whom was a shortage of eligible European women—took Khoi or slave wives, but this practice was soon *outlawed* (as early as 1685), as were inter-racial sexual relations. A white man who *consorted* with a slave was flogged, and a white woman who did so, was jailed. As the number of imported slaves grew, so too did the number of escapees. These escaped slaves usually fled to the then-inaccessible surrounding mountain ranges, and were largely assimilated into Khoi clans. Thus was born one segment of the so-called "colored" (or "mixed") South African peoples.

Punishment for escaping, stealing from, or assault upon their white employers was severe and harshly dispensed at the imposing Cape castle. Equally, bad treatment of slaves by their white owners was also severely punished, one incident even resulting in a slave owner being *hanged* for beating a slave, who subsequently died. A little-known fact is that these slaves were able to *earn their freedom* (at age 25 for the men and age 22 for the women). Their freedom could be *purchased* with wages they earned by being "leased out" as tradesmen or seamstresses to neighbors—or by simply "converting" to Christianity.[4] Escape however, still remained a more attractive proposition for many of them. Slaves who worked as domestic servants were generally well treated, becoming virtually "part of the family." They were *encouraged* and *trained* to become artisans and craftsmen: a legacy which was to serve these "coloreds" well in generations still to come.

Despite the shortage of willing labor, infrastructure in the form of canals, roads, bridges, mountain passes, dams and plantations, was eventually established. The Dutch, however, though fine agricultural engineers, struggled to establish successful vineyards at the Cape. When their very first wine was produced, Jan van Riebeeck proclaimed: "Praise be to the Lord!" but Maria pronounced it "horrible!" However, the pragmatic Company authorities soon found a way to solve this problem. After van Riebeeck was finally granted his request for a transfer from the Cape, they encouraged *French Huguenot* immigration to the Cape, if they would bring their wine-making skills. A number of Huguenots were glad to undertake the adventure, considering the prospect of living

---

[4] This was based upon the misfounded premise that a Christian should not own a Christian slave. However, contrary to what most Christians may have believed, their Bible did not forbid the owning of slaves (white, Christian, or otherwise). The Bible simply commanded the proper treatment of slaves; as even the *New Testament* book of Philemon explained. Obviously, one had to question whether *all* "conversions" were genuine; since freedom was a *fringe benefit* of "becoming" a Christian. However, many slaves were of Muslim origin, and remained so. Today, they form a distinct community in Cape Town.

in a climate similar to some regions of France, and due to the fact that the Cape was a *Calvinist strong-hold*. Many Huguenots lived in Holland, having fled there to escape religious persecution at the hands of their own Catholic King Louis XIV.—after he treacherously revoked the "Edict of Nantes" in 1685; which King Henry IV. had granted to Protestants, ensuring their freedom from persecution (1598). Over 200 Huguenots were thus granted "free" passage on Company ships in 1688, and they were "given" basic farming implements, seed and some cattle upon landing at the Cape. In keeping with the Dutch corporate character of those times, these "grants" were in the form of *loans,* which, of course, had to be *re-paid.* These deeply religious Huguenots were an educated, hard-working people and they were keen to plant the French vine-cuttings they had nurtured on the long sea-voyage south. The first permanent Governor of the Cape, Simon van der Stel (1639-1712), had sent the new Huguenot arrivals inland; where they soon established themselves on land-grants which had been purchased by the Company *from the Khoi.* These Huguenots laid the first foundations of what later grew into the world-renowned *Franschhoek, Paarl and Stellenbosch* wine and brandy region (with its Mediterranean-type climate well-suited to viticulture).

The arrival of Governor van der Stel led to a sudden, though somewhat *unintended* expansion of the land area under white settler control. He was tasked with introducing free-hold land tenure, and soon enough, the vibrant town of *Stellenbosch*— ("Stel's Woods") named in his honor—was established. Another town, named after him, a safer winter anchorage called *Simonstown,* was also founded. Service industries, geared towards supplying and servicing the passing ships and their crews and the burgeoning middle-class of Cape Town, grew exponentially. Cape Town soon came to be known as "The Tavern of the Seas."

Yet another famous shipwreck occurred around this time, when the *Stavenisse w*ent aground in 1686, about 70 miles south of what eventually became Port Natal, and then later, Durban. Sadly, 11 of the passengers drowned, but 47 of the survivors set out on foot for Cape Town, over 1,000 miles to the south. Some 13 elected to stay near the site of the wreck, and were there joined by survivors from *two other* wrecks. They eventually managed to build a smaller ship from the wrecked timbers, naming it the *Centuar.* Some set sail, and amazingly, managed to reach Cape Town. Later, 21 of the original 47 who had set out on foot, also reached Cape Town, but not without extreme hardship. Some of the white women had been forcibly taken as wives by local black chiefs, and their pale-skinned progeny were still evident in that area a century later. However, the *Centuar,* a remarkably seaworthy vessel, accompanied by the *Noord*, set out again, *northwards*, to collect those survivors who might still be found at the wreck-site. These brave souls returned with much valuable information: They determined that the Negroid Xhosa people had migrated as far south as the Kei River, and that the Pondo tribe had settled somewhat further north. The captain of the *Noord* had remarkably, managed to *purchase* the "Bay of Natal" (later Port Natal) from the local chiefs, but the Dutch authorities at the Cape refused to ratify that agreement. How differently South Africa's history might have turned out if the Dutch had indeed taken possession of Port Natal, almost 150 years before white men did eventually, settle there!

The rocky outcrop of *Robben Eiland* which had once supported the large populations of fur-seals and jackass-penguins of Table Bay, now housed *prisoners* of the Company, both white and colored. An escaped-slave uprising occurred near Stellenbosch in 1690, during which a burgher was killed, another was wounded, and a number of firearms were stolen. Military retribution was swift. After a number of the rebels had been killed, a captured prisoner revealed that their intention had been to kill a number of whites and torch their farms, in the hope that those successes would draw more slaves into their ranks. Thereafter, they planned to "seize some white women, and make their way to Madagascar." However, after their first attack and the military response, they panicked and fled to the hills.

In the early decades of the 1700's, by which time Simon van der Stel's rapacious son Willem Adriaan van der Stel (1664-1723) had taken over as Governor of the Cape, more and more free-burghers were taking to cattle and sheep ranching, which required less labor-input than cropping. This meant that the Dutch Afrikaners, now known simply as *Boers* (*Boere* being the Dutch word for "farmers"), needed more extensive grazing lands and pastures. Thus originated the first *Afrikaner Trekboers*—the wandering white African pioneer farmers formed from several European nationalities.

However, virtually *all* the settlers and trekkers spoke Dutch; regardless of which European nation from which they hailed. Dutch was the language of commerce at the Cape, and all official communications were in *the mother-tongue*. It was about 200 years later that *Zuid-Afrikaans* ("South African," a new variant of Dutch, closest to Frisian or Flemish) became an officially recognized language, and the term "Afrikaner" was then applied to the new, *white* African "tribe." However, even in the earliest days this adapted "Cape Dutch" or *Afrikaans*—which was more easily understood by the slaves and the colored servants—was in everyday use, and a number of Cape-born whites were already proudly referring to themselves as *Afrikaners*. The settlers named the Khoi, "Hottentots"—in imitation of the clicking sound of their language. Inevitably, however, fierce clashes arose between the Afrikaners and the Khoi herders as a result of competition for free-range—and because the Khoi routinely stole Afrikaner livestock. The elusive little San Bushmen of course, took advantage of this chaotic situation, and their predations on both the Trekboer and Khoi livestock continued unabated.

Though the Dutch authorities actively discouraged expansion by settlers beyond the *Hottentots-Holland Mountain range,* there was no holding back this sturdy new race of Trekboers. South of that imposing range lay *Klein Holland* ("Little Holland"). To the north of those mountains lived, of course, scattered clans of Hottentots, but more significantly—to the Boers at least—also lay an untamed, sparsely populated wilderness. Soon, wagons were being dragged over the mountains that hemmed in much of the western Cape and the peninsula—and the vast southern interior beckoned unto them. The town of *Swellendam*[5] was established in 1745, and about 40 years later, the eastern frontier town of Graaff-Reinet (named after Governor van de Graaff, and his wife Reinet) came into being. There, wagon-making soon became big business. For the first time, as the 1700's drew to a close, white pioneer farmers began to come into contact with a *black* tribe—the *Xhosa*,[6] who had by then migrated as far south as *die Groot-Visrivier* (the "Great Fish River") in the eastern Cape. From that time on, South African history would forever be characterized by racial conflict over land ownership between the black and white tribes.

In the western Cape however, and especially around Cape Town itself, life in the 1700's had assumed an aura of civilization that rivaled that of many European nations. The arts flourished, grand civic building projects, Dutch-style canals, and the model Company gardens transformed the city at the foot of Table Mountain into an architectural and agricultural showpiece. Equally, the gabled Cape-Dutch manor houses and neat, spreading vineyards of the wealthy landowners transformed the rural landscapes. Cobbled roads bearing fine polished coaches, drawn by matched teams of horses and driven by silk-liveried servants, conveyed their owners into town in grand style. Musical concerts and stylish balls drew the cream of Cape society from far and wide, and the opulent fashions of Europe were everywhere to be admired. Custom outfitters and skilled tailors (many of them staffed with Malay seamstresses and Indian suit-makers), milliners, and cobblers provided the finest in clothing and accessories for those who could afford such luxuries. Prosperous mer-

---

[5] Named after Hendrik Swellengrebel (c.1700-1763); first South African-born Governor of the Cape and his wife Engela ten Damme.

[6] —usually pronounced like "KOR-sah" (a *long* "o" sound). "Xhosa" is *technically* properly pronounced with the "X" as a hollow "click." The clicks in their language were mostly inherited from the Khoi.

chants and colorful vendors thronged the bustling lanes, and on the wide, stately boulevards the shops overflowed with fine wares of every description; brought there by great sailing ships from many far-away lands.

The farms produced vegetables and fruit, mutton and beef of the highest quality, and the little fishing boats which plied the deep, blue waters of *Houtbaai* ("Timber Bay") and *Valsbaai* ("False Bay"—so-named for its deceptive tranquility) brought in fresh fish daily to the bustling harbors. The housewives of Cape Town lacked for nothing, and their fine town houses were kept in pristine condition by their slaves and servants. At the imposing castle itself, which was still the center of life in the town, the Governor reigned supreme, and the Company flourished. Magnificent furnishings, many of them carved and crafted by skilled Malay carpenters and joiners, graced the elegant halls. The wines of the Cape, now largely perfected by the French Huguenot settlers, were exported to the royal courts of Europe. It was said that the wine produced at nearby *Groot Constantia* ("Great Constantia," named after Governor Simon van der Stel's wife) was among the finest in the world, and that whenever possible, the Tsar of Russia purchased the entire year's vintage. Then came *Klein Constantia* ("Little Constantia"), *Hoog Constantia* ("High Constantia"), and the estates around leafy Stellenbosch, planted with oak trees by the Governor himself.

An event occurred on a wintry day in 1773 during a north-westerly gale, which graphically illustrated the vast gulf in "nobility" between the salt-of-the-earth farmers of the Cape, and the materialistic mentality of the wealthy merchants of the DUTCH EAST INDIA COMPANY hierarchy. A heavily laden East-Indiaman, *De Jonge Thomas* ("The Young Thomas") was driven ashore near the mouth of the *Zoutrivier* ("Salt River").

The officials of the Company, paying no regard to the cries of the desperate crew and passengers of the stricken ship, concentrated their efforts on salvaging their valuable cargo, leaving those on board to their fate. Wolraad Woltemade (c.1708-1773), a dairy farmer of German descent, passed by on horseback, and seeing the people aboard the ship about to perish, bravely rode out into the waves. Encouraging the drowning men to cling to the horse's stirrups and tail, he made eight heroic swims out to the wreck, and in this fashion, managed to save the lives of fourteen men. Tragically, he and his horse were themselves eventually overwhelmed by the waves, and drowned, along with about 140 of the passengers and crew. To their credit, the Company generously compensated Woltemade's widow and sons and subsequently christened a ship in memory of this brave soul, naming it *Die Held Woltemade* ("The Hero Woltemade"). This new breed of Boer, made up of many European nations (though predominantly German, Dutch and French) would soon have full opportunity to show their mettle; not against the pitiless waves of the ocean, but against the savage wilderness of the hinterland.

The *Franschhoek* ("French corner") district and *Paarl*—the "Pearl of the Cape" (so-named for the granite domes above the town)—producers of fine wines and brandies in the old French tradition, nurtured a sturdy breed of people who would lead the coming *diaspora* into the interior of the vast southern African subcontinent. Among them, two Huguenot families stood out prominently: the Delarey family of *Sannasrus*[7] near Franschhoek, and the Roux family on their estate alongside the *Bergrivier* ("Mountain River"). In addition to wine, *Sannasrus* also bred fine cattle, and produced plenteous fruit. Susanna "Sanna" Delarey had died in childbirth there, but not before producing a strong son, the first French-Dutch child to be born on that farm. Their new Sannasrus wine label, named in her memory, would soon become known as one of the Cape's finest. Succeeding generations of Delareys would look back to the traumatic birth of that son, named Christiaan Hercules Delarey, as upon the advent of a founding father of this new breed of Afrikaner. He soon lived up to his middle name, growing up into a stern, bearded giant of a man. He would also become the first

---

[7] —"Susanna's Rest." It was a portion of the original farm, named after a young Dutch woman who had married into the Huguenot family.

of their old Cape Afrikaner family to cast his eyes northwards; towards the vast, untamed interior of the country, and then lead a portion of that family into the unknown.

Similarly, the Roux family would one day be able to look back on their *own* lineage, and identify the birth of one particular boy-child as the start of a new, Trekboer dynasty. That child was Johannes Benjamin Roux, born just a few years before Christiaan Delarey. He too, would leave his family farm forever, and join the Boer migration, but that was still some decades into the future; an *exodus* that would become known as the Great Trek.

{Around this time, in Philadelphia, the first capital of the United States, the American colonists declared their independence from Britain, in 1776—and finally won it in 1783.}

Chapter Three

Momentous events were taking place in Europe around the dawn of the 1800's. Likewise, in the southern Hemisphere, trouble was brewing. In NATAL, the first stirrings of a new, militant black tribe, the *Zulu,* were being felt, far to the north of the newly established eastern frontier of the Trekboers. In Europe, the French Revolution was making all the kingdoms of the "Olde Order" shudder, and Napoléon Bonaparte's (1769-1821) star was on the ascendancy. In Africa, Shaka Zulu (c.1787-1828) was still a young boy—commonly called a *picannin* in South Africa (a corruption from the Spanish *pequeño,* "small" and *niño,* "child")—but by the time he grew to manhood, all the Negroid tribes of sub-Saharan Africa would feel the impact of his bloody martial reign.

Shortly after the French Revolution, a French army invaded the Netherlands during the northern hemisphere's winter of 1795, and a new (short-lived) republic (fashioned after the so-called French Republic) was formed: the Batavian Republic. The ruler of the Netherlands, William V. Batavus (1748-1806), Prince of Orange, (the last Stadtholder of the Dutch Republic) fled into exile in England. The megalithic DUTCH EAST INDIA COMPANY was then placed under state control, and was soon reduced to a mere shadow of its former greatness. Fearing that the Cape itself—and thus the profitable sea-route to the East—would fall into hostile French hands, the English, under the *pretext* of "securing it for the House of Orange," occupied the old Dutch enclave, and proclaimed it a "British protectorate" in 1795. The British fleet was led by Sir George Keith Elphinstone (1746-1823). The commander of the landing force was General Sir James Henry Craig (1748-1812), who then became the first British Governor of the Cape; serving for two years.

[One of the few bright points of this "first occupation" was the presence of the gracious and beautiful Lady Anne Barnard (1750-1825), Scottish-born wife of the Irish-born British Colonial Secretary. She had anonymously published the immortal ballad "Auld Robin Gray" (while Lady Lindsay, before her marriage to Andrew Barnard), and her wit and charm soon won over much of the rather stuffy Cape high-society. She wrote a series of enchanting letters (which became a South African classic) describing daily life in the Colony, and is also reputed to have been the first "Englishwoman" to climb Table Mountain.]

However, 8 years later, Britain made a pretense of "handing back" the Cape to the Dutch in compliance with the "Treaty of Amiens." Three years after this, the British *again* occupied the Cape—but this time, they intended to stay. The Dutch authorities of the Cape fomented a half-hearted attempt to resist *this* British *invasion*, but it was soon crushed after a short, sharp battle, at *Blaauwberg* ("Blue Mountain") in 1806. The freeburgers of Graaff-Reinet were partly to blame for this easy British victory, because they refused to respond to the "call-to-arms" of the Dutch Commissioner-General at the castle. In 1814, the CAPE COLONY formally became *part of the British Empire*. Existing Roman-Dutch Law was, however, retained and *all* property rights were guaranteed. This brought into question the delicate matter of the growing tension on the eastern Cape frontier, where frequent clashes between Boer and Xhosa had even escalated into a number of full-scale wars. Finally, the British authorities at the Cape could no longer ignore the pleas of their new Dutch "subjects" for intervention and protection, and built a number of military outposts, and the garrison town of Cradock after the FIRST KAFFIR WAR, which ended in 1812.

It would still be 20 years or so before the British themselves abolished slavery throughout their Empire. Although *they*[8] were, at this stage in history, *still the greatest slave traders in the world,*

---

[8] The only other people whose slave-trade industry came close to the size of that of the British were the Arabs. They reputedly even marched their shackled West African slaves mercilessly across the burning Sahara Desert to the east coast, and thence by boat to Arabia. The remnants of an "avenue" of mango trees (inadvertently "seeded" by these slaves) stretching intermittently for enormous distances reputedly can still be seen from the air. Elephants also apparently followed this "avenue" for shade during their trans-Saharan migrations, and utilized the ripening fruit.

their attitude towards the ill-treatment of slaves or colored servants by settlers was somewhat stricter than that of the previous Dutch authority at the Cape. The British were especially heavy-handed in their punishment upon their new Dutch-Boer "subjects" in what *they* deemed, *improper* treatment of "natives."

However, an event occurred in 1815 which would set the tone for future friction and conflict between Boer and British; which would resonate far into the next century. It was known as the *Slagter's Nek*[9] *Rebellion,* which culminated in the botched execution of some Boer rebels by—of all people—an *American.* Colonel Jacob Glen Cuyler (1775-1854) was serving with the British forces after having fled the U.S.A. where his father, the mayor of Albany, New York, had sided with the British during the American War of Independence. A rough Boer farmer by the name of Frederik Bezuidenhout was summonsed to a British circuit court to answer to charges of ill-treatment brought by one of his Khoi-Khoi servants. The Boer flatly refused to answer the summons and in a ham-handed attempt to arrest him, the British troops shot him dead. His brother Johannes vowed to avenge him, but unwisely sought the support of a *Xhosa chieftain* for his planned rebellion against the British authorities, which was summarily snuffed out. When the Boer rebels were publicly hung, all but one of the ropes snapped! The watching crowd, many of whom were—until then—unsympathetic towards the rebels, then *appealed for clemency.* Unmoved, the steadfast Colonel Cuyler simply called for new ropes and hanged them all again; this time successfully. Cuyler was later promoted to General. These unfortunate men were the first perceived martyrs in what was to become a 150-year struggle for Afrikaner-Boer independence from British invasion and oppression—and their execution was viewed, by the Boers, as a *foretaste* of the "British justice" to which they could look forward.

Christiaan Delarey (now a man in his early 30's) observed the machinations of the British authorities at the Cape with a jaundiced eye. Everywhere, their pervasive influence was impacting on the everyday lives of their new "subjects:" the Cape Afrikaners. Government decrees were now published only in English, and

---

[9] "Slaughterer's" or "Butcher's" "Neck" or "Pass."

court proceedings now, of course, also required an *interpreter* for any matter involving Dutch-speakers. The British attitude towards the Cape Dutch was generally one of superiority, and Dutch resentment of the high-handed British administration began to simmer in the breasts of the independence-minded Boers. Petty officials arrived unexpectedly at farms with grandiose proclamations, which they then read out in English, for the edification of their Dutch-speaking, captive audiences, who were compelled to listen. If they did in fact listen, it was generally in sullen silence. It was on one such occasion that Christiaan Delarey first clashed with English bureaucracy.

An English officer, resplendent in his red tunic and mounted on a fine charger, galloped through the imposing gates of the Sannasrus estate, almost knocking down Christiaan Delarey, who was busy with the task of measuring and marking out spaces alongside the driveway, where he planned to plant an avenue of oak trees. Completely ignoring the master of the estate, the officer galloped up to the manor house, and imperiously summonsed the staff. He advised them that a new court had been set up in the district, and that they were encouraged to report any infringement by their employers of the new ordinances relating to labor relations. He assured them that the British authorities would view their complaints in a sympathetic light, and that harsh measures would be taken against any of their masters who were found to have mistreated them. With that, he re-mounted his horse, and galloped back towards the gates of the estate. However, this time his path was firmly blocked by the imposing figure of Christiaan Delarey, who took firm hold of the horse's bridle, and demanded to know why he, as the master of that estate, was not consulted, nor indeed requested to attend the provocative announcement to his staff, with whom he had, until then, exemplary relations.

"Unhand my horse, you uncivilized oaf!" responded the British officer, "Or I'll have you flogged for insubordination to an officer of the Crown!" With that, he lashed out with his riding-crop, dealing Christiaan Delarey a stinging blow across his cheek. Blood suffused the face of the big Boer, and his eyes flamed with fury, but he wisely held his tongue, and released his hold on the bridle of the English officer's horse. The officer rode off, but Christiaan Delarey never forgot, nor ever forgave that insult. His colored field staff, some of whom had observed the incident, snickered under their breaths, now knowing who were the *real* masters of the Cape. The slaves which had been born into the Delarey household, and then nurtured and trained to become artisans, coopers, or vintners, soon began to show a different attitude towards their patrons. The young colored males became ever more familiar in their dealings with the young white females of the Delarey family, and ever more sullen in their attitude towards the white men. Previously obliging domestic servants, became subversive and insolent; spurious charges of alleged ill-treatment by employers became commonplace.

When British troops, who were assigned to combat Xhosa incursions into the farming areas of the eastern Cape frontier (then called, "British Kaffraria"), met with limited success against tribesmen familiar with the thick, thorny valley-bushveld terrain of the area, the British authorities came up with a totally new strategy. They began by offering incentives to *British* immigrants to settle on the troubled frontier, granting them each 100-acre plots in the *Zuurveld* ("Sourfields") area south-west of the Great Fish River. Upwards of 5,000 British farmers, tradesmen and ex-soldiers jumped at the opportunity: for even to an Englishman of *middle-class*, 100 acres amounted to a *rich gentleman's country estate*. Little did they know what they were in for—and that farming on the rugged African *veld* was a far cry from tilling the lush, green fields back "home" in mother England.

What was even more deceptive, was that these British settlers in 1820 were also not appraised of the fact that they were about to be *used* by their own government as a *human* "shield" to create a "buffer-zone" between the raiding Xhosas and the white-owned farms of the Cape. Nevertheless, they were a doughty, resourceful lot, and after a rather tentative start, they got down to the serious business of carving out many successful farms on the turbulent eastern frontier. The conditions they faced were much the same as those faced by the *Boer* pioneers who preceded them: a hard life, made all the more difficult by the marauding Xhosas. These unprincipled Xhosas stole their ripe crops and their cattle, raped their women, killed them and their children (in unspeakably brutal fashion)—and generally made life on the frontier virtually intolerable. The British authorities, comfortably ensconced in Cape Town, appeared incapable of adequately protecting their "subjects" (or unwilling to extend to them the protection to which subjects were entitled by law). Equally as disgraceful, the British authorities even began to *falsely* brand the Boers as "the aggressors" in most all frontier altercations—to divert attention away from *their own* incompetency to protect their subjects.

The experienced Boer farmers of the eastern frontier *did* have fewer qualms about taking the law into their own hands— especially when it came to driving marauding Xhosa raiders back across the Great Fish River and exacting due retribution—than did the new, inexperienced British settlers. Before long, a bond began to form, in resisting the predations of a common black foe, between those white men who had been born in Africa (of parents and great-grandparents also born in Africa) and the "new-comer" white farmers who had been born in Britain. The British settlers themselves largely began to sympathize with the independence-minded Boers. It also soon became apparent to the Boers that the average *Engelsman* ("Englishman" as the Boers called him, whether he was English, Irish, or Scots—for they all spoke English), was of far different, and more palatable character than the typically unsympathetic, bureaucratic Englishman who held the reins of power in Cape Town. The Boers found too, that their own language was now being relegated to second class, and that they were often "spoken down to" by their new, English overlords.

Nonetheless, many of the new British settlers soon learned to speak rudimentary Afrikaner-Dutch, some rather more quickly than many of the rural Boers managed to master English. A bond of kinship slowly grew between the Boer and British farmers. Independent, volunteer, mounted Boer *commando* units were formed, and they responded swiftly and efficiently to calls for assistance—with equal vigor—from either Boer or British frontier farmers. Notwithstanding, many independence-minded Boers were beginning to cast their eyes further north, away from the long arm of the self-righteous *interloping* British "authorities" in the Cape. The sales of sturdy, covered *ossewa* ("ox-wagons") being built in Cape Town and Graaff-Reinet began, for the first time, to outstrip sales of utility farm-wagons. Old Cape families, some resident there for 180 years, now decided to sell their farms, pack up and emigrate inland *en masse*. In other families, individuals gave up their own portions of farms, and joined trek parties preparing to leave.

Many Boers were already making steady progress northwards—ever northwards—in their flight from British rule by the mid-1830's. Their trek route along the South African east coast had often been thwarted by the dozens of deep rivers, impassable with their covered wagons. The Xhosa tribe, which inhabited the coastal region down as far south as the Great Fish River, was also a constant threat. Therefore, many trek parties turned *further inland,* away from the coast and the scenic mountains of the *Klein Karoo,* and onto the *dry plains* of the *Groot Karoo:*[10] a vast semi-desert that straddles the hinterland. Some trekkers headed due north, across the *Vaalrivier* ("Pale" or "Grey" River); others further west across the muddy *Oranjerivier* ("Orange River") to the fringes of the waterless, red *Kalahari Desert.* Other *Trekboers* headed eastwards toward the *Drakensberg* ("Dragon Mountains") towards NATAL and the land of the Zulu. In all, over the period of a decade, between 12,000 and 14,000 Boers headed north, by various routes, for NATAL, and for the high plains of the interior. Many considered their departure in terms of the Biblical Exodus.

Boer scouts had returned from NATAL—a thousand hard miles to the north—with tantalizing tales of unoccupied, lush grazing and water for their many livestock. They further reported concerning the abundance of thick woodlands for the building of houses and settlements. Trekking as they were across the semi-arid Karoo, with its sparse grazing and infrequent water,

[10] —respectively, the "Little" and "Great" *Karoo. Karoo* is a Khoi-San word meaning, "harsh, arid or sparse."

those reports fascinated the Trekboers, and the "Promised Land" OF Natal beckoned unto them. But they would first have to *literally drag* their heavily laden wagons across the mighty Drakensberg—or *uKhahlamba*, that "Barrier of Spears," as the Zulus called the lofty peaks. Most winters, those peaks were covered with snow; their steep, slippery slopes offering few footholds for men or their oxen. Far across the *Vaal,* other trekkers came upon, for the first time, a river flowing *northwards,* surrounded by pyramid-shaped hills. These rugged *Voortrekker* ("Fore-trekker" or "Foreward Trekking") pioneers had no maps, of course, as the land there was largely unexplored; so they consulted their Bibles: their only written source of knowledge. They concluded that they had trekked so far north, that this must be the source of the Nile![11] So they named that waterway *Nylstroom* ("Nile Stream").

The British "authorities" in the Cape outlawed slavery in 1834. Since very few Khoi relished paid work this left many of the pioneer farmers without any reliable labor. The British government had promised to "compensate" those farmers who *could prove* that they had paid hard cash for their former slaves. However, there was a *catch* to their "generous" offer—the Boers had to collect that money *in person in England!* To the simpler country folk, England may as well have been *in another galaxy.* Much resentment was caused by this very English sleight-of-hand. Thereafter, *all* the inhabitants of the Cape were considered equal before the law.

A number of Hottentots did work sporadically for the white farmers, but many of them were unfortunately very prone to alcoholism: a situation some people believed was exacerbated by wine farmers who dispensed *liquor* as a part of their wages. Some farmers, however, pragmatically rationalized the *virtues* of

---

[11] In reality, the source of the Nile River lay 1,800 miles to the north and would not be discovered until c.1864. The sources of the Nile are Lakes Victoria (on the border of Uganda, Kenya, and Tanzania) and Albert (on the border of the Congo and Uganda), which supply the necessary water to keep the Nile flowing through 2,300 miles of hot, dry land, north to the Mediterranean.

the *"dop* system."[12] They reasoned that since the farm hands were going to buy liquor anyway, it was better to dispense the liquor to their workers *there on their farms,* rather than have their only hired help head into the towns to get drunk—where they could not be supervised, may get into trouble, and may not even return to work. Nonetheless, the insidious legacy of this "dop system" would linger long into the future, until it was eventually outlawed; much to the chagrin of many of the workers!

To add to the labor problems of the white settlers, the British armed forces at the Cape seemed to be patently incapable of protecting their *new* Boer "subjects" or their farms and livestock against raids by black tribesmen—or worse, they were *unwilling* to. The British at this time, who had been the most prominent slave-traders in the world, seemed to have *suddenly* developed a twisted sense of conscience. As if to compensate for their past ill deeds, they invented and perpetuated the myth (and the enduring cult) of the "noble savage." In a queer twist, the struggling white *Christian* African farmers soon found themselves being vilified *by missionaries* and by the emerging British liberal movement and their press: who falsely labeled the Afrikaners as "the aggressors" in the frontier "disputes"—even though they were simply, desperately, defending their own property from theft and their families from rape, torture, and murder by very *un*-Christian, *pagan* blacks.

The Afrikaner-Boer frontiersmen of mainly Dutch, French and German (or even British) descent understandably became restless, and talk concerning possible relocation to the vast, unoccupied rangelands of the interior had grown increasingly optimistic. In 1835, two groups of *Voortrekkers* led by Louis Trichardt (1783-1838) and Johannes "Lang Hans" Jacobus Janse van Rensburg (1779-c.1836), headed first north across the Vaal River, and then east, down towards the coast. The *Shangaan* tribe there attacked van Rensburg's group and annihilated them. Trichardt's party was also virtually wiped out—but by an alto-

---

[12] *Dop* literally means a "shell" or "cap" (such as off a bottle) and became a generic term for *"a drink* of alcohol" (similar to a "tot"). Thus, the *dop system* was so named because the workers received part of their wages in alcohol.

gether different foe: the virulent malaria of the humid, swampy coastal plains of Mozambique (the Portuguese colony on the north-east coast). Other, more fortunate groups of trekkers found the vast, grassy plains between the Orange and Vaal Rivers to be largely devoid of African tribes, due to the genocidal raids of Mzilikaze (c.1790-1868), a renegade *Zulu* general, in his northward expansion.

The only black tribesmen that the trekkers came across were scattered on the fringes of that central area: pitiful remnants of Shaka Zulu's *Difequane* ("the Great Crushings"); followed by the *Difequane* of the merciless Mzilikaze. These surviving peoples were themselves in the process of forming a conglomerate nation— *Sotho*—now reasonably secure in their virtually unassailable, rocky strongholds, in what later became the mountain kingdom of *Lesotho,* under their charismatic leader Moshesh (c.1790-1870).

There were numerous clashes with the rear-guard regiments of Mzilikaze's raiding tribe called *Matabele* (or *Ndebele,* "those who disappear") and the frustrated trekkers finally elected a competent military commander, Andries Hendrik Potgieter[13] (1792-1852). Under his leadership the Boers were able to deal with the predations of the blacks and to recover the livestock which had been stolen from them. Potgieter led a bold surprise-attack on the *Matabele impis* ("regiments") at *Vegkop* ("Battle Hill") in 1836. In this conflict he defeated thousands of their warriors with virtually only a handful of Boer fighters; and they recaptured many of their cattle. In that battle, a very young man of German ancestry by the name of Stephanus Johannes Paulus Kruger[14] (1825-1904) received his *baptism of fire.*

---

[13] "Potgieter" is of German origin, meaning "pot caster." The town of *Potgietersrus* ("Potgieter's Rest") was named after this trekker. It has since been renamed Mokopane by the new, black government.

[14] Kruger would later become the revered *Oom Paul* ("Uncle Paul")— president of a fledgling Boer republic in the *Transvaal.* In later years, Kruger loved to describe in lurid detail how Boer women desperately hacked the arms of savage black warriors who were trying to grab them through the thorn barricades between

[Footnote continued at bottom of next page...]

The Zulus soon took advantage of a very opportune situation. Their king Dingane kaSenzangakhona Zulu[15] (c.1795-1840) launched his own Zulu army and dealt Mzilikazi another heavy blow; further weakening Mzilikazi's *impis*. A few years later, the relentless Boer commandos then drove Mzilikazi's *Matabele* completely out of what was then the *Trans-Vaal*—and eventually further north and beyond the *Limpoporivier* (that "great, grey-green, greasy Limpopo River, all set about with fever trees" as Rudyard Kipling later described it[16]). After this Boer victory, which finally expelled the rapacious Matabele *impis,* Mzilikazi turned his warriors against—and decimated—the resident *Shona* tribe and finally settled his wandering, warlike people in what later became British-ruled *Rhodesia* (which in turn later became the Shona-ruled *Zimbabwe*).

A Boer trek leader by name of Pieter Retief (1780-1838), who had assisted ably in the rout of the Matabele, then decided to head for NATAL. English officials had disgracefully tried their utmost to prevent Piet Retief and his companions from arming themselves with ammunition before their departure on the dangerous trek,

---

[14] [...continued from bottom of previous page.]
the laagered wagons, whilst the Boer children cast lead bullets by the heat of the coals of the campfires. Kruger himself, as a "boy," had fought in the laager at Blood River. Later, as a young man, he was forced to amputate his own thumb, which had been shattered by an exploding firearm while hunting lions. He was fond of sitting on the *stoep* of his modest "Presidential" townhouse in Pretoria where he would enjoy a conversation and a cup of coffee with any of his *Volk* who stopped to visit as they passed by. President Kruger was a veritable "man of the people." The gate of that house is guarded by two stone lions which had been presented to Kruger by—of all people—his arch-enemy, Cecil Rhodes.

[15] Dingane was successor to his half-brother, the great general Shaka, whom he murdered. Dingane and Shaka shared the same father, Senzangakhona kaJama, but Dingane's mother was Mpikase kaMlilela Ngobese.

[16] —which Joseph Rudyard Kipling (1865-1936), who traveled extensively throughout South Africa, commemorated in "The Elephant's Child," in his Just So Stories (1902).

where they would assuredly suffer attacks from black tribes.[17] He had heard that the Zulu king Dingane had ceded land south of the traditional Zulu boundary, the *Tugela River,* to the English traders of *Port Natal.*[18] Retief's scouts reported back from NATAL to say that Dingane apparently had no objection to further numbers of whites settling on the edges of his kingdom, and the enterprising Boer pathfinders had also found a few negotiable passes over the seemingly insurmountable *Drakènsberg.*[19] Piet Retief set out immediately for NATAL ("Nativity") with his own trek party of 54 wagons, and finally camped near a mountain overlooking "the Promised Land" of *NATAL—die groen, groen land* ("the green, green land"). From that viewpoint he christened the region *Blijde Vooruitzicht* ("Joyful Prospect") and recorded in his diary: "From the heights of these mountains I saw this beautiful land, the most beautiful I had ever yet seen in Africa."

From those lofty heights, he and a few companions descended across the NATAL midlands, to the little settlement of Port Natal, where they received a warm welcome from the handful of English traders there. These traders assured him that all he had to do was pay a courtesy visit to the Zulu king, and King Dingane would most likely also give them land (as they themselves had received land first by Shaka, and then later by Dingane). Retief returned to the main trek group, whom he had left behind in the mountains, and delivered the good news to his people.

---

[17] The Boer Fight For Freedom (1902), Michael Davitt, M.P.

[18] The Boers kept the name which the Portuguese explorers had named the area, *Natal* ("Nativity"). The fledgling port later became Durban; which is modernly Africa's busiest harbor. It has a sub-tropical climate, and is a famous beach resort.

[19] Reaching a respectable height of 11,422 feet at their highest peak, this mountain range is the tallest in South Africa. One of its greatest peaks is the towering, amphitheater-shaped *Mont-aux-Sources* ("Mountain of Spring Headwaters"), so-named by French missionaries. It is also known to the Sotho as *Phofung* ("Eland Mountain"). It gives rise to, among others, the east-flowing Tugela River and the west-flowing Vaal (which ultimately becomes the Orange River). The infant Tugela forms the tallest waterfall in South Africa, its upper reaches freezing solid in winter.

Chapter Four

The Christiaan Delarey trek party skirted the land of the Xhosa, covering the broken veld of the Great Karoo at a rate of merely 5 or 6 miles a day. They stopped to camp at any suitable grazing near water, hunted whenever possible, and often camped in the same place for a week or two to rest the weary trek-oxen. They were ever alert for possible attack, these wandering farmers, as they blazed ahead, forging new trails. The Xhosas coveted the Boer livestock and would range far inland to lay an ambush in the hope of surprising the Boers and making off with their cattle and sheep. The Xhosa considered themselves especially successful if they were able to *steal everything,* burn all the wagons and kill every white member of the party, and anyone else, regardless of color, whom they did not consider "useful" to them.

The indigenous Stone-age Bushmen, the *Khoi-San* people, regarded all animals, whether wild or domestic, as "fair game"— and had made an "art" of stealing both Boer and Xhosa livestock, upon which they feasted, before they moved on to "hunt" elsewhere. Their age-old cunning bush-craft was unsurpassed, and their tiny bows, which fired *poisoned* arrows, were greatly feared. The similar (but somewhat taller) early Iron-age *Hottentots (Khoi-Khoi)* were also primarily wandering herders. However, at various times they allied themselves with either the Boers or the Xhosas; depending upon with whom they perceived a better opportunity to steal cattle. There had been virtually *constant* war between the southward-moving Xhosas and the northward-trekking Boers since 1779. The Khoi Hottentots found themselves sandwiched in between these groups, and many either were assimilated into the Xhosa tribe or worked for the Trekboers as herders and servants. Most of these skirmishes took place in the *Zuurveld,* between the lower reaches of *die Boesmans rivier*[20] (the "Bushmans' River") and the Great Fish River, largely due to the fierce competition for grazing. This Zuurveld, soon settled by British immigrants, formed a natural barrier checking southward *Bantu* migration. The Zuurveld was a "climatic transition-zone" which demarcated a change from a *semi-tropical* climate to a *Mediterranean* climate. The *Bantu's* familiar crops refused to grow south of the Zuurveld, due to the cool, wet winters. During the third (and most serious) Eastern Frontier War, which lasted about 3 years (until 1801), many *well-armed* Hottentots, who had deserted their Boer employers, joined ranks with the Xhosa.

Christiaan Delarey[21] was a hard, though principled man. Born in the wine-lands of the Cape, and descended from the French Huguenot religious refugees who had first settled there under Dutch rule in 1688, he had decided to give up his portion of the family farm, Sannasrus, and trek towards wider horizons. He, like many other Boers, wanted to escape the stifling influence of the overbearing British authorities at the Cape. He was now in his early 50's but had the strength and athleticism of a man 20 years younger. Standing well over 6-feet tall, his broad frame had been hardened by many long years of farming—and now, it was further tempered through laborious trekking, hunting and fighting. His craggy, brooding face, tanned to the color and texture of leather, was fringed by a full, dark beard which wafted in the hot desert wind. His fierce green eyes stared out over the wagon train stretching behind him, as he sought and focused upon his own wagon; drawn by his fine team of 12 strong, red *Afrikander* oxen, which were led by a small colored boy. Perched on the wooden chest at the front of the wagon was a blond teenage girl: his beautiful daughter Erika. Delarey's eyes glinted angrily as he recognized the rider of the bay horse walking along-

---

[20] The mouth of the *Bushman's River* in the Indian Ocean is about 30 miles south of the mouth of the *Great Fish River;* they snake along through the veld at roughly the same distance, but come as close as 11.5 miles of each other.

[21] Delarey (or De la Rey) is French for, "of the King."

side the wagon. It was that lecherous scoundrel Piet Roos.[22] Roos had made plain his intention to make young Erika his own; as soon as she came of age—and the young, lustful trekker reckoned that was *anytime now* (Boer girls were considered eligible for marriage by their mid-teens).

"Damn him!" thought Delarey. "His poor dead wife is hardly cold in her grave, and he's already making eyes at my young Erika."

Piet Roos had lost his young wife in childbirth a few months earlier, and their baby boy was now being raised by Roos' childless, also recently widowed sister; who had lost her husband to deadly Xhosa spears. Roos had watched Erika Delarey grow, before his hungry eyes, from a gangly adolescent into a beautiful young woman, in what seemed like only a few months on the trek. Boer girls were generally attractive. Many had fair skin, blue eyes and blond hair—a legacy of their Dutch and German ancestry; but some also had a certain sensuous quality inherited from their French roots. However, Erika's slim, feminine beauty and grace stood out distinctively; since the average Voortrekker girl tended to more commonly display traits of physical strength and resilience (which had been bred into them due to the harsh conditions in which they lived and were raised).

By now, every young man in the wagon train had his eyes on Erika's every move; always finding an excuse to ride alongside her wagon, to check the traces and the wheels, or to offer some advice on the best course around a rough patch of veld lying ahead. Christiaan Delarey was fed up with it already, and certainly did not fancy the idea of that scoundrel Piet Roos becoming his son-in-law. He leaped effortlessly into the saddle of his sturdy black pony—his *Boerperd* ("Boer horse")—and shrugged his old musket onto his back. As he approached his wagon at a trot, he shouted roughly at Piet Roos to stop bothering his daughter, and to get to the front of the wagon train to lead them through a gully which crossed their path. Roos glowered at him, then swung his horse away from the Delarey wagon and gal-

---

[22] Roos is Dutch or Afrikaans for, "Rose." He is later described as a *Takhaar:* colloquially a "backvelder."

loped off towards the sandy *donga* ("ravine"). Erika was already used to the attentions of the younger men by now, and so she just laughed at her over-protective father. She had learned to flirt and dance and enjoy their covetous looks when she wore her best frock to the *Nagmaal communion* ("night meal")—a weekend-long, religious and social event, which brought the trekkers together from far and wide across the rugged veld.

There might be several months between *Nagmaals,* so it was important to get as much socializing done as possible when the opportunity arose. Here, the trekkers made friends and found wives; they traded for goods, swapped often-embellished stories of hunting and skirmishes with the heathen, feasted and sang hymns to their beloved *Calvinistic* God. The *Nagmaal* was a joyous celebration of life—and a sharing of the hardships and wonders of the Great Trek. The Dutch Bible was their *manual* for all things in life, and in its well-worn pages they found ample proof that they, the Boers, *were actual descendants of the Israelites:* chosen and beloved of God; now wandering in a new savage *wilderness,* forging a new nation among a different breed of *heathen* tribes.

The Boers were a strictly moral people: who lived "by the Book." On the trek, however, due to obvious conditions and limitations, marital arrangements could sometimes—under *certain* conditions—be unceremoniously made *en route* on the veld. Such infrequent marriages were later "officiated" by ceremony when the first occasion presented itself. This rare, informal impromptu formation of a sacred union, was allowable (though still frowned upon by some) in *special* cases; such as when a single woman was reduced to having no male family member left alive to protect her. It was considered a necessity, not a frivolous union. Thus, if the young woman had already formed a bond with a capable Boer man, and they consented to become one, they would simply join together and openly live as man and wife—and they would solemnize the arrangement at the next *Nagmaal* or at the first opportunity in which a *predikant* ("preacher") was at hand. This, in truth, was little different from that practiced in Bible times.

The Boer's children were seldom allowed to *wile away* their time in childish pursuits; being a very conscientious and industrious people, denigrating sloth and idleness. The boys were expected—virtually from the time they could walk—to assist with chores, especially the care and herding of the livestock. Their toys were homemade, tiny bone replicas of wagons and oxen, and miniature wooden muskets and cutlasses. But every boy had a *real* hunting knife, and *knew how to use it.* They learned to ride at a tender age, to load and shoot the clumsy smooth-bored flint-lock muskets and pistols, to make bullets, fix wagons, and even kill, clean and prepare game. The young girls, when not assisting their mothers with domestic duties, foraged in the veld and woodlands for wild fruits and berries, roots, shoots and herbs. The children grew up sun tanned, wind burned and tough: babes of the unforgiving wilderness, their natural youthful exuberance kept in check only by the trekker's strict, Bible-based code of conduct (which also firmly applied to the colored servants—one law for *all)*.

The Boers also found ample justification in their Bibles for the God-ordained separation of the races; being a godly people, they endeavored to know God's Will and follow it. God commanded the Israelites to stay separate from all other peoples and not to intermarry.[23] Since the Boers believed themselves to be God's very Israel people, then understandably, they knew God wanted them to remain separate also. The Boers believed (as did many Europeans at that time in history) that the dark-skinned peoples were "drawers of water and hewers of wood" descended from the sons of Ham, who (according to Genesis 9:25,26) were to be either the *foes* or the *servants* of the sons of Shem; but never their equals.

More than once on their trek, the Delarey party had been attacked by roving bands of Xhosas, but had fought off these

---

[23] Though the Boers were in error thinking that the blacks had descended from Ham, they *correctly* understood God's command to His people the Israelites to remain separate from all foreign peoples, and to marry only among their own (Genesis 24:3,4,37,38; Exodus 34:10-16; Numbers 36:5-13; Isaiah 52:11; II Corinthians 6:17,18; Ezra 9; and I Esdras 8:68,69 from the Apocrypha).

opportunistic *Kaffir* raids. The Boers called all blacks "Kaffirs"[24] —all blacks, that is, *except* the fearsome Zulus. Boer scouts in NATAL had reported the Zulus to be a superior military tribe, and who themselves regarded all other blacks as *inferior* to themselves. The tiny apricot-hued *Khoi-San Bushmen* were regarded by all as essentially sub-human, virtually, "creatures of the veld." The somewhat more advanced *Khoi-Khoi Hottentots* (or *Hotnots*, as the Boers called them)—who would often accompany the trekkers as herders and servants—were themselves considered to be on the *lowest* rung of the human ladder. Occasionally a lonely or lustful Boer would impregnate a Hottentot girl, but inter-racial marriage was *anathema*. Any half-caste offspring were seldom assimilated into the family of the white man. They were regarded as objects of shame, to become forever after part of that great amalgam of bloodlines known as the *coloreds*. It was not that the Boers hated other peoples; they simply desired to preserve their own heritage—and to obey God.

The numerous separate trek parties were scattered far and wide over the veld and the iron-shod wheels of their heavy-laden wagons cut deep, parallel *spoors* ("tracks") into the earth; while the rugged veld slowed their progress at every turn. Steep river banks and dry, sandy *dongas* ("ravines") had to be laboriously cut away or filled in to make gentler gradients over which the straining oxen would haul their creaking wagons. The oxen were cajoled, but never thrashed—though stern, the Boers were not calloused "brutes." The Boer drivers cracked their long, platted raw-hide whips sharply—but harmlessly—*above* the oxen's heads. These great beasts were known and loved as individuals, each with its own name, and each indispensable to its

---

[24] Kaffir, an *Arabic* word, simply means, "unbeliever" and has **no** etymological *negative* connotation. Though modern blacks are "offended" to have a white man call them *Kaffir,* they commonly call each other *Kaffir*—even as "African-Americans" casually call each other, "nigger" (though that word does have a negative connotation). The Zulus openly call whites, *umLungu,* which reputedly means, "white scum" (i.e., "of the sea"); others claim it means, "white cockroach" (as in, a white bug found under a rock, never having seen the sun). But no one accuses the Zulus of "racism."

Trekboer owner.

The men ranged over the veld, sometimes many miles from the wagon train, searching for game and birds to shoot for the cooking pots. The women were kept busy cooking, sewing, giving birth and raising their children. Sadly, it was not uncommon for women to die during childbirth, under such austere conditions in which the Boers lived.

Their life was hard. Their rudimentary medicines were restricted to those diverse, traditional remedies brought over from Holland (almost 200 years earlier)—or those concocted from local herbs and barks, which they learned to use from the Bushmen and Hottentots. The Boers discovered that *Kankerbos*[25] ("cancer bush") suppressed cancers, and boosted the immune system. Sap from the abundant Aloes was used as shampoo and as a skin balm, and juice from succulent ground-creepers soothed chapped lips. A plant of the *Salsola* variety known as "ganna" or "kanna," to the Hottentots and Boers respectively, was burned, and its ashes were used in the making of soap. In later years, a large area of the Klein Karoo even became known as "Kannaland." To relieve the agony of a scorpion sting, the offending creature itself was crushed, and then applied as a poultice!

The women also to a large extent, supervised the colored servants; scolding and chiding any insolence, and remedying any laziness or neglect (whether real or perceived). Communication was always carried on in what came to be known as *Afrikaans:* that vibrant "new" tongue born of the African veld— a heady amalgam of mainly Dutch, Flemish,[26] some German, Malay, a little French, English, and Portuguese, and even a few Hottentot words. It was a language that could *roll* and ROAR like an African thunderstorm echoing off the cliffs... or *whisper* and *sing* like the wind through the acacia trees.

---

[25] —*Sutherlandia frutescens,* of the "Pea Family" (in Zulu, *Insiswa).* Today it is cultivated commercially, for medicinal use.

[26] Flemish (Vlaams) is the *Belgian* Dutch of Flanders, which itself had absorbed significant characteristics from French. It is most similar to spoken Afrikaans (which is also spoken by the so-called "coloreds" or *brown Afrikaners,* as well as by whites).

If a scouting rider came galloping in with news of a raiding party of Xhosas, the wagons would be hastily drawn into a protective circular *laager*. The outspanned oxen and other livestock would then be gathered in the middle within the circle. If there was time, acacia-thorn branches were cut and shoved in between and under the wagons. All available muskets and pistols were hastily loaded, and spare lead balls and powder stacked close at hand. Then they would silently, breathlessly wait... many lying under the wagons, straining, through the spokes of the wheels, for a glimpse of their heathen foe. A Xhosa attack would often be preceded by this long, *nerve-wracking* wait, as the warriors crept closer and closer, using whatever broken cover they could, before suddenly charging the *laager* in a frenzied, yelling horde.

The Trekboers knew then, that it was fight—or die. If they failed to drive off their attackers, if they were overwhelmed by the rushing hordes of wild-eyed black warriors, if they fumbled a reload or panicked, a *cruel* death surely awaited them. The white men would be stabbed, slashed, and very often disemboweled. Small children usually met a brutal end: A black warrior would hold a child by his feet and swing him violently, smashing the child's head mercilessly against the iron-shod wagon wheels. The white girls and women would be stripped of their long frocks and sun bonnets and then be repeatedly ravaged by the lust-crazed warriors, before being killed to discourage inevitable rescue attempts by other white men. The exulting Xhosa warriors would roast some of the Boer's sheep or oxen, glut themselves, and swill any brandy they discovered while ransacking the wagons. Other blacks would hack off body-parts from the slain (or living) trekkers. These body parts and especially the long hair from the women were added to their *muti* (the blacks' noxious "black magic" concoctions, with which they made superstitious potions and amulets). The blacks believed that these *muti* gave them supernatural powers over their enemies.

The colored and Hottentot servants too, knew that they themselves would be *spared no cruelty* if they fell into the hands of the black warriors. In this respect, the blacks were "color blind"—they killed virtually all: regardless of color. These unfortunate colored servants shared the same fate as the white men. The males would usually be slaughtered. However, the surviving Khoi females—who were prized because of their prominent buttocks—would be dragged off to become concubines and any older children would become *slaves* to their new *black* masters.[27] When the sexual and blood-lust urges of the victorious Xhosas were eventually sated, the warriors would drive the remaining cattle and sheep, along with their captives, back to the Xhosa *kraals* ("corrals" or "hutted villages") to bask in the adulation of their chiefs and womenfolk, upon their triumphant return. Subsequent cross-breeding, over time, produced more "coloreds" as the paler, apricot-colored skin of the Khoi was infused into the Xhosa bloodlines. As a result of this interbreeding, the characteristic *clicks* in the Khoi-Khoi language passed into some of the black languages, and especially that of the Xhosa. The very name *Xhosa* itself was derived from a Hottentot-Khoi word

---

[27] While the Boers and British initially both had slaves—but later only paid servants—the blacks themselves commonly took slaves as a way of life. However, the modern liberal "revision" is to call the peoples whom other blacks *enslaved,* "clients," and the black *slave owners* are likewise euphemized as, "patrons." Ironically, white people have been castigated for being slave traders and owning slaves, even though blacks owned just as many slaves (if not more); even though the majority of slave traders were actually *Jewish*—and even though the slave traders *bought* the slaves *from the blacks' own chieftains* who *sold their own people* to the slave traders. Overall, whites treated their slaves quite well. The only "abuses" were when they had to administer punishment for severe violations of the law (which punishment they also imposed upon their own white brethren who broke the law). Slave owners were themselves severely punished, if they abused their slaves. However, blacks who owned slaves usually treated their slaves worse than dogs; and even tortured and executed them at their whim. One of the most famous modern books/movies denouncing the history of the slave trade was *Amistad*. The story centers around one poor African slave who eventually won his freedom. However, what the movie does not mention, is the fact that after he won his freedom—*he returned to Africa to become a slave trader himself!*—abusing and selling his own people into slavery! San-Bushmen are today enslaved by the Owambo and Herero.

meaning, "angry men."

The last Xhosa attack on the Delarey party had come suddenly. The forward scout galloped back, breathless and sweating, shouting and waving his hat at the lead oxen, forcing them to turn, to form a defensive circle. There was no time to outspan the oxen, no time to back up the wagons or gather thorn branches. The oxen skittered and bellowed, sensing panic in their drivers. The Boers' great tan dogs growled ominously. The younger children screamed and cried, running towards their mothers, to be swept up and carried hastily to their individual wagons and hidden under the wooden benches. Then the women and girls (both white and colored) instinctively began grabbing the leather pouches of lead musket balls and powder horns hanging from the wagon driving seats, as the men, cursing and shouting, struggled to form a protective *laager* with the wagons. Sensing an easy victory, about 100 Xhosa warriors leaped up, as if out of the ground, and swept down the gentle slope towards the disorganized line of 11 covered wagons.

The dust and sweat already on Christiaan Delarey's face now mingled with the darkness of his fury to create a frightful visage. Out of the corner of his eye he saw his Hottentot herder galloping away from the wagons, and cursed him as a bloody coward. He would have summarily shot him down for stealing a horse and fleeing in the face of the enemy, if he could have spared the shot. The first warrior to break away from his fellows and charge leaping and yelling towards the half-turned leading wagon drew back a muscular arm to hurl his spear at the big, bearded Boer. Before he could unleash the deadly *assegai,* Delarey leveled his musket and shot him through the chest. As he fell backwards, another leaped over his body and swung at the Boer with his *knopkierie,* but the heavy knobbed club was deflected by the now-empty musket as Delarey swung his pony around and charged straight at the oncoming group of warriors. They parted as the pony's thundering hooves crashed through their midst, the powerful Boer rider swinging his empty musket like a long club, cracking skulls and smashing ribs as he vented his fury and indignation. He galloped right through the group of warriors, then reined-in his wild-eyed pony to reload his musket by placing the butt on the ground, pouring a charge of black powder from his bone powder-horn deftly down the muzzle, and swiftly driving the lead ball down the smooth barrel with the ramrod. A dash of powder on the flash-pan, a hasty re-cocking of the flint-lock, and he was ready to charge into the fray again in less than half a minute.

By this time, the line of wagons had been formed into a semi-circle, and Boer muskets opened fire on the advancing warriors. The *phut...phut...* of lead balls piercing cowhide shields and smashing into their bodies was drowned out by the excited yells of the Xhosa warriors. Some broke away from the main group, and dashed across the face of the half-formed laager, attempting to get in behind the defensive line. Two were felled as they ran, by well-aimed shots, but a group of about a dozen got in among the oxen, slashing at the crazed beasts' hamstrings with their razor-sharp *assegais*. The oxen bellowed in terror, straining against their harnesses and shaking their great horned heads to throw off their yokes, their eyes rolling white. The black warriors' acrid *tang* ("odor") and the smells of blood, sweat, dung and dust combined in the heat of the battle with the smoke and stink of the musket discharge.

Those Boers who were still mounted charged repeatedly at the yelling warriors, firing muskets and pistols, wildly swinging their cutlasses and empty firearms, trying to force the flanking Xhosa groups back across the face of the half-formed laager, where the dismounted Boers, servants and women could get a clear shot at them.

Erika Delarey stood stalwartly, reloading the *voorlaaiers* ("front-loader" muskets) and passing them to the old man in front of her, Oom Sarel Delarey (her great-uncle)—and he aimed, fired and passed back the empty gun without looking, took a recharged one from her outstretched hand, aimed and fired again. With each carefully aimed shot, an approaching warrior fell. Erika only looked up from her reloading when the old man failed to hand back his discharged firearm, and only then did she see the long spear protruding from between his shoulder blades. Instantly, a tall black warrior was upon him, stabbing the dying old man repeatedly with his spear. The savage was aware of the slim, blond girl close behind his victim and visions of her soft white body flashed through his mind as he finished his grisly work. He threw aside his long shield, and leaped to his feet to claim his prize; but this was no *shrinking violet.*

Erika raised the hot musket, and shot the looming warrior cleanly through the head. The Xhosa fell at her feet; she stepped over the muscular black body that shone with sweat and took up her fallen old uncle's position. She now had to reload and fire without assistance, but did not falter—and more than one Xhosa warrior fell to her deliberate aim. Assegais sang about her, thudding into the wooden boards of the wagon. Through the smoke, she caught glimpses of her father charging back and forth across the line of wagons, his eyes wild, his beard matted with the fresh blood of Xhosa warriors. He was like a dark avenging angel: shooting, galloping a short distance from the fray to reload; thundering back in, firing, then clubbing with his empty musket and kicking out with his stirrups. Christiaan Delarey also reared his maddened pony in the charge so that its sharp hooves slashed and pummeled the black spearmen as they sought vainly to close with him.

Piet Roos had managed to get in between two smaller groups of warriors attempting to flank the wagons, which by now were in total disarray. Crippled and dying oxen dragged down their span-mates. The sheep, goats and loose cattle had fled; while riderless ponies frantically floundered about wild-eyed, with flapping stirrups, blood-stained saddles and foam-flecked flanks. Roos looked desperately about, seeing no sign of Erika. The Delarey wagon was jack-knifed and in danger of toppling onto its side as the fear-crazed oxen backed up, stumbling over other fallen beasts under their hooves. Roos swiftly clubbed a warrior with his empty musket as he tried to spear his horse, and galloped straight at the lurching wagon, scattering the yelling group that was closing in. Leaping from his pony, he hurriedly tied its reins to a meat-hook on the side of the wagon, whipped out his long, curved hunting knife and peered into the darkened interior, fearing the worst. He was almost speared through the neck from inside of the covered wagon, but he managed to grab the shaft and haul it past his head, with Erika hanging grimly onto the other end. Her frightened blue eyes widened even further when she realized that she had almost dispatched the man who had come to save her, but she clung to the spear shaft, then lunged past Roos to jab at a black warrior who was clambering onto the wagon.

Above the din of battle, a cry was heard "Hulp kom!" ("Help comes!"). The sound of a fusillade of shots in the near distance, and the thunder of galloping hooves raised a ragged cheer from the embattled trekkers as they realized that a group of horsemen was approaching fast, firing from the saddle. They could only be fellow Boers, as the Xhosas seldom used horses or firearms. The galloping commando, led by a big blond rider, swept into view over a low ridge, and charged straight into the fray. The wagons in front of the Xhosa were still belching deadly musket fire and with the blazing reinforcements charging up behind them, the collective nerve of the warriors finally broke. The Xhosas vaulted over wagon shafts, crippled oxen, and speared bodies and fled in disarray towards the broken ground whence they had sprung their ambush. The Xhosas left behind about two dozen of their dead and wounded, and now sprang like gazelles with the mounted Boers in hot pursuit, firing and reloading as they galloped after their fleeing foes.

Piet Roos now stalked from black body to fallen black body, kicking aside shields, grabbing mortally wounded warriors by their woolly hair and deftly slashing their throats. His expression was one of absolute hatred, his cruel eyes glinting with murderous intent. A big tan dog followed him and tore and snarled at the gaping throats of the fallen warriors. Christiaan Delarey eventually galloped swiftly back to his own wagon, and his heart leapt when he saw the frilled blue bonnet and long fair hair of his brave daughter shining as she bent down to gently close the dead eyes of the old man who had fought valiantly by her side. He swung heavily out of the saddle and swept her up into his grimy arms, hugging her close to his heaving chest, and kissed her forehead as he mumbled a breathless prayer of thanks to his merciful God. "Piet Roos came to help me when the Kaffirs were almost upon me, Pa," Erika said through her tears. Delarey glared about him, saw Roos still crouched over a dead warrior, bloodied knife in hand, and shouted "Hey, Roos! Dankie!" ("Thanks!"). His estimation of the young man rose ever so slightly; but he would still keep an eye on him whenever Roos was near his young Erika.

The leader of the rescue commando, Jan Roux,[28] (who was the son of Johannes Roux, a former Franschhoek district neighbor to Christiaan) trotted up to Delarey. The handsome young Boer leaned down from his sweating horse and held out a big, calloused hand to shake that of the older man, who was still hugging his sobbing daughter. Then Christiaan Delarey saw the mounted Hottentot who had fled when the Xhosas attacked, and clenched his fists in fury, his knuckles showing white.

"Wait!" exclaimed Roux. "That *Hotnot* of yours galloped up to my camp to tell us that your wagons were being attacked. We came as fast as we possibly could." Members of Roux's trek party were in the process of breaking up camp at a water-hole a few miles away when the wild-eyed herdsman had raced in, yelling that his master's wagons had been ambushed by about 100 Xhosa warriors. Roux had shouted orders that the men on foot were to stay behind and hold a defensive laager (in case they were also to be attacked), while the mounted men were to follow him and the Hottentot servant. They had then galloped at break-neck speed over the stony veld in the direction indicated by the herder. Roux then looked down at Erika Delarey, and saw the three warriors lying dead near her wagon, the speared body of the old white man, and a fourth warrior lying against the front wheel of her wagon, much of his head blown away by her point-blank shot. Jan took off his broad-brimmed felt hat in respect for the old man lying dead at Erika's feet.

"You fought well, young lady," Jan Roux smiled. "You'll make a fine wife for a good, strong Boer one day." He winked at her, she blushed, and hid her face behind the edge of her

---

[28] Jan (usually short for Johan or Johannes is pronounced, *yahn*). Roux means "ruddy" in French.

bonnet. He then turned back to the older man, his tone now serious. "How many of your people did you lose?"

"Oom Sarel is dead, looks like three others, and two Hotnots," Delarey replied sadly. "About a dozen wounded. Some of our oxen are also now crippled. But we lost no other livestock— the boys are herding them in now. We killed more than two dozen of those damned Kaffirs. *Dankie*—thank you—for coming at such speed. It was looking ugly; they caught us by surprise." Turning to the mounted Hottentot, Delarey said, "Boontjies, I thought you were running away. I almost shot you myself. How did you know that *Meneer* ("Mister") Roux was camped close by?"

The herdsman replied in his lilting Afrikaans that he had once slipped away from the wagons during the night to seek out his lady friend, Saartjie, a servant in the Roux trek, which he knew had stopped over at the last waterhole, and she had told him that they would be staying on there for another half a day or so. When the Xhosa attacked, he realized that they might be overwhelmed, and had galloped back to the waterhole to get help.

"It would be wise to join our trek parties together. The Kaffirs might try again," announced Jan Roux. Delarey looked at him, this rugged young Boer, hardly into his twenties, but already a man matured beyond his years by hardship and adventure. His clear, smiling blue eyes steadily held the older man's fierce gaze. His finely chiseled, tanned young face sported a reddish stubble, his clothing, like all of theirs, was rough and simple, his old *velskoene* ("homemade hide shoes") were tied with rawhide, and his wide-brimmed hat stained by sweat and dust. He was a young man you could count on, Delarey had heard when they still lived in the same district of the Cape, and he had now seen it for himself. All the same he, Christiaan Hercules Delarey, was not inclined to share his leadership. Just then, Piet Roos sidled up to Erika, and took her hand. "It was a close thing, hey my Erika?" he said obsequiously, as her father glared at him.

Piet Roos' attempt to capitalize on his recent actions finally decided things for Christiaan Delarey. He turned to the handsome young Boer still mounted on the white horse. "Good idea, Roux," he announced. "We will wait here for your wagons to catch up. It will give us time to slaughter the crippled oxen and salt the meat, to make *biltong* ("jerky"—literally "buttock-tongue")." Jan Roux seemed to him a much better prospect for his young Erika than that scoundrel Roos, brave as he might be. A brave man was not always also a good man, Delarey had noted on the trek. Some men just liked killing Kaffirs. There were certain traits that Delarey looked for in a man that he did not see in Piet Roos. Besides, Roos drank too much. Moreover, why had Roos not been defending his own infant son and his sister's wagon? Christiaan Delarey had always instinctively disliked Piet Roos, and he had long ago learned to trust his own instincts.

A solemn service was held for the fallen trekkers, but the dead Xhosa warriors were left to rot where they fell; serving as food for the hyenas and vultures—and as a grim warning to other heathen. Delarey read the appropriate passages from his big, leather-bound Dutch Bible[29] and said a few words over the fresh, shallow graves—four mounds of stony earth under a spreading acacia. Two other mounds, a little way off to one side, contained the final remains of the Hottentot servants. The others trekkers stood, heads bowed, hats in hand, some with bandages showing fresh blood from their spear wounds. Jan Roux's small commando stood by with their sweating horses, respectfully waiting for the service to end so that they could hasten back to their own families still camped in the veld.

"Our Lord in Heaven," Christiaan Delarey intoned, "have mercy on the souls of Your humble servants, and their own, even humbler servants. They all fought bravely against the heathen, and fell, happy in the belief that You, Lord, have kept a place for them in Your house. We are wanderers in a hostile land, Your people, chosen from the tribes to spread Your Word. We ask for

---

[29] It would be nearly 100 years until the Boers would have a Bible in their own Cape-Dutch language. Though the first book of the Bible was translated into Afrikaans in 1878, the entire Bible in Afrikaans was completed in 1933 and revised in 1953 by the BYBELGENOOTSKAP VAN SUID AFRIKA ("BIBLE SOCIETY OF SOUTH AFRICA").

Your continued protection, and Divine Providence. Amen."

Delarey thought of his own dear wife, killed just six months ago. He missed her sorely, his companion of sixteen years, and his heart ached when he thought of her lonely grave on the open veld some 300 miles back along the trek route from the Cape. She had gone alone to perform her ablutions down by a stream when she was surprised by a vagrant Xhosa who had hidden in the thickets at the approach of the wagon train. He had waited in the shadows until Delia Delarey began disrobing to wash herself in the cool water, unaware that hungry eyes were watching her. He then grabbed her from behind, and threw her to the ground. As he loosened his filthy loincloth, Delia had scrambled to her feet and attempted to flee up the sandy bank, but he tripped her up and threw himself on her struggling, half-clothed form. She had turned and bitten him hard, badly tearing his ear. When he could not subdue the fiercely struggling, screaming white woman, he had grabbed his rusty spear and plunged it in frustration into her side. The agony of his ripped ear had dispelled any further lust, so he fled, leaving Delia Delarey dying, her life-blood seeping into the white sand of the riverbank. A half-hour later, Christiaan Delarey found the still-warm body of his wife, and by swiftly following her attacker's tracks alongside the river, galloped after and shot dead the vagrant when he burst from cover and fled across the open veld. The hardest thing he ever had to do in his life, was to tell his daughter that her beloved and beautiful mother was no more. Erika had stayed a week inside their covered wagon, mourning and weeping inconsolably while she reluctantly packed away, into a small box, the delicate jewelry, and a few precious mementos of her late mother. A persons life did not come to much, she thought: just a small box of memories, and a larger box of bones in the ground. But her God-fearing mother's soul would live on, and that thought comforted her just a little.

In the loneliness of the night, when Christiaan thought about his dead wife, he felt a strange relief that she had not been ravaged, only to survive, and for them both to have had to live with that shame. He knew that he would not have been able to come to terms with rape by a Kaffir, to be able to desire his wife again as before, if she had been so violated. It was a deep-seated, almost primeval loathing that the white men felt for any of their womenfolk who had been ravaged by other races, willingly or not. They believed that their women were thereby forever tainted, untouchable. It was inconceivable to the white men of Africa that a white woman would *willingly* give herself to a black man; knowing the black's brutal nature—and if she *did*, then she was a reprobate, and deserved to be shunned by her own, and to be treated as an object of disgust.

Delarey had been shocked to the core when he had once come across a drunken white prostitute copulating with a black "customer" in an alleyway one night in Graaff-Reinet, when he had visited that town for supplies earlier in the trek. His immediate instinct had been to destroy them both, there and then, to cleanse the land of this gross abomination. Instead, he had turned away, sickened by what he had seen. "Like should be with like," Christiaan firmly believed. "Each should only be with its own kind; even white whores!" The mixed-race offspring of interracial unions, the so-called *kleurlinge* ("colorlings") were never fully accepted by either race. They lived in a kind of "twilight zone" world: a virtual *no-man's land* of perpetual *limbo* between the pure parent races. The legacy of such disowned people of those times, was one of wandering: either working as servants and herders for the white folk, or being assimilated into one of the Hottentot clans or black tribes—and they were usually considered by the blacks to be "second-class" citizens and discriminated against. Later, these coloreds would form their own distinct "tribe," speaking Afrikaans, and with their own, uniquely colorful culture and traditions. No one in the mid-1830's, at the time of the Great Trek, could have foreseen what a pivotal role these coloreds would play in the politics of a future South Africa.

Chapter Five

The two wagon trains joined up the next day. Their combined ranks now swelled to 19 wagons with over 200 trek oxen, 78 trekkers, 40 servants, and over 500 head each of sheep, *Boerbokke* (Boergoats), and cattle. Over the next few weeks, mounted scouts rode well ahead with their great tan dogs, their *Boerboels* (Boer "bulldogs"), who loped exuberantly alongside their masters. Outriders were placed on both flanks, as well as on the dusty tracks left behind by the wagon train. The Voortrekkers were determined not to be again surprised by the Xhosas. Slowly—as slowly as the oxen could haul their loads over the rugged veld—their wounds and hearts began to heal.

The soulful, rhythmic, squawking chant of the *tarentaal* ("guineafowls") calling for rain, seemed to mimic the rhythmic squeaking of the slowly turning wagon wheels; the sound of the lumbering *ossewa* ("ox-wagon") was now as much a part of the veld chorus as that of its natural denizens. Huge herds of dainty *springbok,* seemingly numbering in the millions, raised towering clouds of dust as they skipped and trotted quite closely alongside the wagons, devouring any edible plant in their path. This species of antelope (which would later become a national icon of the SOUTH AFRICAN REPUBLIC) was soon nicknamed the *trekbok* or "pronkbok" by the Boers. The springbok seemed to delight in *pronking* ("leaping or springing into the air, with their legs extended and their feet held close together"). This pronking resembled a bronco (unbroken horse) when it leaps into the air, back arched and legs down. When a herd of springbok leapt intermittently as the greater mass strode along, it somewhat resembled a pod of dolphins as they swam along while some randomly leapt out of the water. The springbok often seemed to "compete" for speed with the galloping ostriches, which "scorneth horse and rider" (Job 39:18). The wagon trains had eventually left the myriad species of *Protea* flowers of the Cape behind them. Eventually, the species of game and gamefowl changed, as the vegetation and climate changed. Small groups of *bloubok* ("bluebuck") and partly striped *quagga* (a zebra variant) were occasionally to be seen; sadly, these two species would soon become extinct. The piebald *bontebok* ("variegated buck") were left behind as the veld slowly gave way to succulent Karoo vegetation, and then to grassland; home to herds of gamboling black *wildebeest* ("wild cattle") and to the *blesbok* ("blaze buck"), a close cousin of the Cape *bontebok*. Already, settled farmers in the southern Cape were setting aside land for the preservation of the *bontebok,* and then farmers on the Highveld would soon be doing the same for the dwindling numbers of black wildebeest, steadily being replaced by cattle.

The brake-blocks for the wagon wheels, which the trekkers had fashioned from the wood of the *Waboom* ("wagon-tree") or *Protea nitida,* would eventually wear out, and they would have to fashion new ones from whatever species of tree were at hand. *Bloukraanvoëls* ("Blue crane fowls;" which later became the national bird of the SOUTH AFRICAN REPUBLIC) whirled and danced in courtship; their flowing tails sweeping the dust. These cranes laid their eggs carelessly on the open veld, and when the passing teams of oxen trod too closely to their "nests," the cranes would cackle indignantly, raise themselves to their full height, (around 3-4 feet) flap their wings and snap and poke their dagger-sharp beaks at the clumsy, indifferent intruders. Above, Cape *griffin* vultures wheeled and soared on the rising air currents.

Piet Roos noted with much irritation that Jan Roux now often shared the lead with Delarey, and that Erika seemed to be quite taken with the handsome young Boer. She laughed gaily at his antics, like when he tried to make his stocky white pony high-step like a show horse, and when he handed her a tiny *meerkat* he had rescued in the veld.

Piet Roos knew that Jan Roux was now a serious rival for Erika's affections. "Damn," he said to himself. "You would think that after I saved her life, she would show me some gratitude. But along comes that big blond oaf, galloping up like some great hero on his white *Boerperd*, and now she's all a-flutter. Women! Pah!" He stalked angrily back to his wagon, and cuffed the dozing colored boy riding on the lead ox. "Klein bliksem! ("Little scoundrel!") Walk in front and lead Buffel, don't ride on him! You will tire him out, and if he trips in a hole because you are asleep, I'll thrash your backside with my *sjambok,*" he growled, flexing his short rhino-hide whip.

Erika, despite the mischievous company of her tiny new meerkat, keenly felt the loss of her great-uncle, Oom Sarel. He had been a kindly old man, immune to the raw passions that drove younger men. On the trek, as the wagon creaked along, he had told her long, rambling stories about his youth on their family farm (Sannarus) at the Cape, where they had produced wine and raised cattle. He would pause and chew thoughtfully on his tobacco, spit politely behind himself into the dust, and then resume his story. He never neglected to include details about his dear-departed wife and stories about his beloved sister-in-law Sanna, Erika's own grandmother. He would recount how they used to make sweet wines and delicious jams from the plump grapes and juicy fruits that grew so prolifically on the fertile family farm... how they used to occasionally go into Cape Town to buy the exotic spices (to flavor their aromatic stews) brought by the passing merchant ships all the way from Java... and how they would dress up in their lace and finery so that they would not look *out of place* in the fashionable parts of that big, bustling harbor town. Cape Town was the *center* of their growing world, a beautiful, cosmopolitan "Tavern of the Seas." Sir Francis Drake once described it as "a most stately thing, and the fairest cape in the whole circumference of the earth."

Erika's departed great-uncle had recounted to her how the wealthier landowners would compete to *out-do each other* with their fine teams of horses, drawing highly polished coaches; their colored servants dressed in fine silk livery. He once told her how one rich, young fool of a farmer had even *tamed* a team of zebras to draw his coach (or thought he had); knowing that he would be the *center of attention* in the main street of

Cape Town. However, the poor zebras, who were by nature sprinters; not accustomed to long feats of endurance, dropped one-by-one from exhaustion in the traces, and had to be hurriedly replaced by scruffy mules to usher the embarrassed gentleman home! Oom Sarel had explained to her how the unmarried young men—not himself of course—would line the *Heerengraght* (the "Gentleman's Canal"), on blustery days, perchance to glimpse a well-turned leg when a young lady's voluminous skirt blew up by the south-easter. He told her how the great sailing-ships from many distant lands stopped at the Cape to take on fresh water, and to acquire the Cape wines, vegetables and fruit grown there by the employees of the DUTCH EAST INDIA COMPANY, THE "JAN COMPAGNIE" (and later, by the BRITISH EAST INDIA COMPANY; the "JOHN COMPANY").

Oom Sarel Delarey would describe in great detail how the fine wine was made on the old family farm which his, and of course, Erika's own ancestors had begun to build up with their bare hands from the virgin earth a century-and-a-half ago—way back in 1688. He would recount how the Dutch authorities, who had been at the Cape since 1652 (who were a dour lot, with no success at growing vines) had courted the French Huguenots—not so much as religious refugees, but as skilled winemakers. Oom Sarel further related how, after all the *best* wines had finally been bottled and labeled for export to the royal courts of Europe, the baser wines would be consumed with riotous delight by the young men—but *not* by himself, *of course.*

If old Oom Sarel was to *be believed,* he himself was a virtual *paragon* of Christian virtue, surrounded by baser men of weaker moral fiber. His decision to accompany the trek away from English domination at his advanced age was spurred by the passing of his own dear wife; which had left him no reason to stay around any longer on the old family farm. So he had given up his small share of that beautiful farm to join the GREAT TREK with his nephew, Christiaan (Erika's father); to seek greener pastures and new, wider horizons. Oom Sarel also sometimes had spoken of his other nephew whose own family had—so far as Oom

Sarel knew—trekked only to *Winburg* ("Victory town" named after a defeat of Mzilikaze's impis) and who still wrote his name *De la Rey,* in the *old French* fashion. Oom Sarel often wondered how he and his family were doing now.

Oom Sarel could not have known (due to the dearth of news from far-away trek parties) that they had settled for a time there or that his other nephew's wife would, a decade later give birth in Winburg to a boy: Jacobus "Cobus" (or "Koos") Herculaas De La Rey (1847-1914). Young Koos and his family would then trek on to Lichtenburg, that "Town of Light," across the *Vaal River,* where they would set down roots. Koos himself would eventually (a half century later) go on to distinguish himself as a great general; the bravest of the brave generals of the Second Boer War, earning the nickname *die Lig van Lichtenburg* (the "Light of Lichtenburg")—a veritable lion in battle and the scourge of the English in the SECOND FREEDOM WAR. But sadly, Sarel Delarey would never know this.

Oom Sarel also told his niece of how he missed the sight of the soaring Cape-Dutch gables of the mansions and fine homesteads of old *Kaapstad*, and of the beautifully laid out farms, and the lush, fertile fields. After having left it all behind, Sarel Delarey saw only covered wagons and rugged semi-desert— but oh, how he relished the *freedom* of the veld; and the sense of identity that the trek had engendered among the Boers; the harsh trials having forged them together into one strong, cohesive people.

The Boers were fast becoming a *white* African "tribe"—in the true sense of the word: They were forming into a distinct group of people, with their own particular customs and traditions. They even had descended from many a common ancestor, in the same way that black Africans could claim to be part of a "tribe."

Oom Sarel was already an elderly man when the trek started. However, Erika had still *secretly* hoped, as more and more smaller trek parties had joined the *mass exodus* that some widowed *tannie* ("auntie") would catch her great-uncle's eye, and make his last years happy again. Maybe one of these tannies would be from the scenic hills and passes of the Klein Karoo, or from the embattled eastern Cape frontier. But sadly, this was not to be. Oom Sarel Delarey was, with great sadness, lowered into the earth in what was to be his final resting place. Though the Trekkers left him behind in the lonely, barren wasteland, they carried with them fond memories of him which would last for as long as they themselves trod this earth.

Erika felt the tears sting her eyes (and a dull pain deep within) when she spied Oom Sarel's old tobacco tin at her feet; after having heard it rattling on the floor of the wagon, as the ox wagons jolted across the veld, moving onward blazing new trails. As she stooped to retrieve it, the tiny meerkat grabbed at it, and chased the rolling tin around in circles. She laughed at the bright-eyed little creature, and soon found her mood lifted somewhat by the antics of her playful new pet. It hurt a little to smile, but it slowly softened her face of mourning. Shielding her eyes against the harsh sunlight, she adjusted the peak of her frilled cotton bonnet, and looked out over the brawny red backs of the ox team; their horns shining and tossing as they periodically shook their great heads to chase off ever-so-briefly, the blanket of biting flies. The chill desert night had given way to a scorching day; dancing mirages distorted the harsh landscape, and the heat sang in her ears. In the far blue distance, she could just make out the looming grey-blue mass of the Dragon Mountains. A distant thunderstorm swept across the vast African veld like a great, grey battleship, firing its bolts of lightning at the trembling earth.

Jan Roux soon proved himself to be a reliable young leader: adept at choosing safe routes for the clumsy wagons and finding places with good grazing and water for the laagers. His *social* skills rivaled his frontier skills, as he was also competent in *encouraging* the weaker members of the trek party when they seemed overwhelmed from the heat, dust, flies and ticks; when seemingly endless stretches of monotonous stony veld dispirited them, or when social tensions threatened to spin out of control.

As they moved ever forward the Boers would devise *descriptive names* for the various natural features they passed: Because water was so vital to their survival, even tiny trickles were named *fonteins* ("fountains" or "springs"). Thus, they would give each creek they crossed its own name, such as: *Soetfontein, Brakfontein, Bitterfontein, Modderfontein,* or *Doornfontein* (respectively, "sweet-," "brackish-," "bitter-," "muddy-," or "thorny-" fountain or spring). In similar fashion they named mountain ranges as they passed by them, such as: *Rooiberg, Swartberg,* or *Langeberg* ("Red-," "Black-," or "Very Long-" Mountain). This not only had cartographic practicalities, but it also served as a little game to pass the boredom of the lonely trek. The *rhebok* would utter their shill warning whistles as the wagons passed their slopes, and the agile little *klipspringer* ("rock-jumper") would then bound away, from rock to rock.

Jan Roux had come to be in charge of leading his original, smaller trek party only because his widowed father Johannes (a contemporary of Christiaan Delarey) and from the same district, had broken his leg in a bad fall when a *pofadder* ("puff-adder") startled his pony. Now, Johannes was confined to a bed in his wagon, suffering agonies from the infected break as they jolted over the rough veld. In the face of adversity, his son Jan had risen admirably to the task when someone was needed to assume responsibility. They too, had left family behind on their fine cattle and wine farm *Bergplaas* ("Mountain Place/Farm") on the slopes of the Berg River near *Franschhoek*, to join the Great Trek north. They too, like the Delareys, had French Huguenot and Dutch blood running strongly in their veins, and had answered the call of the wide-open veld when they began to feel the sting of British oppression. Though from the same district, they left on their treks at different times, and had taken slightly different routes, but now Providence decreed that they should join forces on their northern odyssey.

For his part, Christiaan Delarey was content to leave the slowly moving wagon train or the evening *laager* ("defensive, circled wagon camp") in the younger man's capable hands while he rode off ahead to scout for hostile natives. He was pleased to see that Erika was much taken by this spirited young man, and that Piet Roos was now spending more of his time with a big, hearty but rather plain girl named Bettie Breedt. Roos himself, however, had not taken kindly to the handsome interloper, and made his resentment clear. Although Piet Roos was *only a few* years older than him, Jan Roux mischievously enjoyed calling him *Oom* ("uncle") Piet—as if paying respect to an older man; but with the emphasis distinctly on *Oom*. Grimly, Roos would glare back at him, but hold his tongue. Roux's steady gaze and confident demeanor, coupled with his youthful, broad shoulders and big hands warned Roos of the great latent strength of his new rival. As the weeks after the Xhosa attack grew to months, Erika and Jan Roux grew ever closer—and Piet Roos ever more bitter at his perceived rejection by the desirable Erika.

The young meerkat, which was now part of the family, was dubbed *Koerie*—named for the strange *chuckling* sound he made when he was excited: such as when he was given a bowl of *pap* ("corn porridge"), of which he was quite fond (and from which he grew ever more rotund). *Koerie* would spend his time scampering alongside the wagons searching for tasty bugs, as the convoy creaked and groaned its way over the seemingly endless plains at the leisurely pace established by the oxen. When the energetic little creature finally grew tired or nervous, such as when one of the big dogs eyed him too closely, he would leap into Erika's arms and cling to her, chattering and whimpering pitifully. She would then place him in a padded open box near the front of their wagon, where he would doze with his fat belly exposed to the warm sun; his head lolling from side-to-side like a little old man who could not keep his heavy eyelids open.

Christiaan Delarey found himself, more often than not, alone with his thoughts, as Erika now spent much of her leisure time chatting to Jan Roux. It was becoming obvious to all in the wagon train—and to none more painfully so than Piet Roos— that the two were becoming a couple. And a very handsome couple they made too; in the opinion of most of the trek party, and especially in the knowing eyes of the more mature Boer women, the *tannies*. Their colored servants too, sized up other servants as potential marriage partners.

Boontjies, the Hottentot servant who was almost shot for seeming desertion in his heroic dash to get help when they were attacked by the Xhosa, courted his colored lady-friend, Saartjie. Saartjie was servant to *Mevrou* ("Mrs.") Hilda Breedt. Hilda, also fondly known as *Tant* ("Aunt") Hilda, was a very large and rather stern *Boerevrou* ("Boer wife").

Tant Hilda was the mother of Bettie: the plump girl whom Piet Roos now found himself courting by default. Bettie was a jolly, noisy type, and she and Saartjie cooked up the best spiced stews in the camp.

The Hottentot Boontjies was very proud of his fine young colored lady; for she was a quiet, genteel girl (of Muslim Malay descent). Her sewing skills were much in demand, and in the little leisure time that Mevrou Breedt allowed her, she made cotton dresses for the other girls on the trek, and smart linen shirts for Boontjies. She had been born a slave into the modest Breedt household in the Cape, had then converted to Christianity, and was thereafter known by the diminutive Dutch form of the Biblical name Sarah. She could have taken her freedom when she turned 22, but even when the British abolished slavery in 1834, when she was 18, she *chose* to remain with the family as a valued servant, and had joined them on their northern odyssey. This in itself was powerful testimony to how the average Boer treated his slaves and servants. Saartjie was a petite, pretty girl, and Boontjies counted the days towards the time when he would be able to ask Saartjie to be his wife; to be officiated in front of a predikant at the next Nagmaal. She loved her mistress as a mother and Bettie as a sister. Saartjie's own family elected to remain in the Cape to enjoy their new-found freedom. All the same, as a respectful servant, she always slept and ate apart from the Breedt family.

Hilda (a common Old Germanic name which means, "battle woman") and *Breedt* (Afrikaans/Dutch meaning "broad") were names which epitomized her person, and she typified the average mature Boer matron on the GREAT TREK. She was indeed *wide:* a stout, rather plain, salt-of-the-earth type woman—and if a monument was ever to be erected to those stalwart, mature trekker women, *she* would have made an *exemplary model* for it. She was married to a somewhat meek man, Koos Breedt, who with his sparse, wiry frame, literally hid in her overbearing shadow. Tant Hilda ruled her mobile household with a sharp look, and if required, an even sharper tongue. She was both loved and feared by all, young and old, who traveled alongside her; a woman not to be trifled with. Her potential future son-in-law, Piet Roos, stayed well clear of her if possible, but did occasionally brave a hearty meal with the family.

Oom Koos Breedt, whose health was not good, and who had been in danger of losing his small farm in the Cape (due to his inability to undertake manual labor, and insufficient means to own more than a few slaves or employ servants), did not relish the thought of his family being obliged to become *bywooners* ("tenant farmers"), so he had elected to sell up, and join the trek to seek new pastures. He was also rather partial to his peach brandy and would soon doze off after supper. Thereafter, Hilda would allow Piet and Bettie to sit up and chat for a while. The length of the visit itself was determined by the length of the tallow *opsitkers* (the "sitting-up-candle") which Hilda would light when she bade the couple good night. However, Hilda was not overly fond of Bettie's choice of suitor; having noticed the lecherous looks he cast at their colored servant girl; so the *opsitkers* was purposely sometimes just a short stub of a candle. She knew that her Bettie was no beauty; but she was a good, strong Christian girl, and would make any Boer man a fine, capable wife. Mevrou Hilda Breedt had decided that she too, would keep an eye on that "no-good, opportunistic scoundrel" Piet Roos, already a *bywooner* himself at the time he joined the Great Trek. He'd had nothing to lose, which did not endear him to his future mother-in-law.

Chapter Six

As the combined Christiaan Delarey and Jan Roux trek party neared the mighty *Drakensberg,* they noticed that more and more of the scattered wagon trains were starting to converge, making contact more frequent between the groups. From far across the rugged veld, the trekkers were beginning to form a "nation on wheels," heading for a common goal—the lush pastures of NATAL. Even as in the Cape, where the Xhosa tribe did not often venture south across the Great Fish River (except to steal Boer cattle), so the Zulus seldom ventured south across the Tugela River into NATAL. The craggy *krantzes* ("cliffs") and *kloofs* ("gorges") that provided the few passes down the Drakensberg soon became silent witness to scenes of great trial and ingenuity on the part of the trekkers. Wagons often had to be *dismantled* down to their component parts and lowered by rope down sheer drops, only to be re-assembled below the cliffs. If the path was wide enough for a wagon, but too steep for the oxen to hold back the heavy load, a full *span* ("team") of oxen had to be harnessed behind the wagon to assist in the braking effort. At other times, the wheels of the wagons would be removed and stout branches tied in their place to act as improvised skids to slow the descent. Men, women and oxen would pick their hazardous way down dizzying cliff paths that had been in use for eons by the great eland antelope. Huge bearded *lammergeiers* ("lamb-vultures") and black eagles circled above, patiently waiting for man or beast to fall to their death; to be dashed on the sharp rocks below. Occasionally, the hungry raptors would fly at a lamb or small calf perched precariously on the loose stones of a ledge, and beat at the unfortunate beast with their wings, causing it to plummet to its death; whereupon they would swoop down to claim their gory prize. Before long, the passes were littered with the wreckage of wagons that had come to grief, and the bleached and broken bones of beasts.

Erika and Jan would often wander away from the laagered wagons in the cool of the evening, sit on a large rock still warm from the day's sun, and look out over the *Promised Land* of NATAL. On clear nights, far below, they could make out tiny pin-pricks of light in the dark blanket of the veld stretching out endlessly towards the east coast: the distant campfires of fellow-trekker groups which had made it over the mountains, and onto the lush plains below. There, they would plan and dream, of what their future house would look like, what color cattle they would breed, and the delicate matter of how many children they would have. They were both rather shy when it came to that particular subject, as neither of them had yet actually mentioned the word "marriage," but they and all the others in their trek party took it for granted that they would indeed marry, just as soon as they could attend *Nagmaal* and find a preacher to solemnize their vows in the eyes of God and the congregation.

After a particularly hard day of dragging wagons and cajoling livestock along one of the mountain passes, Piet Roos rode alone up to a small stream that cascaded over a rocky outcrop, plan-ning to have a cursory wash before making his way back to the camp at an opening in the cliffs. He had once again been invited to supper with his future in-laws, and was looking forward to a good meal. He led his thirsty horse towards the pool at the base of the little waterfall, and was about to step out from the shad-ows of the acacias when he noticed that someone was already bathing in the pool. It was the colored girl, Saartjie. He stopped, and silently watched as she stood naked in the shallows. The sound of the waterfall had masked his approach, and she bathed without inhibition. Her long black hair, a legacy of her Malay ancestors, lay wet against the milk-coffee of her skin. As she bent to gather water in her cupped hands Roos made his move. Delarey had been a good judge of character: Roos had no moral standards when it came to satiating his baser urges.

That evening, alongside the wagon, Mevrou Breedt noted that Saartjie was strangely silent as she served the meal to the family and their visitor, Piet Roos. She saw that the girl had a slight swelling below her eye, and naturally assumed that she had been in an altercation with the Hottentot herdsman Boontjies, whom she knew was madly in love with Saartjie. A jealous lover's tiff perhaps? She thought no more of it, though she did notice that the servant girl had moved her bedroll much closer than usual to their wagon that night when she retired for the evening. "I'll give that *donnerse Hotnot* ("damned Hottentot") a good *klap* ("smack") if he harms her again," thought Mevrou Breedt as she dozed off beside her husband in their comfortable bed in the wagon.

Bettie Breedt had trouble sleeping that night—and the snores of her mother and father emanating from inside the wagon did not help matters any. She lay in her usual place on her bedroll under the wagon, and could see the dying embers of the cooking fire through the wooden spokes of the wheel. Bettie's mind was troubled, but she could not put her finger on what was bothering her. Piet had seemed distant at supper, eating his favorite stew with hardly a word and accepting the plate of food from the Malay servant girl without even looking up. He usually stayed on a while after her parents had turned in, but this night, even though her mother had grudgingly put a new candle in the brass holder on the table, he had left almost immediately for his own wagon. She wondered if he was still serious about courting her, or if he was just using her until a better prospect came along. She knew full well that he had his hopes set on Erika Delarey until that handsome Jan Roux came galloping up and stole Erika's heart.

Bettie had no illusions about herself, and knew that she was no beauty, but she was a strong, vibrant young woman. She did not find Piet Roos particularly handsome, with his *takhaar* ("thatch hair"), his battle-scarred face and large ears; Piet also drank too much brandy, in her opinion. However, he was a fierce fighter, and would hopefully mellow into a more likable person once the ardors and dangers of the Great Trek finally ended. There was no doubt that Piet felt some attraction to her; as he had made several amorous advances toward her in private. Like her mother, Bettie was very capable in all things womanly. No woman could rival her cooking, and her home-making skills were equally impressive.

As Bettie lay awake, under the patchwork quilt, which she herself had crafted, her thoughts turned to little Saartjie; whom she spotted sleeping not far from their own wagon. She was fond of the well-mannered and conscientious colored servant girl. But Bettie disapproved of Saartjie's Hottentot suitor, Boontjies. Despite Boontjies admirable qualities, Bettie did not think it was a good match; primarily due to their stark ethnic difference. She felt Saartjie was rushing into things out of desperation and hoped that she would wait at least until they neared Port Natal: where there would no doubt be a greater selection of suitable men of closer affinity.

The thought of the races mixing was abhorrent to Bettie. "A white rhino does not mate with a black rhino; nor a black wildebeest with a blue. Come to think of it," pondered Bettie, "even those creatures which looked most similar (for instance, the *lean mountain zebra,* the *fat plains zebra* and the pale *quagga)* were endowed by their Creator with the innate understanding— some primal instinct—to recognize that they were different and were ordained to *keep to themselves.*" This was in simple obedience to God's Law of *Everything after its own kind;* which Bettie noticed God had mentioned numerous times in the first chapter of Genesis. "If the dumb animals—God's innocent creatures—know their own (and equally recognized those *not* their own)," Bettie reasoned, "then why do *we His children,* who have been endowed by the Creator with higher intelligence, not recognize such obvious, simple truths established not only in God's Word, but in nature itself?"

Bettie herself had seen the unfortunate products of such unnatural unions, those sad progeny that were—by nature— perpetual outcasts; people with no true identity; who belonged to neither one, nor the other: who were never really accepted by any. Bettie's heart was saddened by such senseless tragedy; but reasoned that if mankind would simply obey God, such unnecessary heartaches would be very few in number.

Bettie further noted that, quite often, instead of recognizing the Creator's Lordship, sinful man made excuses for sin; thus perpetuating it; not halting it. Many people thought *cross-*

breeding had it benefits. However, Bettie considered such notions to be a myth, which was nonexistent in the *natural* world. "Some people *may think* that there are benefits when breeds of live-stock, crops, and even—God forbid!—races of people were pur-posely cross-bred; but that does not make it right. God, as the Creator, certainly had and still has the right to determine how *He* wants His creation to be," Bettie reasoned. "God determined that some things are *immoral;* abominations—violations of what He declared to be holy and good." Bettie also remembered from reading the family Dutch Bible, that in His Law to His people, God forbade *various* "unholy unions;" even including having an ox and an ass yoked together. For some reason, God determined that it is *just not right*. Likewise, Bettie remembered reading that God clearly forbade the cross-breeding of crops or animals. Most importantly, Bettie reflected that God had created the races *distinct* from one another, *separated* them—and even *commanded* His people to retain the purity of the identity with which He created them (in His *own* image).

"In the natural world, cross-bred offspring most often inherit the *worst* traits of their parents." This was a simple observa-tion Bettie had made. She knew that violating God's Law was *not* justified just because some silly person considered the out-come to be pleasant or beneficial. "Man cannot overrule God!" asserted Bettie. She realized that the consequences of disobe-dience could be harsh with *long-term* and *unforgiving* conse-quences. "And did not God Himself forbid the Israelites to marry with the Canaanites, and did He not command them against taking foreign wives?" Bettie recalled how God clearly warned His people, that if they did so sin, that they would be severely judged. "We reap what we sow," she remembered reading somewhere in the New Testament.

Bettie was a simple girl, but observant enough to notice another example from nature. She saw that there were hard-working and industrious *white ants* (termites) prevalent on the veld, who labored to fill the larders of their skillfully built cities. She also recognized how these peaceful, hard-working white ants would then be vio-lently raided by tribes of *black ants* (which the Boers called

Matabele ants)—who *destroyed* the white ant community, and *stole* the food which the white ants had carefully stored up—and *killed* any white ants that did not flee. Bettie had herself observed this on numerous occasions on the veld. "Those black ants could just as easily work and store up their own food. Why, for goodness sake!—killing and stealing is just as much hard work as is honest labor. But those black ants refuse to work; they build nothing of their own and I think they actually *like* to kill and steal from their peaceful neighbors." Though this harsh reality both saddened and infuriated Bettie, she noticed the obvious parallel in terms of peoples; in the behavior of the white and the black tribes on the African veld. Some built cities like Kaapstad (Cape Town), others built *nothing* of substance themselves—and invaded and violated what others had built.

Bettie also considered another parallel in nature, as her eyelids grew heavy. She noticed that her people also had to be ever vigilant against the cunning, stealthy leopards of the *kloofs,* and even against the attacks of *the prey of the leopard:* marauding bands of baboons, who would not only steal everything which they could carry, but whose own sharp, deadly fangs also presented grave danger to people and livestock alike. She wondered if there was something in the soil or climate which made everything so wild and violent. Her people had been raised on this wild continent for nearly two centuries; yet *they* were not wild. She assumed that it was because God had made His people civilized, and further, because He had given them His Word by which they were to live. God placed His Spirit within them, instilling within them the desire to abide by His moral code—and not merely follow whatever base urges may at times overcome them. "Everyone has a choice," she mused.

As her mind pondered these sad realities of life, Bettie finally dozed off, lulled by the distant roar of a lion, the whooping of a hyena and the nervous yelping of a black-backed jackal. A *naguil* ("nightjar," sometimes referred to as "goatsucker") chanted plaintively in reply. As the wildlife continued its ghoulish serenade, she subconsciously drew the warm cover a little closer about her neck.

The days followed a distinct pattern; the times set by the blazing African sun. In the morning, they said their prayers and then consumed a breakfast of *rusks* ("delicious, crunchy aniseed-flavored biscuits") and strong *moerkoffie* ("fresh-ground coffee"). Next, they packed their bedrolls, tables, chairs, and cooking pots and stuffed them into the wagons. Finally, they inspanned the oxen, the signal was given, the whips cracked, and everyone set out across the veld, ever northwards, into the vast unknown.

At midday they paused for a short break under the shade of a tarpaulin stretched out from the side of the wagon where they enjoyed a light lunch. Their afternoon repast consisted of their tasty mainstay—*biltong* ("jerky"); and perhaps a piece of bread and cheese which they washed down with tepid water from a skin bag. Once they were refreshed they would push on again until the sun began to dip below the western horizon.

When camp was made, the weary oxen would be outspanned and led to water before being allowed to spend the night grazing and dozing nearby. If there was any perceived threat of an attack, the wagons would be laagered and the livestock kept in the middle of the circled wagons. Keeping the livestock in the center of the wagons also provided protection against the ever-present danger of lions; whose rumbling roars seemed to shake the very ground. The lions unleashed their unnerving bellows, snarls, and growls in protest and demonstration of their frustration in not being able to reach the cattle. These "Kings of the Veld" were successfully kept at bay and deterred by the constantly burning camp fires, as well as the shouts and gun shots of the watchers. The oxen and horses had learned not to stray too far from the laager when grazing and they, as well as the sheep and the goats, were usually guarded by the alert herders, accompanied by their muscular mastiff-like dogs, their *Boerboels*.

Piet Roos sat and watched as his infant son suckled at the breast of his surrogate mother, Roos' widowed sister, and he wondered if Bettie Breedt would one day take over that role. He still burned with jealousy whenever he saw Erika and Jan Roux together, but had found that Bettie was an ardent lover and a capable young woman, and he knew that she would be a good homemaker when they finally settled in NATAL. He still had dark thoughts about his encounter with the colored girl at the stream a few weeks ago; but was relieved that she did not seem to have told Bettie or her formidable mistress about it. Piet Roos felt little personal guilt for his rape of the servant girl. She was, after all, hardly more than a slave, an unpaid servant to his future mother-in-law. "Who did she think she was," he rationalized to himself, "styling her long hair *like a European,* swaying her hips like that when she walked and wearing her frock so tight around her waist." His darkened heart caused his irrational mind to justify his own sinful behavior; down-playing his own role and laying the blame at the feet of another. "Obviously," he fumed in his mind, "she had in her head the idea of seducing a fine, young Boer like me, and then expecting me to support her and some half-breed child in a grand manner—or even *marry her."* Well, that was not going to happen, not to him, if he could help it. If she was with child and blamed him, he would simply deny it. Everyone would just naturally assume that the Hotnot herder Boontjies was to blame. The Hotnot always proudly wore the shirts Saartjie sewed for him, and followed her around like some love-sick puppy.

In any event, Roos was now planning to ask Bettie to marry him at the next *Nagmaal,* and he had no doubts that she would accept his proposal. That would settle the matter, and that Malay girl would not have the audacity to claim maintenance from him then. She had not looked directly at him since that day at the waterfall, and avoided coming anywhere near him; except to place his plate of food before him when he ate with the Breedts.

Roos stood up, bade his sister and his infant son good night, and strolled around the perimeter of the laager. He passed various campfires, around which sat the older Boers, talking softly, smoking their pipes, and *braaing* ("barbecuing") venison steaks and lamb chops, or their spicy *boerewors* ("Boer-wurst"). At other fires, aromatic venison and *marog* ("wild spinach") stews simmered in *potjies* ("three-legged cast-iron pots"). Some read their old family Dutch Bibles by candle-light; one played a forlorn tune on his harmonica, and others simply sat staring out over the veld, or looking up at the glistening stars in the wide velvety black sky. A short distance away were the campfires of the colored herders, from which direction wafted over the faint, sweet smell of *dagga*[30]—the local "cannabis"—mingled with the acacia woodsmoke from the campfires. When the Hotnots could not obtain the true hemp (brought in by the Arabs to the east coast), they smoked *Bushman* or *Wilde dagga*, which they obtained by picking the leaves of the local plant. When Piet Roos had completed his circuit of the wagons, he took a long swallow of straight brandy from an earthen jug and placed it back under the bench of his wagon. He then shook out his bedroll between the wagon wheels before kicking off his rawhide shoes and settling down to sleep; still in his sweat-stained, dusty clothes.

Huddled in her own bedroll near the Breedt wagon, Saartjie was deeply troubled—her monthly period had not arrived. She now knew that when Piet Roos had forced himself on her at the mountain pool three weeks ago, she had conceived. She had been a virgin, had promised herself to Boontjies, the Hottentot herder, and now she was carrying the illegitimate, half-breed child of a Boer; disgracefully, the very suitor of her beloved mistress. Saartjie waged a battle with herself in her own mind.

Who would believe *her?* Who would believe that it was not *she* who had seduced Piet Roos and that *her* seduction had not been carefully *premeditated* to secure for herself a better future—by entrapping the unfortunate Boer widower in his time of vulnerability? Would Boontjies believe her? Would *Mejuffrou* ("young miss") Bettie believe her?—and most importantly—would Mevrou Hilda Breedt, her austere mistress (who was once even her *owner),* believe her? Would Piet Roos even ever acknowledge that the child was his? She had tried to scream for help when he had grabbed her, but he had roughly

---

[30] Though unrelated to marijuana, and not nearly as potent, *Leonotis leonurus* is a mild euphorbic of the mint family. It is commonly called "Lion's tail" or "Lion's ear" and is a dark green plant which grows to around five feet tall, with bright orange tubular flowers. The Zulu call it *Umunyane* or *Ntsangu*. They also commonly dried this or *Cannabis sativa* for snuff and took it before battle.

covered her mouth, and slapped her hard when she bit his hand. She well remembered the pain when he roughly deflowered her, his hooded eyes, and the strong smell of brandy on his ragged breath. Now, her heart ached, and her soul cried out for solace from *die Here* ("the Lord").

As the combined Delarey and Roux trek party painstakingly negotiated the passes through the formidable *Drakensberg,* which led down to the fertile plains of NATAL, reports began to reach them of isolated wagons that had been attacked by the *Zulus*. Resultantly, small hesitant trek parties began to gather at the foot of the pass, afraid to go on until they could join up with larger groups. Leaders of various treks met to decide which direction to take: *due east* towards the coast, towards the growing town of Port Natal and relative safety...? or *northward,* towards open pastures, but close to the land of the Zulu and certain danger...?

Chapter Seven

The Zulus were exceedingly proud of their untainted blackness. The name *amaZulu* means, in their sonorous tongue, "people of the sky." They considered themselves a *superior* tribe of fearless warriors, with a proud military history. Indeed, the Zulus were a hard people, forged with blood and fire in the savage crucible of nineteenth-century South Africa. The Nguni-speaking *Bantu* peoples had split many times during their migration into Southern Africa from lands much further north; these forebears of the *Zulus* took up residence in present-day Kwazulu-Natal; the *Xhosa* offshoots migrating further south into the eastern Cape, down as far as the Great Fish River; where they later clashed with the white pioneers moving northward, in the late 1700's.

In battle, the Zulu considered himself invincible, and when pitted against other tribes armed only with shield and spear, *he was*. The great general *Shaka,* founder of the Zulu nation, welded disparate clans into a mighty military machine, revolutionizing tribal warfare. Shaka Zulu himself had a somewhat inauspicious start to life. His father, Senzangakhona KaJama (c.1762-1816), was minor chieftain of the then-insignificant Zulu clan. He had at least 16 wives and Shaka was born out of wedlock, in 1788, to Nandi KaBhebhe eLangeni. Shaka was immediately ostracized (as was his mother)—due to the fact that his father and mother were members of the same clan (Senzangakhona's mother was a *Langeni);* which was considered a great taboo. Nandi was forced to flee, with her 6-year-old son, to the neighboring Langeni people, where Shaka grew up. The name *Shaka* reputedly meant "parasite" or "stomach bug;" as his mother initially denied being pregnant—to which her clan sisters replied scathingly that she must be swelling due to a stomach parasite! His childhood among the Langeni was not a happy one. Young Shaka endured much bullying due to his lowly status within the tribe (due to his own mother's disgrace) and because of his reportedly undersized genitals.

Eventually, in 1802, when Shaka was an adolescent, both he and his mother were expelled from the Langeni clan, and found refuge with the more powerful *Mtwetwa* people (with whom the Zulu were confederated), under paramount chief Dingiswayo[31] (c.1780-1817). As a young man (roughly between the ages of 23 and 29), Shaka served with distinction as a Mtwetwa warrior demonstrating outstanding fighting ability. Although initially shunned by his Zulu clan, he was still a son of the chief, and in 1816 Shaka succeeded to the Zulu chieftainship. This was still not a position of any great importance, as the clan numbered just 1500, and were among the smallest and most insignificant of the 800-odd clans that comprised the eastern *Nguni* peoples.

Before Shaka Zulu burst unannounced on the scene like an African thundercloud, tribal warfare had consisted largely of posturing stand-offs, normally resulting in merely a few fatalities per episode. Typically, the weaker force would retire from the battlefield after a bout of warlike yelling and spear throwing (with most of the spears being easily deflected by the hardened cowhide shields). In place of the rather ineffectual throwing spear, Shaka designed a short-handled, long-bladed stabbing spear, or *assegai,* for mortal hand-to-hand combat. The short stabbing *assegai*[32] was known to the Zulus by the name of *iklwa,* due to the sucking sound it made when withdrawn from the bowels of a speared enemy. In addition to the short stabbing spear, Zulu warriors usually carried one or two lighter throwing spears, and the *indunas* ("captains or minor chiefs") also carried hardwood knobbed

---

[31] He was born Godongwana, but changed his name to Dingiswayo (which means, "he who is troubled," "wanderer," or "the outcast") after he was forced to flee when his plot to murder his own father, Chief Jobe, was discovered. Upon his father's death he returned and claimed the chieftaincy.

[32] *Assegai* is an Arabic/Berber word for spear that has come to us through Old Spanish by way of Old French. The short-handled, long-bladed Zulu stabbing version was used much like a Roman *gladius:* a short sword.

clubs for close combat. These *knopkieries*[33] were also used to dispense deadly "battlefield justice" to cowardly or undisciplined warriors. It was said that British officers in the front-lines of war carried handguns for similar reasons.

Shaka also taught his *indunas* to implement a deadly pincer maneuver—the "horns of the buffalo"—to surround and destroy opposing armies. In this maneuver, the entire Zulu army would close with the enemy head-on, and at a given signal, the younger, fleet-footed warriors would break away from the main army in two great "horns," encircling the enemy and driving them against the "anvil" of the older and more experienced, battle-hardened warriors. A *fourth* group of warriors—"the loins"—was held back in reserve, often with their backs to the battle, so as to remain calm and unmoved by the fray. This fourth column stood ready to intervene and enter the battle, should reinforcements be needed.

Shaka's military genius and the ruthless discipline he imposed on his *Amabutho impis* (age-graded fighting regiments) transformed them into a formidable force. Any hint of non-compliance to his orders, or ill-discipline courted immediate execution. His warriors were subjected to a regime of strenuous physical training and deprivation, until they could be relied upon to survive the rigors of extended campaigns under harsh circumstances. They were not permitted even to wear the usual rawhide sandals, which could slow a man in battle; they trod barefoot into battle, on feet hardened by years of merciless training, bare-footed on stony and thorny ground. Shaka re-organized his small army, re-equipped them with his revolutionary short stabbing assegai, and refined the successful age-graded regimental system of the northern Nguni. These regiments, in their *Amabutho* system, each consisted of men of similar age, living apart from the main tribe in their own quarters, and decked out with their own unique regalia and shield-markings. Thus was the Zulu *impi* ("regi-

---

[33] An Afrikaans word meaning, "knobbed-stick." Often incorrectly spelled "*knob*kerrie" (an Anglicization). The Afrikaans word for "knob" is *knop* and "stick" is *kierie* (not *kerrie*, which means "curry"). To the Zulu it was known as *iwisa*.

ment") formed. They fought not just to win—but to *utterly obliterate* their opponent; thus annihilating any *future* threat. Shaka led his "people of the sky" against the surrounding clans; laid waste to entire districts—killing or enslaving the people and assimilating the captured warriors into his rapidly growing army. Soon, his original Zulu clan had grown into the mightiest army black Africa had ever seen. It would not have been too fanciful to call the Zulus "the black Spartans."

[However, later romantic comparisons of Shaka Zulu to legendary military commanders like Atilla the Hun or Ghenghis Khan *are* fanciful exaggerations—some even called him, the "black Napoléon." The Corsican military genius, Napoléon Bonaparte (1769-1821)—only a decade or two before the meteoric rise of Shaka—was in such a different class as to allow nothing but a crude comparison. Napoléon commanded infantry, cavalry, artillery, engineering corps and even navies—on a *continental* scale—in his audacious sweeps across Europe and the Mediterranean. He defeated powerful, long-established nations which had well-organized, modern, professional armies often numerically superior to his own. Shaka, for the most part, merely faced small, scattered, disorganized clans of tribal infantry armed with crude and primitive hand-weapons.

Even Shaka's much-vaunted double-envelopment maneuver (with a fourth force in reserve) was not unique. This military tactic had previously been successfully employed by many great ancient military leaders—centuries, even millennia before—such as:

- young Alexander "the Great" (356-323 B.C.) of Macedon in his conquest of the mighty Persian Empire;
- Hannibal Barca (247-183 B.C.), that wily Carthaginian (North African-Phoenician) general who crossed the Alps on elephant back and became the scourge of Rome; and
- Danish King Harald I., "Hildetand" (8th Century), in a sophisticated maneuver he called the "pig phalanx."

While the maneuver certainly cannot be considered *unique* to Shaka; it was *original* in the sub-Saharan African context—for he obviously did not learn it by studying history or reading classical literature. There is no doubt that Shaka was "head and shoulders" above others of his *own people*; yet his murderous brutality against his *own people* relegates him to a somewhat different class of "greatness."

Indeed, Shaka Zulu *was* unique in the black African context, in the efficient way that he organized his *impis* into age-regiments, with distinctive regalia, and in the firm discipline and training he imposed on his troops.]

It did not take Shaka long to wreak terrible revenge on the clans that had earlier humiliated him and his mother. The arrogant *Langeni* tribesmen were swiftly and brutally butchered—and *rectally impaled* on the wooden stakes of their own stockades.

In the year 1817, the paramount chief Dingiswayo was murdered through some intrigue. Shaka's army had swelled substantially, by this time, and the chief's death left the way open for Shaka to conquer first the prominent *Ndwandwe* and *Qwabe* peoples—then destroy the confederation of *Nguni* clans further south. These conquests set in motion a ripple-like effect, which spread destructively throughout sub-Saharan Africa. This situation was further exacerbated by the equally brutal depravities of Shaka's runaway general, Mzilikazi (1790-1868), which left vast regions denuded and depopulated. The Voortrekkers were surprised when they arrived and found so much vacant land; they were shocked when they learned that the reason the land was uninhabited was because Shaka Zulu and Mzilikazi *had committed genocide against their own people.*[34] In many places, the

---

[34] Sadly, this seems to have been "a way of life" for many black tribes. Decade after decade, the strong preyed (and continue to prey) upon the weak throughout Africa (Kenya, Uganda, Somalia, Rwanda, etc.); massacring their own people and often even *slaughtering every creature* with which they came in contact (including all the animals on game preserves)—just for the sake of killing—leaving most of the carcasses to simply rot in the sun. Though *some* white ivory-hunters were guilty of killing elephants for their tusks alone, leaving the carcasses to rot, whites, in general, did *far more* to *protect* the wildlife of Africa: Whites founded *every* public game preserve in South Africa and whites also founded *thousands* of privately owned wildlife sanctuaries in South Africa. However, today, blacks are claiming those reserve lands (including the northern parts of the world-famous Kruger National Park) for "cattle-grazing." White authorities

[Footnote continued at bottom of next page...]

Boers found the remnants of razed villages, strewn with the skulls and skeletons of hundreds of cruelly slaughtered inhabitants; such places then became haunted by hyenas and jackals.

The renegade Mzilikaze,[35] with ambitions of his own, had defied Shaka by withholding cattle booty, and had to flee for his life—accompanied by several hundred prime Zulu warriors. Mzilikaze initially swept all before him, shattering and scattering those many offshoots of the original Bantu who had migrated southward and who had settled in various disparate areas of Southern Africa. Mzilikaze and his *Matabele* (or *Ndebele;* "conquerors") met their match, however, when they clashed with the northward-trekking Boers. Accustomed to slaughtering panic-stricken, ineffectual tribal militia and unarmed civilians, they were shocked to discover that the Boers whom they attacked were organized, strong, brave and resilient. At the Battle of Vegkop ("Battle Hill") in 1836, just 40 Boer men, women and servants miraculously repelled about 6,000 Matabele warriors. The Boers, in self-defense, eventually drove the Matabele out of the Trans-Vaal area, north across the Limpopo River. This militant black tribe, after finding itself unable to conquer the Boers, preyed on weaker tribes of their own Nguni or Bantu people—especially the long-established *Shona* tribe. The Matabele enslaved the Shona and dispossessed them of their homeland; stealing it for their own—which in time would become *Southern Rhodesia* (and later still, *Zimbabwe*).

A number of early British and European traders, such as the controversial, self-proclaimed "native expert" and later "great white chief" Henry Francis Fynn (1803-1861), (retired, former-

---

[34] [...continued from bottom of previous page.]
also set aside huge tracts of scenic, fertile land for the sole ownership of the blacks as "tribal homelands." Yet the Boers are now despised, seemingly, for trying to "bring law, order, and civilization to a dark continent, and make *just a part* of it livable for Christian white men and women."

[35] Mzilikaze's name means, "the great road." His was succeeded by his equally barbaric son, Lobengula (c.1836-1894).

Lieutenant) Francis George Farewell[36] (1774-1829) and some missionaries had made contact with the new regent Shaka. They were cordially received by the Zulu king, who was intrigued by their scientific and medical knowledge; which gave rise to the belief that white men were *tagati* ("wizards"). Some were granted land and trading rights around Port Natal, which later became *Durban,* a largely English settlement (soon to be the busiest port in Africa). A few of the traders were invited to witness a Zulu "hunt" which actually consisted of propelling a very long cordon of shouting warriors across the veld, and then driving the panicked herds of antelope into prepared pits studded with spikes, or over cliffs, whereupon the crippled, mangled, and dying beasts could be easily slaughtered. Various Christian missionaries tried earnestly to convert the Zulu, but with little success. The superstitious Zulus venerated their dead ancestors, and lived in fear of their *sangomas* ("witch doctors"), who could reportedly *sniff out* so-called *tagati* whom they claimed to be responsible for any particular misfortune. These "wizards" were accused of having brought curses on individuals, families, or even livestock and crops—and once "found," they were then subjected to cruel deaths. Obviously, anyone the *sangoma* did not like, would eventually be accused of being a "wizard." Certain trees and species of bird (owls and *hamerkops)* were regarded as tokens of ill-fortune; frogs and chameleons were particularly feared, and hyenas were regarded as bewitched.

In 1827, Shaka's beloved mother Nandi died. Driven almost to insanity by his grief, Shaka struck out in a blood-bath orgy of killing. Cows nursing calfs, as well as pregnant women and their husbands were put to death, so that they too, might know the pain of losing a mother. Shaka's brutal bodyguards ranged far and wide through-

---

[36] Farewell had impressed Shaka with his medical knowledge after a failed assassination attempt on the Zulu king, and was granted land near Port Natal. His attempts to get Britain to recognize and annex the area were unsuccessful, as Farewell was a civilian. Later, of course, when the Boers moved into the area, Britain *then* decided to "annex" the region—and *forcibly took* Port Natal from the Boers. Farewell, in the end, was murdered by natives.

out his kingdom, cruelly impaling or bludgeoning any person, young or old, who was perceived to *not* "mourn sufficiently" for the dead Nandi. Shaka reportedly murdered over 7,000 of his own people for allegedly not showing due observance to his decree for national mourning. The Zulu king's mother was entombed with a number of maidens—*buried alive* alongside her (their arms and legs were broken; yet they were still expected to serve her in the afterlife). Shaka never really recovered emotionally from the loss of his mother, and descended into morbidity and even greater brutality.

A year later, after an extended campaign in the south, Shaka's warriors returned home exhausted, only to be ordered immediately to attack his enemies to the far north. Fear and rebellion in the ranks at his obsessive thirst for military victories, and revenge on both real and perceived enemies, led to Shaka's murder by his own half-brothers Mhlangana and Dingane, who succeeded him. Dingane then murdered Mhlangana and all other of his own family, whom he considered might be a threat to his throne. Dingane went on to consolidate the Zulu nation, but was to make a fatal mistake some 10 years later (which can be recognized as the first stumble on the road to the destruction of the fledgling Zulu empire; which would itself end in another half-century). Dingane had decided to try and destroy the encroaching Trekboers. This ill-fated attempt culminated in 1838 at what came to be famously known as the *miraculous* BATTLE OF BLOOD RIVER.

Chapter Eight

"We have not trekked this far across the veld to end up in another *English* town," growled Christiaan Delarey. "We left the Cape to escape the damned English and their haughty laws: to found a new, Boer nation based on God's Laws—and for freedom! I say we go north, and to hell with the Zulus."

Delarey looked around at the assembled leaders for support. Bearded, weather-beaten faces looked back at him: men who had fought the Xhosa, hunted and trekked, loved and married and buried their loved ones on the open veld. They would never again be able to adapt to town life; least of all under the jurisdiction of the English. Behind them younger, fresher faces eager to speak up, edged forward.

One Boer spoke up and declared, "I say we find the first good pasture and fresh water, settle down, grow some crops, raise our children, and defend our farms against the Zulus. Its as simple as that." It was Jan Roux. Several of the older men turned to look at this brave young Boer. "People say that the NATAL midlands are lush and well-watered, that the climate is good, and that the Zulus don't cross over the Tugela River in any great numbers, only in small raiding parties to try and steal cattle. We can deal with them."

A tall, angular Boer with a fringed beard stepped forward. He had the bearing of a leader, and looked slowly across the assembly before speaking. "My name is Piet Retief. I led a large group from the eastern Cape, and they have asked me to represent them here at this meeting. They will accept what is decided here, for better or for worse. But they will not go east to Port Natal, to be again ruled by the British. I believe that the best course of action would be to go directly to the Zulu king Dingane, and make a treaty with him. If he promises to order his warriors to stay away from our wagons, we will set a boundary between them and us, build our farms, and live in peace as good neighbors."

A murmur of assent went through the assembly. "Do we agree?" Piet Retief asked. A vote was held and Retief received their mandate to approach the Zulu king. Pieter Retief (c.1780-1838) was of French descent, born in the Cape. He had settled on the eastern frontier as a young man. He had fought well against the Xhosa in the frontier wars, had soon been elected to commandant, and had become something of a spokesman for the trekkers in their difficulties with the British authorities. He had also been instrumental in issuing a manifesto explaining to the British authorities in the Cape exactly why the Boers were migrating to relocate. He was also greatly responsible for helping the Trekboers in Winburg to form a sort of administration. He then led a large trek party over the *Drakensberg* into NATAL, where they were now congregated.

Among the points Retief had made in his "Manifesto" (published in 1837), was that the eastern Cape frontier was unstable largely due to Hottentot vagrancy and Xhosa raids; that the Boers had sustained heavy losses, and that the British authorities appeared unable—or unwilling—to protect them, their subjects. They therefore had no option but to seek new pastures to the north, which was largely unoccupied. The Boers also promised not to enslave any tribesmen they encountered; leaving no reason for the British to try and impose their will on the Boers in the future—and giving the British no excuse to invade any new sovereign Boer nation.

Before long, Retief had assembled a small commando, and set out for *Gindgindlovu* ("Swallow the Elephant"), capital of the mighty Zulu king. They rode for two days, crossing the Tugela River, the traditional boundary between NATAL and Zululand; led by a Zulu *induna* (a minor chief) they had prevailed upon to take them to Dingane's *kraal* ("corral"). As they approached the sprawling settlement, their eyes surveyed the thousands of grass beehive-shaped huts, the huge herds of speckled Nguni cattle, and the extensive fields of millet and pumpkins. Black, unsmiling faces lined the path as they rode by, bare-breasted women clutching naked babies, young warriors with long cowhide shields, scowling old men, bemused children and skinny village dogs, which barked at the unfamiliar scent of the white men and their horses.

They were eventually led into the presence of the Zulu monarch—a gross, rotund figure seated on a carved wooden throne. Behind him stood his bodyguards, muscular hand-picked warriors, each armed with a *knopkierie* ("heavy, wooden club"). In front of him stood rank upon rank of warriors, impi after impi, each regiment with its distinctly colored shield pattern. They stood silently, the sun glinting on their razor-sharp stabbing *assegais*. A faint breeze stirred the tall feathers on the head-rings of the *indunas* ("captains"). At a glance, Piet Retief estimated that about 10,000 or more warriors covered the hard-ened-earth parade ground. On the fringes of the clearing stood the women, children and old men, equally silent. The group of armed and mounted Boers, numbering only about 70, approached the throne, and at a hand-signal from Retief, stopped and dismounted.

To their surprise, a sun-burnt *white* man dressed in a worn brown suit stepped out from behind the throne, and approached the Boers with his hand outstretched to Retief. "Greetings from the 'Great Elephant,' Dingane. I am Francis Owen,[37] the resident missionary, and aid to Dingane's interpreter. Please show due courtesy by bowing to his majesty."

Retief then noticed a teenage *white* boy standing calmly behind the Zulu king's throne. Owen later informed the Boers that this white youth was named William Wood (c.1823-c.1865). In August of 1836, young William had visited Gindgindlovu (formerly spelled, "Mgungundlovu") with his uncle (also named William) and the Hottentot trader Jan Brouwer. King Dingane, when he heard of the lad, had invited the youth to stay with him at Gingindlovu because he "wanted to see a white child." Young

---

[37] (1802-1854); he was an English missionary with the Church Missionary Society (Church of England).

William began to learn the Zulu language within the first few months, and soon became so fluent that by 1837 he was serving as interpreter for both Dingane and Owen.

[This remarkable youth's personal account of the events that were to follow would later be published in Durban. Wood had arrived in NATAL in 1835 with his father, Richard and his family, and Richard's brother, William (the elder).]

William had even "tutored" Francis Owen, a little, concerning the basics of the Zulu language. Owen himself was thus able to make himself understood (clumsily) by the Zulu monarch, in the vain hope of eventually converting him to Christianity.

Retief stood as stiff as a ramrod, glaring at the white man as he shook his hand, and then nodded curtly in the direction of the Zulu monarch. He did not remove his hat, but stood with his musket at his side, his level gaze on the king's expressionless face. "We are not here to grovel to the Zulu king, we are here as emissaries from our people, the Boers. Tell your king that we have come to forge an agreement with him and his people, to establish clear boundaries between them and us, so that we may live in peace as good neighbors."

Francis Owen turned to the Zulu king, smiled nervously, and then spoke carefully, albeit hesitantly: "Mighty king, 'Great Elephant,' *Swallower-of-Elephants,* the white men, who call themselves *Boers*—farmers—say that they have come to make a land-treaty with your majesty. They say that they wish to live in peace on their own land, alongside your kingdom. What shall I tell them?"

The young white boy then whispered in the Zulu monarch's ear. Dingane nodded, rose slowly, heavily from his seat, and raised his right arm, holding a white wildebeest-tail fly whisk. The crowd before him fell utterly silent. Dingane stared at Retief as he spoke in the sonorous tones of the Zulu tongue, his deep voice rumbling over the vast assembly of warriors. "I see that these Boers are proud men, and do not crawl on their bellies before me, as do my very own people. I see that they are few, and that we are many; yet they are not afraid. What magic do these white men have that they can approach the 'Great Elephant' to ask his favor—armed—and yet without any gifts, as is the custom?"

Francis Owen, looking perplexed, scurried over to the white boy, and held a brief, whispered consultation with him. He then went back, and stood with Retief, obviously hesitant to pass on the king's guarded response.

Dingane had heard reports of the final defeat of his renegade general, Mzilikaze, in the Trans-Vaal, by a commando of only a few hundred of these Boers, and he thus feared them. But he also noted that the few colored, or *brown* men accompanying them, *also* rode horses and carried fire-arms. This gave him courage for the future, when perhaps the Zulus themselves would be able to field a force of mounted men, so armed.

A barely audible sigh from tens of thousands of black throats was the only indication that the assembled masses had heard and understood their king's ominous words. Suddenly, a hunched, grotesque figure, covered in a bizarre assortment of reptile skins, charms and bone necklaces threw himself prostrate on the earth at the king's feet. The ancient *sangoma* ("witch-doctor") writhed and squirmed and gibbered, foam flecking his toothless mouth and chest. Raising himself on one arm, his face to the sun, his eyes rolled back in his head. He froze in that position, like a hideous lizard.

"Speak *Madala*,* Old One, Ye-Who-Sees-All," said Dingane.

[* —a term of respect, which literally means, "toothless one."]

Francis Owen paled visibly, and whispered to Retief, "This is not good."

The ancient *sangoma* spoke in a shrill, quavering voice. "O, 'Great Elephant,' King-of-All, mighty warrior, slayer of thousands. These white men are *tagati* ("wizards"). They come to bring death to your people; to gobble up the grass like locusts, to steal your land. *Bulala!—Bulala!*" ("Kill them now!—"Kill them now!") He spun about and then pointed a bony finger at the Boers, his unseeing eyeballs white in their sunken sockets. He inhaled great shuddering breaths into his scrawny chest, as if trying to absorb the scent of the feared white men.

Dingane's expression did not change. He sat down again, flicked his whisk, without showing any trace of emotion, and said, "It would not be our custom to send these visitors away hungry. Let them eat and rest, and tomorrow we will talk further of their petition."

Owen then consulted with young William, who translated the king's words. Owen passed the message on to Retief, who replied, in typically gruff, to-the-point Boer fashion, "We did not come here to feast or sleep. Our people are impatiently awaiting our return. Let us present our treaty to the king, let him sign, and let us be on our way."

Owen's hand grasped Retief's arm tightly. "Do not insult Dingane by refusing his hospitality. Please, stay. It is the Zulu custom to eat and rest, and to enjoy the king's largesses, before discussing business."

Retief shrugged off his hand. "What did that old witch-doctor say?" he asked.

"He warned the king that you have come to take his land." Owen then looked down at the ground, and shuffled uncomfortably.

"What else did he say?" Retief asked suspiciously.

"He said Dingane should kill you all while he has a chance."

Retief looked hard at Dingane, but the king's serene expression betrayed nothing as he idly flicked at a fly with the wildebeest tail he held casually in his hand. "You may kill me and my men," said Retief, "—but other Boer fighters will come, then more and more. And they may not be as willing as I am to make treaties. We seek ownership of the land between the *Tugela* ("Startling") and *Mzimvube* ("Hippo") Rivers, and the *Drakensberg*. Better that you sign a treaty now, so that there can be no conflict over boundaries in the future. What does the King have to say to that!"

"Please, do not speak so to Dingane; it is not safe!" Owen's distress was obvious, the sweat breaking out on his brow, his hands clutching at his sleeves. "Powerful as he is, the king cannot simply ignore the advice of his *sangoma*. The people heard what the old man said. They fear him, perhaps even more that they do their own king. Wait, please, let the king entertain you, eat, rest. Tomorrow you may try to convince him that a treaty is in his interests."

Grudgingly, Retief turned to his men, and ordered them to sit—with their loaded firearms alongside them. Immediately, scores of bare-breasted young Zulu maidens appeared, carrying bowls of water for the men to wash their hands in. No sooner had they done so, than another file of maidens appeared from the maze of huts bearing earthen containers of sour millet beer, which they presented in small gourds to be passed from man-to-man. The white men sipped the beer cautiously, and many found it to be surprisingly refreshing. Then the king clapped his hands together once, and the first rank of warriors, who had stood rigidly up until that moment, sprang forward, and commenced a whirling, leaping dance. They clashed their assegais in unison against their shields, their bare feet stamping on the hard-packed earth. The drums that accompanied the movements of the warriors throbbed out a deep rhythm, faster and faster, until the dancers were a whirling blur of shields, feathers and shining black bodies. Spinning, jumping forward towards the seated Boers, leaping back, all in perfect unison, the Zulus pounded out their fearsome war dance.

This continued for upwards of an hour in the hot sun, the ranks retiring and replacing each other in perfect order. Then, on an unseen signal, the Zulu drums fell silent, their echoes rolling out across the hills like distant thunder. Dingane stood again, and said: "Do the white men, who come empty-handed, wish to show us how *they* can dance?" Owen again had a brief exchange of words with the white boy, then hurried over to Retief, and passed on the king's words.

Retief held a whispered consultation with two of his lieutenants. "We'll show Dingane who's empty-handed," he muttered.

They in turn then spoke quietly to their men. Each man then untethered his horse, and leaped nimbly into the saddle. They formed three ranks, wheeled about, and galloped to the far end of the parade ground. There, they turned their ponies to face the king, each man raised his musket, and they then galloped at breakneck speed directly towards the throne. As the three ranks of horsemen thundered up to the king, his bodyguards edged nervously forward, as if to protect their monarch from the charge, but he briefly held up a hand to them, and his warriors stopped where they stood. At the last moment, when it seemed that the Boer commando might gallop right over the Zulu king, they wheeled their agile ponies about, fired their muskets, rank by rank, in three thunderous volleys over the heads of the warriors and galloped back to the far end of the parade ground to reload. For a moment or two, the Zulus were dumb-struck, then the hitherto silent assembly murmured like a great swarm of bees. The king again raised his hand, and again the ranks fell silent.

Francis Owen appeared as if about to suffer a stroke, but managed to clap his hands in feeble applause, the only sound to be heard in the vast expanse of Zulus. "Very good, very good!" he cried, before turning nervously to the king, who had remained unmoved during the entire performance. "Does the 'Great Elephant' wish to show the white men any more of his great power?" he asked, wringing his hands. Again, the white boy, his face now shrouded by a deathly serious expression, showed evident anguish as he whispered in the king's ear.

"No," replied Dingane. "It has been a hot day, and my many wives are awaiting my presence. Tell the Boer farmers to sleep well, and that I will consider their petition in the morning." With that, he rose and with slow, dignified steps, made his way towards the royal enclosure, followed by 4 bodyguards.

The following morning, the Boers again rode up to Dingane's kraal from their small camp on the outskirts of the Zulu capital. They had turned down the king's offer of huts the previous night, preferring the *clear air*—a safe distance away from the over-powering *miasma* of cattle dung, sweaty bodies and a thousand Zulu cooking fires. As the sun rose, Francis Owen hurried over to Piet Retief to inform him that the king required, as a test of good faith, that the Boers mount a punitive raid on the *Tlokwe* clan of chief Sekonyela, whose warriors had stolen thousands of his best cattle the previous month. The request irritated Retief, but he realized that it would be a small price to pay for such a huge expanse of land on which to safely settle his people.

They set out at once for Sekonyela's rocky stronghold far to the north, in the valley of the Caledon River. They rode hard, and by nightfall on the last day of that week, had set up an ambush at the narrow defile that led from the village to the nearby grazing lands. A stroke of good fortune enabled them to actually arrest chief Sekonyela when he was surprised and surrounded by the Boer commando on the outskirts of his kraal. They also confiscated eleven guns from the chief's bodyguards, and a good number of horses. It was easy to spot the huge stolen herd of several thousand pure-white royal Zulu cattle being driven towards the pastures in the early morning by a handful of herders. The Boers began to drive the beasts southwards, but were then swiftly attacked by about 100 fleet-footed *Tlokwe* warriors as they forded a shallow stream. The warriors flung their throwing spears from a distance at the Boers, who galloped about shooting and reloading; while also trying to prevent the cattle from stampeding in panic at the unaccustomed sound of gunfire.

Few of the assegais found their mark, but the Boer musket fire was deadly accurate and the Tlokwe soon fell back. Three wounded Boers had their gashes bound, and the commando made haste to clear out of Sekonyela's territory. By sunset at the end of the following week, the stolen cattle had been returned to the Zulu king as agreed, and Piet Retief received

Dingane's thanks via Francis Owen. Owen did point out, however, that the king was upset that Retief had not *executed* Sekonyela and because Dingane had heard about the rifles and horses which the Boers had confiscated, and the Zulu king wanted those for himself. Retief politely refused, as their deal only entailed recovering the cattle, asserting that the guns and 60 horses were theirs by virtue of conquest and were only just compensation for the casualties they suffered while doing Dingane a favor. Besides, the horses had been stolen from Boers in the first place.

That night, the Boers sat huddled around their campfires on the outskirts of the royal kraal. It was not a cold night, being mid-summer in early February 1838, but their fires burned late into the night, and a sense of foreboding gripped them. An owl hooted ominously from a nearby acacia tree, and in the distance a lonely jackal sang his mournful song. Retief tried to lift the spirits of his men by reassuring them that they would be well on their way back to their families by midday, with the signed treaty safely in his pocket. Nonetheless, few of the men slept soundly.

At sunrise they saddled up, and were about to ride up to the royal enclosure for the last time when they were stopped by Francis Owen. The missionary appeared even more agitated than usual, and appealed to Retief and his men to leave their weapons—at the request of the Zulu king—near the entrance to his kraal. "Dingane was a bit rattled by your rather unwise blasts of gunshots the other day, and would consider it an insult if you were to be again armed at the signing of the pact, which he, in any case, regards as more of a petition than a treaty," he explained anxiously.

Reluctantly, the Boers stacked their loaded muskets against the wooden stockade surrounding the royal enclosure, and posted the few colored horsemen who had accompanied them, to guard the weapons. Dingane soon appeared, and when the treaty was unfurled before him, made his mark on it with a flourish. Retief smilingly tucked the precious paper into a leather pouch, thanked Dingane and turned to thank Francis Owen for his part in settling the future boundaries between the Zulus and his own people. However, the Boers had not noticed the *impi* in full battle regalia filing in behind Dingane's row of large huts while the signing formalities were taking place.

Suddenly, the hideous old *sangoma,* who had cavorted in front of the Zulu king at their first meeting, leaped at Piet Retief and spat full in his face, screaming and shaking his head-dress of dried gall-bladders and porcupine quills like a giant rattle. The king raised a hand to signal the concealed *impi* and shouted *"Bambani, bulala aba Tagati!"* ("Grab and kill the wizards!") and when his hand fell back to his side, the warriors ran swiftly forward and surrounded the startled Boers. Those who had hunting knives drew them, and formed a tight group around Retief, even managing to dispatch a few of the warriors, but they were soon overwhelmed by the sheer mass of muscular black bodies. In the *mêlée,* some Boers tried to force their way through towards their stacked muskets, but were held back by the massive weight of the many warriors pressing in. They then heard the agonized screams of the colored guards as they were speared before they could use their own weapons. The Zulu monarch then rose, and ordered that Piet Retief's heart and liver be brought to him. That would give him power over his new, Boer enemies.

Piet Retief and his men were dragged by their arms and legs from the royal enclosure as Dingane disdainfully turned away towards his hut. As the Boers were frog-marched to the place of execution outside the Zulu capital, they struggled and fought, but to no avail. Each man in turn was then impaled through the rectum the length of his body with a sharp hammered wooden stake—and Retief, their leader, was forced to watch. His own agony was finally ended by having his skull crushed with heavy blows from many *knopkieries.* Their broken bodies were left in the open veld to the scavenging of vultures and jackals. In the inner pocket of Retief's jacket lay the treaty with the Zulu king's mark.[38]

Retief and his doomed men had not known that young William Wood's uncle, and 3 other white traders were being held captive in a darkened hut in Dingane's kraal—and listened with horror to the mayhem and bedlam, fearing for their own lives, as Retief and his men were dragged off to the place where they would be brutally massacred. While they were sitting in the dank, acrid smoky hut, with a tiny fire providing the only, dim light, one of the traders picked up a hollow cow horn, filled it with tallow, inserted a twisted cloth wick, and lit it. Thus was the first *lamp,* or "artificial light" introduced to the Zulu kingdom!

---

[38] Both Francis Owen and the young William Wood gave witness to this "Land Treaty" document and its signing by Dingane. The document was well known and witnessed by many people for over 60 years, until it was "lost;" presumed to have been destroyed in a house fire during the SECOND ANGLO-BOER WAR. Photographs of it still exist, though some *liberal* "revisionists" claim the story and document was "invented" by the Boers. [An ANC cadre, and later Minister of Communications, Jay Naidoo (born 1954) infamously published a dissertation in 1985 claiming that the *entire story* of the "treaty" episode was fraudulently concocted.] Nonetheless, a similar treaty signed shortly thereafter with Zulu King Mpande is still in existence—and no one (yet) disputes its authenticity. Mpande (1798-1872) was half brother to Shaka, Dingane and Mhlangana. Although Dingane murdered Shaka, Dingane did not bother to have Mpande murdered, because Mpande was not feared as a future rival. However, in 1840, Mpande (with the aid of Andries Pretorius and 600 Boers) overthrew and expelled Dingane, who fled to Swaziland (where he was murdered in 1841). Mpande succeeded him as king of the Zulus. Later in 1884, King Dinizulu KaCetshwayo also gave a major land-grant to the Boers, for helping him defeat his brother Usibepu. Thus, the Boers *earned* any land they were "given." Liberal revisionists would incorrectly have one believe that the Boers "stole" their land from the Zulu. Nothing could be further from the truth. Yet these formal land-treaties, signed before many witnesses by the kings of the largest, and most powerful black tribe in South Africa, are today disregarded by the ANC-dominated South African government.

Dingane later sent word to Wood's party that they need not fear, as he "still wanted to trade with them." A week after the execution of Retief and his men, when the first safe opportunity presented itself, Francis Owen,[39] young William (and his uncle, William, the Elder),[40] and the other whites fled from the Zulu capital; most of them heading back to Durban, whence they had come. However, they were obliged to leave behind one of their wagons and most of their trade-goods and possessions which Dingane had taken from them. Upon reaching the port, young William Wood wrote his eyewitness account of the events at Gingindlovu (which document exists to this day).

---

[39] After fleeing the Zulu, Owen attempted to convert the *Hurutse* (or *BaHurutshe),* a dynasty of Tswana (Central Sotho). The Hurutse had many savage customs, such as when a mixed set of twins was born, the female was buried alive (which custom the Hottentots also practiced). Incidentally, many African tribes, and notably the BaSotho, to this day, either put the old folk out for the hyenas to finish off, or drive their herds of cattle over them while they are in their kraal, and then bury them under all the dung in that enclosure. That way, the *spirits of the ancestors* will "protect the cattle!" Most of Owen's missionary efforts were a dismal failure [as were those, largely, of other missionaries, including the famous David Livingstone (1813-73), of the LONDON MISSIONARY SOCIETY]. Owen then returned to England in 1840. His diary was later published by the VAN RIEBEECK SOCIETY (1926), officially recording for posterity all the historical details of his encounter with the Zulus. Owen, like Livingstone, reputedly had little regard for the Boers, and thus he would have had no reason to *fabricate* the Zulu-Boer Land Treaty story.

[40] Young William's father Richard, and young William's uncle William (Richard's brother) both died in battle against the Zulus at the Tugela River in 1838. William (the younger) then fled with his mother and siblings to Grahamstown. William later made his way to the United States and served in the American Civil War; along with his own, adolescent son. His descendants live there to this day, and have possession of (and copyright on) "The Diary of William Wood, Interpreter to the Zulu King Dingane."

Chapter Nine

Immediately after the execution of the Boer emissary Retief and his men, thousands of Dingane's warriors streamed out in their regiments over the countryside, seeking out the lightly defended Boer laagers. A few laagers along the *Bloukrans* ("Blue Cliffs") and the *Boesmans*[41] Rivers were warned by fleeing riders (mostly Boer women) concerning the approaching Zulu impis on the warpath. Those laagers with sufficient warning feverishly prepared to fight for their lives. One of these laagers was the combined Christiaan Delarey-Jan Roux trek party. Fortunately, neither Christiaan nor Jan had accompanied Piet Retief and his men on their fated mission. However, Christiaan knew one thing for certain—this time, there would be no rescue party coming to their assistance. A tight laager was hastily formed near *Saaiplaas* ("Sown Farm"), where a few optimistic Boers had already sown crops. Their cattle, sheep and goats were herded inside the circle, then acacia branches with their fearsome thorns were hastily shoved and stuffed beneath and between the wheels and the wagons. Powder and shot from the munitions wagon were stashed alongside each fighter. Then they waited in breathless silence.

They did not have to wait long. They heard the Zulus before they saw them—the rumbling thunder of thousands of feet running over the veld, came to them on the breeze, along with the unmistakable acrid, hircine-like tang of the black warriors' sweating, smoke-stenched bodies. They charged in the classic Zulu battle formation—"the horns of the buffalo"—with the experienced warriors in the center, and the younger, fleet-footed warriors forming the horns. The main body swept up to the laager, then came the humming of hundreds of assegais flying through the air, striking

---

[41] —a different "Bushman's" River from the one at the Cape. The San-Bushmen are the "original" inhabitants of South Africa. The black tribes arrived relatively recently by land, and the whites by sea. Both blacks and whites are thus "settlers."

the wagons like a heavy hail. Then the Zulus were upon them. The sheer weight of the impact from the initial massed charge almost overturned the wagons that were broadside to the attack, and the Boers instantly found themselves in a bitter, merciless hand-to-hand struggle. They fired, passed the smoking, empty muskets backwards, and fired again as newly loaded muskets were thrust into their hands by the women and servants. A heavy black tide rolled against the wagons, then flowed around the beleaguered laager as the two horns closed and came together.

The bellowing of panic-stricken cattle in the midst of the laager was drowned by the terrifying hissing of the Zulu impi and the ragged yells of the fighting Boers. Blood-crazed warriors leaped into and over the thorn barricades. Razor-sharp stabbing assegais slashed through the thick sun-bleached canvas covers of the wagons, and wild-eyed warriors scrambled in through the gaping rips. Boer women hacked at the groping black arms with knives and swords, and fired pistols at point-blank range into the warriors' faces. Terrified children, both Boer and colored, shrieked as they were dragged by their legs from the clutching arms of colored servants, or from their own, frantic mothers, to then have their fragile young skulls smashed against the iron-shod wagon wheels. One or two of the warriors tried to ravage struggling Boer women and girls whom they dragged into the long grass during the heat of battle—only to be discovered by their own indignant *induna,* who then cracked such foolish warriors' heads open with his heavy *knopkierie.*

Christiaan Delarey fought grimly, his back against the wooden side of his wagon. These disciplined Zulu warriors were a much more formidable proposition than the disorganized Xhosas he had fought on their long trek north. The enclosed circle of wagons now held a mass of struggling Boer and Zulu bodies, milling cattle and screaming women and children. Delarey knew that if the laager was fully breached, death would come quickly to the Boers. Above the din of battle, he roared to Jan Roux to turn his fire inward, to kill those Zulus already inside the laager. Erika was feverishly loading hot muskets, passing them to her father, ducking under flying assegais, loading and passing without pause.

There was no time even to swab out the glowing embers left in the hot barrels, exposing Erika to the very real danger of severe injury—even death—from the premature ignition of a fresh charge of powder... no time even to drive the musket ball firmly home with the ramrod. In their desperation, some Boers were even dropping two loose-fitting balls at a time down the smooth barrels, for a shotgun-type effect at the point-blank ranges at which they were firing, throwing caution to the wind and ignoring the risk of bursting a barrel.

Jan Roux, Piet Roos and many of the colored herders now turned their aim inwards and concentrated their fire on those black bodies they could make out through the dust. Some strapping young Boers dropped their empty muskets, drew their long, curved hunting knives, and sprang into the wagons to clear them of Zulus.

Those Boers still alive and shooting from under and between the wagons kept up a steady rate of fire despite the press of warriors, but Delarey soon noted that the volume of shots was not as great as at the beginning of the battle. His fighting men were being speared, and he knew that they could not survive this rate of attrition for much longer. Suddenly a huge explosion rent the air, sending broken bodies flying in all directions. A Zulu warrior had grabbed a firebrand from a smoldering campfire and hurled it into one of the wagons which contained numerous barrels of gunpowder. The resulting blast completely destroyed the munitions wagon, and ripped a huge gap in the laager.

As the smoke of the explosion cleared, the Zulu captain, a royal-blood induna, and a forefather of the future king Dinuzulu KaCetshwayo, held aloft his shield and signaled. As one, the main body of the attacking *impi* made straight for the yawning breach. Erika Delarey saw the gap between the wagons filling with scores of warriors, and knew that their embattled laager must surely now be doomed. She raised her tearful eyes heavenward, and prayed out loud for a miracle.

The panicking oxen, terrified out of their wits by the din of the pitched battle and then the mighty blast, instinctively flowed towards the gap in the laager and fled for the open veld. The stampeding herd met the rush of Zulus head-on. Warriors were gored by the sweeping horns and trampled under the thundering hooves. The agonized screams of the dying warriors mingled with the bellows of the oxen, their blood, likewise, mixed with the churned red earth. Shields were flung aside as warriors dodged vainly between the crazed beasts. Their *induna's* shrieking commands to fall back were drowned out by the deafening cacophony; regardless, the Zulus needed no further encouragement to flee. A hoarse cheer went up from the Boers as the tide of battle turned. Erika's miracle had been granted, and just in time.

Christiaan Delarey seized the initiative. Roaring out to his men to mount their tethered, rearing horses, he sprang into the saddle and led the charge through the gap in the wagons, hard on the heels of the fleeing oxen and Zulus. Firing, clubbing, reloading, firing, hacking with their cutlasses, the Boer horsemen relentlessly pursued the warriors, running them down, scattering the *impi,* wheeling away to reload, then charging again into the fray. Those remaining Zulus who had managed to penetrate the laager were mercilessly killed by vengeful Boers.

The dust and smoke of the blast and the battle began to drift away on the breeze as the Boer horsemen made their way back to the shattered laager, driving back those few oxen that they had managed to round up. Erika Delarey moved from one dying Boer to another, cushioning their heads, praying a few words over each one, gently closing the eyes of those already expired. A tiny infant lay beneath Piet Roos' wagon, his skull shattered. Alongside, with an arm draped protectively over the tiny corpse, lay the skewered body of the child's surrogate mother, Piet Roos' sister. Erika looked up to see Roos approaching the wagon. Wordlessly, she backed away to allow the bereaved father and brother the privacy to mourn the loss of his son and sister—the only family he had. He removed his slouch hat, and knelt beside his battered wagon, his head bowed in grief. After a few minutes, Piet Roos rose, and was soon busy at the grim work of finishing off wounded warriors. This time, in addition to deftly slashing black throats with his curved blade, he neatly severed an ear from each dying Zulu, until he had a wet, bloody string of the grisly, ebony trophies.

The retreating Zulu impi regrouped a few miles beyond the Delarey laager, and counted their losses. The royal induna Dinizulu strode up and down the reformed but depleted ranks, berating one warrior after another. "Cowards!" he roared. "A handful of *farmers* thrashed you! Defeated by women and oxen! What message will I send your king tonight?" A low voice reminded him that he himself had called the retreat. Dinizulu stalked swiftly up to the offending warrior and struck him down with one blow of his knopkierie. "Fools! Better that you die now, by my hand, than be skewered up the backside by Dingane's bodyguards. We go on! There are other laagers along the river. Perhaps you can still regain your honor, and wash your spears in fresh Boer blood before we return to Gindgindlovu."

The remaining impi set off at a brisk trot, led by their indomitable induna. The badly wounded warriors were left behind to slowly die (or to be finished off by the Boers); while the less-wounded managed to straggle back to their own camp. That day, laager after laager fell to the marauding impis, and by sunset the eagles and vultures were circling. As darkness fell, exulting hyenas prowled the shattered laagers, and jackals howled throughout the night; feasting on the flesh of the dead. In all, 40 Boer men, 56 women and 185 of their children were slaughtered, along with over 200 of their faithful colored servants. It was impossible to count the number of wounded.

Forever after, the Boers called that district *Weenen* (the "Place of Weeping"). Piet Retief's young daughter Deborah, not wanting to forget the face of her beloved father, tearfully etched his initials and a portrait of him on a rock. It was still there—150 years later. The Zulu regiments drove off many thousands of stolen Boer cattle and other Boer livestock, guiding them back to their king (as a present to hopefully allay his wrath), and a great victory feast was held in the Zulu capital at Gindgindlovu.

Chapter Ten

The Boers' trek into NATAL was in disarray. Piet Retief was dead, the Boers had suffered dreadful losses, and much of their livestock and trek oxen were gone. They heart-brokenly tended to their wounded, buried their dead, dragged Zulu bodies into *dongas* ("gulleys") to rot, and repaired their wagons.

Although Dingane had achieved a great victory over the Boers, had executed their leader and his men, and smashed many laagers with his surprise attacks, the Zulu king was still uneasy. He had smiled indulgently as returning warriors re-enacted their exploits in the battles, and nodded approvingly when droves of fat Boer cattle were paraded past his throne. But behind his smile, he knew that the real war had only just begun. These tough Boers would regroup, and he would have to fight them again... and again. He knew that he still had to strike the decisive blow, to draw them into open battle, where his huge superiority in numbers could overwhelm and completely annihilate them, once and for all.

In early April 1838, the remaining Natal Boers launched a hastily planned, ill-conceived and ultimately unsuccessful counter-attack. It was a desperate move born of anguish—an urgent need to show the Zulu monarch that they were not cowed by his bloody massacre of their emissaries and the subsequent surprise attacks on the vulnerable, unsuspecting laagers; most of whom were comprised 5/6ths of women and children. Many laagers had not learned of the treacherous murders of Retief and his party, and believed that the "Land Treaty" was being approved, and therefore, were not prepared for an attack. A two-pronged Boer commando totaling about 350 men led by two rival trekker leaders, Petrus "Piet" Lafras Uys (1797-1838) and Andries Hendrik Potgieter (1792-1852), was ambushed by 6,500 Zulus at Talana Hill,[42] after they crossed the Buffalo River.

Christiaan Delarey and the young Jan Roux rode and fought side-by-side through the deadly ambush, barely escaping with their lives. In all, 10 Boers, including Piet Uys and his teenage son Dirkie were killed, the brave youngster riding back into the fray to try and defend his fallen father. The Natal Boers had wanted to show Dingane that his treachery could not go unpunished. In fact, it did rather the opposite. Since the Boers had been driven back so easily, the Zulu chieftain assumed that the white men had given it their best shot, and therefore, was convinced that the next time they met in battle, he would deliver the final, deadly hammer blow upon them.

A group of English-speaking traders, in an effort to show solidarity with their Boer white brothers, had formed their own, small commando to attack the Zulus. They mounted a brave, but largely futile, raid into the heart of the Tugela valley—but found it largely devoid of Zulu warriors: who were all away attacking the scattered Boer laagers. Nonetheless, the traders managed to capture about 4,000 cattle, and took a large number of Zulu women and children hostage. They later released their hostages and divided up the cattle among themselves; but not without a fair amount of wrangling.

Then a second group of only 17 English settlers, no doubt encouraged by the cattle spoils of the earlier raid, recruited 800 "Natal Kaffirs" (as they called all *non-Zulu* tribesmen in the area), and launched their own raid. They attacked and destroyed a large kraal just across the Tugela River, but were themselves ambushed by a force of 7,000 Zulu warriors. In the ensuing one-sided battle, 13 of the settlers and most of their native recruits were slaughtered. The 4 surviving settlers barely made it back to Port Natal, where they took refuge on a ship and then an island in the bay, along with most of the other

---

[42] This same hill (which was also the site of major battles between blacks in earlier years) would host another bloody battle 6 decades into the future; but that sad battle would be white men fighting white men, on October 20, 1899: the Battle of Talana between the Boers and the *British*.

inhabitants of the tiny settlement. The pursuing Zulu army then ransacked and burnt all the buildings in the town.

In the months following the massacre of Retief and his men, the devastating Zulu surprise assault on the lightly defended Boer laagers, and their failed reprisal attacks the Natal Boers remained largely disorganized and leaderless. Delarey was too taciturn a man to engender a large following, and Jan Roux was too young. Rebuilding their wagons and their lives, hunting for buck and fowl, and fishing for catfish in the muddy rivers kept their hands and minds occupied. The long, hot summer days with their fiery sunsets, velvety starlit nights and glorious dawns, had given way to the russet hues and cooler days of autumn. The fine, falling leaves of the thorny acacia trees blew like confetti across the veld, and collected on the broad hat-brims of the trekkers as they sat in the dappled shade of those sweet-scented trees. Truly NATAL was the *Promised Land,* but the question of the dire Zulu threat to their new, as-yet unsecured borders, still had to be decisively answered.

As the days grew shorter and the early snows appeared on the mountains behind them, many trekkers became discouraged by the hiatus and turned back, scaling the mighty *Drakensberg* once again, but this time in the *opposite* direction, heading up towards the Trans-Vaal. The Boers who had stayed where they were, remained laagered; in case of further attacks from the Zulus. The Zulus would make one more major attack on the now-concentrated Boer laagers, in August of that year.

The trekkers had formed two fortified camps, at *Maritzlaager* ("Martiz's laager") and *Gatslaager* ("Gap laager"), on the upper reaches of the Bushman's River. These two fortified wagon camps combined contained 640 men, 3,200 women and children, 1,260 mostly colored servants, 40,000 cattle, almost 300,000 sheep, and some 3,000 horses.

A huge Zulu army surrounded one of the camps after killing a lone scout, but kept well out of range of the deadly Boer musket fire. The Zulus then captured a number of Boer livestock, and spent the night feasting and dancing within sight of the laager. The following day, the Zulus tried unsuccessfully to set fire to the wagons with bundles of burning grass tied to their thrown assegais, before the Boers drove them off with well-placed shots.

Then slowly, surely and inevitably, a firm resolve began to build and swell in the indomitable hearts of the Natal Boers— they would not simply allow themselves to be slaughtered. They were not yet sunk; their ship was intact; yet they were rudder-less. Then, Providentially, a popular leader emerged. This cou-rageous, charismatic Boer had been scouting for new lands be-yond the grey Vaal River to the north, and fighting the renegade Zulu general Mzilikaze (who had fled there during the late reign of Shaka to avoid retribution for retaining some looted cattle for himself). Returning from a foray across the muddy Orange River towards the Kalahari Desert, the northern Boer scouts finally caught up with the vanguard of the Natal trek in late November 1838. They were ably led by a tall, imposing figure in a well-cut suit, sporting a pistol and cutlass on his belt. With him were his 60 hardened volunteer fighters—experienced, fearless men, many of whom had lost their *entire* families to Mzilikazi's murderous at-tacks. These bereaved men now had *nothing left to lose;* except perhaps, their own lives (which seemed vain to them, now that their families had been butchered).

"This man," declared the widow of Piet Retief, "has been sent by God. He will help us take revenge." That man was Andries Wilhelmus Jacobus Pretorius (1798-1853), a dynamic, swashbuckling farmer from Graaff-Reinet. He had already earned himself a reputation among the Boers as a natural leader and an experienced battle commandant. He was accompanied by his son Marthinus, who would later become Commandant-General of the TRANSVAAL, and then the *first president* of the fledgling SOUTH AFRICAN REPUBLIC. Within a week, Andries Pretorius had recruited a commando of 468 volunteer fighters. Among them were a number of English trekkers, who, after initially settling in the Eastern Cape, had also grown dissatis-fied with the British indifference concerning protecting British "subjects" from murder by marauding blacks.

Andries Pretorius climbed onto a gun carriage, and detailed

his battle-plan for a final showdown with the Zulu nation. Christiaan Delarey and Jan Roux immediately volunteered. Pretorius' avenging force, tiny in comparison to the huge Zulu army, was armed with the usual array of clumsy muzzle-loader muskets and old naval cutlasses. They also had 3 small cannons and 57 wagons to form a fighting laager. They fondly called their flintlock muskets *"Sannas"* ("Suzannas"[43]) and their little cannons *Ou Grietjies* ("Old Gretas"). Although the old flintlocks and single-shot pistols were rather unreliable, misfiring at least once in every ten shots, the Trekboers still preferred them to the newly invented, more efficient cap-primed firearms; which had recently become available in the Cape. The simple reason was that flints or their stone equivalent, could be picked up off the ground in the veld; whereas caps had to be manufactured in a factory. There would be one major difference in *this* up-coming battle—there would be only *male* combatants in the fighting laager.

On December 9, 1838, Pretorius urged the assembled Boers to take a solemn vow to Almighty God, that if they were victorious over their enemy, they would forever honor the day of the battle as a holy day—as a Sabbath—and also build a church to commemorate the vow. They bowed their heads and knees in submission to God, and prayed fervently that His hand would be with them, in their struggle against the black heathen. The Boers, the few dozen English-speaking farmers who had joined them, and all the colored servants made the vow:

"Hier staan ons voor die Heilige God van hemel en aarde om 'n gelofte aan Hom te doen, dat, as Hy ons sal beskerm en ons vyand in ons hand sal gee, ons die dag en datum elke jaar as 'n dankdag soos 'n Sabbat sal deurbring; en dat ons 'n huis tot Sy eer sal oprig waar dit Hom behaag, en dat ons ook aan ons kinders sal sê dat hulle met ons daarin moet deel tot nagedagtenis ook vir die opkomende geslagte. Want die eer van Sy naam sal verheerlik word deur die roem en die eer van oorwinning aan Hom te gee."

---

[43] Similar to American frontiersmen, who, in time, referred to their muskets as "Ole Bessie" or "Betsie" and British soldiers to theirs as "Brown Bess." In steady hands, some of these old muskets were remarkably accurate, even out to 300 yards.

("Here we stand before the Holy God of heaven and earth, to make a vow to Him that, if He will protect us and give our enemy into our hand, we shall keep this day and date every year as a day of thanksgiving like a Sabbath, and that we shall erect a house to His honour wherever it should please Him, and that we also will tell our children that they should share in that with us in memory for future generations. For the honour of His name will be glorified by giving Him the fame and honour for the victory.")

After 7 days of fervent prayers to the Almighty, they would confidently and defiantly confront the mighty Zulu nation. The site that Andries Pretorius so carefully chose would come to be known thereafter as *Bloedrivier* ("Blood River"), and the actual day of the ensuing battle, Sunday the 16th of December, which was thereafter officially recognized as a National Holiday: *Geloftedag* "the Day of the Vow" or "Covenant Day."[44]

On Saturday, December 15, Boer scouts reported a large Zulu army converging on the column. This was exactly what the shrewd tactician Pretorius had anticipated, although the Zulus had come a day earlier than expected. Immediately, he ordered the wagons into a tight "D" shaped laager on his chosen ground: a cunningly sited killing-field between the strongly flowing *Ncome*[45] *River* (which would be renamed "Blood River" after this battle) and a deep converging *donga* (washed-out ravine). Pretorius left one "unprotected" flank facing open ground. As this was grassland, with no thorny trees in the vicinity, he had his men weave many *veghekke* ("battle gates") with latticed canes which they fastened between the wagons. At 3 small openings in the defenses, he placed their 3 small cannons. Lanterns were placed at every wagon, hanging from long whip-stocks. The trek-oxen were as usual, kept within the protective laager, along with the tethered horses. Some col-

---

[44] In 1994, the "new government" regime officially renamed this Boer holiday as, "Day of Reconciliation." There is today a fine laager of 2/3-scale bronze replica wagons at the site of the Battle of Blood River. Ceremonies by both Boer and Zulu are held on site, every anniversary.

[45] Providentially, this Zulu name for the river was to be a sign of God's faithfulness, for it meant, "worthy of praise."

ored men were detailed to tend to the trek-oxen, their presence there a calming influence on the beasts. A service was then held to honor the Lord's Sabbath, and the sound of prayers and hymns floated over the veld. An eerie silence then descended over the laager, and the muted glow of the lanterns in the night-mist created a surreal scene.

It was a sleepless night for many of the laagered Boers. They knew full well that they were facing a disciplined Zulu force at least 20 times larger than their own. Their frail defenses could not withstand a prolonged, determined assault. Christiaan Delarey ran through the battle plan again and again in his mind. He did not voice his concerns to Jan Roux, sleeping soundly beside him, oblivious to the restlessness of the older man. The bravery of the young Boer was heartening to Delarey, and again he knew that his confidence in him was justified, but he prayed silently nonetheless, that God would watch over Jan Roux especially—for Erika's sake. What if the Zulus managed to set fire to the grassy veld, and burned their wood and canvas barricade down around them? What if it rained heavily, and their muskets were drenched and unable to fire reliably? What if the Zulus did not attack across the open ground in daylight, as expected, but instead crept up close under the cover of darkness? The Boers knew that their only real advantage lay in their superior firepower—and their unshakable faith in their Covenant-keeping God.

Early on the morning of Sunday, December 16, 1838, out of the thick mist, came the Zulu attack. The main impi had crossed the swollen Ncome River by the thousands, well downstream at a ford. Then a large body of warriors crept close to the flat-lined apparently vulnerable "rear" of the Boer D-shaped laager by using the cover of the steep *donga* which Pretorius had earlier surveyed. The two Zulu "horns of the buffalo" crossed the donga further up, where it was less steep, but then charged as one mass across the open ground, dividing into two distinct horns only when they came within range of the Boer guns, ostensibly to split their field of fire. What happened next at the Battle of Blood River was—and remains—*unprecedented* in the worldwide annals of military history.

An estimated 12,000 or more of the best, bravest and most disciplined warriors in Africa attacked the Boer laager, manned by less than 500 men. The first rush of Zulus cascaded towards the wagons like a black tsunami, but was cut down by the accurate and sustained musket fire of the Boers. Few Zulus actually managed to get close enough to the barricades, to hurl their throwing-spears with any accuracy, before falling back. The second wave came on at pace in closed ranks, leaping over the bodies of their downed compatriots. Then the little cannons spoke, spewing grapeshot, which scythed through the Zulu ranks, cutting great swathes in their lines. Again they fell back. Yet after regrouping, again the Zulus pressed bravely forward; the third wave slipping on the blood and stumbling over the bodies of their fallen comrades. The large impi advancing behind the "D" was cut down again and again by accurate fire from the laager as the Zulus clambered out of the congested donga.

As one Boer later wrote: "Nothing remains in my memory except shouting and tumult and lamentations. We scarcely had time to throw a handful of powder in the gun and slip a bullet down the barrel, without a moment even to drive it home with the ramrod." Andries Pretorius was in his element, riding this way and that behind the wagons, waving his tall hat and urging his men to stand firm, to fire only when they were sure of a kill with every shot. Assegais flew about him, but he remained oblivious to the danger. Everywhere, the Boers hoarsely shouted encouragement to each other, grinning macabrely through the smoke of battle with sooty, sweat-streaked faces as they saw their hated enemy falling to their deadly fire. Most did not even bother to duck under the flying Zulu spears, so strong was their faith in their all-conquering God, and their inevitable destiny as victors.

The Zulu co-commander Dinizulu was astounded at the decimation of his ranks. Every charge of his impi was being cut down well before it could storm the Boer laager. Those few brave warriors who managed to reach the barricades were summarily shot at point-blank range, or clubbed and hacked by exulting Boers. Some of his wounded warriors were even being dragged bodily over the barricades by strong arms and bludgeoned to death with gun butts. Dinizulu had listened carefully to his king's strategy, to lure the Boers into mounting a campaign in numbers into Zululand, to trap them against a river where they could not escape, and then to smash them, to "eat them up," as Dingane had worded it. Yet *not a single Boer* had so far fallen, as best he could make out through the smoke and haze of battle. Just before his impi, tasked with storming the laager from the donga, had launched their attack, a brown hyena was inadvertently flushed from its den in the embankment by their war-cries—and suddenly ran across the front of the Zulu ranks. The hyena, as "death's attendant," was a very bad omen for the Zulu warriors. Surely the old *sangoma* had been right, he thought, that these white men were indeed "wizards." Their new leader, a tall man wearing a tall hat, rode through hail after hail of assegais as if invulnerable. Dinizulu looked up to the sky and saw the hungry vultures gathering.

Jan Roux had fired dozens of well-aimed rounds and had seen one Zulu, and often two, drop to every shot, so thick were their ranks. He counted them as they fell to his steady fire, *"een... twee... drie..."* Yet they kept coming. His musket burned hot in his hand, and his breath roared ragged in his chest and rasped dry in his throat. The acrid white gunsmoke hung thick in the air, displacing the morning mist, which had begun to evaporate in the strengthening sunlight. Beside Jan Roux, Christiaan Delarey was also loading and firing steadily; making every shot count. The older man concentrated on those warriors with feather head-dresses and head-rings, reckoning them to be commanders. He could not have known in the heat of that battle that one of those indunas was Dinizulu, the very captain who had commanded the abortive surprise attack on his own laager earlier in the year, or that one of Dinizulu's descendants would later become king of the Zulus.

The gunners manning the 3 little cannons worked manfully with their eyes down, ignoring the flocks of assegais flying in their direction, lifting their gaze only to aim and fire their *Ou Grietjies*. With every blast of grapeshot, they smashed a gaping hole in the Zulu ranks. Soon, even the bravest of the warriors were avoiding those sections of the laager where the cannons were placed. Finally, the Zulu assault began to waiver, and neither the shouts nor the threats of their commanders could make them charge in again to certain death at the hands of the indomitable Boers. Then Andries Pretorius, always full of surprises, did an astounding thing. He ordered an opening to be made in the besieged laager. By manhandling two wagons aside, his men created a gap, and he led a mounted charge to scatter the Zulus. Stunned warriors fled in every direction in the face of this audacity.

"Kom, Oom Christiaan!" yelled Jan Roux as he leapt onto his white Boerperd. "Let's finish them!" With that he galloped for the widening gap in the wagons, spurring his horse to overtake those mounted Boers who had already set off in pursuit of the fleeing Zulus. Swinging a cutlass wildly above his head, he hacked down two fleeing warriors in quick succession. Christiaan Delarey was hard-pressed to catch up with the younger man, but finally charged up beside Jan Roux, then paused to shrug his musket off his back and take a long shot at a tall, muscular warrior with plumes on his head. Dinizulu saw the big blond Boer wielding the cutlass, then saw a puff of white smoke spurt from the musket of the older man beside him. The Zulu *induna* had a fleeting awareness that the older, bearded Boer looked vaguely familiar, before the musket ball struck his head a glancing blow, and darkness overwhelmed him.

The Zulu army was in full flight before the charging Boers. Some warriors fled back the way they had come, others hid in a dry donga nearby and huddled fearfully together, hoping they would not be discovered. Many leaped into the swollen Ncome River and vainly attempted to swim to safety, clutching at, and clambering over one another, drowning others to save themselves. The vengeful Boer riders, knowing that few blacks could swim well, herded the panic-stricken warriors like stampeding wildebeest towards the swirling river, then shot them as they struggled in the water. Soon the river ran red with the blood of Zulu warriors. Hundreds of demoralized warriors hiding in the donga were soon spotted by the mounted Boers, and dispatched where they were. No prisoners were taken.

In the aftermath of the Battle of Blood River, the Boer chaplain Sarel Arnoldus Cilliers[46] (1801-1871) noted that "when it was all over, they lay on the ground like pumpkins on a rich soil that had borne a large crop." He counted over 3,000[47] dead Zulu bodies. Incredibly, inconceivably, *not a single* Boer was killed— and neither was any of their livestock. Besides the gash on their leader's arm sustained in a hand-to-hand struggle with a Zulu, only two others had received flesh wounds. The chaplain, recognizing Divine Intervention when he saw it, commented that the Word of the Lord had been fulfilled:

"By one way shall your enemies come, but by the blessing of the Lord, they shall fly before your face."

The tough Boer spiritual leader and soldier may well have added an appropriate verse or two from Psalm 91:

"Thou shalt not be afraid for the terror by night, nor for the arrow that flieth by day.... A thousand shall fall at thy side, and ten thousand at thy right hand, but it shall not come nigh thee.... Because thou hast made the Lord, which is my refuge, even the most High, thy habitation."

However, the Boers were not the only ones who noted God's hand in the battle. South African author Dirk van der Merwe and Afrikaner historian P. C. Venter, recorded:

"Old Zulus who took part in the battle as young warriors were later to tell that what decided the battle against them was not the Boers shooting from between the wheels of the wagons, but '*giant white warriors*' shooting from the white cloud hovering above the laager all day... Afrikaners know their survival is completely dependent on Divine intervention."

---

[46] Sarel (Charl or Charles) Cilliers (or Cilje) was a prominent member of the GEREFORMEERDE KERK ("REFORMED CHURCH"), an offshoot of the DUTCH REFORMED CHURCH. Modernly, the *Nederduitse Gereformeerde Kerk* (N.G.K., "NETHER-DUTCH REFORMED CHURCH") is the largest Afrikaans-language Christian church in South Africa.

[47] Some sources estimate the Zulu army was 30,000 strong and record as many as 12,000 Zulu casualties. Even if each of the 450 Boers (in the day-long battle) scored *only* 10 kills that is 4,500. Some shots killed 2 or 3 and the cannon fire was also effective.

Chapter Eleven

The victorious Boers did not rest long on their battle laurels; they soon pushed on towards *Gindgindlovu*—the Zulu capital— to consolidate their stunning victory: by striking at the very heart of the beast. But all the fight had gone out of the Zulu king and Dingane fled. Andries Pretorius and his jubilant men found that the sprawling settlement had been torched, and that the thousands of grass huts were already burnt to the ground: reduced to piles of smoldering ash. The scattered remains of Pieter Retief and his men were discovered, and on searching through the clothing of the executed Boer emissary, the precious land treaty (signed 10 months earlier) was found intact. Pretorious and his men gave a proper Christian burial to the meager earthly remains of Retief and his company. The Boers then recovered around 5,000 of their cattle which the Zulus had stolen, yet which they had hastily left behind in their frantic, mass evacuation. However, a few lingering Zulu regiments ambushed the Boers and Andries Pretorius ordered his commando to return to the relatively greater safety of their laager. After hiding in nearby forests for some time, Dingane finally made his way north to the neighboring kingdom of *Swaziland;* but was murdered there in 1841 by members of the Swazi royal clan.[48]

Despite their many losses, through the bitter crucible of trial, the Boer Republic of *NATALIA* had finally been born—of blood and fire and steel. The Boer's named their tiny new Republic in keeping with the original Portuguese name for the region (Bay of Natal)—but in so doing they named it in honor of the birth of Jesus Christ, the Son of God, who died a cruel death so that His people might live through His sacrifice. Thus, in the naming of

---

[48] The *Dlamini-Nkhosi* are the royal clan of the Swazis, even as the *Usuthu* constituted the royal clan of the *Zulus,* (as the *Tudors* were, and as the *Windsors* are to the British). The members of some royal Nguni clans chop off the last joint of their little finger, as an act of courage, and a "mark of royalty." The Swazis are related to the Zulus.

their Republic, the Boers expressed their gratitude to God for honoring the Covenant which they had made with Him in their darkest hour—and symbolized the new birth they themselves were experiencing as a people.

The Boer republic also enjoyed a better black African neighbor since a new, "more compliant" monarch—who vowed to honor the land-treaty—*Mpande,* was duly installed as king of the Zulus. It appeared that the Natalia Boers had achieved their objectives brilliantly and the surviving trek-parties wasted no time in happily settling in their Promised Land. A *Volksraad*[48] was established and apportioned the land granted by the Zulu king. Farms were soon marked out, usually by riding in one direction for a set time, turning ninety degrees, and then riding the same distance again. *Cairns* ("stone monuments") were raised on the farm boundary corners.[49] The battered wagons were unpacked, and temporary shelters were erected, using the canvas covers to keep out the warm rain. Then the mighty trek oxen were inspanned once again—but this time to drag ploughs through the fertile, virgin earth of NATAL. Little stone farmhouses began springing up; usually sited close to water, and the beginning of *die lekker lewe* ("the good life") seemed to have finally dawned—earned through the blood and sweat of the Great Trek. Hundreds of lonely trekker graves dotting the veld, stretching back the 1,200 miles to the Cape, bore silent testimony to their travails.

---

[48] —an elected governing body; "Folk's Council."

[49] This was actually an old Hebrew-Israelite custom of measuring (Joshua 1:3) and marking land. Scripture also commanded that these sacred landmarks were not to be deceitfully moved (Deuteronomy 19:14; 27:17; Proverbs 22:28; 23:10). Wherever the Israelites travelled, they erected these stone cairns (and even larger dolmens and cromlechs) and left place-names as testimony of their having passed through such areas. They practiced this both in *Biblical* times (Genesis 28:18-22; Deuteronomy 27:2; Joshua 22:10,22-29; Jeremiah 31:21) and post-Biblical times in their various migrations. See the well-documented, historical study of ancient to modern times, <u>Uncovering the Mysteries</u>... in the "Recommended Reading" section in the back of this book.

However, all was not well in paradise. The thousands of Trekboers had left the Cape to remove themselves from the presence of the reviled British "authorities." The Natalia Boers were, however, infuriated by the fact that the *British government* had easily leap-frogged their way by ship up the east coast, and were now ensconced in Port Natal. To add insult to injury, the handful of English settlers there had renamed the area *Durban;* to curry favor with Sir Benjamin d'Urban (1777-1849), then British Governor of the Cape. Nonetheless, the Boers held a great feast, calling all together for a Natalia *Nagmaal* ("night meal"—a joyous time of fellowship and communion feast).

Their very first Nagmaal was held in *Pietermaritzburg,* the newly established Boer capital 50 miles north of Port Natal (named in honor of deceased trek leaders *Pieter* Retief and Gerhardus "Gerrit" Marthinus *Maritz* (1798-1838). This presented the ideal opportunity for Johannes Paulus Roux and Erika Delia Delarey to be joined in holy matrimony or as the Boers called it *troue* ("troth" or "trust"). A disgruntled Piet Roos also finally proposed to Bettie Breedt and, as he anticipated, she accepted. On the site of the simple church that was to be built in honor of the DAY OF THE VOW, they duly appeared before the *dominee;* as did Boontjies the Hottentot herder, and his beloved Saartjie, both dressed in formal wedding attire, thanks to Saartjie's sewing skills. Her sleek black hair contrasted beautifully against the white lace mantilla she wore, but she had to insist that her groom remove the blue veld-flowers he had enmeshed into his own, tight curls!

One of the other colored servant girls held Saartjie's squalling, *green-eyed, straight-haired* infant boy, who had been born a few months earlier, for the duration of the short ceremony. Saartjie herself had made sure that Boontjies succumbed to her charms as soon as she had discovered that she was pregnant as a result of her rape at the hands of Piet Roos, in the hope thereby of avoiding the inevitable scandal. Although the simple Hottentot herder was unable to calculate the exact duration of his bride's pregnancy with any accuracy, he was intrigued—and not a little disappointed—that their baby boy bore no resemblance to him at all. A second dominee was busy conducting baptisms at the far end of the common, so Saartjie insisted that they both go over and have their infant son christened there and then.

Saartjie, born of Muslim Malay slave parents at the Cape, and formally named *Sarah,* had long since adopted the Calvinistic Christianity of her beloved employer, Mevrou Breedt, as well as her employer's surname; as was fairly common practice at the time. Boontjies, however, was an adopted orphan Hottentot who never had a surname. He acquired the Dutch sobriquet *Boontjies* ("Little Beans"), due to his inordinate fondness for saucy legumes as an infant. Just before their wedding, it had suddenly occurred to him that he had better "choose" a surname very quickly, to enable the pastor to inscribe one on their certificate of marriage. So he had blurted out Boontjies *Ryer* (colloquial Afrikaans for "rider") to the dominee. Their son was thus duly christened *Krisjan Ryer;* his first name being a loose, but flattering combination of the names of the colored couple's Boer patrons, *Christiaan* Delarey and *Jan* Roux. The coloreds were somewhat more inventive when it came to naming their offspring than were the Boers, who regularly christened their sons, quite often, with the father's own name. It was not unusual for grandfather, father and son, all to bear the same first name (or at least the same *middle* name).

Christiaan Delarey stood proudly alongside his fair daughter (who was radiant in her simple cotton wedding gown and garlanded hair), before handing her over to a beaming Jan Roux. Jan was now almost unrecognizable in his formal black suit, clean-shaven and with his own fair hair neatly combed. Jan Roux's widowed father Johannes had only recently succumbed to a lingering infection from the broken leg sustained in the fall from his horse during the trek, and, sadly, had not survived long enough to see his only son married. Johannes' simple burial had taken place just within sight of the Promised Land and Jan Roux now proudly, but solemnly, bore his fathers mantle upon his broad young shoulders.

Erika's meerkat Koerie, now fully grown, managed to briefly disrupt the nuptial ceremony by escaping the clutches of his designated attendant, and then squirming under the wedding dress of his giggling mistress. The stern Dutch Reformed Church dominee was not amused, muttering under his breath something about, *"diere van die veld"* (beasts of the field) not being welcome *"in die Here se Kerk"*[50] on such a solemn, sacred and God-ordained occasion. Nonetheless, the irrepressible meerkat, resplendent in a tiny, blue bow-tie, soon made his presence felt again when he darted out from behind the folds of Erika's gown and nipped the preacher sharply on the ankle as he leaned forward to kiss the bride.

That *Nagmaal* was the most joyous yet held on the trek; coming as it did, at the end of a long odyssey often dotted with tragedies. The campfires on the village common burned brightly —and late into the night—as the Boers celebrated the many weddings that had been performed that day. Their wagons were again formed into a huge laager, this time not to defend against marauding tribesmen, but to engender a sense of togetherness. Lanterns hung from long, bent canes, providing a soft glow between the covered wagons. Boer accordions and fiddles provided the lively tunes to which the trekkers, both young and old, danced. Delicious *boerewors* and juicy lamb chops sizzled on the many *braais*, and aromatic stews simmered in the many black *potjies* (3-legged, cast-iron pots).

Oom Koos Breedt (Piet Roos' new father-in-law) passed around, in earthen jugs, his remaining, copious supply of potent peach *mampoer* ("brandy") and *witblitz* ("white-lightning")— until he himself passed out, rather unceremoniously, in the shadows under the wagons. Many a doughty Boer also eventually succumbed to the Breedt's liberally dispensed home brews. Mevrou Hilda Breedt soon took up her new role as the formidable mother-in-law, and roundly scolded a somewhat inebriated Piet Roos for "looking too deeply" into the brandy jug on his own wedding night. The former Juffrou Bettie Breedt— now Mevrou Bettie Roos—wearing a considerable yardage of white linen wedding attire, eventually dragged her new husband bodily off to their conjugal wagon, there to enthusiasti-

---

[50] —"beasts of the veld... in the Lord's Church."

cally consummate her marriage.

Jan and Erika Roux, who had slipped away to their own wagon when an opportunity finally presented itself later that evening, shyly undressed each other with much anticipation in the flickering light of a single candle, as it was the very first time that they had been physically intimate. Their joyous new union that night was, in due course, to produce a blond son. In a break with tradition, they decided to baptize him Benjamin *Sarel* Roux; in honor of his mother's great-uncle who had died on the trek, bravely facing the Xhosa attack. When that long Nagmaal weekend finally drew to a close, the trekkers, who had formed so many close bonds of friendship and camaraderie during their journey to the Promised Land, inspanned their oxen once again, and set out separately for their new farms, scattered far and wide over the lush midlands of NATALIA.

The Boer commandos continued, with some effort, to recover their stolen herds. Unfortunately for the other indigenous inhabitants, this created a domino effect: the scattered Zulu impis in turn, preyed on the much weaker *Pondo* tribe on the south coast of NATAL. After receiving complaints about this situation from the chief of the *AmaPondo*,[51] the new British Governor of the Cape, Sir George Thomas Napier (1784-1855), decided to move all his available troops to Durban; ostensibly to keep the newly independent Boers "in their place." Talk of the British siding with the Natal Kaffirs, and even the possible *annexation* ("political theft") of their fledgling republic, finally reached the dismayed ears of the new Natalia Boer *Volksraad* ("leadership"). The Boers appealed to Napier to abort such plans but their petitions were ignored; so, with disgust, the Boers prepared, once again to fight it out.

Taking the offensive initiative, in May of 1842, the Boers rode down to Durban, drove off the British transport oxen, commandeered 700 head of cattle, beat off a night attack by the British, and then besieged about 500 British troops and civilians

---

[51] The prefix *ama-* means "people of" in Zulu. In the Nguni dialects, the prefix is sometimes *aba-*.

in a hastily erected stockade under the command of Captain Thomas Charlton Smith (1794-1883). It had been a dizzyingly fast transition from the white men of NATAL fighting the blacks, to the white men of NATAL fighting each other. The British "authorities" were quite bitter concerning the *loss* of many thousands of those whom they had considered to be *their* Boer "subjects"—who had the *audacity* to move to a new land and live as their own sovereigns; outside of British control. Some Boers imagined that is how Pharaoh felt when "his" Israelite *slaves* left Egypt in the Exodus under Moses, on their way to *their* Promised Land. The Boers firmly, and correctly, believed that the British would never accept their independence and that the British would try to steal their new homeland of NATALIA; as they had stolen *Kaapstad* (Cape Town).

Captain Smith's fragile defensive position lacked both sufficient water and food, but the surrender of proud British troops to rural Boer farmers was unthinkable. A young man known by the name of Richard "Dick" Phillip King (1813-1871) then stepped forward, and bravely offered to undertake what appeared to Smith to be "mission impossible." With two good horses and his young Zulu servant Ndongeni KaXoki (1826-c.1911) as a guide, he slipped through the Boer cordon by wading across the shallow bay, and then rode the 600 miles to the nearest British garrison in Grahamstown—in only 10 days—arriving there in a state of utter exhaustion. More British troops were immediately dispatched towards Durban, and the swift arrival of the warship *HMS Southampton,* with 5 companies of infantry, soon tipped the balance of power in favor of the besieged Durbanites. Dick King became a local folk hero and was rewarded with £15[52] and a farm at *Isipingo* (named after a local fruit). Ndongeni was likewise rewarded for his services to the British Crown by being given a farm on the *Mzimkulu* ("Big") River.

Andries Pretorius withdrew his commandos and the reinforced British troops, now under the command of Lieutenant-Colonel

---

[52] £370 or $740 in today's currency.

Abraham Josias Cloete[53] (1794-1886), backed up a demand that the Boer Volksraad return any captured British property—and *submit* once again, to the rule of Queen Victoria. After their protracted quest for full independence from British rule in the Cape, their long and arduous trek, their stunning victory over the mighty Zulus, and their joyous investiture of NATAL—the ultimate Boer humiliation was the forced signing of their "surrender" to the British on July 15, 1842. Pretorius had vainly hoped that the Netherlands[54] would send a warship full of troops to assist them—but even their fellow Boers, who had trekked to the Highveld, did not respond to his pleas for commando reinforcements in their hour of need. Over the next century, the Afrikaner Boers would find that expectations of "help from abroad" would be just as much of a pipe-dream as it was then—and that they would have to rely upon *their own,* limited resources (and their faith in God) to sustain and maintain their independence. They also realized the necessity of engendering a solidarity amongst *all* Afrikaners.

Three years later, NATAL itself was formally "annexed" to the British CAPE COLONY. A decade of travail had come to naught for the Natalia Boers. The British then appointed Sir Theophilus Shepstone (1817-1893) as Diplomatic Agent *to the various black tribes* of the area, and "the writing was on the wall" for the Boers. They would now have to contend, not just with the predations of blacks—but their own avaricious, white cousins now appeared to be taking sides with the

---

[53] —who would come to be called, "Father of the British Army."

[54] However, it seems that the Kingdom of the Netherlands, which had been on shaky terms itself with the British over the past several centuries, did not want to risk a major war between Britain and the Netherlands, over some tiny, "unofficial" Dutch colony on the other side of the world. By the end of the 17th Century the Dutch had driven the British out of the East Indies, cutting the British off from the very lucrative spice trade (nutmeg, mace, cloves, cinnamon, ginger, turmeric, and black pepper—which once was so costly it was sold by the *individual peppercorn).* The desire for *retribution* possibly explains the reason why Britain chose to *steal* the "Cape Dutch" settlement, and later, the two fledgling republics from the peaceful, freedom-loving Afrikaner Boers.

blacks against them (even as they had in the eastern Cape). Many Boers simply *once again* dismantled what they could of their homesteads, gathered their flocks and herds, inspanned their trek-oxen, and set out north across the mountains for the vast, largely uninhabited interior of the continent. This trickle of wagons heading north again (out of their stolen republic) continued *for the next decade,* as the British slowly tightened their grip on NATAL.

[In later years, in the Boer Republic of the ORANGE FREE STATE a life-size statue of a barefoot woman would be erected next to the Retief Pass, honoring the courage and determination of the Voortrekker women. The statue would commemorate the time when, after the British declared their intention to "annex" NATAL in 1842, Susanna Smit (wife of minister Erasmus Smit and the sister of Gerrit Maritz) declared:

"We would rather walk barefoot back over the Drakensberg before we yield to the British yoke."]

Chapter Twelve

It was mid-summer, and the rich, red earth and humid climate of NATAL had produced luxuriant growth in the new couple's fields. Hardy vegetables and stout corn had shot up rapidly after Jan Roux had ploughed the plots and Erika had planted the seed. Boontjies Ryer, the herder, reveled in his new responsibilities: riding his horse busily to and fro across their sprawling rangelands, delighting in the births of his young master's calves and lambs. He would gallop home for a simple midday meal of bread and cheese with his beloved Saartjie and their little son Krisjan, before rushing off again, imagining that he had heard the distant call of a jackal that might threaten the flocks. Saartjie had tearfully requested Mevrou Hilda Breedt and Bettie to allow her to resign and then accompany her Boontjies (whom she had recently married) to also work for his employer, Jan Roux and his new family. Piet Roos was mightily relieved to see the colored girl leave, and take his ill-conceived bastard son with her; to save him from possible further exposure as the immoral cad that he was.

For his own dwelling, the middle-aged Christiaan Delarey had built himself a small, reed-thatched adobe cottage alongside the stream that flowed through their farm; having sited it a short, but discreet distance from the stone house of the newlyweds. The imminent arrival of his first grand-child had done much to lift the spirits of the widowed trekker, but he had paced anxiously on the stoep, distressed as the agonized cries of his daughter in labor rang out from within her bedroom. Saartjie had been a great comfort to her young mistress during the birth of baby Benjamin, as had Erika been to her, during her own recent travail. Little master Benjamin Sarel Roux was soon capable of toddling rather unsteadily along the path—watched anxiously by his doting mother—to visit his gruff but loving grandpa. He would suck on, until it was soft, one of the aniseed-flavored *rusks* ("crisp, oven dried bread") or chunks of salty *biltong,* which his mother had asked him to deliver to her father, and then generously offer the *soggy* "treat" to his grandpa, who would invariably make a show of accepting it from his grubby hand, and then sneak it under his rocking-chair to the grateful meerkat. This once-formidable Boer warrior, hero of many battles, now liked nothing more than to sit and watch his fair-haired grandson play at his feet.

Krisjan, just a year older than Benjamin, was soon big enough to occasionally ride on the front of Boontjies' saddle when he set out to check on the livestock, and little Ben, watching them ride off, would plead tearfully with his mother—to no avail—to allow him to go along. She would sweep the little tyke up onto her hip and ruffle his mop of blond curls, promising him that soon, he too would be big enough to accompany his own father during his chores. Jan Roux appeared larger than life to his little son, who, with his big blue eyes wide in wonder, would look up in awe at the sheer size of his father. Although he had been a large young man to begin with, Jan's already broad frame burgeoned under the large portions of Erika and Saartjie's delicious, aromatic stews and sweet puddings. Jan also now sported a full, red beard, and when he stood, tall and solid in front of the small boy, he appeared to the toddler as some ruddy giant.

Jan's battle-scarred firearm was a thing of beauty and wonder to his young son. Ben would beg to be allowed to play with the musket balls that hung in the leather pouch alongside the powder horn; promising with his pleadings that he would put them all back where they belonged when he finally tired of his game of lead marbles. The long, shiny cutlass that had dispatched many a foe was now mounted above the big stone fireplace, but Benjamin knew that he was forbidden to touch it, on pain of a spanking. So his father made him a smaller, wooden replica of the sword and a miniature musket (its "broomstick barrel" blackened for authenticity), complete with a leather strap, wherewith the young tyke could sling it over his little shoulder.

The little colored boy Krisjan was equally proud of his own loving father, and would listen in open-mouthed awe when Saartjie related his favorite tale of how his father Boontjies had saved the Delarey trek from disaster at the hands of the treacherous Xhosas: in which Boontjies galloped to the Roux laager and guided the mounted commando to their rescue just in the nick of time. Krisjan would savor Boontjies' vivid descriptions of wild-eyed, black warriors leaping over thorn barricades into embattled laagers, only to be driven back by the indomitable Boers and their faithful colored servants. It did not occur to the young boy that the house which his own parents had built was even humbler than the simple dwelling where old Meneer Christiaan lived alone; nor did he recognize that it was sited a fair distance away from the homes of the white people. That was just the way things were—they were the faithful colored servants, who, while they loved their employers, also realized the two races were different and that, therefore, a little distance was proper to give both parties the privacy they each deserved. It also represented the fact that they were servants, not slaves. When off duty, their time was their own and a little distance safeguarded that. However, both employer and servant were willing, at an instant, to help the other in time of need.

When Benjamin was just three years old, his mother gave birth to a baby girl. He would stand next to her wicker cradle peering in at the gurgling infant, and hold out his finger so that baby Delia (named after her murdered grandmother) could clutch it with her surprisingly strong, chubby little hand. When she was a little older, he would pass her one of his rusks to teethe on, and hold the squirming meerkat up for her to admire. The great tan Boerboel often took up a guard position near the cradle, but seldom had the chance to enjoy any crumbs that fell; the lightning-fast meerkat[55] beating him to the snack every time. In fact, the meerkat, having lost his initial fear of the big dog, now *ruled the roost,* and would fearlessly latch on with its sharp

---

[55] —also called a *suricate* or *stokstert* ("sticktail"), it is officially known as, *Suricata suricatta.* They can live for 17 years or more in captivity. Interestingly, for some reason the Boers named this little relative of the mongoose, *meerkat,* meaning, "monkey-cat." While *meer* literally means, "sea" in Old Dutch, it also was used as slang for *monkey* (since the monkey was not native to Europe and came from *overseas).* *Meer* can also mean "lake" in Afrikaans, but the *meerkat* itself is seldom found near water, being virtually independent thereof; preferring the semi-arid areas.

teeth to the massive jowls of the dog named *Wagter* ("Watcher" or "Guardian"), if there was ever any contest over dropped food. The gentle dog simply accepted the higher-strung, tiny mammal's inability to share. At age 4, Benjamin was given a grey Boerperd foal to look after, and the two soon became inseparable.

Several times a week, Jan Roux and Boontjies Ryer would ride their horses side-by-side, armed with their muskets, and patrol the long boundaries and the firebreaks of the sprawling farm, ever alert for stock thieves. Many non-Zulu Natal Kaffirs had taken to "making a living" from cattle and sheep thievery, or even from stealing the crops into which the Boers had invested significant time, labor, and resources. Quite often, just before the Boers harvested their crops, the Kaffirs would steal them and then sell them to their fellow Kaffirs. After the back-breaking work of ploughing, sowing and weeding, it was heart-breaking to find the bulk of the ripe crop stolen. This particularly incensed the hard-working Boers, who realized that such theft was an *abomination* in God's eyes: for Scripture declared that it was the *sacred* right of a man to be the first to eat of his own harvest. In fact, in Israel, men were even exempted from military duty if they had not yet eaten from their newly planted orchards or vineyards (Deuteronomy 20:4-7).

Other *wild tribes* also devastated the Boers' crops and orchards: the ever marauding, fierce baboons from the *krantzes* ("cliffs") and *kloofs* ("gorges") and vervet monkeys from the riverine forests. The Boers' grain crops of corn, sorghum, wheat, and peanuts were also routinely vandalized by large flocks of hungry Egyptian geese and the enormous spurwing geese (one of the largest members of the goose family; ganders weighing up to 20 lbs.). While a careful shot occasionally put a plump, corn-fed goose on the Boer dinner table, it could not even come close to "settling the score" of the crop eaten up by the large, gluttonous water fowl.

Such predations were a *constant* problem. The Boers did what they could to protect their crops from any thief—and frequently, commandos were raised from the affected districts to mount punitive raids against, and recover livestock stolen by the blacks. The British government, of course, did not "approve" of these "vigilante" actions, and threatened to *arrest any Boer* found "taking the law into his own hands." Yet, the British government itself *did virtually nothing* to *stop* such crimes, apprehend the criminals, or reimburse their Boer "subjects" for losses incurred due to the *inadequate* British maintenance of law and order (which they the British were *duty bound* to provide for their "subjects").

The conquered Zulus themselves kept largely to the boundaries of the Tugela and Buffalo Rivers. However, inevitably, the Zulu nation slowly rebuilt their martial state.

Events far to the north had taken a new, and bewildering turn. The British, not content with snatching away NATAL from the newly independent Boers, now cast their eyes further afield. The northern Trekboers had, by then, also established themselves in the TRANSVAAL and the TRANSORANGIA.[56] The Boers in the TRANSVAAL had made short work of driving the renegade Zulu general Mzilikaze and his *Matabele* north across the Limpopo River. The Boers thereafter lived in relative harmony with the remaining black tribes. The *Transorangia* Boers however, were having more difficulty consolidating their own rule, mainly due to the number and variety of other population groupings living on the outskirts of that area. A mixed, colored tribe of *Griquas* (formerly known as the "Bastards" or "Basters"—as *they called themselves*) had established themselves under Adam Kok III. (1811-1875) in the south. Another clan of Basters migrated to SOUTH WEST AFRICA (now NAMIBIA) and established themselves there as the *Rehoboth Basters;* by which name they distinguish themselves, even to this day. To the east lived the *Rolong* under chief Moroka (?-1880) and the newly consolidated nation of *Sothos* under the "enlightened" leadership of Moshesh (c.1790-1870). The *Sotho* were a *conglomerate* tribe, made up of refugees from both Zulu and Matabele rampages in the interior, as well as a fair number of bandits and cannibals from various different

---

[56] —the regions beyond, respectively, the Vaal and Orange Rivers.

clans and tribes. The Sotho were distinct from other black tribes in having a great number of horses, now called *Basotho ponies*, which they bred from the hardy Boerperds they had originally stolen from the Boers.

A small group of Boers under the obscure Michiel Oberholzer inexplicably then sought British patronage; but a second, much larger grouping under Andries Hendrik Potgieter (1792-1852) remained fiercely republican. However, *all* the Transorangia Boers were outraged when, in 1843, the British Governor Napier of the Cape signed treaties with both the *Griqua* and *Sotho* tribes—in the face of which the proud, independent men and women of the almost two-century-old white tribe of Africa suddenly found themselves ostensibly in a subordinate political status to *black* tribes for the very first time in their history!

The Afrikaner Boers had of course, every right to now call *themselves* a "tribe"—and to demand recognition as such. The Zulus, Xhosas or Sothos could not claim to be any older as a distinct tribe in the region than could the Afrikaners. The Zulu tribe itself was *only 3 decades old* and the Xhosas were not much older: both "originated" out of the forced consolidation of many branches of Nguni-speaking *Bantu*. The Boers too, though a "tribe" formed from many different European "tribes," were by now as "African" as any black tribesmen—and were, like the Bantu, descended from many a common ancestor (the very definition of a "tribe"), hence their many common surnames. They had also been settled, at least in the huge area loosely called "The Cape," *for more than a century longer* than any Bantu tribe. The TRANSVAAL and the ORANGE FREE STATE had been "cleared" for their occupation by Mzilikaze's genocides, until the *Matabele* and Mzilikaze himself were, in turn, "cleared" from the area by the Boers.

To show their refusal to accept this new, oppressive situation, a small group of armed Afrikaner trekkers engaged in a skirmish with British troops at *Swartkoppies* ("Black Hills"), in May of 1845, but were ambushed and repelled. In the summer of 1848, Sir Henry "Harry" George Wakelyn Smith[57] (1787-1860), a flamboyant and brave (but controversial) character, "annexed" the vast territory lying between the *Drakensberg* and the Vaal and Orange Rivers, to the British Crown. Sir Harry, a career soldier who had fought against the United States of America in 1812, and against France at Waterloo in 1815, had personally pursued and captured Hintsa kaKhawuta (1789-1835), "the Great," paramount Chief of the *Gcaleka* (a sub-tribe of the Xhosa) during the *Sixth* "Frontier" (or Kaffir) War; just before the Boers had embarked on the Great Trek. However, under the leadership of the less-able Lieutenant-Governor of the Eastern Cape Colony, Colonel John Hare[58] (?-1847), another British force had subsequently been repulsed by Xhosa chief Mgolombane Sandile (1821-1878); son of Ngqika, paramount chief of the *Rharhabe)*.

During the SEVENTH KAFFIR WAR[59] (1846-48), which was triggered by the arrest of a Xhosa axe-thief (who was later "liberated" by chopping off the hand of the unfortunate Hottentot to whom he was shackled), Sir Harry Smith made his personal attitude towards the Xhosas perfectly clear. He literally placed his boot on the neck of a rebellious chief, and declared that he was going to "educate the Xhosas," by building schools, and would "not allow them to remain as evil, lazy savages!"

In the winter of 1848, Andries Pretorius mounted a determined attack on a British army in the south of Transorangia; but

---

[57] Two towns were later named after his *Spanish*-born wife Juana: Ladysmith, in Natal, and the smaller but more scenic Ladismith in the Klein Karoo. Juana was much revered by the common people (due to her beauty and pleasant nature).

[58] Hare built numerous outposts, including, "Fort Hare." He died on the island of St. Helena, while on his way back home to England. Ironically, a "black" school, FORT HARE UNIVERSITY, was named after this colonial officer, and would a century later number among its *alumni,* both Zimbabwean "dictator" Shona Robert Mugabe and South African "liberator" Xhosa chief Nelson Mandela. Sir Harry Smith had thus kept to his promise; i.e. to "educate" the "lazy, evil" Xhosa!

[59] Also known as the "War of the Axe."

even *his* military expertise was not enough to defeat Sir Harry's troops and the British won a decisive victory against the outnumbered Boers at the BATTLE OF BOOMPLAATS ("tree-flats"). However, the British soon found that fighting the Xhosa in the viciously contested, 3-year-long EIGHTH FRONTIER WAR OF 1850, while at the same time trying to consolidate their control over their *Orange River Sovereignty,* was a difficult and costly business. The astute Andries Pretorius saw his chance and this time: by seizing a *diplomatic initiative,* he managed to persuade the hard-pressed British authorities to recognize the independence of a TRANSVAAL Boer Republic; which was legally formalized by the SAND RIVER CONVENTION of January, 1852. Thus, at long last, the Afrikaner Boers finally received recognition as a *sovereign nation*, by Great Britain (the greatest power in the world at that time). It had taken almost two long, hard decades of trekking and fighting—against both black *and* white foes—for the Boers to finally achieve a *recognized* independence. The Boers changed the name of the TRANSVAALSE REPUBLIEK ("Republic of Transvaal") to ZUID-AFRIKAANSCHE REPUBLIEK (ZAR) ("SOUTH AFRICAN REPUBLIC") in 1853; which housed a growing population of 15,000 whites, and about 100,000 blacks of various different tribes.

At the BLOEMFONTEIN CONVENTION two years later, the British also begrudgingly "granted" independence to a fledgling ORANJE VRYSTAAT or ORANJE VRIJ STAAT.[60] Thus, the white Afrikaners were now recognized internationally as being sovereigns of *two* independent nations.[61] The population of the new ORANGE FREE STATE consisted of among others, 12,000 Boers.

---

[60] —named in honor of the Dutch statesman and defender of the Protestant Reformation, William I. (1533-1584), "the Silent," Prince of Orange and Stadtholder of the Netherlands.

[61] In May 2008, a full century and a half later, the Afrikaner would be obliged to present this written proof to the UNPO (UNREPRESENTED NATIONS AND PEOPLES ORGANIZATION) in Brussels, Belgium, to gain legal status as an "unrepresented minority" *in their own land;* which had by then, been "democratically" stolen from them by a ANC-dominated black government.

Their capital, *Bloemfontein* ("Flowering Springs") was home to 2,500 inhabitants.

After the white men (Boers and British) established communities and built cities, the populations *burgeoned rapidly* because blacks and coloreds flocked in droves to these areas of civilization and safety, where they could obtain work, be taught trades, and also enjoy the benefits of education, medical care and general law and order—conditions which existed nowhere in black Africa.

A mere 30 years later, while the white population had *trebled* in the ZAR—the blacks' numbers had increased an astounding *sevenfold.* This disparity in population growth was due, in part, to the blacks' common practice of polygamy (which helped stabilize the population after the deaths of many males from war or executions by their own chiefs), and due in part to the more active libido of the black man (with little thought of consequences), which naturally resulted in more prolific progeny. In both Boer republics, citizenship and voting rights were extended only to whites, because the non-Christian and overwhelmingly illiterate blacks were not considered capable of making rational political or administrative decisions in regard to the administration of the Christian Boer nations (even as any whites living in the Zulu nation had no say in the governance of that nation), and because the whites and blacks harbored diametrically opposed moral and religious notions.

The Boers resented the British trying to tell them how to govern their own nation. The Boers considered the nation to be an extension of the family. If one had a "family business" and gave *all* employees (family members or not) an "equal say" in the running of the business, in a very short time it would no longer be a *family* business. The ancient Greek concept of a true Democracy, the Boers noted, works *only* in a community of a *homogeneous* people who share similar political, moral, and religious convictions. Further, the Boers believed they were the *people of God*, and lived "by the Book," in which God commanded His people—"thou mayest not set a stranger over thee, which *is* not thy brother." (Deuteronomy 17:15)

Some outspoken Boers may have argued with the British government, expressing:

"We have nothing against the blacks enjoying civilization—but let them build their own; not try to take what we have built through our own blood, sweat and tears. What right has anyone to take what someone else has built? *We* built these farms, these towns, this nation—we carved it out of the wilderness. If others do not like the fact that only *we* have a say in how it is to be run—let them go elsewhere and build their own nation; where of course, they alone will have a say in how it is administered. We don't recall any Zulu chief offering to the Boer leaders 'an equal say' in how *the Zulu nation* was to be governed. We would never have been so presumptuous, and we never would have even accepted such a proposal. We did not want *their* nation; we simply wanted *our own* nation: where we might live peaceably, albeit, geographically alongside them. Yet Piet Retief and his men were ignominiously deceived and savagely butchered and Boer laagers comprised mainly of women and children were brutally attacked, violated, and massacred. Besides, we do not tell the blacks how to live in their own tribally segregated territories; they are self-governing there. Further, why do the British think they have the right to invade our republics and tell us how we ought to live? What gives them the right to invade black nations and tell the blacks how to live? We have never committed such reprehensible acts against the blacks or the British; yet we are depicted as the aggressors. It is just not right. How can our British cousins, who are supposed to be Christians, treat us so maliciously? We have never done anything to Britain to warrant such inexcusable treatment."

While the ORANGE FREE STATE was, by now, a model of stability and good governance under President Johannes Henricus Brand (1823-1888), their brothers north of the Vaal River—dismayed at the deaths of both of their two most experienced leaders, Andries Pretorius and Andries Potgieter—fell into bitter wrangling over control of their fledgling republic (as men so often do after strong rulers die). Their first president, Martinus Wessel Pretorius (c.1818-1901), son of the hero of Blood River, was eventually forced to resign when supporters of the late Andries Potgieter preferred as a successor Stephanus Schoeman (1810-1890)—and marched on the capital, Pretoria, to install Schoeman as Acting State President. Shamefully, a civil war then ensued in the northern Boer republic, and it was only when a new, strong leader by the name of Paul Kruger (a big, lion-hunting farmer) defeated the rebels, that the diplomatic Martinus Pretorius was reinstated, and was then able to reconcile the warring groups of white farmers.

[This inherent individualism and resultant in-fighting would cost the Boers dearly in their future political machinations. Of course, their decision not to include *even the leaders* of their black citizens in decision-making would also cause problems down the political road. However, the Boers held firmly to their religious convictions; seeking not the approval of man—but the approval of God. The more educated of the Boers recognized that the Imperial British had been invading sovereign nations in the four corners of the globe, for some time now; subjecting those sovereign peoples and telling them how they ought to live in their own countries. "Why, then," some Afrikaners wondered, "were the Boers considered 'evil' for desiring to retain the integrity of *their own sovereign nation* by not extending "equal rights" to those blacks who had encroached to live *within the Boer nations* as "uninvited guests"?]

Chapter Thirteen

Life in NATAL for the Roux family had in the interim, settled down to a reasonably peaceful, almost idyllic existence on their beautiful farm. The many abundant crops of corn and vegetables, and sub-tropical fruits, were duly harvested at the end of each summer, and the surplus transported for sale in the new town of Utrecht. When the flocks and herds proliferated and began to denude the veld, their excess numbers were driven to the distant auction-yards and sold off. This income from their farming activities, however, was seldom enough for luxuries, and their lives on the farm were simple, but wholesome. They never had much spare *cash in hand,* but their hard work and resourcefulness ensured a good quality of life. Christiaan Delarey, initially dismayed by the British "annexation" of their *NATALIA* republic, had finally settled down into taciturn old age. He pragmatically decided to simply ignore any British official who would occasionally arrive uninvited at the main house to conduct a census of Boer "subjects," impose some new tax, or warn them of possible threats of rebellion by disaffected Zulus and Natal Kaffirs.

As the years passed on by, the two boys, Krisjan the colored herder and the tall, blond Benjamin, had both grown into strapping young men before the old trekker's eyes. Krisjan was a comely lad, thanks to his mother's good looks. However, he was also taller and larger framed, than his "father" Boontjies would have expected (since his *biological* father was not the slight-framed Hottentot herder, but the shameful Boer, Piet Roos). Little Delia, now in her mid-teens, was the image of her mother: a beautiful and gracious girl who (with a sense of humor of her own) delighted in teasing her grumpy grandpa about his profound dislike for *"daardie verdomde Engelse duiwels"* ("those damned English devils"), as he called them.

"But some of those English officers are *so* very handsome, Oupa!" she would say coquettishly. "Look at their smart red uniforms, and their shiny boots, their fine English thoroughbred horses, and their good manners! So different from the local Boer boys who visit here, with their rough clothes, and their brusque, awkward manners, riding their scruffy Boerperds! Why can't I even *talk* with the English officers, maybe even marry one some-day, and then sail off to England, to have tea with the queen?" Christiaan Delarey could stomach his granddaughter's joking—to an extent—but whenever any English would arrive at the farm unexpectedly on some "official" business, he would simply turn his back stiffly towards them and stomp off to his cottage, mut-tering under his breath things best not repeated.

Ben and Krisjan had largely taken over the duty of patrolling the farm boundaries, and like their own fathers had done before them, they would ride side-by-side, muskets slung over their backs, searching the fire-breaks for any signs of strange *spoor* ("tracks"). The cattle herd was flourishing; their sheep dotted the green koppies like so many fat, white ticks, and their ver-dant crops stood thickly in the well-ploughed fields. The cattle were allowed to wander over the open veld, grazing as they went; large predators seldom presented a threat during the daylight hours. Even the leopard of the kloof, a cat quite capable of pulling down a large calf, preferred to hunt at night. The sheep and goats, however, were subject to predation by both jackal and *rooikat* ("red-cat")[62] and were thus regularly checked upon by Boontjies or the two boys, and were always brought in to the kraal at nightfall.

Saartjie Ryer had by then produced a daughter, Sarie, and the four females spent many hours in the kitchen of the stone farm-house, pickling and preserving the wide range of vegetables and fruits that the fertile farm produced. Above the big hearth hung smoked meats, spiced and dried sausages, and salted beef and game *biltong*. Their two old trek-wagons now stood forlornly alongside the stone barn, which housed the milking-cows and chickens at night, their canvas covers now utilized to keep the warm rain off the haystacks. The mended rips in the canvas, which had been made by the sharp assegais of both Xhosa and

---

[62] —a type of lynx, *Felis caracal* (*caracal* in English); agile and efficient predators, they can weigh up to 40 pounds.

Zulu warriors, bore silent, solemn testimony to the hardships that the Roux family and their faithful colored servants had endured on their long trek to NATAL.

Jan and Erika Roux, now both in their thirties, savored the many privileges of a happy marriage and a settled family life. Their farm was doing well, their children were a constant delight, and their unshakable faith in *die Goeie Here* ("the Good Lord") provided an anchor for their souls. Nightly, Jan Roux would open their big, leather-bound Dutch Bible and then read aloud a few verses, mostly from his favorite Psalms, about the goodness and mercy of the Lord. Lonely old Christiaan Delarey, near the start of the *Great Trek*, had completely lost touch with his combative cousin—who wrote his name De La Rey, in the old, "fancy" French fashion; a decade and a half had now passed since he had last heard news of him. That cousin had settled briefly at Winburg, before trekking on to the western TRANSVAAL. Though Christiaan was himself no longer a warrior, and patriarch of only a tiny clan, he particularly enjoyed the stirring tales of the great Israelite warriors of the Old Testament, and especially the ones of David and Jonathan. When Jan read the passages of how those warriors of ancient times smote the Philistine hordes with the edges of their swords, Christiaan Delarey's eyes would burn with a fierce new fire, his old, warlike trekker spirit rejuvenated by the blood-and-thunder narratives. However, Christiaan (as most Boers) reveled not in war *itself;* but fully embraced it when it was just and unavoidable. In this he followed the Biblical principle: "Whatsoever thy hand findeth to do, do *it* with thy might; for *there is* no work, nor device, nor knowledge, nor wisdom, in the grave, whither thou goest." (Ecclesiastes 9:10) In life, it was nice to think that one could change one's own fate, by the power of one's own hands (especially when being oppressed); however, as the Voortrekkers learned, "not by might, nor by power, but by My Spirit, saith the Lord" (Zechariah 4:6).

However, late one evening, after complaining of sharp pains in his broad barrel of a chest, the old Boer warrior rested his tired head on his arms, and breathed his last. With him died a large part of the Delarey trekker history, he being the one who had the courage to leave behind much of what he knew; give up a comfortable life on his farm in the Cape, and set out into the unknown. He was buried under a spreading acacia tree on a *koppie* ("hill") overlooking the farm; at rest—at last—in the Promised Land.

The passing of their larger-than-life patriarch had left a big gap in the close-knit fabric of their lives, but Jan Roux was now the new center of their rural existence, and he soon took up this role, providing a sense of stability and safety to his own family, and their faithful servants. Life had been peaceful for over a decade now that the Zulus had been largely subdued; but the Roux family was nonetheless vigilant (even though there was no real sense of danger on their farm). Though the vagrant Kaffirs would pilfer their crops, they had, thus far, presented no physical threat to the lives of the Boers or their colored servants.

However, sadly, Africa itself was not a place that *stayed* peaceful for long. A year after the passing of her beloved Oupa, Delia Roux was busy putting fresh flowers on his grave when she noticed a column of smoke arising in the far distance. Her keen blue eyes could just make out black specks running in groups towards the homestead, and those groups soon materialized into small, scattered herds of black Natal wildebeest galloping panic-stricken through the veld in their efforts to escape the grass-fire. Making her way quickly down to the stone barn, she alerted her father to the threat. He wiped the sweat off his brow, and put down the pitchfork he had been using to throw fodder into the milking cribs. Walking swiftly through the big barn doors, Jan Roux shouted to his son and to Krisjan to saddle up their horses, and ride over towards the veld-fire to investigate the situation. He was concerned that a distant neighbor may have been busy with the burning of a fire-break—and may have carelessly allowed it to burn out of control. There was a real danger that the breeze might carry the blaze across the fire-breaks to *their own* fields, and he had yet to gather in the bulk of the drying hay and *teff* (a small African grass-seed used for livestock-fodder) for the winter feed.

Ben and Krisjan, who had been busy oiling leather bridles and saddles under the big thorn-tree near the barn, soon had their horses ready, and set out across the fields towards the rapidly approaching column of smoke. As they neared the blaze, which had by then already jumped across the narrow fire-break they had created on the far eastern boundary of their land, white egrets could be seen picking off grass-hoppers and other insects which were also fleeing the fire. The two riders had encountered a fair number of the black wildebeest, who galloped about, swishing their long white tails, *jinking* this-way-and-that as they characteristically did when agitated, and blowing through their noses with that strange, almost metallic sound that had earned them their Bushman name of *gnu*. A honey-badger growled fearlessly at the mounted men, and stood defiantly with one sharply clawed paw on the neck of a fat puff-adder. The badger had ambushed the viper as it wriggled slowly away from the encroaching fire, towards a patch of rocky ground where it found refuge; but the serpent was way-laid by the *ratel* (as the Boers called the feisty black-and-white badgers), in its haste to flee the wildfire. Despite the looming threat of the veld-fire, the two young men paused briefly to laugh at the courageous little beast, before leaping off their ponies, and stripping branches from a nearby tree to begin beating back the flames licking their way swiftly through the dry grass.

When they realized that they were not making much headway against the veld-fire, Ben suggested that they set the grass alight near the riverbank behind them, in the hope that by back-burning a wide enough strip before the main fire got there, they could thereby prevent the blaze from jumping the narrow stream, the last natural barrier before their croplands themselves came under threat. They galloped the few hundred yards over to the riverbank, and Krisjan quickly used the flint from his musket and a small quantity of powder from the powder-horn on his saddle to do just that, and the two young men watched from the safety of the shallow stream as their back-burn took hold, and the fast-encroaching veld-fire eventually died out from a lack of combustible material.

It was only on their ride back to the farmhouse that they noticed a small herd of their own cattle being driven off over the far ridge by a group of blacks, taking advantage of the confusion caused by the wildfire. The stock-thieves had separated about two dozen cattle from the main herd, which had been allowed to graze unattended on the open veld, quite far from the homestead. The rustlers obviously had hoped that they could complete their criminal activity without being discovered. In fact, it was *they* who *had started* the fire as a distraction; but they did not set the fire far enough away from the cattle pastures to assure themselves ample time to commit their crime unnoticed and make a quick, clean getaway. Setting veld-fires was a common ploy used by cattle thieves, but it had been some years since any of their cattle had been stolen by Kaffirs, and the Rouxs had become a little complacent. Ben and Krisjan spurred their ponies forward, and had soon narrowed the distance between themselves and the small herd. They arrived in time to estimate that there were about a dozen Kaffirs, armed with spears, who were making straight for a *kloof* ("small gorge") which led into a thick patch of natural forest. They galloped hard to try and cut off the herd, prodded on by the stock-thieves, before they could enter the narrow defile. Benjamin and Krisjan knew that if they did not manage to block the thieves' entrance to the forest, it would be very difficult to flush out the Kaffirs and the cattle once the approaching night fell.

Ben and Krisjan succeeded in their dash to cut off the stolen herd before they were driven into the forest; but two of the Kaffirs, on seeing the riders coming, had slipped away from the others, and concealed themselves in the shadows of the thick bushes at the narrow defile. The two young men galloped up to the entrance to the kloof and fired warning shots over the heads of the approaching herd and their drivers; however, as they then quickly began to reload their muskets, the two hidden Kaffirs took their chance and attacked. They speared the colored youth first, who was closest to them, and then leaped toward the big, blond boy to kill him. To their surprise, instead of attempting to flee, he sprang down from his horse and swung his now-empty musket in a wide arc, clubbing the first attacker senseless, and then drew his long, curved hunting knife. When the second Kaffir lunged at him with his assegai, Ben deftly parried the thrust with the arm still holding his musket, and plunged his knife deep into the chest of his attacker. The spearman fell at once; his shocked, bulging eyes and white, gritted teeth contrasted starkly against his black face. Crouching protectively over the bleeding body of Krisjan, Ben quickly reloaded both their muskets, and then shot down two of the fast-approaching cattle-thieves in quick succession. A few assegais sang over his head while he crouched down to load again, but he quickly completed his task, and again dispatched two of the encircling Kaffirs. The survivors then broke off their attack and fled into the forest, leaving the stolen cattle milling about at the entrance to the kloof.

It was Boontjies who had first noticed the lone, fair-haired rider driving the small herd of cattle back towards the farmhouse in the last glow of daylight. The Hottentot, standing on the covered *stoep* ("porch") of his humble cottage, recognized the lone rider as Ben, and strained his eyes to see if he could also catch sight of his own son, but the lingering heat-haze of that day, and the dust raised by the hooves of the cattle, made it impossible. Then, as the little herd drew nearer, his heart sank. Ben was leading Krisjan's horse by its loose rein, and the limp body of his own son was tied across the saddle. With an anguished cry that could be heard from the stone farmhouse, Boontjies Ryer ran down towards the approaching herd and rider. Young Ben Roux stared wordlessly at him with haunted eyes, as the Hottentot herder fell to his knees in tearful despair. By then, Jan Roux had run down to join them, and together, he and Ben untied the body of Krisjan Ryer from the bloodied horse, and carried it up to his own mother Saartjie, who now stood in front of the stone farmhouse wringing her hands in her apron. When the men gently laid the limp form before her, she knelt down next to the pierced body of her only son, and gently kissed his still-warm forehead. That night, her wails of anguish were drowned out only by the mournful howling of the great tan *Boerboel*.

Chapter Fourteen

At the exact moment that Krisjan had died, almost 100 miles away from that *kloof,* Piet Roos suddenly sat bolt-upright in the chair in which he had been dozing in the shade on the stoep of his reeking, squalorous shack. Two sharp, searing pains had shot through his slumped body, startling him awake. One of the pains had come from his back, and one from his side. He stood up unsteadily, his head throbbing, and felt carefully under his ribs, then reached backwards and felt for the cause of the pain under his shoulder-blade. Both pains were now slowly subsiding. He reached under the rickety wooden chair in which he had been sleeping, and took a long slug of the waning raw brandy in the big earthenware jug. Flopping back into the chair, he belched loudly and scratched his scruffy beard while he tried to remember the dream he had been having while dozing through the heat of the late afternoon.

It had been a vivid dream and its lingering, salient visions now slowly returned to his memory. He had been fighting Kaffirs—something about which he still often had nightmares; even though over 15 years had transpired since the completion of his trek from the Cape. In his dream the Kaffirs he was battling had no ears; just bloody holes where their ears should have been. He remembered that in his dream, he stood with a string of freshly severed ears hanging from his left fist, and in his right hand he held his long, curved hunting knife. Its blade was smeared with sticky, dark blood and with short, tight, black kinks of hair. Roos was defiantly brandishing his long knife at the earless, bleeding, fallen black warriors—and they stared back at him with dull, hollow eyes. Then he saw a white girl, in a frilled cotton bonnet, her flaxen, platted hair falling softly out from the back of her loose headgear. She looked at him, in his dream, with her blue, smiling eyes and then, reaching out with her pale hand, she had beckoned him to follow her; smiling back over her shoulder as she walked slowly away towards some shady trees near a small waterfall. In his dream, Roos dropped the string of grisly trophies at his feet and eagerly followed her. She reached out to him, pulling him gently onto her slim body as she settled back into the soft, green grass. Then his pale, beautiful dream-girl *suddenly transformed* before his eyes. Somehow she became naked, then her white skin grew darker and her blond, cascading locks turned black and sleek—and wet. Shocked, in his dream he recoiled and staggered backward. Though he stumbled in retreat, in revulsion, the girl who had been holding his left hand with her right hand—then clutched his hand more tightly and tried to strike him with her free hand. He tried to pull away, but could not, then in shock realized that he had plunged his long knife deeply into her slim, smooth belly. The look in her eyes instantly changed from anger to bewilderment, and her grip loosened as she silently fell in slow motion to the ground and lay lifelessly with that expression frozen on her face. Until that final, unconscious act, he had forgotten that he had still been holding his hunting knife. *That instant* in his dream he had been shocked awake by the pains shooting through his body.

Shaken and disturbed by his bizarre dream, Piet Roos looked warily about him. His farmyard, with its rusting, dented buckets and broken spades, looked much the same as it usually did. The few chickens that he still owned (one lying dead by a rotting tree stump) were scratching busily at the manure heap, as they had been doing when he had dozed off. As usual, his two scrawny, brown cows were slowly wandering back to the farmhouse for milking, as they always did towards sunset. Everything now looked as normal to him as it usually did; though the dream still had partial hold of him—and he peered around to examine everything to prove to himself he was no longer dreaming. He was then reassured of his pathetic reality. His wife Bettie had left him 3 years earlier—immediately after finding him drunk, and in the arms of a colored prostitute behind the churchyard at the *Nagmaal* (which they had attended for the purposes of christening their infant son!). Shortly after Bettie had left, the Roos farmyard began to look pretty much as it did now, as he neglected his duties and spent more and more time sleeping with his only companion: his brandy jug. Roos now lived alone on the tiny ramshackle of a farm, doing only as little work as he could get by with, to provide for his basic, immediate needs.

Whenever he needed money, he had sold off portions of the original, much-larger piece of land that he had been granted by the Volksraad. His early attempts at cattle ranching had been thwarted as much by his own frequent drunkenness, as by the predations of Kaffir cattle-thieves. He seldom had any idea where his meager herd was wandering; how many calves it ever produced, or even whether any calves were missing; many may have been been dragged down and consumed by predators or stolen and roasted in the kloofs by vagrant Kaffirs—but he never knew it; not caring enough to keep track or investigate. Regardless, his herds had not prospered and his brutal manner had dissuaded any colored herders from working for him. Eventually, there was no more land left to sell off and little upon which to graze his few remaining livestock around his rundown cabin. Therefore, he had sold off the last of his cattle to purchase more brandy and a few essentials; though he kept two milk-cows to supply his own needs. He also had a few chickens remaining (which were generally as poorly cared for as his cattle). The cows usually managed to push through the broken gate that feebly guarded his sparse vegetable patch, and they would often consume whatever vegetables he did manage to grow (infrequently watered and weeded as they were).

[Bettie had written to him once, about a year after she had left him, and informed him that she had joined one of the treks that had left NATAL, migrating once more: this time for the eastern TRANSVAAL. He received this news during one of his frequent visits to the hotel bar, which had been established at Weenen. While there, a letter was handed to him, in which she informed him that she had joined the trek—and that, not wishing to be married to him any longer, she was taking with her their teenage daughter and infant son. Her aging, now-widowed mother, Mevrou Hilda Breedt had also gone with her. They were hopeful of starting a new life in the eastern TRANSVAAL; where she could perhaps get work as a housekeeper in the new town of *Ohrigstad.*[63] That shameful night in Weenen, when Bettie had found Piet drunk and forni- cating, she had later stood, without her husband, before the dominee with her infant son (and heartbroken daughter) and chose to christen him *Breedt,* her maiden name (rather than Roos). While without Biblical precedent, the dominee, dis- gusted after her explanation of her husband's reprehensible sin, chose to grant her request.

Back then, in the hotel bar at Weenen, after having read the unhappy news, Piet Roos had crumpled the letter in his fist and flung it angrily into the fire. He then gruffly ordered another brandy and sucked it down while cursing irrationally under his breath. Roos then, seething with anger, lashed out at another drunk for having "smirked" at him (or, so Roos imagined). A brawl ensued and Roos ended up spending the rest of the night in the local jail.]

The disturbing nightmare Roos had dreamt while slothfully dozing on his porch during the heat of the day had caused him to reflect upon his sad condition. He had then remembered how his wife and children had vanished into the unknown and walked out of his life without any good-bye; other than that brief, hastily written, impersonal note. It left a large lump in his dry throat, which only exacerbated how miserable he felt having been jolted awake in fear, sweating, with his heart pounding wildly in his

---

[63] —named after Andries Potgieter and Andries Ohrig in 1845 and originally called Andries-Ohrigstad; shortened to *Ohrigstad.* Ohrig was a Dutch merchant who, while in Delagoa Bay, having heard of the Boers' plight, had donated supplies to the Voortrekkers. Thus, the town was named after its leader and in honor of their kind Dutch benefactor. *Staat/Stad* is the Dutch/Afrikaans word for "state" or "city." It was briefly the seat of a little *republic,* with its own Volksraad. Mswati, a young Swazi king had sold the land to the Boers for 110 cattle. He also wanted Boer protection against Zulu cattle raids, and the Ohrigstad Commando *did* rout the Zulu raiders. Mswati also agreed to allow a railway through his territory to the coast, but because of tribal wrangling, this never material- ized. Many other Swazi chiefs sold land to Boers; but liberal revisionists claim the chiefs had no right to so sell the land. Regardless, Ohrigstad was badly sited: it was too low, and thus prone to malaria and horse-sickness. It was later abandoned, but is again occupied today.

chest. "Go to the ant, thou sluggard," he abruptly shouted out loud, authoritatively and melodramatically, as if he was preaching a sermon. "That's probably what she would say to me if she saw me now... quoting the Bible at me instead of showing me respect!" he declared, while looking at the cow now staring at him—as if the cow was supposed to take his side. "Well, good riddance! The ingrate!" Roos spit out in disgust. "Who needs you anyway! Certainly not me." Roos tried to shift the blame off himself to make himself feel better, as he drained the remaining brandy from the jug. "And another thing...!" he shouted out as an afterthought, raising his arm in the air (rather unsteadily as he was now a bit tipsy), with his finger pointing upward as if he about to make some profound statement, "—good riddance to that fearsome old battle-axe of a mother of yours; she'll at least be useful to *you*—by scaring the lions away! I pity the poor lions... they won't be 'King of the Veld' as long as *she's* around!" It seems, in his dejected state, that the brandy gave Piet a little courage to get off his chest and verbalize out loud what he had thought about Mevrou Hilda Breedt, which he would have never dared utter if he was sober, and certainly not while *daardie ou Harpy* ("that old Harpy") was still around! Now noticeable wobbly, as an exclamation point to his tirade, Piet flung the empty brandy jug against the dead tree stump, which shattered its shards among the fleeing chickens. Feeling smug and rather pleased with himself, he then dozed off fitfully once more.

Later that night, once the brandy wore off, he realized that he was still haunted by that vivid nightmare. It also finally dawned upon him, as he took stock of his life, that he had *lost everything* and that his miserable life of sin had caught up with him. He felt something like *die Verlore Seun* (the "Prodigal Son") mentioned in the Gospels: who having squandered his fortune in riotous living, was then reduced to serving as a hired hand feeding someone else's swine—and so desperate that he fought the hogs for scraps of food he would notice in their slop. Unable to suppress it internally any longer, the floods of emotion overcame Roos and he surrendered to them. Then the light dawned upon him—even the Prodigal Son, at his lowest, most-shameful, dejected state, *awoke from his sinful life* and declared, "I will arise and go to my father and beg his forgiveness..."

In a moment of true repentance, entirely out of character for Piet Roos, he knelt and prayed that night. He sobbed and cried out, in the darkness, to the Good Lord, to forgive him for his misspent life and for his many sins: against his wife, everyone else who ever passed through his life—and against God Himself. He implored God to forgive him, for Christ's sake—who had died to redeem His people and pay the judgment a righteous God demands for sin: death.

Piet made his peace with his God, timeously, by the Grace of God—for just a few days later, while out chopping fire-wood in the *kloofs,* he was waylaid by vagrant Kaffirs. They had surprised him after he had laid down his axe to wipe the sweat from his brow (and some fresh tears from his eyes). After stabbing him in the back and in his side with their assegais, they then turned his own axe against him to hack and mutilate his corpse; which was left in the forest to rot or be scavenged as carrion. They had taken trophies of some of his body parts, including the lips, nose and genitals for their heathen *muti* ("black magic medicine"). As an after-thought, just as they were about to leave, one of the Kaffirs had noticed Roos' protruding ears, and deftly sliced them off, with Piet Roos' very own hunting knife.

It was perhaps an appropriate end for one who had so lustfully lived by the sword (and in an altogether unholy manner in general): and as Scripture declares:

All those who live by the sword shall die by the sword (Matthew 26:52); and

We reap what we sow (Galatians 6:7,8).

Two weeks later, some neighbors came upon what was left of his corpse and gave him a proper burial; though no one ever knew that he had been truly converted to Christ, before he met his terrible end. Sadly, he passed from this life into the next, without any honor and though he would be *one of the least* in the Kingdom of Heaven (Matthew 5:19)—at least he would be there.

Chapter Fifteen

Saartjie Ryer stood at the fresh grave of her teenage son Krisjan, situated some way off from the gravestone of old Meneer Christiaan Delarey.

[When that old trekker had died, he had not been aware that his cousin in Winburg (the one who still spelt his name in the old fashion) had already fathered a son. That boy, christened Jacobus Herculaas "Koos" De la Rey, would grow up to become a great Boer general—hero of two liberation wars against the British: who would himself capture an English lord on the field of battle. Such were the hopes that all mothers held for their sons, that they would become great men, no matter how humble (or even sometimes shameful) their origins.]

Saartjie Ryer had never told her husband Boontjies—nor anyone else for that matter—that he had not himself fathered Krisjan, but that her son was the product of her rape by Piet Roos on the Great Trek. Now, that terrible secret had been buried with the body of her son. He would not become a great man; he had yet even to achieve manhood.

The dead colored boy's father Boontjies had been inconsolable after Krisjan was killed by the Kaffirs. He now spent much of his time riding *alone:* patrolling the farm boundaries—armed with his old musket. He now harbored a cold, yet burning bitterness in his heart: an abiding hatred for the thieving, blood-thirsty Kaffirs that lurked in the dark thickets (and in his nightmares). He asked the Lord—repeatedly and frequently—to allow him to take his revenge by killing as many of them as he could; with his own hand. But the Lord seemed to have reserved that vengeance for Himself, and Boontjies Ryer was not granted the satisfaction that he so fervently sought.

Boontjies' daughter Sarie, now a young lady, bore her father's features; though his son mysteriously had not. The Hottentot herder cherished his daughter, but she could never adequately fill the void in his heart created by the loss of his son. Meneer

Jan Roux had given Boontjies a number of cattle of his own, and they now grazed alongside those of his employer. The Hottentot herder now also owned a small flock of sheep, likewise granted by Meneer Roux. Boontjies and Saartjie also grew many vegetables for their own table, from the garden behind their humble home. Boontjies Ryer had not questioned the fact that his son had been buried quite a distance from the grave of old Meneer Christiaan Delarey, the first white man to die on the farm. That was just the way things were (and as many believed, the way they should be; peaceful cohabitation was desired and sought, but proper boundaries needed to be defined, drawn, and maintained).

Benjamin Roux sorely missed his childhood friend. Although Krisjan was the son of their Hottentot herder, Ben had considered the colored boy, in some respects, to be like a brother. Though racial lines were clearly understood and considered sacred, Boers and their faithful servants, regardless of color, formed close bonds. The two boys had grown up together on the farm, being transformed from infants into young men; riding their ponies, hunting and fishing and exploring. Having been a year or so younger than Krisjan, Ben had literally looked up to the colored boy while they were still young. However, after he outgrew Krisjan in their teens, and when it came to riding and shooting, Benjamin realized that he himself was the one to whom Krisjan looked up. The violent death of his childhood friend at his very feet, weighed heavily on the heart of the Boer boy, and his only solace was in the knowledge that he had himself killed at least 5 of the Kaffirs who were responsible for Krisjan's death. He watched Boontjies ride off, again alone, to patrol the fire-breaks, and felt the tears sting his eyes as the lonely figure of their faithful herder grew ever smaller, as his horse carried him over the ridge in the distance.

Erika Roux brushed the long, blond hair of her teenage daughter, which lay thick and sleek against the girl's slim back. Delia had grown into a beautiful, gracious, young woman, and the young officers of the nearby British garrison were well aware of this. They had been stationed in the midlands of NATAL to deter the sporadic cattle-raids of the detribalized blacks who had made the kloofs and thickets their refuge. The Zulu nation itself was relatively peaceful at that time, ruled by Mpande, who himself owed his very throne to the patronage of the Boers. Life in the Promised Land of NATAL had finally settled down into something resembling tranquility—compared, at least, to the travails of the *Great Trek*.

When the British martial officer came to investigate the murder of Krisjan Ryer, and the subsequent shooting dead of the murderous cattle-thieves, he adopted a rather superior attitude towards the rustic Natal Boers. He made it very clear where the British authorities' sympathies now lay—and it was not with the Boers. Little did the English officer know, that less than 25 years hence, his own army would face the might of a resurgent Zulu army and nation—and suffer the worst military defeat by "native" forces in Britain's colonial history—at nearby *Isandlwana* (meaning, "little hand," in Zulu).

The haughty British officer also stiffly pointed out that non-tribal blacks were no longer to be called *Kaffirs* ("unbelievers"), but they were to be referred to as, "detribalized natives." Jan Roux reminded the English officer (in a rather *unsubtle* fashion) that the officer's own British countrymen had fought at least *eight* "Kaffir Wars" in a region which *they themselves* referred to as "Kaffraria"—names which the *British themselves* had chosen to describe those conflicts and that area of the Eastern Cape. The officer's expression showed he did not appreciate the "history lesson."

Jan Roux himself spoke barely passable English, with a strong Zuid-Afrikaans Dutch accent; but young Delia's English was quite good. She and Ben had enrolled at the local farm school, where the medium of instruction was English, with Dutch being treated as a second language. They attended classes at the nearby village of Utrecht, which was still rather like a *wild frontier town*—with only one, long main street. Law and order was maintained there by Meneer Johannes Christiaan Klopper (1809-1891) and his huge, powerful wife, Anna Fransina (Labuschagne) Klopper (1841-1874), who would challenge all comers, both male and female, to an arm-wrestling match; which she invariably won with ease. School attendance by Boer children was restricted to the winter months, as the youngsters were required to assist their parents with farm work during the long, hot summer days. Delia delighted in acting as translator when the British officers made their sporadic visits to their farm—and she would carefully set out her mother's best tea-set before serving them home-baked *beskuit-rusks,* cookies and cakes.

Initially, young Ben Roux had kept his distance when the British officer visited to investigate the deaths of Krisjan Ryer and the cattle-thieves. He hoped that his father and Boontjies Ryer would, with the help of Delia, explain all that had to be explained. But the officer imperiously summonsed him to the stoep of the stone farm-house, and listened carefully as Ben, in his halting English, gave a more detailed account of the tragic events. The officer interrupted Ben's discourse to ask: "Why did you have to kill *five* of the natives? Would it not have been sufficient to kill only the two who actually speared your friend?" To this, Benjamin replied that he had to stab the one who attacked him and was forced to shoot at the others when they began hurling their assegais at him. He had been alone, crouched over the speared body of his dying friend, and was facing about a dozen savage, *adult* attackers. He did what he had to do, to save himself. Apparently satisfied that no unjustifiable deadly force had been utilized in the incident, the English officer finally left.

Small though it still was, Durban had already become an important harbor, and the surrounding areas soon sported their first few substantial homes, rising above the wattle-and-daub hovels that had housed the first, pioneer traders of Port Natal. The independent Boers had briefly flown their flag over the area, and their Volksraad had tried manfully to launch NATALIA as a fully fledged republic; but the true character and language of NATAL after the British annexation grew inexorably more English than Dutch. Their two northern republics were now the focus of the Boers, and although the fledgling Boer States' treasuries remained rather obstinately empty, all the trappings of nationhood were soon in place.

Occasionally, the Roux family heard reports of conditions in those northern republics—and those reports were not always good. The fiercely independent Afrikaner Boer character did not lend itself to good governance; internal squabbling between aspirant politicians and civic leaders often frustrated their own attempts to govern their rather unruly citizens. A Boer on his farm, in relation to property rights, was little different than an Englishman in his home (which according to the COMMON LAW, was his "castle"—regardless of how meager). The independent Boer was sovereign ruler over all he surveyed: the vast tract of land he had carved out of the wilderness. He did not take kindly to interference from even his own, elected officials.

Unfortunately, the tone for future fraternal strife within the now white-ruled country, was cast. Little Boer "republics" *within* Republics had sprung up at every turn; only to, in turn, again sink back into oblivion—as the bigger picture of life on the veld unfolded and as an independent nation emerged. The very fact that *two* Boer republics, in the TRANSVAAL and the ORANGE FREE STATE, had now been established, and existed alongside each other, spoke volumes about the factional nature of white Afrikaner individualism.

The black tribal groupings which had managed to retain some level of integrity during the ravages of the "Great Crushings" by Shaka Zulu and Mzilikaze, now also sought their own independence. The British authorities in the Cape Colony did not see the Boers—their former "subjects"—very differently from how they viewed the various black tribes of Southern Africa. This characteristically British attitude caused them to consider themselves racially superior to every other nation or people—even their own European cousins! Despite the abolition of slavery throughout the British Empire in 1834, the average Victorian Englishman still considered *darker* races to be vastly inferior—and they even considered every other white nation, which was *not British,* to be "beneath them." Negroids in particular were objects of ridicule, and it would be another few decades before the modern *myth* (and subsequent cult) of the "noble savage" began to take over in many English minds—and when it did, it served largely to indoctrinate the growing liberal conscience with the notion of some nonexistent fantasy ideal. The popular phenomenon of circus live "freak-shows" (which later were regarded with infamy) often featured pygmies from various jungle tribes, or even primitive-looking pickled Negroid heads (some of which were the actual heads of certain tribal chiefs who were killed in battle) Just a few decades earlier, the infamous (and so-called) "Hottentot Venus," Saartjie Baartman (1789-1815), was paraded naked (which was her accustomed costume) before crowds in London, and then Paris. The shocked Europeans stared aghast at her over-sized, elongated genitals, pendulous breasts and hugely protruding buttocks. "Scientists" of the day speculated over the possibility that she was the product of a mating between a Khoi and an African ape. She died a destitute drunkard. Her remains were still on public display at a museum in Paris over 150 years later (in 1974).

The British, in their egocentric quest to expand their sprawling, global Empire, adopted imperialistic and militaristic attitudes which caused them to view other lands ("their colonies") beyond the coasts of the British Isles, simply as *reservoirs of raw materials* to supply the burgeoning mills and factories of the Industrial Revolution in their own nation. The "scramble" for Africa by Great Britain and other European powers resulted in the novel delineation of sweeping new boundaries (sometimes arbitrarily drawn with the edge of a ruler on their cabinet-room maps, which could only truly be considered, at best, *semi-accurate*). Great rivers and mountain ranges, which had throughout time, formed natural boundaries and barriers between many peoples and tribes, were often ignored in favor of more expedient means of dividing up the "Dark Continent" (such as, the drawing of a straight line).

Chapter Sixteen

Jan and Erika Roux were largely unaware of the momentous changes taking place in the world beyond the narrow confines of their own, rural existence in NATAL. They were indeed, totally oblivious to the fact that very powerful men in England, Germany, France, Belgium, Italy, and elsewhere were facing each other across boardroom tables, and strategizing, plotting, and bartering over the carving-out and dividing-up of other peoples' countries in Africa and beyond. The CAPE COLONY, which was now flourishing under the "stabilizing" rule of the British authorities, was still home to the largest numbers of white Afrikaners, most of whom had basically resigned themselves to being "British subjects" (although they still retained their character as a distinct people; recognizably different from the English-speaking British settlers).

Although many "Cape Dutch" secretly admired, even envied, the independence of their northern brothers in the two new Boer republics, some men justified, in their own minds—as men often do—their own lack of adventurous spirit by considering the tough Trekboer's courage and enterprise as something rather "less than noble." This was also due to ignorance in not really knowing all that which the Trekboers had unjustly suffered at the hands of both the British and the blacks, on the far-flung eastern Cape frontier, and later in NATAL. Some English arrogantly held the opinion that many of the trekkers had fled to escape from *any* form of authority in the Cape (even their own earlier Dutch-Afrikaner government). Thus, many self-righteous people in Cape Town thought that the settlement was actually "better off" without that "rough, ungovernable element" in their midst.

The wealthier English land-owners compared the soaring gables of their own, beautifully laid out and finely constructed houses and their flourishing vineyards (mostly established by, and purchased from the Dutch and French Huguenot settlers) to the modest, even lowly, rustic dwellings and coarse veld pastures of the now largely settled Trekboers (many of whom had built only rudimentary cabins). Truly, these English "Johnny-come-latelys" brought with them a sense of entitlement. They considered themselves to be South Africa's new aristocracy and they looked down their noses at all who were not British. Many of the "Anglicized" Cape-Dutch (who paid a terrible disservice to their rugged brothers on the veld) shared the same snobbish sentiments. Most Cape English were soldiers, sailors, or government employees. While only few were wealthy, they still retained the in-bred air of British superiority.

It has been observed that when a people forget their humble roots, they develop blind spots of arrogance and an inflated estimation of self-worth. Thus, many wealthy Cape whites considered it "beneath them" to even perform simple tasks which they now hired "domestics" to do; so they never had to *soil* their own hands. Anyone who *did* soil his hands, was considered of *far inferior* status; be he black or white. It did not help the pioneers' image, of course, that the English, took the Dutch word for farmer, *Boer,* and twisted it into the new English words *boor* and *boorish,* which mean "rude or unrefined"—such was the English conception of the honest, hard-working Afrikaner Boers (the people who were the actual *backbone* of the nation).

This sentiment seems to have "rubbed off" on many successful Afrikaners too. It was even gratifying to Cape *Afrikaners,* to contrast their own, *sophisticated* Cape culture with the *crass* "frontier mentality" that pervaded the minds of the Trekboers—to compare their own fine homes, farms, and vineyards to the more rustic, humble accomplishments of their northern brethren. It is true, that many of the Trekboers were *bywooners* ("tenant farmers"), mere *serfs,* who owned little and therefore, left little behind them as they trekked northward and took a chance to hopefully make a better life for themselves with a fresh, clean start. However, there were many who also left behind considerable wealth—*despising it,* in the face of oppression; preferring instead to completely "start over," if it meant independence and freedom.

The Cape Afrikaners were understandably also far more informed concerning the goings-on in Europe and the rest of the world, than were their rustic brothers on the veld. This, while perfectly natural, added to the general conception that the Boers were "ignorant;" but it was a false and illogical assumption. Obviously, any Afrikaner living in the city (and especially on the coast), in those early days before mass communication and high-speed transportation would be well informed concerning current events: due to the many different foreign ships which arrived frequently in Table Bay, bearing news (albeit sometimes a month or two out of date) from abroad. However, the average hard-working, remotely located Boer (busy sun-up to sundown, with raising crops and protecting his livestock—rather than going to operas and parties), dozens of miles from the coast, could hardly be expected to be "up to date" with anything that was happening beyond his own little world. The Western world was progressing in leaps and bounds; new inventions and discoveries were being made on virtually a daily basis—but that affected the remote Boers only minutely and slowly.

Across the Atlantic, far beyond the sunset, New York—which was itself founded within a year or two of Cape Town—was busily growing into the great bustling city that would one day become the virtual center of the brave "New World." However, during the early 1850's, *London* was the capital of the British Empire and the *center* of the *Olde World,* and this meant that what was decided in *Whitehall* in London, became law in the CAPE COLONY and NATAL, which were then, comparatively, merely tiny beacons of light in a still very dark, vast, Third-World African continent. All the citizens (white, brown and black) of that colony were considered "equal" (at least in the eyes of the British authorities—for they were all "subjects" of the CROWN; yet those haughty English who constituted the new nobility, of course, fancied *themselves* "above equal").

If that "political equality" had so remained, somewhat further into the next century than it did, the South Africa of the Twentieth Century would have turned out somewhat differently to what it did, in fact, become. Sweeping changes were yet in store for the British Colony.

All the trappings of civilization were very evident in Cape Town itself, but once a traveler left the confines of the Western Cape, he was faced with the raw realities of Africa. To the north, the Boers had instituted legislative measures, from the very beginning, to insure that the nonwhite populations would be excluded from participating in the governing of their Christian Afrikaner Republics.[64] Black nations had the same laws safeguarding their governments too (if their primitive, monarchial dictatorships could truly be considered "governments"). Their "laws," however, were not set forth in writing, but clearly understood to exclude whites. In the Zulu nation—only Zulus had any semblance of "rights." Whites could not deign to move to the Zulu nation, find work, receive government assistance, and enjoy equal rights. If any whites did find themselves isolated within the Zulu nation, they were most often, with only a few notable exceptions, brutally killed.

The vast majority of tribesmen were in any case still illiterate and superstitious, and even their chiefs, again, with only a very few notable exceptions, were considered impulsive and almost childlike in their cognitive functioning—and also prone to emotional outbursts of unimaginably barbaric cruelty; even against their own people. Many were also greatly inclined toward lasciviousness, sloth, drunkenness, and other vices. It was perhaps understandable then, after the many bloody clashes of the *Great Trek* (which had left a trail of lonely graves and bleached bones stretching all the way back to the Cape), that the Afrikaners had no qualms about relegating less civilized peoples to a lower political status within their newly established Boer republics. This was not a Boer invention; it was the same *caste system* which had been practiced in India for millennia. Any hint of stirring up rebellion and strife against the Boer government was quickly quashed, and the strong arm of the white man would

---

[64] See **Appendix A** for a brief discussion of this decision.

hold absolute power there for the next 140 years.[65]

In the eastern Cape, land of the Xhosa, fighting often characterized the relationships between the various larger clans like the *Gcaleka,* the *Bomvana,* and the *Tembu.* The Tembu (from whose ranks would arise Nelson Mandela) were at one stage threatened with war by the British authorities after their *inkosi enkhulu* ("paramount chief") Gangelizwe Qeya (1840-1884) murdered a Gcaleka woman. But these, and the smaller tribes which inhabited that area of the country (including the *Pondos, Pondomise, Cele, Xesibe* and *Fengu)* soon faced an unexpected phenomenon—in the form of a *young girl:* who would be partly responsible for the devastation of their land and people which would destroy them as a military force and even threaten their very existence.

Nongqawuse (1842-1898)—or *Nonquase,* as the whites called her—was only 14 years old when she managed to convince her people to commit what amounted to *national suicide.* In 1856, the rather plain-looking, uncharismatic young girl was sitting staring into a pool of water along side the Gxara River, when she allegedly saw a vision of her Gcaleka ancestors. They told her, in her vision, that they were prepared to return, and drive the hated white men back into the sea from whence they had come, but first, as an act of supreme faith in their ability to achieve this, the Xhosa would have to kill all of their own cattle and consume all their own crops. Those tribesmen who refused would be magically transformed into frogs, mice and even ants, and then blown into the sea themselves, by a powerful whirlwind conjured up by their ancestors. Nonquase told her uncle, the village *sangoma* ("witch doctor") about her vision, and he, duly impressed, approached the tribal chiefs with her in tow. There, she repeated what she had "seen" in her vision and her uncle added

---

[65] Yet, the various black peoples were perfectly free to go and live among their own people any time they wanted, if they did not like living in the caste system—they were not slaves. They *chose* to move to the civilized settlements the Boers had built and had the liberty to leave any time they wished, and to establish their own towns and farms in their *own* tribal homelands.

his own notion that "the Russians" (whose army he had presumably heard had recently engaged England in the Crimean War), would arrive timeously to assist the Xhosa in driving out the whites. Of course, due to his scant knowledge of the world outside of the eastern Cape, Nonquase's uncle did not realize that the Russians were themselves "white" men.

Delighted at the prospect of ridding the land of the whites, the Xhosa enthusiastically set about slaughtering their own herds, killing an estimated 200,000 beasts. Great feasts were held—and for the rest of that year, they partied as if there was no tomorrow. They soon consumed all their own crops, winter arrived, and they continued feasting on their cattle. Spring arrived, and they did not bother to plant any crops; convinced that they would never have to work again—once they "inherited" the fat herds and grain stores of the whites (whom they believed would be driven back to the sea whence they had come). Summer came, and their fated day of destiny, February 18, 1857, finally dawned. Their teenage "seer" had confidently predicted that a blood-red sun would rise that day—but would stand still above the sea, and then *change course* and immediately set in the east, and the hated whites would flounder and drown in the waves; leaving all their wealth to the Xhosas.

As the sun rose on that fateful day, her people sat waiting expectantly, but the sun continued along its normal course through the summer sky high above them, and finally set—*in the west,* as it ever had since creation. Darkness fell on the ruined Xhosa tribe. Starvation soon stalked the land, and the sight of skeletal tribesmen and their families flooding into the settler towns begging for food from the whites, became commonplace (and the theft of cattle and crops became more frequent). Despite the best efforts of the kind-hearted whites in feeding the starving Xhosas from their own, rapidly depleting stores, that *self-induced* famine claimed the lives of 55,000 Xhosas—about half of their entire tribe! This became known as "The Great Cattle-Killing Delusion."

Nonquase, understandably unpopular by that stage, fled to King William's Town for refuge, and the British authorities arrested and then shipped her off to Robben Island, for her own safety. She could not have known that a little over a century later, one of her own tribesmen, Nelson Rolihlahla Mandela (whose middle name, colloquially, meant "trouble-maker") would also be incarcerated on that very same bleak, rocky outcrop in the sea overlooked by Table Mountain. Mandela would be imprisoned for attempting to start a *race war* that would also—his supporters hoped—drive the whites back into the sea; leaving to the blacks all their wealth, homes and farms; free for the taking. He too, although ultimately more successful in his endeavors, would in a remarkable twist of fate, also look to Russia for assistance.

Such were the recurring themes and cycles of life and death on the African continent. The Xhosa tribe, though devastated by the self-induced famine, would rise again, and ultimately, one of their own sons, a royal of the Tembu clan, would become the first "black" president of a future and "new" South Africa.

Chapter Seventeen

In NATAL, about 500 miles from the scene of the devastating famine in the EASTERN CAPE, Benjamin and Delia Roux were enjoying a picnic lunch on the banks of the river that flowed through their farm. On the out-spread cotton cloth lay a steaming plate of juicy, just-boiled, buttered *mealies* ("ears of corn"), freshly drawn from the small *potjie* (3-legged cast iron pot) boiling over a tiny camp fire. There were other delicacies which awaited them: freshly baked bread, a bowl of shredded biltong, fruits from their orchards, jars of sweet jams, cold, sliced roasted beef and venison, and a jug of home-brewed beer. Ben, having now grown into a responsible young man, was occasionally allowed by his father to have a pint of the heady brew for himself, and he leaned comfortably against his sister, who was sitting on the cloth with her back to him. Being Sunday, Delia Roux had brought along her Bible, and she sat reading quietly from the Book of Job. When she came across the verses which described the ferocity of a warhorse, she began reading a few verses aloud, for the benefit of their old white horse grazing nearby, and of course, for her brother's enjoyment also.

That old Boerperd was the one their father Jan had ridden into battle against both the Xhosas and the Zulus on the Great Trek into the Promised Land. Once a fierce young warhorse, the fire in the stallion's belly had grown cold since they had settled peacefully on their farm. The assegai scars on his flanks still showed through his thinning fur and the fetlock that had once been pierced, now troubled him on colder days. The old horse limped a little now, but was still willing enough to carry their baggage along the footpath beside the river. Delia read aloud:

"He paweth in the valley, and rejoiceth in his strength: he goeth on to meet the armed men. He mocketh at fear, and is not affrighted; neither turneth he back from the sword. The quiver rattleth against him, the glittering spear and the shield. He swalloweth the ground with fierceness and rage... it is the sound of the trumpet... and he smelleth the battle afar off, the thunder of the captains, and the shouting." (Job 39:21-25)

The aged horse, sensing he was being spoken to, snorted, then majestically raised his head into the air and retorted with a whinney and pawed the ground in front of him.

Their big, tan dog lay with his head on his paws, eyes rolling longingly in their sockets, occasionally—towards the bowl of biltong, as he silently coveted a morsel of the savory treat. Finally, Ben relented, reached over to the meat platter, took a large bone from it and gave it to the grateful dog, who lazily, but with satisfaction, meandered off a short distance where he flopped to the ground to enjoy his prized possession. Ben then poured the water from the *potjie* in which he had boiled the *mealies* to give it time to cool. The jug of beer and the spread of food were much depleted by the time the sun began to settle behind the *Drakensberg*. Ben, having doused their smoldering fire, began to pack up their picnic. He gathered in his fishing line, and saw that the hungry *barber* ("catfish") had managed to strip the piece of bread off the hook. Then he whistled softly, and their old white horse lifted his head from the green grass on which he had been grazing, and walked slowly over to Ben. The teenagers would walk the mile or two back to the farmhouse, leading the horse laden with their supplies which Ben now strapped to its saddle.

A faint, strangely familiar scent wafted to the old warhorse's sensitive nostrils from the thicket above the riverbank, and from deep in the recesses of his equine memory, an alarm signal was sent to his stiff old muscles. At almost the same instant, the big, tan dog behind them dropped the bone he had been holding in his jaws, and growled ominously, his powerful shoulders and thick neck bunched and tense while the hair along his spine bristled to attention. The horse and the dog both looked intently towards the thicket whence came the acrid stench of woodsmoke and the sweat of unwashed bodies, which had alerted them to the presence of the hidden blacks.

Ben Roux spun about as the rumbling in the deep chest of the Boerboel reached his ears. He drew his knife, the only weapon he was carrying—the same one he had used to carve the meat at their picnic. Delia clung to her brother's belt, peering fearfully over his broad shoulder. At first, Ben thought that perhaps one of the leopards from the kloofs had strayed onto their farm in search of a small calf or a sheep for an easy meal, and was resting up in the shade of the riverine trees. But then he saw the black faces peering at them from the shadows. He grasped his sister by her slim waist, and lifted her easily onto the laden horse's back, before smacking the beast smartly on its rump. The horse leapt forward, scrambling up the riverbank and onto the fields of *eragrostis* ("lovegrass"), which lay alongside, while Delia clung desperately onto his halter. Once on even ground Delia looked backwards to see if her brother was following. Two black figures suddenly lunged at the leather halter, trying to grasp it to stop the bolting horse. The Boerperd reared up, as he had done so many times during the battles on the trek, and struck out at the black men in front of him. His hooves crashed down onto the bare shoulders of one of the men, sending him spinning away, to fall writhing in agony on the ground. But Delia, unable to keep her grip on the halter, fell off the rearing horse, landed hard on her side, and lay winded on the ground as the horse galloped away across the fields in the direction of the farmhouse.

Again, it was Boontjies Ryer who spotted the old white Boerperd galloping riderless towards the homestead. The pack on its back had come loose, and only the picnic cloth tied to its girdle now trailed behind the horse as it slowed to a trot. The Hottentot herder ran swiftly down the dusty track to intercept the sweating horse, which slowed, and then stopped when it recognized him, allowing him to grasp its halter and lead it towards the stable. Boontjies called out to his employer, who was working inside the stable, and Jan Roux stepped out into the fading sunlight. On seeing his old horse with the tablecloth trailing from its back, he paled visibly, and then ran towards the stone farmhouse. Erika Roux, startled by her husband bursting in through the front door, and then grabbing his musket, shot-bag and powder-horn off the rack on the wall, nervously asked what the problem was. Jan replied that maybe there was no problem, and that the horse had simply bolted home after being startled by a puff-adder on the pathway back from the river. But he would take his musket along, just in case. Erika Roux and Saartjie Ryer, with her young daughter Sarie alongside her, stood in their aprons on the stoep of the stone farmhouse, watching their husbands galloping off down towards the bend in the river where the two older children had gone for their Sunday-afternoon picnic. The women did not speak, and were still standing there an hour later, anxiously watching and waiting, when they saw Jan and Boontjies slowly leading the two laden horses home through the twilight.

It had been the hardest thing Jan had been forced to do in his life, closing his daughter's dead eyes, and then lifting her young, half-naked body onto his horse, to take home to her mother, waiting on the stoep. Harder even than helping Boontjies tie the body of Benjamin to the other horse, and then lead them both slowly back to the stone farmhouse. The sun was just beginning to set behind the peaks of the *Drakensberg* when he and his herder had discovered the bodies of the two teenagers, as well as that of the tan dog. Ben had obviously put up a fierce fight, armed only with his knife, after being surprised by the Kaffirs on the riverbank. The dead, stabbed body of one of his attackers lay near where they found Ben's lifeless body. They discovered another dead Kaffir, also stabbed—and with his throat torn out by the Boerboel—not far off, near the speared body of the big dog, which was itself sired by Wagter, the original childhood guardian of the murdered teenagers.

It had been young Delia's torn clothing that they had first spotted as Jan searched the riverbank in the fading light. She lay there, his once-beautiful daughter, with her throat slit, her staring blue eyes wide open, her slim, pale legs apart and exposed. He had quickly covered her, and then held her still-warm body to his heaving chest. The Kaffirs—and it appeared that there had been quite a few of them, judging by the tracks leading off towards the *kloofs*—had obviously had their way with her, once they had speared her brave brother and his dog. In his grief and despair, the only thought which provided any comfort for Jan was that the Kaffirs, no doubt fearing swift retribution from the nearby farmhouse for these seemingly sense-less (or perhaps vengeful) murders, had not taken the time to slice off body-parts from their victims: for adding to their vile *muti* ("black-magic concoctions").

Jan Roux then sadly undertook the most lonely and devastating chore the human heart could ever have to bear: the slow task of digging the graves of his beloved children. Jan dug three holes that day: one for each of his children and one for the brave, faithful dog who gave his life in the futile attempt to save the two youths. It was a bitter day, when on the following morning, they lowered the bodies of their offspring into the ground, as the rain drizzled down upon them. When the graves were covered, they held a short, solemn ceremony and Jan read some of the favorite Bible verses of his departed children.

Koerie, the playful *meerkat* was now well advanced in years, having spent a part of his youth on the Great Trek to NATAL as Erika's pet, and then over 15 years as a family favorite. Delia and Koerie had grown up together and been almost insepa-rable. Heartbroken, Koerie crawled up onto Delia's fresh grave, forlorn, and refused to leave. A few days later he breathed his last weak breath and expired atop Delia's grave; wherein Jan buried him over Delia's heart.

Their mother had been inconsolable at the loss of her chil-dren, and had wept bitterly, in their dark bedroom, refusing even to eat, for what seemed to Jan like *weeks*. When Erika Roux had finally emerged, pale and thin, into the morning sunlight on the stoep of their stone farmhouse, she had firmly announced that she no longer wanted to live there, on that farm: forced to see the graves of her children every day. Erika wanted her husband to fix up the trek-wagon, and inspan their oxen again, so they could leave that place—with its haunting memories and heartache—forever. Jan sadly agreed.

It was not long after Jan and Erika Roux had buried their two teenage children alongside the grave of old Christiaan Delarey, that they abandoned their beloved NATAL farmstead forever and trekked on to the eastern *Lowveld* ("lowland fields"). Jan had first ridden into Utrecht with Boontjies Ryer to see the magistrate, the *landdrost,* where Jan formally signed over the title deeds of the farm to his faithful herder. Then he went into the KLOPPER'S TRADING STORE, and purchased a squat, wooden barrel of black gunpowder, and 30 pounds-weight of musket balls. Meneer Klopper tried to interest him in one of the new, rifled muskets which had recently been brought up from Port Natal, of the sort that utilized a percussion cap instead of a flint to ignite the charge of black powder. But Jan Roux was not about to give up his old "Sanna" flint-lock. Then he spotted a double-barreled firearm with ornate hammers standing on the rack behind the store-keeper's large-framed wife: the very woman who had once challenged him to arm-wrestle her on the shop counter. Jan had wisely declined the challenge, as he was well aware of Mevrou Klopper's reputation as the unbeaten arm-wrestling champion of the NATAL midlands. Jan took the well-balanced "Cape gun" from her big hands, and peered down the barrels. One of the two slim barrels was smooth-bored for buckshot and birdshot, and the other, neatly rifled for a single bullet. An ivory bead served as the front sight, and adjustable metal leaves, the rear. The metal side-plates were skillfully engraved with stylized depictions of a deer, and of game birds.

"It's the latest thing from England," announced Meneer Klopper. "It's made especially for someone like you—a farmer who might need a shotgun for shooting guineafowl now and then, and a rifle for buck and Kaffirs. Kills two birds with one stone, so to speak."

On hearing the words "from England," Jan Roux instinctively started to hand the firearm back to the shopkeeper, but then noticed that the gun was clearly engraved "Made in Glasgow"— which as far as *he* was aware, was actually in *Scotland,* a country somewhat to the north of England. Well now, that was a different matter entirely. Besides, Jan himself had once met a Scottish *predikant* ("evangelist") who had learned to speak Afrikaans Dutch reasonably well (in his own rolling brogue) and Jan had quite liked the man. The Synod of the DUTCH REFORMED CHURCH in the Cape (not being impervious to political intrigue itself) had not "officially approved" of the Great Trek. The Synod regarded the trekkers as essentially "renegades" against authority, and had thereby discouraged many of their own *dominees* from accompanying the Trekboers on their northern odyssey. Their vacant places had however, been filled by more than a few Scottish Presbyterian ministers, who were soon accepted by the Boers as their own. So Jan Roux bought the fancy Cape gun, and also a new cotton sun-bonnet for Erika, in the pale blue color that matched his wife's eyes—and his late daughter's eyes, he reminded himself. When Jan came over the rise on the homeward journey and saw the farm, resplendent in the setting sunshine, and knew that he no longer owned it, he did not feel sorry for himself. It was time to move on, and he felt glad for Boontjies, that he now had a farm of his own. At least, the *"verdomde Engelse"* would not be able to "take" the farm.

Early the next morning, Jan slaughtered a *tollie* ("young ox") and sliced it up to make *biltong,* drying the salted meat in the breezy shade of the stoep, within the wire mesh cage he had fashioned, in which he always dried his meats. He then took the patched canvas covers off the haystack, and pulled one of the old, battered wagons out from where it had stood, unused, for nearly 17 years under the tree next to the stone barn. He oiled the dry wood of the wagon, and then re-made the leather traces that would harness the oxen that would pull them back over the mountains, through the steep passes that led to the Highveld. Boontjies helped him to harvest the onions growing in their fields, then braid their green stalks and hang them, to dry them out for the long journey that lay ahead of them.

Jan was not exactly sure which direction they would take once they reached the Highveld; but he had heard that there was much game to be hunted on the eastern Lowveld, which they could reach by trekking through Lydenberg, then down the escarpment, and onto the sandy plains that stretched east, to the Lebombo Mountains and the Indian Ocean. Perhaps that was thither they would trek. Perhaps there he could make a living by hunting for and harvesting ivory, and by hunting game from which he would make hides and biltong. They would there, hopefully, sadly, start over: erecting a new cabin on a parcel of land which hopefully he could purchase from the new Boer government there. It would be an empty home; but perhaps, in time, they would find some solace. Besides, what other choice did they have? They had saved a little money over their years in NATAL, by selling their calves and crops in the town, and perhaps they could use that to buy some land on the plains of the eastern Lowveld. Jan had heard that there was *malarial* fever on the Lowveld, and that few white people could survive there—but that meant that there would also be *fewer Kaffirs* there, because the Kaffirs always migrated closer to white settlements (much the same way that seagulls follow a fishing boat). If there were no whites in the Lowveld, due to the prevalence of fever, then there should be few Kaffirs there as well. To Jan, *the Kaffirs* were the greater danger. Jan and his wife would take their chances with the fever.

Shortly before the morning on which the heart-broken couple set off for their new, unknown home, a British officer arrived at the farmstead to investigate the tragic deaths of Benjamin and Delia Roux. He was the same young British officer who had previously questioned young Ben after he had fought off the murderous stock-thieves (and killed 5 of them). He did not receive his usual cup of tea served on the stoep. He had not even been offered a chair after his long ride from the garrison. Instead, he stood in his hot, red uniform in the blazing sun, outside the stone farmhouse. He was shown the two fresh graves, scribbled a few details in his notebook, and then mat-ter-of-factly suggested that perhaps the murderers were survi-vors of the previous band of cattle thieves, avenging their fallen comrades whom Ben had killed in self-defense. The officer then feeling rather unwelcome (and perhaps a little guilty), unceremoniously rode off again.   Before he left though, he did take off his white helmet, and offered his sincere condolences to "Missus" Roux on the tragic loss of her two children, and solemnly vowed that his men would hunt down the surviving perpetrators, and then bring them to trial in Utrecht.   Erika Roux nodded silently, and then turned away to go back into the kitchen, where Saartjie and Sarie were busy pickling condiments for their *former* employers' lonely, one-way trek to the Lowveld.   The fresh tears in Erika's blue eyes were not caused by the steaming pots in the kitchen, full of onions and carrots, but by the aching emptiness in her heart, which seemed to reach with its gripping pain to the deepest reaches of her soul.

Chapter Eighteen

When Jan and Erika Roux reached Lydenburg after 3 months of trekking, they made discreet inquiries at the general store about some of the other Natal trekkers whom they knew had also trekked on up to the TRANSVAAL after abandoning their farms in the NATAL midlands. They were informed that Bettie Breedt (Piet Roos' ex-wife, who had returned to using her maiden name since the christening of her infant son) had arrived in Ohrigstad a couple of years earlier, along with her toddler son, teenage daughter, and elderly, widowed mother Hilda. Sadly, the tough, aged trekker lady had succumbed to the fever there, not too many months after their arrival. When that badly sited village was abandoned, and the inhabitants had all moved to higher, healthier climes, Bettie and her daughter then worked for some time as housekeepers in Lydenberg; but had since left, apparently for the eastern Lowveld. Ohrigstad was one of the many evanescent, little trekker *republics* that had sprung up in the veld (seemingly overnight) only to disappear again just as quickly.

After stocking up their wagon again with basic essentials, Jan and Erika made inquiries at the local magistrate's office about the possibility of acquiring some land on the Lowveld. They were informed by the Boer landdrost that it was indeed possible, for the then-princely sum of £200[66] (pounds sterling), to stake out a farm there of 2,000 morgen[67] in size. He went on to caution the couple that "swamp-fever" was rife there, the soil was sandy, and that the many wild animals made both cattle-ranching risky and crop farming virtually impossible. Not easily deterred, Jan Roux asked the landdrost to show him on the big government survey chart pinned to the wall, which portions of land there were still available.

---

[66] Approximately £4,625 or $9,250 in today's currency.

[67] 1 *morg* = 2.1 acres; thus 2,000 *morgen* = 4,200 acres.

Jan stared at the chart, and then pointed to an unshaded portion alongside the *Sabierivier* (from *uluSaba,* meaning "river of fear" due to many the many crocodiles which inhabited it). "What about this piece?" he asked. "It looks to me like there is a track leading past it. Is it passable by oxwagon?"

"Haven't a clue," replied the landdrost candidly. "This survey map is not particularly accurate. There is also another, much larger portion available alongside that parcel you like. It's about 8,000 morgen.[68] It has a few *koppies* near the river and a range of hills to the north, which also cross into *your* piece. Why don't you take them both for £1,000? They would together form one good-sized farm, which could support a lot more game, that is, if you are interested in hunting for a living."

Jan Roux had to confess that even the money being asked for the much smaller portion would virtually clean out their life-savings, leaving them very little with which to live, let alone establish a new farm. Jan realized that the average independent, *established* Boer family could live *a whole month* on *one* pound-sterling. The landdrost sympathized, but could only suggest that they approach the local bank for a loan if they needed more capital. Jan and Erika Roux then told him that they would like to give the suggestion some thought, and promised to return the next day. That night, they camped next to their wagon on the *uitspan* (the "outspan" common) on the fringes of Lydenberg, surrounded by their humble possessions: their small herd of trek-oxen and cattle, their few horses, their flock of sheep and *Boerbokke* ("Boergoats") and their little, portable coop full of chickens. There, as they lay still awaiting sleep, they agonized about the possibility of getting themselves into debt to secure both parcels of land. They knew that the combined parcels would have a much greater chance of bringing in a viable income than just the smaller piece alone; but the thought of owing such a huge sum of money to a banker frightened the rustic farmers. Nonetheless, they decided to pay a visit to the local bank the next morning, and then weigh their options.

---

[68] 16,800 acres.

Hiram Goldberg sat comfortably in his plush leather chair, surveying the Boer couple sitting opposite him over the gleaming desk. They were a handsome pair, the man big and rugged-looking, his fair hair and beard neatly trimmed for the interview. He had an honest solidity about him that made a good first-impression on the banker, and his petite wife was quite beautiful, and had gracious manners. A fine couple, thought the banker, his soft hands clasped, and resting on his belly, which strained the buttons of his waistcoat. "They seem more likely than most to make a success of their farm and then be able to repay a loan," he thought to himself. He inquired closely as to where they had come from, to where they were heading, what their future plans were, and how they intended to make a living on the Lowveld. He listened with great interest as Jan Roux described their trek from the Cape, their farm in the NATAL midlands, the decision to trek again after losing both their children, and the hope that he would be able to hunt for ivory, hides and biltong along the Sabie River.

The banker was surprised to learn that they had recently given away their farm in the midlands to their colored herder and his family, pointing out that the property there could have been used as collateral for a loan. In their turn, the couple explained that the farm held painful memories, that they had turned their backs on it after the tragic loss of their children, and that their herder was a deserving, new land-owner after he, and later his wife, had served their family for decades with little remuneration. It had just seemed to be the right thing to do at the time, and it was better than letting the British usurpers take the abandoned farm.

Hiram Goldberg explained to them that a mortgage of say, £1000[69] pounds sterling, at an interest rate of 4% *per annum,* would require them to pay back at least £60[70] a year, to make any headway against the loan, and around 20 years to pay it off entirely. The couple realized that it would be a burden too

---

[69] £23,133 or $46,266 in today's currency.

[70] £1,388 or $2,775 per year in today's currency.

great for them to risk carrying. It had taken them all of 15 years to save just over £300,[71] and they now dreaded the thought of having to pay back such a huge loan. When the banker *pointedly* consulted his shiny gold pocket-watch, they thanked him for his time, and then walked slowly back towards the office of the landdrost, deep in thought. They realized that their sudden and emotional, rash departure from their farm in NATAL had left them very short of any real capital, and once again adrift on the veld in their ox-wagon. But now, at least, they were again free to go anywhere they wanted to, and start a new life.

"I have you, my Erika," announced Jan Roux, "and you are far more precious to me than all the money in Meneer Goldberg's bank. Don't worry, my *liefling* ("darling")—we will be fine. After all, we now own a fancy new Cape gun, that can kill two birds with one stone!" He laughed, and hugged his wife, and for the first time since the violent deaths of their children, he saw Erika brave a smile.

"And I have you, my man," she replied. "I found you on the Great Trek, and you were my hero then, and you are still my hero now. I know that there is nothing we cannot achieve if we love each other, and trust in the Good Lord." Jan then declared, "Come, let's go and have a nice lunch at the hotel, like the rich folk do! But only after we have given Meneer Landdrost his £200 for the smaller farm on the Sabie River—the one we can afford."

It did not take long for the landdrost to carefully inscribe the name of "Johannes Paulus Roux, born Franschoek district in 1815," on the title deed-of-transfer for the farm *Olifantshoek*[72] of 2,000 *morgen* in size, alongside the Sabie River, and bounded in the north by the range of hills known as the Sabie Ridge (named after the nearby *Sabierivier),* situated in the eastern Lowveld region of the SOUTH AFRICAN REPUBLIC, formerly called the TRANSVAAL REPUBLIC. With that, the landdrost placed the seal of the new republic on the corner of *die akte van transport*

---

[71] £6,947 or $13,894 per year in today's currency.
[72] "Elephant's" "hook" (literally, a "corner" or "bend" in the river).

("the deed of transfer"), and handed it over to Jan Roux, after having collected the £200.

Their celebratory lunch at the Lydenburg Hotel extended well into the afternoon, and by the time they strolled arm-in-arm back towards the outspan common, they were both giggling a little from the effects of the bottle of sparkling-sweet Sannasrus wine which they had enjoyed. The waiter had obligingly managed to find one for them, after they had specifically requested it; hoping that some of Erika's ancestral vineyard's fine produce had made its way as far as the eastern TRANSVAAL.

That evening, after having paid a shiny shilling to the local Boer boy tasked with guarding their *ossewa* ("ox-wagon") and livestock at their campsite (which comprised all their possessions in the world), Jan had warmed up a tub of water, from the nearby river, for his wife to bathe in. He sat smoking his pipe, their big dog, (another descendant of Wagter) at his feet, and watched her comb her long, fair hair by the firelight. She was still a very beautiful woman, he thought—and even the travails of the Great Trek, the hard life on the farm in NATAL, the tragic loss of their two beloved children, and now the daunting prospect of establishing a new life (from scratch) on the sandy plains of the Lowveld, had not dimmed the light in her eyes, nor etched many lines in her fair skin. Soon, a mist rolled in, and so they decided to sleep inside their dry, covered wagon that night, instead of on their canvas cots between the big wheels. In the soft glow of their one paraffin lamp, on the goose-down bed in their old wagon, Jan Roux made gentle love to his wife near the newly established eastern TRANSVAAL town named *Lydenburg* ("town of suffering").

On the trek to the long pass that led down to the Lowveld, Jan and Erika stopped at a spectacular viewpoint, from which they could see, stretched before them like a vast green canvas, the plains that bordered the Indian Ocean, itself invisible in the hazy distance. They sat side-by-side on a large, sun-warmed rock that jutted out over a 2,000-foot drop. Below, they could see ancient trees festooned with yellow-grey moss, like an old man's beard. Fat brown dassies scurried busily among the boulders, warily watching the big black eagles that glided silently past their rocky stronghold. Their new world lay spread below them, and for the first time since the deaths of their children, Jan and Erika Roux's hearts soared like the eagles.

"Is it not beautiful, Jan?" asked Erika. "It is like God's window, where He can look out over His creation, and be glad that He made it. From here, one could imagine that there are no troubles in this world, and that all things are wonderful and new again."

Their 10 oxen stood patiently in the traces, their yokes resting lightly on their massive necks. Behind the trek team stood their wagon, old and battered, the scars of many battles showing on the boards and in the patched canvas. All their worldly possessions were now contained in that old wagon—a lifetime of collecting whittled down to the bare essentials which would fit in the wagon; mostly, practical things, such as pots and pans, picks and spades, buckets and tools with which they would build their new home on the sandy plains near the Sabie River. They had brought some vegetable and grain seed from their Natal farm, to plant alongside the new farmhouse that they would build, and their small herds and flocks would serve as breeding-stock, if they survived the diseases of the Lowveld. It was only a few days later that they reached the Sabie Ridge via the narrow, stony track and camped there, overlooking the farm that now lay before them, sloping gently down to the forested banks of the verdant Sabie River. In the far distance lay the Lebombo Mountains, and beyond that, the Indian Ocean.

When they reached the river and saw the great trees laden with wild fruits and figs, inhabited by chattering grey monkeys and colorful birds, they knelt side-by-side, and prayed that the Good Lord would bless their endeavors there, consecrating their new homestead to Him. They prayed that they would remain strong and wise, God-fearing and honorable; that their crops would flourish, and that they would be blessed with abundance in all things according to their faithfulness. Then Jan Roux rose, and helping his wife to her feet, turned to look at the range of *koppies* ("hills") to the north, the boundary of their farm. A small stream, whose waters were clear and fresh, flowed from those hills down to the Sabie River. On a rocky outcrop alongside that pristine stream, they decided to build their home. Jan used the oxen to drag their wagon, now uncovered, through the soft, white sand, to haul rocks from the koppies with which to build the foundation of their cottage. He had stretched the canvas wagon-covers between some large trees, and in this shade, Erika sat on a milking-stool and sewed together the lengths of cloth that they had bought at the trading store in Lydenburg. She made tablecloths and bedding, curtains and covers for their home, and watched contentedly as the few chickens they had brought with them scratched in the sand nearby. Their great, tan dog lay at her feet, dozing peacefully.

Soon, the sound of an axe (the only sound of human habitation) could be heard ringing through the shady glades, as Jan Roux chopped down 7 tall, straight trees for beams on which to lay the thatch which they had cut from the grassy plains. Although it was winter,[73] the weather was warm and dry, and there were no mosquitoes or flies to bother them. At night, they slept on the ground under the canvas, their goose-down mattress cushioning them comfortably. Day by day, the stone walls of their cottage grew slowly higher as Jan carefully laid the stones, securing them with *dagha* ("mud") dug from the edges of the muddy pool that the hippos had churned out in the bed of the great river. The hippos, with just their noses, eyes and ears protruding from the water, watched suspiciously as the man with the bucket labored up the sandy bank with each load of mud. But other than grunting indignantly at the intruder to their watery world and opening wide their gaping jaws, showing their long,

---

[73] The Lowveld of the Transvaal (in the southern hemisphere) has hot, humid summers (during the time of winter in the northern hemisphere), averaging approximately 18-38° C. (65-100° F.) and mild dry winters (during the northern summer), averaging approximately 8-28° C. (46-82° F.). Rain mostly falls in their springtime or early summer.

white teeth to remind him it was *their* river, they took no aggressive action—still, Jan was ever cautious of the incredibly dangerous creatures. At night, however, the hippos left their pool, and lumbered along the double-laned paths that their big, widely spaced feet had worn through the grass—and as they passed they peered at the firelight that flickered through the trees. Jan was ever alert at night, also: for he knew that hippos (and rhinos), having a natural loathing of fire, would, on occasion, *attack* and *stamp out* campfires (presumably to save their grazing site)—and anyone or anything in the way risked being trampled by the 3-ton behemoths.   If one of the ever-watchful, lurking crocodiles ventured too close to the pod of hippos, a huge bull would bare his banana-sized ivory tusks lining his gaping jaws and then madly rush at the reptile, causing it to dive and flee for its life.

Occasionally, a herd of elephants would stop to drink at the pool, spraying water and mud over their backs, vigilantly watching their young frolicking between the legs of the great matriarch of the herd. The smallest calf would reach up and suckle from her two breasts, which hung between the *front* legs of its mother, then run squealing back into the water, splashing and rolling about gleefully in the mud. Jan watched the elephants silently from behind the buttress roots of a massive wild-fig tree, his musket at his side. He knew that he would have to wait for the great bull tuskers to arrive before he could fell one of those mighty beasts for its ivory; to sell to the traders in the new Lowveld towns. But he also knew that it would not be easy, for money's sake, to take the life of one of these majestic creatures—for its tusks alone—leaving the majority of the massive carcass to rot and be eaten by scavengers. It was with mixed emotions that Jan would consider it forgivable to take the life of an elephant, from-time-to-time, for its valuable ivory, which he could sell to pay for the necessities of life. As with many wild species, a thinning out of the herd, when judiciously implemented, was actually *good* for the health and vigor of the herd; and to keep the vigorous creatures from over-populating the region, thereby destroying their own habitat. He stood waiting and contemplating, but Jan just could not bring himself to pull the trigger. He finally resolved, *"Die Goeie Here"* will provide for our needs in another way." Jan thought to himself, "I won't wastefully violate His beautiful creation just for an easy pocket of coin."

At sunset, Erika would gather the chickens into the latticed coop that Jan had built, to protect them from the *muishond,*[74] which had been lurking around their camp after dark; and from the feisty honey badger, which dug under the roots of the trees, searching for rodents and snakes. She asked her husband, "Is it correct, in English, to call more than one mongoose: 'mongooses,' 'mongeese,' or 'mongi'...?" He replied, *"Die Engelse taal* is not a language I choose to speak, but if I must, I am uncertain which word is correct. Should the situation ever arise, I imagine, to be safe, I would say: 'The other day, I saw a mongoose—no, actually I saw two!'" Erika thought that solved the conundrum rather nicely and they both had a little chuckle over it.

When they heard a lion roaring his boastful challenge to the darkness of the night, the oxen would crowd towards the center of the sturdy palisade *kraal* ("corral"), which Jan had erected, safe behind the thick screen of thorny branches. The young leopard that patrolled its territory along the great river at night had seen and scented the big dog that now lived within "his" domain; but the leopard did not approach too closely, not knowing what manner of beast it was. It was the first dog the leopard had ever encountered, and its tan coloring was not unlike that of the fierce lionesses, which inhabited the grassy plains. So the spotted cat kept its distance, and satisfied its hunger as it always had: by ambushing the chocolate-colored bushbuck as they crossed the sandy riverbed, or by snatching a grey monkey from the large troop which came down from the trees to drink from a shady pool at the edge of the stream.

Now and then, large herds of buffaloes would make their way past the camp through the riverine forest, their hulking black shapes

---

[74] —literally, "mouse-dog;" the grey "mongoose" (one of the many species of mongoose inhabiting South Africa).

moving steadily along as they peacefully grazed and browsed the lush vegetation. The massive bulls would glare balefully at the man standing, watching them from the river bank. They would throw their heads powerfully up into the air, roll their eyes back, and snort loudly in defiance. Then, they would take up their guard on the fringes of the herd, as the cows ushered their calves towards the center, where they were safer.

A big *kudu* bull, with long, spiraled horns, fell to the first rifled bullet which Jan fired from his fancy new Cape gun and immediately thereafter a guineafowl, which had been flushed from the tall grass, by the gun's loud report, then crashed down through the branches of a tree, stopped in mid-flight by a charge of birdshot from the other, smooth barrel. Jan knew instantly that he had made a good purchase—and smiled warmly with satisfaction, with a lighter step in his gait as he sauntered over to collect his prizes. He cut most of the meat from the kudu into short strips, which his wife soaked overnight in a salty vinegar brine, sprinkled the wet meat with pepper and crushed coriander, and then hung to dry in the shade. They enclosed the guineafowl, feathers and all, in a big ball of mud, which they then baked within the coals of their campfire until the muddy shell was dry and hard. When they cracked open the hard ball after a few hours of baking, it split in half, detaching the feathers from the cooked bird (and the innards, which had shrunk and dried, were then pulled out in one piece). The succulent fowl was a good starter for their meal of roast kudu fillet that night, which they ate with the warm bread that Erika had baked in a heavy iron pot, likewise, under the coals.

Erika's stock of flour was not great, but she carefully rationed it out; knowing that it would be some months before they could harvest their first *mealies* to then dry, grind, and make cornbread. The big, whiskered *barbers* were easy to catch, slithering as they did in the shallow, muddy pools left by the river, which eventually slowed to a trickle during the dry winter months. Some of the catfish would encase themselves in the drying mud, and lie there dormant until the spring rains fell and flooded the riverbed again; whereupon those primitive fish would emerge, and then use their pectoral fins to "walk" overland from pool to pool; wriggling, wrestling and spawning in the spreading shallows. Ugly as they were, the catfish made excellent, boneless eating, particularly when smoked.

By the end of that winter, the little cottage was ready for the couple to occupy. Jan Roux carried his petite wife effortlessly across the threshold, and they embraced in front of the big, stone fireplace. Erika lit the first fire in their new hearth, and soon, smoke could be seen coming from the stone chimney that rose above the new, yellow, thatched roof. The grey, striped and fringed kudu hide lay on the hard, mud floor of the cottage, and its great spiraling horns were now attached to the wall of the stoep. Jan and Erika had fashioned the floor by mixing fine sand from termite mounds with water and cattle-dung, to make a kind of concrete, and then, while the floor was drying, colored it with blood from one of the older oxen, which they had slaughtered after it became lame. They had dried, smoked and pickled the large amounts of beef, and boiled the copious fat to make candles and soap. When polished, the cottage floor shone a rich blood-red, and here and there, Jan had closely embedded many hard fruit *pitte* ("seeds" or "pits") into the floor, which gave a pleasing pattern.

Erika's new curtains were hung above the small windows, which let in a soft light through the cotton fabric "panes" which had been impregnated with tallow (the same tallow that was used to make their rather smoky candles). Their soap, which was imbued with astringent lye made by dripping water through wood-ash, was then scented with aromatic herbs, such as lavender, thyme, or rosemary.

Jan had also softened the big hide of the slaughtered ox by using the brains of a *waterbok* ("waterbuck") he had just shot (animals brains being full of a kind of lanolin fat), after he had soaked the ox skin for many days in water containing a measure of saltpeter-rich gunpowder and urine, as well as tannin, which they had boiled from the bark of a suitable acacia tree.

From the hide of the waterbuck, he fashioned a rain-proof cape. The fur of that animal was known to remain oily for years, even after being tanned, but the scent thereof was rather acrid; some believing it repelled crocodiles. However, Jan was subject to Erika's mirth every time he wore his new cape: The waterbuck has a white ring around the rump, and it made Jan look as if he had a target painted on his posterior! He had scraped the hair from the ox hide with a sharp blade, and when the leather was fully cured, had cut long, thin *riempies* ("straps") to make thongs. He then laced these, in a grid pattern, through small holes which he had bored in the frames of the rustic wooden chairs and benches, which he had fashioned from one of the local hardwoods. When the first warm, spring showers arrived from the Indian Ocean far to the east, Jan (resplendent in his new "oilskin") and Erika Roux planted their first vegetable and grain seeds in the sandy soil of the bushveld.

198

Chapter Nineteen

Life for the trustees of the government of the new ZUID
AFRIKAANSE REPUBLIC (ZAR) in the TRANSVAAL was difficult.
The mainly agricultural economy did not generate much in the
way of taxes, and the country itself was landlocked. Goods had
to be imported by ox-wagon via NATAL, Mozambique, or even
the far-off, CAPE COLONY. Their first President Marthinus
Pretorius had made an attempt to establish both a corridor to
the east coast, and a railway to serve it; but it had come to
naught. Far across the sea, a young boy destined for fabulous
wealth and greatness, by the name of Cecil John Rhodes (1853-
1902), was born to a vicar in England, the same year that
President Pretorius' illustrious father, Andries, died. In 1871,
Rhodes arrived in Southern Africa. In *that same* year, another
young man, Alfred Aloysius Smith (1854-1931) would also
arrive in Southern Africa from Glasgow, and work as a prospector and trader, later becoming famous as the adventurous hero
known as "Trader Horn." Before becoming famous though, he
would be reduced to selling mouse traps from door to door! The
vacant presidency of the new republic in the TRANSVAAL, upon
the resignation of Marthinus Pretorius, was initially offered to Sir
Johannes Hendricus Brand, who was at that time the President
of the model ORANGE FREE STATE; but it finally was given, in
1873, to a hard-working young clergyman by the name of Thomas François Burgers (1834-1881).

Burgers set about founding a small standing army, fostered
education, and established good diplomatic ties with a number
of the European powers. He, like Pretorius before him, envi-
sioned the Portuguese east-coast port of Delagoa Bay[75] as the
best and closest option for import and export, and thus kept
close links with the authorities there. Their dream of total Boer

---

[75] —now *Baía de Maputo;* an inlet in the Indian Ocean on the coast
of Mozambique.

independence—especially from Great Britain—was initially encouraged by the discovery of rather limited reserves of gold in the eastern Transvaal (around Lydenburg, Pilgrim's Rest and Barberton). However, ironically, a real "problem" arose, about 15 years later—when *vast* reserves of gold ore were discovered on the *Witwatersrand* ("the Ridge of White Waters"): for upon this discovery, Great Britain cast a covetous eye toward the fledgling Boer Republic, jealous of the immense wealth lying in the ground, just waiting to be mined.

{Around this period in history, the tragic American Civil War (1861–1865) was fought in the United States, where brother killed brother, as the North attempted to destroy the South (after the southern Confederation of states wanted to secede from the Union to maintain their independence). The Federalists of the North used their quest to "abolish slavery" as the excuse to invade, subjugate, humiliate, and oppress their southern brethren (even though there were over 300,000 slave-owners in the Northern armies, including General Ulysses S. Grant himself).}

Previous to this gold find, diamonds had also been discovered by two children playing on the banks of the Orange River, at Klipdrift in the Orange Free State in 1867. The area containing the diamond deposits had been purchased 6 years earlier from the "colored-tribe" leader Adam Kok—but the discovery there of the glittering stones quickly led to new "claims" of ownership by *various* individuals, tribes, and even the governments of both Boer republics. Being a powder keg, the matter was sent to the Governor of Natal for his arbitration. He decided in favor of one Nikolaas Waterboer (1819-1896), paramount chief of the *colored* Griquas, who then, strangely unconcerned about the wealth lying all around, handed the area over to the Crown! The British authorities in the Cape quickly annexed the diamond area to the Cape Colony, thereby depriving the little Boer republic of a major source of future income. However, geographically, the main diamond area was clearly part of the Orange Free State, in that it lay *east* of both the Vaal and Orange Rivers. A later Land Court (1876) declared Waterboer's "claim" to ownership to have been *invalid* and the Crown paid over the then-huge sum of £90,000[76] to the ORANGE FREE STATE in compensation. This turned out to be a pittance compared to the actual value of the diamonds subsequently recovered in the area.

The diggers, who had flooded into the area from the far corners of the earth by whatever transport was available, soon turned their attentions to a newly discovered—and incredibly rich—volcanic blue *"kimberlite"* pipe, at what became Kimberley. What was originally a hill, was then excavated, to become the largest, deepest *hand-dug* hole in the world. Cecil Rhodes would make his fortune as a young man in Kimberley by consolidating the many small and dangerously unstable claim-digs there, to form the DE BEERS COMPANY; then he moved on to the new Witwatersrand goldfields—and finally ended up as Governor of the CAPE COLONY.

An Imperialist to the core, Rhodes would make waves in Southern African history, which would reverberate well into the second half of the next century—but a big Afrikaner, a staunchly religious man and a lion hunter, Paul Kruger, would stand firmly in Rhode's way at every turn. Vice-president Kruger himself eventually became, in 1883, the third President of the SOUTH AFRICAN REPUBLIC—a post he would hold for 4 terms. The dour and formidable Boer leader, who had fought as a youth in the laager at Blood River (well before Cecil Rhodes was born), would die just a year or two after Rhodes died. However, they would die in very different circumstances, and of different causes: Kruger of old age and a broken heart—*in exile* in Switzerland; and Rhodes of ill-health, and in some disgrace, but comfortably at his seaside cottage in the Cape. Kruger's body would eventually be "brought home," to be buried in *Helde Akker* ("Hero's Acre") in Pretoria, but Rhodes' body would be interred in the Matopos Hills of Rhodesia.[77]

---

[76] £1,675,000 or $3,350,000 in today's currency.

[77] Southern Rhodesia was originally called *South Zambezia;* it then came to be known as *Rhodesia* c.1895, but was renamed *Zimbabwe* c.1979/80, when Robert Mugabe took power; it is currently in economic meltdown due to seizure of whites' farms.

About seventeen years before the gold-rush started near Lydenburg, at the age of 40, Erika Roux found to her great surprise, that she was pregnant. Her husband was delighted when in April, Joshua Benjamin Roux—the son of their middle-age—was born. Later that night Jan got drunk for the first time in his life. Jan had helped to deliver the boy after Erika's long confinement and difficult labor, and although he was well-used to the bloody business of skinning buck, Jan had almost fainted after their *laat-lammetjie* ("late-lamb") emerged from his wife's womb, when he had to cut *his own child's* umbilical cord.

Up until she realized that she was pregnant, Erika herself had believed that her womb had long since closed up; but baby Josh soon became the delight of their lonely lives on the farm alongside the Sabie River. He grew up into a sturdy, adventurous youth, hunting with his father and fishing in the river. The boy could ride almost before he could walk properly and longed for the day when his father would give him his own horse. That great day, his 6th birthday, finally arrived, and his father presented him with a fine young foal: born of a salted mare, immune to the diseases that regularly struck down weaker horses on the humid plains of the Lowveld. Joshua Roux immediately named the shiny-coated foal "Jasper," after the blood-red quartz pebbles he so admired—and because, as he was taught, by his devout mother, that the Almighty God who watches over His children, has a radiant, burning countenance which is described as follows: "And He that sat [upon the Throne in Heaven] was to look upon like a *jasper*..." (Revelation 4:3) Thus, whenever Joshua was on his horse, he was reminded of God's vigilant, watchful protection over him.

Boy and horse soon became inseparable, and when he was just 10 years old, Joshua was allowed to venture alone on horseback onto the plains above the farm. When he hunted with his father, seldom did the speedy antelope escape the young Boer lad's unerring aim. His hunting success supplemented both their larder and the family's income: since he and his father would sell their dried meat and hides in the towns now springing up on the escarpment, and here and there on the Lowveld itself. The Roux family only harvested what game they needed to support themselves, and then only shot the old, weak, or unproven specimens; a practice which actually strengthened the herds. But Jan was not the only landowner to practice conservation in the area: a copy of the TRANSVAAL *Staatskoerant* ("Government gazette") recorded that by the mid-1860's all of 62 farmers in the Lydenburg district protected their game populations, with a total of 200 farms in the Boer republic having established such "safe havens" for wildlife.

Malaria or *koors* ("fever"), as the Boers called it, was a real obstacle to white settlement on the eastern Lowveld, and most preferred the cooler, healthier climes of the higher altitudes. Very few black tribes inhabited the area either, and if they did, it was generally on the coast, and in nearby Mozambique, where they lived under firm Portuguese rule. Consequently, the Roux family lived in relative peace and safety on their farm there. To ward off the virulent malaria Erika regularly brewed a concoction from the bark of specimens of the yellow *Koorsboom*[78] ("fever tree"), which grew in the swampy areas; which she then mixed with the bitter quinine that was obtainable in the town stores. The Boers observed that wherever malaria occurred, the fever trees also grew. However, since that species of acacia was so common in the swampy regions, *originally* the explorers actually thought that the *trees themselves caused* the swamp fever (not realizing that they were actually the cure for it). It was only later discovered that *mosquitoes* hosted the virus—and thus the myth was also dispelled that the malady was caused by "bad air" *(mal aeria);* though the misnomer *malaria* has never been extinguished. Erika's foul-tasting concoction was, however, very effective, and neither she, her husband or their young son ever contracted the deadly fever. They did occasionally suffered from *tick-bite fever,* a kind of *biliary;* but other than causing a splitting headache for a few days, it soon passed. Erika gratefully noted that when creation fell from perfection, the Good Lord graciously provided for mercy. Quite often, the herbal *cure* for

---

[78] —*Acacia xanthophloea*, of the "Pea Family;" a yellow-barked, thorny tree (in Zulu, *umHlosinga*).

certain ailments grew in close proximity to the cause of the ailment itself.

The tales of fortunes both won and lost in the same week by the gold-panners around Pilgrim's Rest, Lydenburg and Barberton, soon reached the ears of the young Joshua Roux. On one of the many trips that he and his father took, to sell their dried game-hides and biltong, to the burgeoning trader population of the eastern TRANSVAAL, they were standing in a newly established trading store in the gold-rush town of Pilgrim's Rest. Jan Roux and the friendly Irish proprietor were haggling, good naturedly, over the price of hides, when in marched a large, important-looking man by the name of Stafford Parker (1833-1915). He was accompanied by his mistress: a pretty girl who went by the sobriquet of "Cockney Liz." She had made the long journey from the streets of London to the TRANSVAAL in search of her fortune-seeking fiancé, who had since disappeared. Unable to find him, Stafford Parker had then taken her under his wing. Parker himself had briefly been "President" of the tiny KLIPDRIFT DIGGERS' REPUBLIC far to the west: one of the myriad such little "republics," which, like a desert blossom, had sprung up virtually overnight in the veld, only to disappear again just as quickly. Their sprawling camp at Klipdrift (which stood on the bank of the Orange River, opposite that of the previously isolated BERLIN MISSION STATION of Pniel), had been "declared" a "republic" by the diamond diggers there: who had even formed a small army to ward off claims to the area by the then-president of the SOUTH AFRICAN REPUBLIC, Marthinus Wessel Pretorius. Stafford Parker, sporting a fine top hat and a magnificently styled beard and mustache, now loomed large over the Boer teenager, surveying the boy's simple home-made clothing and rawhide shoes.

"I say, young fellow," he began in his clipped British accent. "You look like an honest young man. I have need of strong fellows like you to work my claims along the river. What would you say to a shilling a day, with a tent thrown in for good measure?"

Joshua Roux looked up at the big, well-dressed man and his pretty companion. "A shilling a day, meneer! *Dis baie geld!* ("That's a lot of money!") The boy then glanced at his father, who had just settled on the price of one shilling for a rawhide, with the storekeeper. Jan Roux placed his big hand on his son's shoulder, and informed Stafford Parker that his boy was too young to work in a town full of fortune-seekers and scoundrels, and besides that, he was needed on their farm. Parker hauled out his gold fob-watch by its chain from his waistcoat, checked the time, and then loudly announced that he had better be off, as he had to weigh the gold dust and nuggets being brought in at that very moment by his panners and diggers. He then marched out, followed by Cockney Liz, who first put her soft hand on Joshua's blushing cheek, and told him that if he ever needed a job, or even just some company, he now knew where to come. That night, Joshua sat alongside his father's wagon on the outskirts of Pilgrim's Rest, staring up at the bright stars in the black, velvety night sky, occasionally touching his cheek where the perfumed hand of Cockney Liz had caressed it. A yearning deep inside him had been triggered by that chance encounter, and he would never again be quite the same, simple Boer boy that had grown up hunting alongside his father.

When they got back to their farmhouse at Olifantshoek on the Sabie River, Erika Roux came out to greet them. She had stayed alone on the farm, armed only with the Cape gun, while her husband and son had trekked to the escarpment to sell their wares. After hugging them both happily, she told them that all had been quiet on the farm, except one night when she had been forced to shoot dead a leopard that had attacked a small calf, after having climbed into the kraal by using an overhanging tree. She felt sad about killing such a magnificent animal, but had been left with no choice. Their massive dog, his hair bristling at the strange scent, had awakened Erika with his growls, and alerted her to the presence of the fearsome, stealthy cat. Its yellow, spotted pelt now hung drying over the fence rail.

Her husband, relieved that no harm had come to her, handed over the small leather bag containing the remainder of the 10 pounds-sterling worth of coins that he had received for the wagon-load of hides and biltong. Erika was delighted with the money, and with the bolts of cotton cloth, bags of flour and packets of spices that her husband had bought for her. It was only when they were preparing for bed that night that Jan told his wife about their encounter with Stafford Parker, and his job-offer to their son. Her brow furrowed with concern, because she felt sure she had noticed something odd about the boy: a strange, new light in his eyes, which she had not seen before. Jan laughingly told his wife that he believed that Joshua had merely been smitten by his close encounter with the pretty young woman, and had felt the first stirrings of manhood.

In the halls of power in the capital of Pretoria[79] their new President Burgers was having a rather difficult time. Foreigners were flooding into the new Boer republic in search of wealth, and these *Uitlanders* ("Outlanders" or "foreigners") now formed a sizable proportion of the population. A *Pedi* chieftain by the name of Sekhukuni (later murdered, in 1882, by his own brother, Mampoer[80]) was busy raiding Boer farms in the eastern TRANSVAAL, and the Zulus, who had been quiet for some time, were now also starting to make rumblings along the Boer's border with NATAL. The death of the Zulu king Mpande had led to succession by Cetshwayo, who had reported to the British Natal authorities that he was in dispute with some Transvaal Boers over boundaries and grazing rights. Some of the gold-digging foreigners, who had also suffered from frequent raids by the Pedi tribesmen, now appealed to the *British* authorities,

---

[79] —named of course, after that hero of Blood River, Andries Pretorius; it was founded in 1855 and became the capital of the TRANSVAAL in 1860. It would also later become the capital of South Africa in 1910. The ANC recently changed the name of Pretoria to *Tswane*.

[80] —whose name meant, "hooch" or "booze," which probably gives insight into his character.

in nearby NATAL, for assistance, doubting the ability—or the willingness—of the Boer government to protect them.

The astute British Foreign Secretary, Lord Carnarvon,[81] saw an opportunity to promote a federation of CROWN territories with the two Boer republics and had the backing of British Prime Minister Benjamin Disraeli (1804-1881). President Burgers was patently and understandably opposed to the idea, but Carnarvon, not to be thwarted, urged NATAL's Secretary of Native Affairs, Sir Theophilus Shepstone (1817-1893), to go immediately to Pretoria and propose annexation anyway; providing he had majority support among the whites there. The Boer Volksraad, taking heart from the defiance of their new Vice-President Paul Kruger, refused to budge, or to institute any of the civil reforms proposed by their powerful British neighbor. An over-confident Shepstone went ahead, in 1877, with the *annexation* ("governmental theft") nonetheless, and to the despair of the Afrikaners, hoisted the Union Jack over their capital. Once again, the Boers found themselves under British rule.

While the British did not like the Boers ruling over the indigenous Africans, the British thought themselves "self-appointed masters" who had no qualms about ruling over *everyone:* the Boers *and* the "indigenous" Africans. In fact, in order to keep tightly tied the hands of their fearful Southern African rivals (the Boers), the British passed and enforced laws which favored the blacks (and turned a blind eye to their crimes against the Boers). By keeping their Afrikaner rivals in chaos and subjection, they kept them weak. The British employed this same tactic against her other "rebellious colony," the young United States of America, by employing American Indians to commit acts of terrorism against the white settlers (including scalping them). Lord Carnarvon had gambled on the ORANGE FREE STATE also joining the confederation, in the realization that they could not realistically survive alone.

---

[81] Henry Howard Molyneux Herbert (1831-1890), 4th Earl of Carnarvon.

However, Shepstone—nicknamed *Somtseu* ("Great Hunter") by the Zulus, in an attempt to curry British favor—had no more success in ruling the unruly Boer republic and its various *Uitlanders* or the local *Pedi;* nor could they control the resurgent Zulus any better than Burgers had. Paul Kruger, in an effort to retain the integrity and sovereignty of the Afrikaner Republics, rallied Boer support against Shepstone. The stage was set for a clash, as the storm had been brewing and the time was ripe. It came in an unexpected form, and took an unforeseen direction, when a commission, set up to arbitrate in the land dispute on the south-eastern border between the Boers and the Zulus—ruled *in favor of the Zulus!* Boers had no choice but to abandon their farms in the disputed area, in the face of increasing attacks by the now-emboldened Zulus. Boer resentment seethed, but the Imperialists had other *fish to fry*.

Shepstone himself feared that a strong military state in the form of the Zulu nation would be a threat to his dream of British hegemony over the whole of Southern Africa, and that sooner or later, they would have to confront the Zulus and bring them to heel. But he needed a semi-credible justification to go to war against the Zulu nation. This *raison de guerre* finally presented itself in late 1878. Two of the wives of a minor Zulu chieftain were in the habit of crossing the Buffalo River into NATAL near *Rorke's Drift* at night to consort with their secret lovers. When he discovered their infidelity, the chieftain had his own sons beat the promiscuous wives *to death*. The crux, to Shepstone's delight, was that *the chieftain's posse* had crossed into NATAL to apprehend the women, whom they then executed. Another incident, in which two British surveyors were harassed and robbed by a group of Zulu warriors while working on the NATAL side of the river border, was also used as an excuse to present an ultimatum to the Zulu king. The British did not seem to care if the Zulus killed *Boers* or stole valuable Boer livestock; but when it served their own purposes, the British postured and assumed a condescending, "morally superior" attitude when even the lowest of peoples were killed or if even insignificant "Crown property" was pilfered.

Under what became known as the *Ultimatum Tree*[82] on the banks of the Tugela River, the British demands, formulated by Governor Sir Bartle Frere (1815-1884), were presented to a dismayed group of Zulu senior *indunas* belonging to King Cetshwayo. The conditions set by Frere were onerous, and practically impossible to meet. In addition to a *fine* of a huge sum of cattle, Frere and Shepstone basically demanded that the Zulu nation immediately disband its decades-old military system, and that their king submit to the BRITISH CROWN. He also insisted that all Zulu men be free to marry. At that stage, they were only allowed to marry after the age of 35, and then only with the king's blessing. It did not seem to occur to Frere or Shepstone that the enlisted men in their own British Army were not free to marry either!

Cetshwayo himself wanted, at all costs, to avoid war with the mighty BRITISH EMPIRE, but his younger warriors had other ideas, and wanted to "wash their spears" in white men's blood. So the stage was set for war, and Frere[83] and Shepstone refused to waste any time by waiting to see if the Zulu monarch would comply with their outrageous demands. On January 11, 1879, Shepstone summarily ordered their military commander, Lieutenant-General Lord Chelmsford,[84] to invade Zululand in 3 long columns: from the north, the center and the coast. After a brief, but sharp skirmish, the big central column of British troops—accompanied by a good number of Natal Kaffirs and white colonial volunteers—crossed into Zululand and successfully routed the clan of the chief who had ordered the execution of his unfaithful wives. However, the overconfident British then made a fatal mistake. Lord Chelmsford *split his column*

---

[82] Sadly, a century later this significant tree was felled during the construction of a highway.

[83] Ironically, a major *hospital* in Durban was later named after the "war-monger" Frere (who was responsible for many people *needing* a hospital).

[84] Frederic Augustus Thesiger, 2nd Baron Chelmsford (1827-1905).

and set off in futile pursuit of elusive groups of Zulu warriors, who then deliberately and skillfully drew Chelmsford's main force ever deeper into their own territory. The rear-guard of the British column, still shuttling scores of wagon-loads of supplies across Rorke's Drift from the NATAL bank of the Buffalo River, then camped below a strangely Sphinx-shaped mountain called *Isandlwana*. They did not bother to dig-in, mainly due to the rocky nature of the ground, and then spread their meager forces thinly around the long perimeter. As far as *they* were concerned, the main British columns were on their way to attack the new Zulu capital at Ulundi, and the threat of the Zulu army actually attacking *them*, was never even considered. But that is precisely what happened.

On the morning of January 22, 1879, scouting British riders came over a rise, and there before them, in a hidden valley only a few miles from their temporary camp at Isandlwana, sat a Zulu army of well over 20,000 warriors. On realizing that they had been spotted, the Zulu impis rose as one and surged towards the British camp. The scouts fired a few shots into the massed Zulu ranks, and then galloped back towards Isandlwana. The several hundred mounted, but mostly poorly armed, Natal Kaffir volunteers serving with the British forces took off in fright soon after seeing the overwhelming numbers of Zulus attacking them, and fled back towards NATAL, leaving the camp to be defended by only about 1,000 soldiers of the 24th Regiment of Foot, and some Natal Carbineers. A few rockets were hastily and inaccurately fired at the advancing black horde, but on they came. Lieut.-Col. Anthony William Durnford (1830-1879) and his men, who had been some distance from the camp on their way to join up with the main British column under Lord Chelmsford, now retreated to a *donga* that ran across the face of the camp. There, they held back the Zulu advance for a short time, but then they also had to fall back towards the camp. Two small cannons kept up a steady fire, cutting holes in the densely massed ranks of the warriors every time a shell burst among them. The impis then split into the classic Zulu *horns of the buffalo* battle formation, flowed around the Sphinx-shaped hill, and soon had the British camp surrounded. The red lines fell back under the onslaught, and the embattled troops had soon fired off most of the 70 rounds of Martini-Henry breech-loading ammunition that they each carried in their pouches; while the troops in the rear struggled feverishly to open ammunition crates and then distribute cartridges along the stretched lines. Soon, hand-to-hand combat ensued, and the Zulus, who had been taking severe casualties from the sustained and accurate volley-fire of heavy .450-caliber British bullets, then came into their own and the tide of the battle turned. When the British troops in the long and thinly spread defensive lines began to run low on ready ammunition, and their previously high rate of fire began to slacken, the Zulu impis surged forward in an unstoppable black wave.

However, just as the main body of Zulus broke through the thin red lines of British soldiers and invaded the camp, the sun *darkened*. It had been a *cloudless* day with a clear blue sky and burning sun—but an *unexpected partial solar eclipse* occurred, and the combatants on both sides momentarily stopped fighting, and looked up at the dark shadow blotting out the sun. A deathly silence fell over the battlefield. Then the sun began to brighten again as the eclipse passed, and immediately, the battle resumed. Red-coated soldiers formed tight groups bristling with bayonets, and tried to work their way towards other embattled knots of soldiers surrounded by the sea of black warriors. When the Zulus were halted by the long bayonets, thrust through their shields, they fell back to a safer distance and then hurled their light throwing-spears at the exposed British soldiers. Quite a number of the Zulus also had firearms, and although most of these were antiquated muskets and the Zulu's aim was not very accurate, many bullets still found their mark. One by one, the redcoats fell, and the size of each remaining group of redcoats began to shrink steadily. Some Zulu warriors, not trusting their cowhide shields to deflect the sharp bayonets, lifted the dead bodies of fallen comrades onto their heads and shoulders, and then advanced towards the desperate groups, using the bodies to entangle the bayonetted rifles.

A handful of British Imperial troops and Carbineers, realizing that their position was untenable, and that their camp was about to be overwhelmed, began to peel off from the shattered lines, and flee through the only remaining, narrow gap in the Zulu ranks, which led down towards the Buffalo River. But the ground was rugged and rocky, and the fleet-footed Zulu warriors easily kept pace with the mounted fugitives; even running alongside their horses and spearing them. Lieutenant Teignmouth Melville (1842-1879), in an effort to save the battalion's "Queen's Color" from capture by the Zulus, rode hard for the Buffalo River with the cased flag across his saddle. When he finally reached what became known as *Fugitive's Drift,* he and Lieutenant Neville J.A. Coghill (1852-1879) helped each other to cross the flooded river (nearly drowning), under heavy fire from Zulus on both banks. Exhausted, they abandoned the heavy flag[85] in the swirling waters, and made a fighting last stand before being killed on the opposite bank.

The Zulu *induna* Dabulamanzi KaMpande (1839-1886), a half-brother of the Zulu king, had earlier been trying desperately to hold back his reserve *impi* from charging recklessly into the face of the faltering but still-disciplined British lines, which were at that stage, still firing fairly steadily. But at the forefront of the battle, another *royal* Zulu named Dinizulu, a descendant of the induna Dinizulu (who had been felled, but not killed, by a glancing shot from the musket of Christiaan Delarey at the *Battle of Blood River*, 41 years earlier), urged his men on. His own regiment had been badly mauled by the accurate British rifle-fire in the first half-hour of the frenetic battle—and they were forced to scramble over their fallen companions to get at the white men, as they slipped and slid on the grass made slick by the blood,

---

[85] This flag was recovered 10 days later by a British patrol where it had washed up on a sandbank downstream, and shipped home to their regiment, where its return greatly raised morale. It had been enclosed in a leather cylindrical case or tube.

brains, and guts of their fallen comrades. The heavy bullets would sometimes punch through two or even three warriors and their shields, however, the Zulus pushed slowly, but steadily forward. Then Dinizulu saw a bold young British officer, sword drawn, his red tunic drenched with sweat and caked with dust, standing back-to-back with a dozen of his men, who lunged with their bayonets at any Zulu who came too close. They had by then obviously run out of rifle ammunition, and Captain Reginald Younghusband (1844-1879), with his sword in one hand, fired the last round from his revolver through the shield and into the chest of a charging warrior, before flinging the empty handgun at another, and then skewering him with his long, curved sword.

"What a brave warrior is this," thought Dinizulu. "The young redcoat induna fights like a lion. But he shall fall like a rock, where he stands, when I reach him with my spear!" With that, Dinizulu leapt forward over the fallen warriors lying in his path, and made for the small group of redcoats still holding out on a slight rise at the base of the hill. All around him, Dinizulu saw other small groups of redcoated soldiers completely surrounded by his own warriors, fighting with the long bayonets attached to their empty rifles, and when the warriors pressed too closely, the desperate British would hack and stab them with their swords and knives. Slowly but surely, the knots of British soldiers grew smaller and more scattered as they were overwhelmed by the Zulu warriors. Dinizulu finally reached the last stand of the young redcoated officer, who now had only 3 men still with him. Dinizulu flung his spear at the wild-eyed white warrior. The light throwing-spear caught the officer on his shoulder, and he spun about to face his attacker, his pale eyes blazing.

Dinizulu rapidly closed the short distance between them, and when the young officer charged desperately at him, whirling his sword and slashing at the Zulu's throat, Dinizulu deftly parried the long blade with his hardened cow-hide shield, then lunged with his short stabbing-assegai, piercing the redcoat below his breastbone. Yet still, the young officer did not fall, and the sucking *iklwa* sound that the assegai made when Dinizulu withdrew it was followed by the agonized roar of the mortally wounded man, who again lashed out at Dinizulu with his sword, before slowly sinking to his knees, and then toppling forward. Dinizulu's men quickly speared the last of the red-coated soldiers, who had stood over their fallen officer, and skillfully disemboweled them. Some of the warriors reached into the rib-cavities of the white men, and then sucked the warm fluid from their gall-bladders. This would, they believed, give them the strength and courage of the fallen, brave, white soldiers. Soon, they too were running back down to the camp to join in the looting which was already in full swing. In their blood-frenzy, the Zulu warriors were spearing everything they came across, including the oxen, horses, tents and wagons. Some warriors were using their razor-sharp assegais to split the stomachs of the fallen British, ostensibly to "release their spirits," while others were slicing off the lower jaws of bearded soldiers for trophies.* Only 55 of the white men (very few of them regular British soldiers—and only those wearing blue jackets) had managed to flee the terrifying carnage. Not a single red-coated soldier escaped.

[* After this battle, most British soldiers shaved their beards and kept themselves clean shaven.]

In the aftermath of the battle at the foot of Isandlwana Mountain, the jubilant Zulu warriors ransacked the British camp. A drummer boy, no older than about 16, was found alive under a pile of bodies of older men, including that of his grizzled sergeant, who had tried in vain to protect the youngster. Incongruously, the boy was still clutching his drumsticks, and his wide, frightened eyes scanned the grinning black faces surrounding him, desperately searching for any sign of clemency. But he found none, and was stripped of his uniform, then hoisted up and hung from the meat-hooks attached to the field-kitchen wagon. The sharp hooks easily pierced his tender body, and skewered under his shoulder-blades, he hung agonizingly under his own body weight, while his many laughing tormentors jabbed at him with their assegais. His suffering was finally cut short when a warrior stepped forward, plunged his spear deep into the boy's stomach, and then ripped hard downwards, spilling his entrails. A small pet dog, one of the regiment's mascots, had also some-how escaped detection by hiding under a canvas cover near one of the fallen tents. When a warrior poked at the shape under the canvas, the dog yelped, and then fled across the body-strewn battlefield. Half-a-dozen warriors took off after the terrified dog, flinging their throwing-spears at the fleeing canine, which dodged desperately left and right before one spear finally found its mark. The body of the little dog was then hoisted high on the tip of that spear, and waved triumphantly over the heads of the surrounding warriors. All around, Zulus were stripping the bodies of the fallen British soldiers, trying on their red tunics, and mock-ing each other when the white helmets fitted awkwardly over their bushy hair.

Dabulamanzi KaMpande rode purposefully across the battle-field on his white horse, rallying his reserve impi, most of whom were busy plunging their assegais into dead British bodies, in frustration at not having "washed their spears" in *live* white man's blood. Soon, he had gathered most of his men, and sensing their mood, signaled for them to follow him. He set off at a trot, heading for the crossing above Fugitive's Drift, and then turned north towards the staging-post and field hospital at Rorke's Drift. He knew that the few British survivors of the massacre would surely flee to the tiny outpost at the mission station there, and his men might still have the opportunity to kill white soldiers. Dabulamanzi had received direct and explicit orders from his half-brother, King Cetshwayo, not to cross into NATAL, nor ever to attack the red soldiers if they were in a fortified defensive position, but the familiarity that came from being kin of the regent gave him the boldness to ignore those orders. Cetshwayo feared that an attack into NATAL would give the British the excuse they needed to mount a full-scale inva-sion of his kingdom; but he did not understand the British mind. They already *had* found cause to invade—and the humiliation of the rout at Isandlwana would serve merely to strengthen their resolve to completely crush his Zulu nation.

Dinizulu's own impis, who had been at the forefront of the battle, now enjoyed the spoils of war. They looted the wagons and the fallen tents, swilling any liquor they came across, and when they found some untouched crates of ammunition, which had not been opened in time to change the course of the battle, they began firing into the air with the rifles of fallen British soldiers. Inexplicably, their shots were suddenly answered by a shot from a small cave on the mountain behind them, and a Zulu warrior busy disemboweling a body at the base of the Sphinx-shaped outcrop fell, shot through. All eyes then turned towards the cave, as another shot rang out, and yet another warrior fell. It appeared that there was still at least one British soldier holed up in the small cave, and in despair at seeing the carnage and mutilation taking place below, he had opened fire on the exulting Zulus. Immediately, Dinizulu ordered a detachment of a dozen warriors to storm the cave and kill any surviving red-coated soldiers still holding out there. The band of warriors set off up the slope of the small mountain, but had not covered more than a hundred yards before two of them were shot down in quick succession. The rest of the small group at the base of the mountain took cover, and then began working their way up carefully, dodging from boulder to boulder. A warrior suddenly broke cover and ran towards the cave, but was immediately felled by a well-aimed shot. In frustration, 3 of the warriors who were armed only with their spears, ran back down the slope, snatched up fallen Martini-Henry rifles and handfuls of cartridges from the smashed ammunition cases and then hurried back towards their detachment. Again, one of the Zulu warriors was felled as he ran, the rifle clattering over the rocks as it slipped from his lifeless hand.

As Dinizulu bent down to unhook the scabbard of the sword from the belt of the young captain who had fought so bravely, he noticed the regimental emblem which was attached to the collar of the soldier's red tunic. It was a small, gold Sphinx, almost identical in profile to Isandlwana Mountain. "Aah," he nodded, "these brave red soldiers came here, to this very mountain, to die.

It was their destiny as warriors." He reverently took the blood-ied sword from the white hand that still clutched the embellished grip, and then slipped it into the scabbard before attaching it to his own waistband. As he bent again to detach the Sphinx emblem from the young officer's tunic, a shot whistled close past his head, and he suddenly realized that the marksman in the cave had now directed his fire *at him*. Taking cover behind a large boulder, Dinizulu flinched involuntarily as another heavy bullet buzzed through the feathers of his head-dress, which protruded above the rock. Shouting to his men, who were now closing in on the sniper in the cave, to start firing into the dark interior, Dinizulu himself now dodged from boulder to boulder as he made his way cautiously up the slope. Brave as he was, Dinizulu saw no point in exposing himself to the deadly and accurate rifle-fire still coming from the cave.

Lying side-by-side behind a rock at the entrance to the shallow cave was one British soldier, and Joshua Roux. The Boer boy, who had just turned 18, had begged his parents to allow him to join the scores of wagons heading down to Port Natal in order to provide transport to the cumbersome British columns preparing to invade Zululand. His mother Erika had fearfully begged her son not to even consider going, but the youth was adamant. Many times during his childhood, he had listened in awe as his father had described Boer battles against both Xhosa and Zulu on the Great Trek. Joshua also cried hot, childish tears of anger and frustration when his mother told him of the violent deaths of his two older siblings—whom he had never met—at the hands of vagrant Kaffirs on their first farm in NATAL. Deep within his youthful heart, he felt compelled to avenge his murdered brother and sister, despite his God-fearing mother's assertion that vengeance belonged to the Good Lord alone. Joshua's father Jan had been only slightly more sympathetic of his willful son's compulsion to spread his wings at such a tender age, but had promised the boy that he would consider his request.

Unable to stand upright because of the danger of incoming fire, Joshua now acted as spotter, and used his hunting knife to pry a jammed cartridge out of the chamber of the British soldier's rifle as they lay flat on the floor of the cave. It had been less than 4 hours since the scout riders had galloped into the British camp just after noon, with virtually the entire Zulu army hot on their heels. The contingent of mounted black troops had quickly fled when the Zulus had attacked, abandoning their white comrades to their own bloody fate. The out-lying rocket battery commanded by Brevet-Major Francis Broadfoot Russell (1842-1879) had been the first British unit to be overwhelmed, after firing only a few of their spectacularly noisy but rather ineffectual missiles (which were known by the British merely to inflict *psychological*, rather than any *real* damage on the enemy). The only thing that had held the Zulus back for any length of time was brave Colonel Durnford and his men (who had retreated to the donga that ran across the face of the camp) and the two light cannons (still on the main line of battle) firing their small but devastating 7-pounder, case-shot fragmentation shells into the advancing hordes.

The camp itself had fallen in less than two hours, and the Battle of Isandlwana would come to be known as the *worst defeat* which the mighty British army had *ever* suffered *anywhere* in their *colonial* empire at the hands of *native* forces. But all this was academic to the last two survivors of that terrible battle: who were now fighting for their lives on the heights of Isandlwana Mountain. Joshua Roux looked into the eyes of the British soldier lying alongside him, and saw not fear, but a calm resolve. When, during the heated battle, the self-possessed soldier, realizing that all was lost, had filled the pockets of his red tunic and refilled the depleted pouches on his belt with cartridges from a spilled ammunition crate, before he ran and scrambled up the rocky slope to the cave. He had fought bravely alongside his own commander, Brevet-Lieut.-Col. Henry Burmester Pulleine (1838-1879), until Pulleine himself was wounded and they were about to be overwhelmed. At that moment, the Colonel had ordered him to take off his conspicuous red jacket, and try to make his escape through the long grass and boulders. Before sneaking away, he took off his red jacket, turned it inside out, rolled it into a ball, and tied it around his waist with a gunstrap he had taken from a rifle lying by the corpse of a British soldier.

"Tell Lord Chelmsford that all *our* men fought bravely, but that the odds were overwhelming. Go quickly now, Private, and don't look back!" Those were the last words that Colonel Pulleine had shouted to him over the din of battle. But the lone soldier *did* look back, just as he breasted the low plateau that formed the base of the rocky outcrop that soared upwards into the blue Zululand sky. He then saw his brave commander fall under the heavy onslaught of dozens of spear-wielding Zulu warriors, the backs of his last few remaining men pressed protectively against him.

The private had sustained a wound to his leg, which was caused by a stray Zulu musket ball, and it was still bleeding profusely. The lone, wounded soldier soon realized that he would not now have the strength to escape on foot. Besides, the narrow gap, through which the handful of fugitives had fled down towards the Buffalo River, had now been effectively cut off by the Zulus, and the only other possible escape route, over the back of the mountain and down towards Rourke's Drift, was also still swarming with Zulu warriors. So clutching his rifle in one hand and his cartridge-filled tunic in the other, he had crawled towards a small cave that he had spotted in the rocky outcrop. The British soldier's heart had skipped a beat when he first saw the dark shape of another person already crouched in the cave, but the wide-eyed, sun-tanned face staring back at him was that of a Boer teenager.

Chapter Twenty

Joshua Roux had been almost delirious with excitement when his father had finally relented, and allowed him to accompany, as a driver, the many private wagons heading for Port Natal. Erika Roux had made her son solemnly promise that he would stay well away from any actual fighting. She did not want to again lose a child—her *only* child to Zulus; as she had lost both Benjamin and Delia to Kaffirs in NATAL. Young Joshua had truly tried hard to keep that promise to his distraught mother. He had ridden his horse Jasper, alone up to Pilgrim's Rest, and had then driven one of the wagons belonging to the friendly Irish storekeeper there (for a shilling a day plus rations), all the way down the rugged mountain passes to Durban, without mishap. Josh had gained more than enough experience in handling a team of oxen and a wagon while assisting his father on their numerous trips to the small towns to deliver their loads of dried meat and hides. Joshua had even managed to catch another glimpse of Cockney Liz while in Pilgrim's Rest, where she now entertained the riotous crowds of thirsty diggers at the new saloon that had been opened by her benefactor, Stafford Parker. Joshua thought that she sang and danced beautifully, and she had even winked at the blushing Boer teenager standing shyly in the far corner of the crowded saloon. The diggers would roar their appreciation when she paraded on the billiard table and impishly snapped her garters at them.

However, it soon came time to join the dozens of empty wagons heading south to NATAL. As they approached the busy port at Durban, crowded with British troop-ships and supply vessels for the forthcoming invasion of Zululand, more and more empty private wagons joined their convoy. They were then bellowed at by red-faced, red-jacketed British quartermasters, directing them to the loading bays. Soon, Joshua's wagon was heavily laden with canvas tents, poles, pots and the other accoutrements necessary for an army on extended campaign. Then they turned north again, and made their way slowly up through the verdant NATAL midlands. When they camped for a night not far from his parents' former farm, Joshua Roux saddled his horse, and galloped over to see that legendary homestead for the very first time. He came over the last ridge shielding the farm, and saw the stone farmhouse and barn, which his own father had built. Nearby was the little wattle-and-daub cottage that the grandfather he had never known—that fierce Boer warrior Christiaan Delarey—had occupied in his old age. Some distance off, stood the crumbling cottage once inhabited by the colored herder and his wife; which now served as a chicken coop. When Joshua reined-in his horse, in front of the stone farmhouse, he was met by a middle-aged Hottentot man, his petite colored wife and adult daughter. Joshua introduced himself.

Boontjies Ryer looked upon the son of his former employer, with wonder. *"Jy lyk net soos jou Oupa!"* he announced, commenting on Joshua Roux's striking resemblance to his late grandfather, as the herder remembered him from two decades earlier. The same intense green eyes and light-brown hair had been passed down, skipping a generation, to the grandson. *"Jy gaan net so groot en kwaai word as ou Meneer Christiaan. Kom, Meester Josh, kom sit nou, en drink tee met ons."* ("You will grow up to be just as big and fierce as old Mister Christiaan. Come Master Josh, sit now and drink tea with us.")

They duly sat on the stoep of the stone farmhouse, which Joshua's parents had graciously given to the faithful colored couple—before Jan and Erika left forever: trekking off to the eastern TRANSVAAL Lowveld. Joshua drank in the loving stories they told as he drank the sweet, hot tea and consumed the freshly baked rusks, similar to those which Saartjie Ryer had served to his parents so many years ago. Behind her skirts a pair of tiny twins, boy and girl grandchildren, peeped shyly out at the Boer boy. When they had finished their tea, Boontjies asked Joshua if he would like to visit the graves of his siblings, as well as that of his grandfather, on the *koppie* near the farmhouse. He graciously and solemnly accepted—and keenly noticed with profound appreciation that the little graveyard was neatly kept, and that the grave of Krisjan Ryer, as well as those of his maternal grandfather and his brother and sister, bore fresh flowers. Joshua looked out over the lush farm, over the fields, and down towards the river described by his parents, where Benjamin and Delia Roux, whom he had never met, had been cruelly and vengefully slain by vagrant Kaffirs. Something changed in the heart of the Boer teenager that day, and when he rode off again, back towards the transport-camp, he was no longer just a fresh-faced boy with stars in his eyes. He was now a young man with a past, and with a future.

By the time Joshua Roux galloped in to the transport camp, about 200 wagons were being inspanned for the haul up to Rorke's Drift on the Buffalo River, the tributary that formed the northern boundary between British NATAL, and enemy territory. As evening fell a few days later, they arrived at the rocky ford: a rustic watery gateway to the Zulu kingdom. Once a trading store owned by an Irishman (who had committed suicide in a fit of depression when his gin stocks did not arrive), Rorke's Drift had then become a mission station, and was now a staging-post and field hospital for the British force preparing to invade Zululand. The small collection of buildings in the shadow of the *Oskarberg*[86] was a hive of activity, and as Joshua's wagon approached, the commander, Lieutenant John Rouse Merriott Chard (1847-1897) bellowed at him to get his wagon lined up in the direction of the drift just half a mile away.

That night, the troops were in high spirits and their eyes shone at the thought of the fire and the steel that they would unleash on the Zulus the next day. The leather of their boots and saddles gleamed, and soldiers sat in excited groups, sharpening the points of their 18-inch long bayonets: their *lungers*. Their officers strode purposefully this way and that, alternately shouting at some soldiers who were using a full sack of mealies

---

[86] "Oscar Mountain" is 680 feet high. It was known to the Zulu as *Shiyane* ("Eyebrow"), but the isolated butte was named *Oskarberg* by Rev. Otto Witt, in 1878, who had acquired the land on behalf of the Swedish/Norwegian Mission. He named it Oskarberg in honor of the reigning king of Sweden, Oskar (II.) Friedrich Bernadotte (1872-1907).

for bayonet practice. Other soldiers were joking with their rugged corporals and sergeants, who also walked around the sprawling temporary camp, handing out small waxed-paper packs of cartridges to the eager troops, who each filled their belt pouches with 70 rounds. Due to the jostling and shaking of the wagons over the stony tracks, the British army had seen fit to manufacture stout mahogany ammunition crates with a sliding lid secured with a screw, in which the waxed cartridge cartons were tightly packed. The individual .450 cartridges also reputedly bore a thin coating of wax, to prevent the summer humidity of NATAL from contaminating the powder charge.

Officers carefully honed the edges of their long, ornate gleaming swords, and checked the actions of their heavy revolvers. Then, the veterans slept, but the younger soldiers, and Joshua himself, found sleep elusive. When the strident bugle sounded in the still darkness before dawn, and the smooth-cheeked drummer boys began rapping out a staccato martial marching beat, Joshua Roux was already waiting impatiently in the driving-seat of his wagon, his stallion Jasper stamping and snorting alongside.

—*Now,* however, Joshua Roux lay on his stomach, shielding his head with his arms as shards of shattered stone and pieces of hot lead whined off the walls of their shelter every time a bullet pierced the shadowed entrance to the cave. The Zulus on the slope below the cave poured an erratic, albeit inaccurate hail of musket balls and captured British bullets at them; but the ricochets in the interior of the cave threatened to tear into their bodies just as effectively as any well-aimed shot. More and more warriors had grabbed fallen British rifles and handfuls of scattered cartridges, then joined their comrades in firing at the last survivors of the battle holed up in the cave. The Martini-Henry rifle with its single cocking lever was easy to operate, and the Zulu warriors had observed during the battle how the red soldiers pulled down the lever to extract a spent cartridge, before inserting a fresh round, and then pulled the lever up again to chamber it and then fire again. The rifle clutched in the hands of the British soldier in the cave was now getting so hot from his continuous firing that the moisture-proof wax coating on the cartridges melted as soon as they were chambered, gumming up the action, and making it difficult to open. The normally substantial recoil of the Martini rifle was exacerbated by the fouled barrel, and now cruelly bruised his shoulder with every shot. Occasionally, when a fired cartridge stuck fast and refused to budge, he lay on his side, and used his boot on the extraction lever to force it down; as he had seen other, doomed British soldiers do while standing upright in the heat of the battle earlier that day. When that exertion caused the blood to again begin flowing freely from his wound, Joshua cut a strip from the British soldier's red tunic, and tightly bound his companion's pierced leg.

The Boer teenager now lay alongside that last surviving redcoat in the dust, at the dark mouth of the cave on Isandlwana Mountain on January 22, 1879. As Zulu bullets smashed chunks of rock off the walls and roof, Joshua prayed quietly for a miracle, and wondered if he would ever see his parents again. They had a good supply of cartridges in the cave, but only one rifle between them, which might fail at any moment. The wounded British soldier was keeping up a steady fire on the groups of Zulus advancing up the slope towards them, and when the rifle jammed and the lever would not extract the spent cartridge, he began handing it to Joshua, who pried the hot case out with his knife, and then handed the firearm back. The fire from below slackened a little, and Joshua peered cautiously around the rock in front of him, noticing that the exulting warriors looting the wagons and stripping the bodies of the fallen British soldiers seemed to have been distracted by something they had seen in the distance. From the heights, Joshua's keen eyes could just make out what looked like a rider in a red coat and white helmet galloping hard towards the shattered camp. As the rider drew closer, he slowed, and then stopped. From a distance, the British scout, perched on his horse, thought he could see red-coated soldiers moving about the camp at the foot of the mountain, and assumed that the troops had driven off the Zulu attack of that day. He had been sent back by Lord Chelmsford to investigate the faint sounds of shooting and occasional cannon fire, which the main column had heard from 12 miles away; as they pursued the elusive groups of Zulus who kept making feints towards them. In the gloom, however, the scout's eyes finally discerned, dishearteningly, that in fact, the red-coated figures were not British soldiers, but Zulus. The victorious warriors had donned the jackets and helmets of the fallen British troops. The British scout wheeled his sweating horse about and galloped back over the ridge, as a few Zulu bullets whistled harmlessly past him above his head.

"Quick, laddie!" hissed the wounded British soldier. "Here's your chance to escape, while the Zulus are distracted. It will start getting dark soon, and you can make it back to Rorke's Drift if you keep to the shadows. I'll start firing again to keep their heads down. Go now, and God speed!" Joshua Roux looked briefly into the eyes of that brave man, whose name he had not even had time to ask, solemnly shook his hand, then scrambled to his knees, and slipped into the long grass, which grew right up to the mouth of the cave. He then wriggled and crawled his way carefully the 200 yards around to the back of the rocky outcrop, where he noticed that the Zulus were now fast departing from the corpse-strewn battlefield. He lay very still until he saw a clear gap down to the wagon trail that led back to the river crossing 12 miles away.

When he eventually reached the rutted track undetected, he again heard heavy firing from the far side of the mountain, and then the firing stopped abruptly. Joshua feared that the brave, lone British soldier had finally run out of ammunition, or had himself been killed. A dark shape under a tree gave him an awful fright, until he realized that it was a runaway horse, which had got its reins caught in a thorn tree. Joshua whistled softly, and the horse whinnied in reply. Joshua's young heart leapt with joy when he realized that it was his own stallion Jasper, who had fled in panic during the terrible battle.

[The horse had been tied to the side of the transport wagon, which Joshua had been busy re-loading, at the temporary, tented camp below Isandlwana Mountain, when the Zulus had first attacked. His horse Jasper was spooked by the sudden shouting and rocket fire, broke loose and fled up the slope of the mountain. Joshua had then made an effort to catch his precious mount; but the panic-stricken horse had soon disappeared over the ridge, and down the other side. When Joshua turned to go back to his wagon, he saw that the camp was being overrun by Zulus, and since he was unarmed (having been hired as a wagon driver, not as a soldier) he had looked desperately around for refuge. It was then that he had spotted the mouth of the small cave in the mountain, and Joshua wisely crept toward it under the cover of the tall grass. He had promised his mother that he would not engage in battle—but circumstances would eventually overrule that promise.]

Soon, the Boer youth was galloping like the wind towards the Buffalo River. His horse's hooves splashed through the shallows as he forded the stony drift upstream of Rorke's Drift, just as the sun began to set.

As Joshua Roux approached the outpost at a gallop, he heard desultory rifle fire. Then he saw that Zulu warriors had already breasted the looming *Oskarberg,* and were firing down on the tiny outpost. Just then, the surviving members of the Natal Native Contingent—who had shamefully abandoned their post at the onset of battle, and escaped to Rorke's Drift—grabbed any horses they could and deserted *once again!* They fled past him up the track towards the distant village of *Helpmekaar*—which, ironically means, "Help Each Other." A white, locally recruited corporal who ignominiously fled with them was summarily gunned down by one of the outraged British troops who were by now firing back at the Zulu snipers on the mountain. The Zulu commander, a large, very black warrior on a white horse—the same *induna* that Joshua had seen marshaling his frustrated rear-guard warriors at Isandlwana earlier that day—suddenly dismount when he realized that British snipers had now found his range. Lieutenant Chard, who recognized the Boer boy as a wagon-driver from two days previously, waved his white helmet at Joshua, and bade him enter the make-shift fortifications around the outpost. He did so just in time, for the two "horns" of the Zulu impi closed around the mission station only minutes after Joshua had dismounted. A grim-faced sergeant then held out a Martini-Henry rifle to the young man, but Joshua Roux hesitated.

"What's wrong, laddie? Did your mammie perhaps tell you that you shouldn't shoot at poor, innocent darkies? Well, they are about to shoot at *you,* if you don't get your young head down!" A few of the redcoats chuckled at Sergeant Frank Bourne's (1854-1945) joke, and then Joshua took the rifle from his big hand. Just an hour before Joshua Roux had galloped in, another witness of the carnage at Isandlwana had galloped straight past the outpost, yelling out, "The Zulus are coming—thick as grass, and black as hell!" The 100 or so men there, many of whom were sick or wounded themselves, were then joined by the very few fugitives who had managed to escape across the flooded Buffalo River well below the mission station. They had immediately set about throwing up defenses with the only materials available to them—big bags filled with mealies, and biscuit crates. The newly arrived Boer teenager then took up a position behind one of the sacks of mealies that had been built up into a wall, and chambered one of the big .450 cartridges. Peering over the mealie bag, he saw a warrior ducking from tree to tree as he made his way closer to the outpost. Steadying the rifle on the hessian bag, Joshua waited until the Zulu re-appeared, and then dropped him in his tracks. A cheer went up from the soldiers around Joshua, and a huge corporal slapped him on the back, and smiled at him through his red beard.

"Where did you learn to shoot like that, young fella?" Corporal Christian Ferdinand Schiess (1856-1884), a valiant Switzer, asked. Joshua replied in his halting English that he had hunted many times with his father, and that buck seldom stood still for long; thus he had learned the necessity of quick, steady shots.

The main Zulu impi then charged the mission station. Heavy firing broke out all around him, and the men began hastily fixing their long, sharp bayonets onto their rifles. Soon, the first wave of warriors reached the fragile fortifications, and tried to scramble over. They were driven back by the soldiers' rifle fire, then their bayonet lunges—and finally when the soldiers resorted to clubbing at the Zulus with their rifle butts. Again the Zulus attacked, and this time, two or three made it over the biscuit boxes stacked on Joshua's right. A warrior raised his heavy club to strike the boy, but fell backwards as he was impaled by the bayonet of the big, red-bearded corporal. A grim hand-to-hand struggle soon ensued, as waves of warriors charged again and again at the thin red line of British soldiers fighting desperately to hold them back. Some tried to grab hold of the barrels of the rifles as they protruded over the flimsy defenses, only to be shot at point-blank range, or skewered by bayonets. Completely surrounded by over 4,000 yelling and hissing Zulu warriors, the British soldiers fired and reloaded, fired and lunged with their bayonets. Soon, their rifle barrels grew hot, and some men wrapped rags around their hands to protect their blistering fingers. The shots from the Zulu snipers who were still firing from their raised positions on the *Oskarberg* were not very accurate, and they had about as much chance of striking *their own* warriors, as any redcoats. Nonetheless, every now and then, a British soldier fell backwards, shot through his exposed head, neck or shoulder. Already outnumbered nearly 40-to-1, these losses began to take their toll on the beleaguered defenders of the tiny outpost.

Night had fallen, and it was now becoming increasingly difficult to distinguish the black warriors through the gloom, and the smoke of the shooting. Then one of the Zulus threw a firebrand onto the thatched roof of the make-shift hospital of the mission station, and despite the increasingly precarious position of the few soldiers and wounded men trapped inside, the light from the burning roof now made it easier for the soldiers at the barricades to pick out their targets. Inside the hospital, a grim, room-to-room struggle was taking place: The men trapped therein were hacking their way out through the mud-brick walls as the Zulus warriors infiltrated the building. More than a few heroic rescues took place that night in the confines of that hospital, as some men dragged the wounded through one hole in a wall, into a clear room, while their comrades held off the Zulus with their bayonets—as the warriors tried to get at them through the hole they themselves had just come through from an adjoining room. Eventually, the thatch roof was fully ablaze, and starting to collapse upon the occupants. As the last of the surviving defenders of the blazing building tumbled out through a window into the midst of the shrinking British position, warriors streamed over the fragile barriers, and had to be driven back again by a bayonet charge. It seemed that the Zulu warriors had more respect for the cold steel of the British bayonets, than they had for the hot, lead bullets. Again and again the Zulus tried to overwhelm the defenders with massed charges, only to be driven back repeatedly by the bayonets and clubbing rifle butts.

As the night wore on, the British soldiers were forced to fall back into ever-smaller sections of their redoubt, as well as from a small, but well-built stone kraal, and Joshua Roux found himself cramped between struggling redcoats. His rifle barrel was now so hot that it glowed a dull crimson-purple color in the dark, as the roof of the hospital slowly burned itself out. Darkness now again began to swallow up the fringes of the defenses, and the tired soldiers feared that they might be overwhelmed by a sudden rush from the gloom of the deepening shadows.

However, the Zulus had sustained fearful losses and, therefore, their attacks began to gradually lose momentum. Warriors' bodies were piled up deep against the outside of the line of bags and boxes, and their impetuous induna, Dabulamanzi KaMpande, began to have doubts about his own tired men's ability to mount any further successful assaults. They had been on the move virtually non-stop since before noon the previous day, after having run a long distance to try and join the fight at Isandlwana—and then they had run many miles to attack the tiny outpost at Rorke's Drift, with the hopes of washing their spears in the blood of white men. He also knew that he would have to account for these extra losses to his king; having squandered the lives of *hundreds* of his brave warriors in this failed attack—which he had launched *in defiance* of standing orders *not* to cross into NATAL, nor ever to attack white soldiers who may be holed up in any defensive position.

Just as the first glow of dawn began to lift the veil of darkness over the *Oskarberg,* one of his lookouts ran up to report that a strong British column had been spotted approaching in the far distance. Dabulamanzi finally gave the order to call off the attack, and mounted his white horse. As the Zulus departed Rorke's Drift, the long lines of warriors paused briefly, silhouetted against the rising sun on the Oskarberg, raised their assegais, and thrice shouted *"bayete!"* ("hail") in salute to the brave handful of British soldiers who had managed to repel their massed, ferocious attacks, all night, against all odds.

Lord Chelmsford's main column had finally reached the battlefield of Isandlwana after nightfall, and they were thus spared the full, graphic reality of the extent of the carnage that had taken place that day. But when a burial party was eventually sent to inter the fallen, they counted about 1,000 dead British soldiers and camp-followers, and about 4,000 Zulu corpses. At the subsequent desperate and heroic defense of Rorke's Drift, miraculously only about 20 of the defenders fell, compared to Zulu losses of almost 400. When Zulu king Cetshwayo heard of his own bitter losses, he sadly commented that an assegai had that day been "thrust into the belly" of the Zulu nation. As a warrior himself, he would have known that such a wound signified a very painful, lingering death. He had initially miscalculated the depth of British resolve to destroy his martial nation—but he was wise enough to now know that those two battles were *just the beginning* of a greater war. Cetshwayo would be proven correct: The mighty Zulu army would be *smashed*—and his proud nation brought to its knees well within that same year. But his warriors would still strike *one more,* isolated blow, which would reverberate across the waters to Europe, and strangely, even change the course of late-Napoléonic France's history.

For their part, the British had initially retreated back to NATAL to lick their wounds; leaving their own southern column *trapped* in Zululand, besieged in a makeshift fort. But when a distraught Lord Chelmsford (who was refused his request to be relieved of his duties) had recovered, he re-invaded Zululand a few months later—and his fresh army re-supplied and well armed, *swept clean all Zulus before him.*

"Back home" in Britain, an *outraged* populace reacted to the news of Britain's defeat at Isandlwana—the worst defeat Britain ever suffered at the hands of native forces in any of "their" colonies. In an attempt to mollify public opinion, 11 "Victoria Crosses" were subsequently awarded to the indomitable defenders of Rorke's Drift—the most ever awarded for a single battle.[87]

[By comparison *only one* such medal was awarded for the disastrous conflict of the previous battle at Isandlwana. Its sole recipient (out of 1,000 dead, and 50 survivors) was Private Samuel Wassal (1856-1927), who had unselfishly helped to save the life of a drowning comrade while crossing *Fugitives' Drift,* under heavy enemy fire. It was rare in itself, that such an award was conferred on a *private:* for the British military of that era, considered the lowly enlisted men as mere *cannon fodder;* not worthy of recognition, as if they were incapable of any valiant or exceptional act.]

The annals of military history vaguely record that an "unknown" British soldier, *in a cave,* on Isandlwana Mountain had held off the Zulus for some hours after the battle was over. Likewise, history records simply that an "unknown" rider had joined the beleaguered outpost of Rorke's Drift at the last moment before the Zulu attack and that he had fought bravely through that long, terrible night. However, the memory of that brave man in the cave, the horrors of Isandlwana and the triumph of Rorke's Drift would remain forever seared into the young mind of the Boer teenager Joshua Roux.

---

[87] In classic posturing, the British government began issuing *belated* posthumous Victoria Crosses in 1907. Among some of the first of these new posthumous VCs awarded, were those awarded to Lieutenants Melville and Coghill, who died at the hands of the Zulus after crossing *Fugitive's Drift,* in their attempt to save the Queen's colors. They were somehow overlooked when the *first* round of medals was initially dispensed, reputedly due to speculation that they had "fled the field of battle."

Chapter Twenty-one

When Joshua finally reached his home on the banks of the Sabie River, he was no longer a boy, but a man. His mother Erika, and father Jan Roux welcomed him home; though their delight at his safe return was jaded somewhat when they learned that their son was now a blooded warrior himself. Any dreams they may have cherished of him staying on the peaceful farm with them for the rest of his life, soon dissipated. Joshua (which name loosely means, "deliverer"), like his namesake—that great Israelite general of the Old Testament—had now experienced the fire and steel of battle; even hunting with his father now seemed *tame* by comparison. He commented to his mother that, ironically, he had never "felt more alive," than when *facing death*. He explained that he had done his utmost to keep his promise to her: not to engage in any actual fighting against the Zulus, but fate had decided otherwise. He would probably now be dead if he had not taken up arms to help repel the Zulu attack on the mission at Rorke's Drift—it was kill or be killed. He had emerged physically unscathed, but a fire now burned in his heart and in his eyes, which would not be quenched; except, perhaps, by a soldier's death on a battlefield, facing the enemy.

The wages Joshua had earned for driving the transport wagon down to Durban, and then up again to Isandlwana via Rorke's Drift, he soon spent to purchase *his own* .450 caliber Martini-Henry rifle.[88] Joshua's former employer at the trading store in Pilgrim's Rest had been well-compensated by the British army

---

[88] The actual caliber designation was .577/.450. The .450 was a modified form of the .577 ammo for the "Snider-Enfield" breech-loading rifle, which had a hinged, swing-out chamber. The British troops irreverently referred to this earlier compromised loading system as the "Suicide Breech"! Col. Jacob Snider (1811-1866), an American, devised the first "enclosed metallic cartridge" with a primer in the rear. The British then "necked down" the .577 to .450 for the Martini-Henry* rifle. [Footnote continued at bottom of next page...]

for the loss of his wagon, and he even gave the Boer boy a good discount on the rifle and ammunition. As young Joshua Roux, hunter, wagon-driver and Zulu fighter, stepped out onto the stoep of the store with his new rifle slung over his shoulder, Cockney Liz beckoned surreptitiously from the window of her cottage across the muddy main street. When Joshua later re-crossed the road to the saloon for an ale, there was a spring in his step, that did not go unnoticed by proprietor Stafford Parker.

Joshua Roux used his fine new rifle to hunt the herds of buffalo that inhabited the riverine forests of the Sabie River, and he once took a bead on the massive forehead of a great bull elephant, just before his father stopped him from firing at it. Jan Roux had come to love and respect the elephants that roamed that area of the Lowveld, and could never bring himself to kill one. So, his modest income was derived only from the wagon-loads of hides and biltong that he and Joshua regularly delivered to the burgeoning towns on the escarpment—and the monetary lure of ivory was put aside. Joshua soon grew bored with the quiet life on the farm, however, and his gaze was now firmly fixed on the distant blue horizon, where dark war-clouds were again beginning to gather, but this time, the Boer teenager would face, not Zulu warriors—but British redcoats.

In the aftermath of the disastrous battle at Isandlwana, and the subsequent heroic defense of Rorke's Drift, another young man, born only a few years before Joshua Roux, tried to persuaded his own, very reluctant mother to allow him to sail to South Africa and join the British army there. However, this young man was not some rustic hunter-farmer—but went by the more illustrious name of *Prince Louis ("Lou-Lou") Napoléon Eugène Jean Joseph* (1856-1879); son of Emperor

---

[88] [...continued from bottom of previous page.]

* It was originally called the "Peabody-Martini-Henry" Rifle. It was a breech-loading rifle with a lever action which was designed by the Swissman, Friedrich von *Martini,* who modified the rifle developed by the American Henry *Peabody,* with the rifled barrel designed by the Scotsman Alexander *Henry.* Regardless of its lengthy name, it was a powerful, sturdy weapon.

Napoléon III. and the Empress Eugénie[89] of France. He had already received his baptism of fire at the Battle of Sarrebruck[90] (1870) at the tender age of 14 and had subsequently received training at the British military academy at Woolwich (London).

Not long after Sarrebruck, France's empire ended with their surrender to Prussia at Sedan (Ardennes, France). When his father died in 1873, Louis, the Prince Imperial, represented the *last* of his royal line. Having received a solemn promise from Lord Chelmsford not to allow her son to get in harm's way, his mother finally relented and the young prince sailed for Durban. He was attached to an artillery battery, with the non-insignia rank of lieutenant. At the Royal Hotel in Durban, he purchased "Percy," a fine but rather skittish horse. He was briefly stationed at Utrecht, where the late Benjamin and Delia Roux had attended school some 20 years earlier. Louis Napoléon went into KLOPPER'S TRADING STORE in the main street to purchase materials to sketch-in details on some military maps.

[Fortunately for Louis, by this date, the imposing Mevrou Klopper had passed away: for most certainly she would have irreverently challenged the prince to an arm-wrestling match. The simple fact of her passing certainly saved Louis some Imperial dignity—for after eying up her imposing girth, the lightly built Prince, no doubt, would have found *some excuse* to wisely decline the challenge.]

The young prince smiled at a middle-aged colored couple standing with their daughter and twin grandchildren on the stoep of the trading store in open-mouthed awe of the immaculately uniformed prince as he strode out, mounted, and then rode regally by them on his fine charger. This colored couple was none other than Boontjies and Saartjie Ryer, in town, buying some supplies. Louis Napoléon was a handsome, enthusiastic and rather engaging fellow, and thus well-liked by the general

---

[89] A Spaniard of partial Irish descent, who before her marriage was Doña María Eugenia Ignacia Augustina de Palafox de Guzmán Portocarrero y Kirkpatrick, 18th Marchioness of Ardales, 18th Marchioness of Moya, 19th Countess of Teba, 10th Countess of Montijo and Countess of Ablitas.

[90] —Saarbrücken: the capital of Saarland, Germany.

public, his comrades and mess-mates. Unfortunately, as were many high-spirited youth, he was also reckless.

When he departed the safety of Utrecht, having been allowed to accompany Lord Chelmsford in his second invasion of Zululand, Louis left camp on the first day of June, 1879—without his commander's knowledge—and "led" an 8-man mounted patrol deep into enemy territory. Captain Jahleel Brenton Carey[91] (1847-1883) was ostensibly in command, but soon deferred to the Prince's strong will. Against the advice of Carey and his men, the Prince ordered the troopers to dismount to brew coffee at an apparently deserted Zulu kraal. Noticing that the ashes in the fireplace were still warm, the men became uneasy, but the young Prince was relaxed, and insisted on taking his time about things. When Louis finally felt inclined to leave, he imperiously called out to his little detachment: "Prepare to mount!"—but was still in the process of doing so himself, when suddenly, shots rang out from close range within some tall grass. Forty Zulus then attacked the patrol and the horses of the small British detachment bolted. All except two troopers and the young Prince himself managed to hold on to their frantic horses, mount and flee. The Prince was dragged some distance by his horse, but then fell, damaging his right arm under Percy's flying hooves. Louis had lost his sword in the fall, so he drew his revolver, and turned to face the Zulus.

A warrior hurled his assegai, piercing the prince's thigh, but Louis plucked it out, and then charged bravely at them, wielding the spear. He also tried to fire his revolver, but his mangled right hand would not function. Another Zulu warrior, named Zabonga, then speared the prince through his left shoulder. Thus immobilized, Prince Napoléon was then swiftly hacked to death. When the naked, mutilated body of the young heir to the lost Napoléonic throne of France was recovered the following morning, it showed 17 fearful assegai wounds—and in Louis' clenched fist was a handful of woolly Zulu hair.

The death of Louis Napoléon at the hands of the Zulus was

---

[91] —an Englishman who, because he spoke French, was chosen to accompany the Prince.

highly embarrassing for the British army high command and it led to a surge of anti-British sentiment in France. The unfortunate Captain Carey, who had the *misfortune to survive,* was court-martialed and dishonorably discharged from the army. A week later, the Prince's corpse was hastily embalmed and shipped out from Durban, to be returned to his grieving mother in England.[92] The following year, after the subsequent destruction of the Zulu army, Empress Eugénie made a pilgrimage to the site of her son's death, and planted a cross and a few trees, which were still growing there over a century later. Thus savagely ended the illustrious Napoléonic blood-line.

A month after the death of Prince Louis Napoléon, the mighty Zulu army was finally destroyed at the Battle of Ulundi, near king Cetshwayo's capital. The road to Ulundi, however, was paved with the bones of both British and Zulu warriors. Lord Chelmsford himself had studiously ignored king Cetshwayo's belated peace overtures, refused his gifts of elephant tusks, and was determined to avenge the bloody defeat at Isandlwana, as well as avoid the embarrassment of being replaced at the moment of victory by Sir Garnet Joseph Wolseley (1833-1913), who had been sent from England to take over his command.

At the end of March, 1879, Lieutenant-Colonel Redvers Henry Buller (1839-1908) was awarded the "Victoria Cross" for his gallant rescue of men trapped in Devil's Pass on Hlobane Mountain. They had been hemmed in by a Zulu army of 22,000, commanded by the Zulu "premier" chief Mnyamana Buthelezi[93] (1809-1892). Colonel Redvers Buller, an exceedingly brave but

---

[92] Sometime later, in what seemed an honorable gesture, Louis Napoléon's sword was returned to the British, when the Zulus found out, to their amazement, that they had killed a French prince!

[93] One of his direct descendants, Mangosuthu Gatsha Buthelezi (1928-) would, just over a century later, unsuccessfully challenge Nelson Mandela for leadership of a "new," *black* South Africa. Mandela's Xhosa-dominated AFRICAN NATIONAL CONGRESS (ANC) had the overwhelming support of the liberal West (and the support of most nonZulu blacks and many coloreds), and therefore easily triumphed, leaving the Zulu-dominated *Inkatha* party briefly in control of only KwaZulu-Natal. The ANC later took control there.

rather pedantic commander, would himself gain infamy and become unflatteringly known as Sir "Reverse" Buller, in the second of two later wars against the Boers.

Meanwhile, the coastal column of Chelmsford's first invasion of Zululand had initially established an earth-walled fort on the north bank of the Tugela River—which was then ably commanded by Colonel Charles Knight Pearson (1834-1909). The column then advanced to Eshowe, defeating a ferocious attack led by chief Buthelezi, whose own 5,000 men were now well-armed with modern *British* rifles. But the Zulus lacked familiarity with firearms, they were not intensively trained and therefore, were not proficient with this weapon; thus, the British soldiers were still at an advantage. This battle was so fierce —and the accurate and sustained British volley-fire so effective—that the Zulus later told of having to "wipe the blood and brains of their fellow warriors off their bodies and shields." The British troops had only just managed to dig in at their newly established fort at Eshowe, when they received news of the massacre at Isandlwana, and the subsequent heroic defense of Rorke's Drift. A month later, Pearson himself launched an audacious attack on the kraal of Dabulamanzi KaMpande, the royal induna on the white horse at Rorke's Drift. Their thus-far, largely successful war against the British had finally "come home" to the Zulu commander. On the same day as the Battle of Hlobane, Lord Chelmsford set out from their "beach-head" on the Tugela, to relieve the besieged force at Eshowe. This time, however, he prudently established a string of small forts to protect his supply-lines in the rear. Finally, his defensive square was attacked by 10,000 Zulus, led once again by prince Dabulamanzi, at Gindgindlovu (the old capital of the late Zulu king Dingane of Blood River-infamy). This time, the British were armed with 9-pounder cannons, and new Gatling[94] rapid-firing "machine guns." The Zulus, who had managed to advance to within 20 yards of the square, suffered 1,200 casualties in the 90-minute battle; while the British sustained just a few dozen. Chelmsford then unleashed his cavalry, and they

---

[94] —the genius of American inventor, Dr. Richard J. Gatling, which gun (a devastating weapon) first became available in 1861.

pursued the fleeing Zulus for 4 miles; cutting them down mercilessly with their sabers and running them through with lances. They then advanced to Eshowe, and lifted the 10-week Zulu siege of Pearson's fort there.

The day after Hlobane, Redvers Buller had managed to provoke the Zulu army into an attack on his defensive positions at Khambula; ably assisted by the "Flying Column" of Colonel Evelyn Wood (1838-1919), they drove them off with accurate artillery, rifle-fire and the bayonet—but not before Buller first finishing his lunch. Over 2,000 Zulus were killed, and many more wounded. The Zulus never really recovered from these defeats. Chief Buthelezi's subsequent report to his king brought home the realization that the British road to the Zulu capital—and their final defeat of the Zulu army—*now lay open,* with no obstacles standing in Britain's way. Less than 6 months after the first, failed invasion of Zululand by the British army, the final reckoning was at hand: at the king's kraal itself.

At daybreak on the 4th of July, 1879, as the citizens of the United States of America were preparing to celebrate almost a century of independence from Britain, the British army in South Africa formed a square, and with their regimental bands playing stirring marching tunes, advanced in formation across the open plains towards the Zulu capital of Ulundi—in their efforts to subjugate another sovereign nation. Their force consisted of just over 4,000 white combatants, 1,000 black volunteers, 12 small cannons, and 2 Gatling guns. The opposing Zulu army totaled about 20,000 warriors, many of whom now carried British rifles, and was commanded once again by prince Dabulamanzi KaMpande, as well as his brother Siwedu, chief Ntshingwayo KaMahole "Khoza," and premier-chief Buthelezi.

Wave upon wave of Zulu warriors attacked the British square, clashing their spears against their shields, and shouting their chilling war-cry of *"Usuthu! Usuthu!"* (the name of their royal clan). But they were mown down by the artillery shells and rifle bullets of the British. The two Gatling guns, supported by sustained volley-fire from the British square, cut great swathes through the tightly massed Zulu ranks. After little more than half-an-hour of this mayhem, when Chelmsford sensed a slackening of the Zulu assaults, he opened a gap in the defensive square, and the mounted Lancers sallied forth to pursue the fleeing Zulu army towards the Mahlabatini plains, sparing not even the wounded. The British troops, enthusiastically assisted by the Natal Native Contingent, then burned king Cetshwayo's Zulu capital to the ground. The once all-powerful Zulu king and his close family had fled rather ignominiously to the Ngome Forest, but he was eventually betrayed by Zulu enemies, captured and then imprisoned in CAPE TOWN's castle. Thus had the might of the Zulu nation finally been broken.

When Sir Garnet Wolseley finally arrived to take over command in NATAL, the military show was, of course, over. Wolseley nonetheless set about the onerous task of administrating the newly conquered territory with vigor and then divided Zululand into 13 chiefdoms. One of these went to an infamous white man, John Dunn (1834-1895), who had already been long established as a "white chief" himself—who had dozens of Zulu wives, scores of children by them, and great herds of cattle. His loyalty to his adopted Zulu nation had been severely tested at the start of the invasion, but he had eventually settled on the side of the white men, and assisted ably in their war effort. His reward was a coastal "kingdom" of his own. But the new arrangements in Zululand were satisfactory to *no* one. Cetshwayo was eventually awarded an audience with Queen Victoria, who then graciously allowed him to retain and rule a portion of his original kingdom. But discord and then civil war broke out in Zululand, and Cetshwayo fled to Eshowe—ironically for British protection—where he died, broken-hearted.

The Zulu throne then passed to his eldest son, Dinizulu KaCetshwayo (1868-1913). Eventually Britain "annexed" the territory in 1887, but it was another 10 years before peace finally settled. Zululand was then incorporated into NATAL. In the interim, a Zulu chief by the name of Uzibhebhu KaMaphitha (1841-1904) another son of Cetshwayo, who had fought bravely for his father, now turned against the royal house of Usuthu. Dinizulu KaCetshwayo, became involved in a struggle for succession against this brother. In a quirk of fate, Dinizulu called on the Boers for assistance. General Louis Botha (1862-1919) was in charge of the Boer contingent, which joined with Dinizulu's volunteers. Together, at the Battle of Ghost Mountain (a.k.a. the Battle of *Tshaneni)* they defeated Uzibhebhu and killed the warriors of his army to the last man. Thus, Dinizulu was established as Supreme Chief of the Zulu nation.

Dinuzulu then granted his white allies a large piece of land (almost 1/3 of Zululand), on which they established the town of *Vryheid* ("Freedom"), near Utrecht in 1884. Vryheid was the capital of the short-lived "New Republic," which was itself soon curtailed by Britain's "annexation" (political theft) of the area. Dinizulu subsequently revolted against the British when they extended their rule over the whole of Zululand in 1887; but he was captured and banished to the remote island of St. Helena (between Africa and South America); where Napoléon Bonaparte himself had spent his last years as a prisoner. Dinizulu was eventually allowed to return to Zululand. However, he again became involved in an uprising and was eventually again banished, to Middelburg in the TRANSVAAL; where he eventually died.

The rise and fall of the Zulu Empire itself had lasted scarcely 60 years; but during that short reign of conquest and bloodshed, *millions* of individuals and scores of tribes had either been displaced, destroyed or absorbed by the Zulus. It would take a full century before the Zulus themselves could again challenge for leadership of the black tribes in South Africa, via the political ambitions of a direct descendant of the premier-chief Buthelezi, who had fought so bravely against the mighty British Empire. But this time around, it would be in a very much-changed country and in a vastly different political context. Further, a well-educated and popular Xhosa chieftain by the name of Nelson Rolihlahla Mandela (born 1918), would stand firmly in their way.

Chapter Twenty-two

Having brought the mighty Zulu nation to heel, Imperial Britain now turned its avaricious attentions to another independent, "unruly," and "militant" African tribe; but this one was composed entirely of *white* men—the Afrikaner Boers. The earlier British "annexation" of the TRANSVAAL in 1877 had proved extremely controversial and unpopular: both in South Africa and abroad. European nations, large and small, made it their business to protest Britain's "gobbling up" of independent peoples in Africa (and elsewhere). Some of these protests, perhaps, were born out of envy concerning Great Britain's far-reaching empire on which "the sun never set"—but most were probably motivated by republican ideals and basic morality. The Boers took advantage of this international anti-British sentiment by sending a delegation first to Lord Carnarvon, and then to his successor as Colonial Secretary, Sir Michael Edward Hicks Beach[95] (1837-1916), to convince them that the "annexation" was *unjust*—to no avail.

So once again, the Boers were forced to prepare to *assert themselves* and fight for their country and freedom. In both the CAPE COLONY and the ORANGE FREE STATE, a ground-swell of public opinion against Britain grew, and after 8,000 Boers met at *Paardekraal* ("Horse corral") under the leadership of Paul Kruger, Petrus ("Piet") Jacobus Joubert (1834-1900) and Marthinus Pretorius, the restoration of the Republic was declared. On December 16, 1880—the *anniversary* of the DAY OF THE VOW—the old *Vierkleur* ("four-colored flag") was proudly flown once more.

The British governor, Colonel Sir William Owen Lanyon (1842-1887), not known for his mental agility, was militarily unprepared for this event; his troops being scattered far and wide. In an ill-considered show of might, he tried to forcefully collect delinquent

---

[95] 1st Earl of St. Aldwyn.

taxes in the town of *Potchefstroom,*[96] but an angry Boer commando under General Piet Arnoldus Cronje (1836-1911) surrounded the British infantry there, and after a few shots were fired, forced their surrender. This successful, though small act of defiance gave the Boers heart, and they, with a commando of 200 men, then confronted the 94th Regiment of Foot on the road to Pretoria. Commandant François "Frans" Gerhadus Joubert (1827-1903) informed the British column under Lieut.-Col. Philip Robert Anstruther (1841-1880) that the country was now again a Republic, and that any further British advance would be considered *an act of war.* When the colonel refused to turn back, firing commenced. His regiment took heavy casualties; Anstruther was himself mortally wounded, and his column surrendered.

Governor Lanyon was now besieged in Pretoria with a force of some 1,700 men, facing about 7,000 armed Boers, and all of his nearest possible troop reinforcements were at least 100 miles away. His only hope was for the Natal garrison to invade through the difficult mountain passes into the TRANSVAAL; but the hastily assembled Natal Field Force under Sir Garnet Wolseley's replacement, Maj.-Gen. Sir George Pomeroy-Colley (1835-1881), was only 1,200 strong. Nonetheless, Colley's column marched north to confront the Boers. News of the planned British "invasion" spread like wildfire, and soon reached the eastern Lowveld.

The first indication that Jan and Erika Roux's 21-year-old son Joshua would want to join the fighting came one summer morning in January 1881, when he confronted his father on the stoep of their cottage alongside the Sabie River. "Pa, I heard from a trader in Pilgrim's Rest that the British plan to invade the TRANSVAAL, and that the Boer *commandos* are now looking for volunteers. Personally, I have no argument with the British myself; but Pa, I am a soldier now—in my heart—and I want to fight for my country. Can I take Jasper and join the commandos to stop the British from invading?" Joshua Roux stood before his father,

---

[96] Most likely named in Dutch, *Potscherf-stroom* ("Pot-sherd Stream"), since a collection of Bantu clay pot fragments was found there. Some believe it was named after trek leader Andries Potgieter; but this is unlikely (see footnote 13).

now tall and strong, his green eyes burning with the same fierce fire that his grandfather, Christiaan Delarey, had possessed. Jan Roux knew that it was futile to resist his strong-willed son in his quest for military honors, and he sadly broke the news to his wife Erika. She was distraught, but knew that the same warrior spirit that had infused her own father, now simmered in the breast of her son. His asking for permission to join the commandos was merely a "formality," out of respect to his father and mother, and she sensed that he had already made up his mind, and would leave regardless of their blessing. So they gave him their permission. Erika made him promise that every day he would read from the small, handwritten collection of Psalms, Proverbs, and other choice passages from the New Testament (which she had copied from their Dutch Bible) that she pressed into his hand. She also made him promise that he would daily pray for the Lord's protection, as she too would. She also admonished him that if he ever came across a British soldier face-to-face, to remember that the *Brit* too, had a mother who would also be praying for her own son's safety.

Jan then counseled his son, reminding him: "War is a terrible thing; though sometimes unavoidable. All we can do is trust that we are in the right and that the Lord will ultimately protect and give victory to those who are in the right. Yet, though our enemy at times, the English are still our cousins. Though they may act disgracefully, you must always behave with honor." Erika agreeing, also encouraged Joshua to show mercy to his foe, whenever possible—as she prayed the *Brits* would do if the situation was reversed. She finally entreated her son to call to remembrance the lone British soldier who had sacrificed his life at Isandlwana so that Joshua could live; and to also remember those redcoats who had fought so bravely alongside him against the Zulus at Rorke's Drift.

With his compassionate mother's words ringing in his ears, Joshua Roux saddled up his mount Jasper, slung his Martini-Henry rifle over his shoulder, and galloped off to war. He soon arrived at the Boer entrenchments under Commandant Nicholas Jacobus Smit[97] (1837-1896) at Laing's Nek, just as the British column tried to force its way through. A sharp engagement then ensued, and the young Boer had his first taste of fighting against white men. The joke at the time was that the British troops wore red tunics so that their enemy would not see the blood stains, and that the Boers wore brown trousers for similar reasons! However, their joking aside, if the Boers were actually afraid, their valiant fighting didn't even hint of fear. The British were driven back, and then Commandant Smit led his 300 men on a raid into NATAL towards Newcastle, where they ambushed an armed mail convoy. Immediately, the British launched a counter-attack at a crossing on the Ingogo River, but were again driven back, with heavy losses. The Boers casualties thus far were light, and the engagements had taken place mostly at long-distance rifle range, so Joshua Roux could still safely state that he had not yet met his British foe face-to-face. That would all soon change however, at the forthcoming Battle of Majuba.

General Colley was in an uncomfortable position. Besides the military setbacks his forces had suffered, with more than a quarter of his men already casualties of Laing's Nek and Ingogo, things on the political front had also taken a turn for the worse. It was rumored that the British Government was considering a *reversal* of their annexation of the TRANSVAAL: news which might dishearten his troops, whose sacrifices so far now began to look *even more futile*. So, when reinforcements finally arrived, he was determined to gain at least one convincing battle victory over the Boers. His eyes turned to the strategically important, flat-topped mountain of *Majuba* (Zulu for "Hill of Doves") thus far unoccupied by the Boer forces. In a daring night advance, his troops occupied the mountain, and now overlooked the Boer positions as far back as *Volksrust* ("Folk's Rest")—just over the border into the TRANSVAAL itself. This lofty position now felt much more comfortable to the eccentric General Colley, so he removed his boots to relieve the many

---

[97] Smit was already a *veld-kornet* ("cavalry officer") by 1864, and an experienced "Kaffir-fighter." He was later a member of the "Independence Delegation" sent to Queen Victoria (c.1883) and Vice-President of the SOUTH AFRICAN REPUBLIC (1886).

blisters he had earned on the night-climb up the mountain, and put on his comfortable slippers. His men, now looking down on the Boer forces, foolishly gave away their position by hurling insults down upon the Boers. However, the Brits had been unable to drag any of their cannons up the steep slopes and the incensed Boers soon realized this. They also noticed that the British troops had failed to dig in well. General Piet Joubert, who held overall command, gave the order, "Get the English off the mountain!" So some of the younger men with Commandant Smit, including Joshua Roux, elected to make the assault. The Boers began to climb Majuba.

General Joubert ordered some of his men to take up positions at Colley's rear to cut off any retreat, while he then directed covering fire, to keep British heads down while two groups of Boers scaled the northern slopes. The group that Joshua Roux had joined soon breasted a knoll on the north-west face, whence they had a good view of the British forces—and for the first time, Joshua was able to actually see the individual faces of the enemy. Although the Martini-Henry .450 round carried for about a mile, accurate shooting of the heavy bullet was limited to about 400 yards. Boer rifle-fire was thus only able to drive the British more towards the center of the saucer-shaped depression on the top of the mountain (from where they would not be able to fire down upon the Boer camp), though without inflicting very many casualties. However, there was one Boer sniper who consistently found his mark at *well over* 400 yards, and that was Joshua Roux. His expert marksmanship was soon noticed by his comrades, who encouraged him to try and pick off the British officers, and thereby sow confusion and fear in the enemy's ranks. This soon had the desired effect, and the beleaguered British force's troop movements became even more erratic and ineffective.

Casualties among the British were mounting fast, and General Colley seemed to be at a loss as to what to do next. Boers were encroaching on every side, and their marksmen were far superior to his own. His men had been under sustained and devastating Boer fire for 4 hours, and of the 365 men that he had taken to the top of the mountain, about half now lay dead or wounded. But he would not surrender. It did not seem to occur to Colley that a bayonet charge may well have cleared a path for an honorable retreat, as the Boers, like the Zulus before them, had a distinct aversion to facing cold British steel. Instead, as he walked about encouraging his troops, he exposed himself to the full view of the Boer snipers, and when British General Sir George Pomeroy-Colley was shot above his right eye, he fell dead with his revolver still clutched in his hand. It was rumored after the battle that the general had committed suicide in despair at his hopeless situation; but Joshua Roux knew better. Needless to say, the British surrendered. Altogether, British losses were about 100 killed, 134 wounded, and 60 taken prisoner. The Boers, on the other hand, suffered only 3 dead and 5 wounded. It was another astounding victory for the Boers—more evidence that the Lord God was on their side. The British were forced to treat for a humiliating peace.

Talks held at a rustic homestead called O'Neill's Cottage, sited directly below Majuba Mountain, led to the CONVENTION OF PRETORIA, where it was agreed that the Boer's independence of the TRANSVAAL REPUBLIC would be recognized by Britain; but they would have to accept a British Resident to oversee both African and Foreign Affairs. Britain also insisted on retaining control of the eastern border native districts, a move which again re-enforced Boer perceptions of British partiality towards the black tribes. Despite their posturing at the Convention, it was clear and obvious to all that Great Britain had suffered a *major* embarrassing, political and military defeat—and at the hands of a "rabble of Boer farmers." British blood spilled at the Battle of Majuba coagulated to bond all Afrikaners in a cohesive nationalism. In 1884, the CONVENTION OF LONDON ratified the earlier agreement, but their defeat deeply wounded Victorian pride, and the stage was set for a far more devastating war that would ignite between Brit and Boer before the close of that century.

Chapter Twenty-three

The discovery of vast reserves of gold in the TRANSVAAL held the prospect of great prosperity for the hitherto virtually penniless Boer republic; but as the numbers of *uitlanders* ("foreigners") seeking their fortunes in the new city of Johannesburg grew, so did President Paul Kruger's concerns that his own people would soon be outnumbered by the immigrants, and their own Boer culture threatened. At one stage, it was estimated that of the 100,000 inhabitants of the boom-town, half were white, and of that, only 10 percent (5,000) were Boers! Although most foreigners hadn't the slightest interest in political affairs, there was a small but vocal group of apparently ungrateful foreigners who *demanded* "their civil rights"—including the right to vote. Liberals in Britain took up their cause and political pressure increased. Kruger commented sadly that pressure from imperialist Britain was not aimed merely at gaining political concessions for *uitlanders*—but at taking over his country, and of course, "liberating" its goldmines. Some may have thought Kruger was paranoid; but Britain's past track record of hostilities, aggression, and avarice spoke for itself. In his rural simplicity, Kruger also had no real conception of the magnitude, might and diabolical deviousness of the international financial forces ranged against his fledgling republic. Despite his friendship with Sammy Marks (*formerly* Marx), it seemed that he was largely unaware that many of these, mostly non-British financiers were European Jews, who were eager to promote political strife, for their own rapacious ends.

To make matters worse, the *Volksraad* kept "shifting the political goalposts" concerning voting rights. They initially changed the qualifying period of residence for voting privileges from 5 years down to 2 years; however, they then had second thoughts and raised it again to an outrageous 14 years—and these voting rights were extended only to those 40 years old and over. Serious political unrest began to seethe. Some malcontents "alleged" that there was corruption among petty government officials; which was claimed to be *responsible* for making the already-difficult life of the diggers, even harder. This propaganda stirred up dissension among the foreign workers (a similar tactic used to incite the devastating riots which culminated in the so-called "French" Revolution). That was when the ambitious Cecil Rhodes began to implement his far-reaching political schemes. The steadily increasing wealth, strength, and prestige of the Boer SOUTH AFRICAN REPUBLIC was an impediment to his grand vision and that of his superiors in the British government. His stated imperialistic aim was to, "paint the map red" (i.e. *British* red), "from Cape to Cairo." The British *still* thought they would have no trouble overthrowing a nation whom they ***still*** considered to be a backward rabble of rustic farmers.

[An amusing story made the rounds—true or not—that on a visit to Queen Victoria, Paul Kruger, after having made the long sea voyage to England to plead the cause of his Boer people (as had Zulu king Cetshwayo, to represent his own tribe) sat awkwardly at the sumptuously laid dinner table in the Queen's palace. When a little *finger-bowl* containing warm water and slices of lemon was placed before the rustic Boer, he began sipping it with a spoon, assuming that it was some kind of thin soup! The Queen, being the genteel lady that she no doubt was, then also began to sip hers, to avoid embarrassing her guest. However, things reportedly escalated—according to the story—when, after the excellent meal, Kruger hauled out his smelly old tobacco pipe, and was hurriedly ushered out onto the verandah. As was the norm in those days, he occasionally spat on the floor alongside the bench on which he sat. A horrified footman then placed an ornate *spittoon* at the correct spitting distance—but Kruger leaned over and again spat on the floor; but this time on the side opposite to the spittoon. Again, the footman moved the spittoon to that side, whereupon Kruger, now slightly irritated, announced to the poor footman that if he did not stop constantly moving that "fancy vase" around, he might inadvertently spit in it!

Those who had become spoiled with inordinate overindulgence and excess, forgot that the rest of the world (especially a nation of relatively poor farmers) was not accustomed to ostentatious displays of luxury and opulence. Rather than being embarrassed at their own hedonism; they mocked others whom they considered, "beneath" them.]

Victoria Regina listened politely to Kruger's plea for the BRITISH CROWN to recognize, and then honor the independence of his fledgling Republic; but she did not give him any overt assurance that she would. Thus, he had received somewhat less sympathy for his cause than had the Zulu king before him.

[King Cetshwayo had visited the "Great White Queen," to plead his own cause, in 1882—having been so encouraged by white liberals such as Bishop John William Colenso[98] (1814–1883) and CAPE COLONY parliamentarian Saul Solomon[99] (1817-1892). While in England, Cetshwayo was *fêted* wherever he went on his conducted tours of London. Resplendent in a European suit, he was soon dubbed "the Ladies Man" and a popular ditty advised white British dandies to "get away-o, to clear the field for Cetshway-o!" The British queen had "diplomatically" pronounced her lunch with the deposed Zulu king "enjoyable," and had then cleared the way for him to be re-instated, briefly, as monarch.

However, on the other hand, Bishop Hans Paludan Smith Schreuder (1817-1882) of the NORWEGIAN MISSIONARY SOCIETY (formed in 1842) described this African "Ladies Man," by reporting that he was, "An able man, but for his cold, selfish pride, cruelty and untruthfulness, worse than any of his predecessors." Further testimony to the real nature of this *chic* Zulu "society man," is the fact that in 1876, he ordered the *execution* of many young Zulu girls who had married men *of*

---

[98] —the first Anglican bishop of Natal; who was not then generally popular among the white population due to his support for the blacks. Ironically, Colonel Durnford, a close friend of the Bishop's daughter, was killed by the Zulus at Isandlwana. To his credit, the "good Bishop" was also sometimes critical of British interference in *Boer* political affairs. The town of Colenso was named in his honor.

[99] —the leader of the LIBERAL PARTY. He was called the "Cape Disraeli." He was a physical dwarf, (but a mental "giant") and the fact that he was a liberal Jew, and a vociferous supporter of "nonwhite" causes made him rather unpopular with conservatives.

their own age-group—without having first sought his blessing—instead of marrying the 35-year-old men whom he *had* granted them permission to marry. This butchery was one of the reasons used by Britain in the "Ultimatum" given to the Zulu nation (which was of course, merely a pretext for war).]

Cecil Rhodes, having earlier made a vast personal fortune on the diamond fields of Kimberley, had soon also become a major player on the goldfields, and by 1895 his NEW CONSOLIDATED GOLDFIELDS had a virtual monopoly on exploiting the deep, difficult-to-extract veins of gold. The days of the lone happy-go-lucky prospector with donkey, pick and shovel, were ostensibly over. Rhodes' friendship with wealthy *Randlords*[100] Alfred Beit (1853-1906) and Sir Lionel Phillips (1855-1936) also added greatly to his financial muscle. Occasionally, Rhodes would refer patronizingly to "his Jews" and asserted that wherever they went, prosperity would soon follow—or that perhaps it was the other way around! A Jew by the name of Barney Isaacs (1852-1897), once an English *Cockney* comedian and prize-fighter, had also made a fortune in Kimberley, by buying up "played out" diamond mines and working them. He then changed his name to *Barney Barnato*. Rhodes later bought Barney's Kimberley diamond mines with a check for well over £5,000,000[101]—which was, reputedly the largest "private" check ever written within the BRITISH EMPIRE, at that time. Rhodes then merged the Kimberley mines with his own to create DE BEERS company. It was rumored that the "incentive" which swayed the deal was the promise to Barney of membership in the elite KIMBERLEY CLUB!

Another prominent man of the time was Sir Abraham "Abe" Bailey (1864-1940), of Irish descent, who made a fortune in the Barberton gold rush. Most of the men who had made their fortunes on the *diamond* fields, would also soon move to the newly discovered *gold* fields of the Witwatersrand, and become

---

[100] Powerful men (many of them Jewish financiers) who controlled the monopoly on gold and diamonds in South Africa.

[101] £118,300,000 or $236,600,000 in today's currency.

known as the *Randlords* or "Goldbugs."[102]   The animosity raised by the Battle of Majuba had spelled an end to any real co-operation between the two main, white South African populations represented by the English administration of the CAPE COLONY, and the Afrikaner leaders of the two Boer republics—and Cecil Rhodes was about to cynically exploit this growing tension.

Elected to the CAPE COLONY legislature as the MEMBER OF PARLIAMENT for Barkley West as early as 1881, Rhodes was a young, but seasoned politician by the time he became PRIME MINISTER of the CAPE COLONY in 1890—at which time he im-mediately set about placing obstacles in the path of Boer repub-lican endeavors in general, and interfering with the SOUTH AFRICAN REPUBLIC's affairs in particular.   Rhodes had already, with his strident voice and autocratic manner, successfully persuaded the British Government to "annex" neighboring *Bechuanaland,* (now called Botswana) to the north of the TRANSVAAL, to forestall any possible Boer expansion in that direction.   His own BRITISH SOUTH AFRICA COMPANY (BSA) had been chartered with "administering the newly conquered territo-ries of Mashonaland and Matabeleland" (which were also north-ern neighbors of the Boers), in what would soon become *RHO-DESIA* (named, of course, after Sir Cecil himself).

Rhodes would one day be able to claim much of the credit for developing South Africa into an industrial and mining giant. How-ever, in his single-minded and often-ruthless quest to further the aims of Britain in Southern Africa, Rhodes would steadily drive a wedge between Englishman and Afrikaner, which would ultimately devastate the country. The point of that wedge initially *came to a head* in "the Jameson Raid"—which was led by a close friend of Rhodes, Leander Starr Jameson (1853-1917). Jameson was a populist with great ambitions of his own: which sometimes ex-ceeded his own strength of character. He was one of a clique of Imperial functionaries (and *effete* male secretaries) who orbited around Cecil Rhodes—some of whom thought and acted more like

---

[102] "Goldbug" was quite possibly a word-play on the name "Goldburg/ Goldberg."

overgrown English schoolboys.

Rhodes and many of these rather queer characters were singularly despised by the Boers; but the Afrikaners were not alone in their disdain. Some manly British also had no stomach for these arrogant, effeminate politicians. Lieutenant-General Sir William Butler (1838-1910) intimated a certain dislike for Rhodes, commenting particularly on Rhodes' irritating falsetto-pitched voice and his odd facial expressions which suggested that Rhodes was suffering "peculiar mental pain."

It was commonly known that Rhodes had little time for the "fairer sex" and so, in an effort to improve his public image, he was advised to obtain the services of an attractive "hostess" to officiate at his parties and to accompany him to social functions. A mysterious European aristocrat, Princess Catherine Radziwill[103] (1858-1941) appeared to fit the bill splendidly, but her free-spending ways soon provoked Rhodes' ire. After Princess Radziwill had spent over £100,000[104] of his money in little over a year, he cut off her allowances. Undeterred, the

---

[103] She was a Polish-Russian noblewoman, Countess Ekaterina Adamovna Rzewuski, the daughter of Polish General, Count Adam Adamovitch Rzewuski and Anna Dmitrievna Voronztev-Dashkova. She married into the famous Lithuanian-Polish high noble family of Radvila (in Polish, Radziwiłł), marrying (1873) Prince Wilhelm Radziwill (1845-1911; in Lithuanian, Kunigaikštis Vilhelmas Radvila) when she was 15, and moving with him to Berlin (divorcing in 1906). The Radvilas were staunch defenders of the Protestant Reformation in the 1500s and 1600s.

The Princess wrote numerous books, including: Cecil Rhodes: Man and Empire-Maker (1918). She also received infamy modernly, due to her efforts to expose the *Protocols of the Learned Elders of Zion* in New York in 1921, where she gave a lecture on them. She told people she was engaged to Rhodes or that they were having an affair. Reportedly, she asked Rhodes to marry her and he turned her down. Some claim the Princess was responsible for ruining Rhodes' career. She took Rhodes to court for "loan fraud" and Rhodes had to appear to answer to the charges; he died shortly thereafter.

[104] £2,575,000 or $5,150,000 in today's currency.

Princess forged his signature on a check to pay some of her bills, whereupon he had her arrested and she served time in jail. She eventually left the country in some disgrace, but not before "borrowing" the cost of her first-class passage back to Europe!

Unconfirmed rumors about Rhodes' bedroom-orientation did nothing to help his poor image among the overtly manly, and ostensibly moral Boer leadership: which leadership was epitomized by their very plain-looking and bearded, ex-lion-hunter president, Paul Kruger. The *First Lady* of the republic—Gezina (du Plessis) Kruger—was herself, rather plain-looking; but she epitomized the solidity of the Boer women, and was much loved by her people. She was adored as the *Mother of the Nation*, until her death in 1901. However, the republican Kruger and the imperialist Rhodes eyed each other with mutual suspicion and hostility: like two lions circling and sizing up their rival, fighting over a coveted carcass. The stage was set for a "clash of the Titans" and the glittering prize was of course, the fabulously rich goldfields. The Boers simply wanted to defend what was theirs; the British wanted to take what was not theirs.

"Doctor Jim," as Jameson was known, hatched a plot with Rhodes—with the complicity of Randlords Lionel Phillips and Abe Bailey, Cecil Rhodes' soldiering brother Colonel Francis ("Frank") William Rhodes (1850-1905), and allegedly, with the new British Colonial Secretary Joseph Chamberlain (1836-1914), unlovingly nick-named, "Pushful Joe." The scheme was to *invade* the TRANSVAAL goldfields from Bechuanaland (where Jameson was the Colonial Administrator) with a column of 500 well-armed men, who would be supported by an uprising of "disaffected" *uitlanders* (who had also been secretly armed and worked into a frenzy of hate through anti-Boer propaganda), led by a "Reform Committee." But nothing for the raiders went as planned. The anticipated general uprising did not materialize—mostly due to *uitlander* apathy—but in the vain hope of precipitating such a rebellion, Jameson's column, commanded by Major Sir John Christopher Willoughby (1859-1918) invaded anyway, in the last days of 1895. His men then incompetently cut *the wrong* telegraph wire leading to Pretoria, where

Kruger resided and continued to receive regular updates on Jameson's progress—courtesy of Doctor Jim's own telegrams to the *uitlander* plotters on the goldfields! The column was soon surrounded by a Boer commando and forced to surrender near Krugersdorp, and the rest of the plotters were arrested on January 2, 1896. In the resulting furor, Joseph Chamberlain protested that he *knew nothing* of the abortive raid, and the blame fell squarely upon Rhodes: who was forced to resign. The Boers were outraged at the attempted *coup*. Despite some Boer die-hards wanting to bring the infamous gallows from Slaghter's Nek all the way up from the Cape to hang the plotters in symbolic retribution for the Boer rebels who had been mercilessly hanged there, Kruger showed remarkable magnanimity and statesmanship by dispatching Jameson and 5 officers to Britain for trial—and then commuting the death sentences of the "Reform Committee." Instead, he imposed stiff fines. Despite the rugged nature of the Boers, they were generally considered courteous gentlemen, even in war; often to their own disadvantage: for they were seldom given the same gentlemanly treatment by a nation (Britain) that had long prided itself in being the *epitome* of refinement and chivalry. The British CROWN later responded by *knighting* a number of the "rehabilitated" plotters for their "*exemplary services to the Realm*"!

The animosity that Afrikaner citizens of both Boer republics now felt towards Britain, was palpable. The heat was raised still further by a rather tactless telegram from Kaiser Wilhelm II., of Germany to President Kruger congratulating him on foiling the attempted coup. It read:

"I express to you my sincere congratulations, that, without appealing for the help of friendly powers, you and your people have succeeded in repelling with your own forces the armed bands which had broken into your country, and in maintaining the independence of your country against foreign aggression."

This dispatch, it seems, was like rubbing salt in an open sore: insulting further an already wounded British pride. The previous, tentative, uneasy public opinion held by Englishmen in both Britain and South Africa, concerning the connivings of their newly elected conservative government—suddenly changed to wholesale support for Jameson and Chamberlain. Mutual hostility between Afrikaner and *Engelsman,* mounted even further.

Once again, Boer and Brit would face each other over the barrel of a gun, but this time, it would not be restricted to skirmishes and a *minor* battle like Majuba, but would escalate into a *full-scale war*. Chamberlain, while protesting at home that war with the SOUTH AFRICAN REPUBLIC would be long and costly, redoubled his own political pressure on President Kruger. "Pushful Joe" apparently secretly wanted war, but professed *outwardly* that he would prefer *federation*. Therefore, he skillfully manipulated events and perceptions to make Kruger look like the aggressor; which gave the false appearance that war was "forced" on the *British*. His appointment of Sir Alfred Milner (1854-1925) as High Commissioner, a brilliant administrator who held an abiding hatred for the Boers, was a master-stroke. Less masterful, however, was his appointment of the brave but pedantic General Sir Redvers Buller as the new Commander-in-Chief of British forces in South Africa. Realizing that the path to war with Britain was now being covertly paved by Lord Milner, the wily, old Boer president Kruger, alerted to the TRANSVAAL's military vulnerability by Jameson's raid, set about arming his young republic.

Kruger transformed the military capabilities of the new Boer Republic virtually overnight, by the ordering of military equipment to the tune of £1,000,000[105] (a staggering sum in those days). He imported 37,000 of MAUSER's excellent bolt-action magazine rifles from Germany and state-of-the-art 155-mm "Long Tom" Creusot artillery pieces (among others) from France. He also mustered a potential 25,000 mounted Transvaal burghers, 15,000 Free State sympathizers, and the many expected additional "Cape rebels."

The British Lieutenant-General Sir William Butler, on the other hand, was, until then, Commander-in-Chief of only about 10,000 scattered Imperial troops. He realized that his forces were woefully inadequate to confront the Boers—but he refused

---

[105] £23,650,000 or $47,300,000 in today's currency.

to call for reinforcements, since the arrival of such might precipitate the war. Instead, he wisely tendered his resignation to an increasingly *jingoistic* British high command. Butler's resignation was quickly accepted, and Buller stepped in.

The British had been searching for any "pretext" to declare war on the Boer Republics and President Kruger himself gave the British Government their *raison de guerre* ("reason of war")— when he presented them with a bluntly worded *ultimatum* to immediately *desist* from their rumored movement of large numbers of troop reinforcements. After this ultimatum from Kruger, war became inevitable.

Chapter Twenty-four

By late 1899, the Boers were just as determined as the British to take the offensive. But they had failed to learn a valuable lesson, which they *should have* learned from their *first* "War of Independence" (1881)—that of *not* wasting valuable manpower and resources in besieging strategically unimportant, small and scattered British garrisons. The Boers invaded the CAPE COLONY, and laid siege to Kimberley—trapping Cecil Rhodes himself. The Boers also trapped in the town of *Mafeking*[106] its British military commander, Colonel Sir Robert Stephenson Smyth Baden-Powell[107] (1857-1941). Colonel Baden-Powell's orders had been to "invade the Transvaal!"

The Boers also thrust into NATAL, and besieged the town of Ladysmith. The fact that they had invaded British-ruled NATAL and the CAPE COLONY confirmed, at least *in the minds of the British public,* that the Boers were indeed the "aggressors." Boer General Joubert's highly motivated young fighters were dismayed when their aging commander (who had been a hero at Majuba) instead of decisively defeating the remaining British forces in NATAL, and occupying the strategic port at Durban, allowed his once-mobile and effective commandos to settle down to a series of drawn-out sieges. This wasted effort on senseless sieges would eventually prove to be one of the major causes of the ultimate lack of success of the Boers in this war. However, the Boers would still record some resounding victories over the

---

[106] —meaning, "Among the Stones," in *Baralong,* a Sotho/Tswana tribal dialect; now spelled *Mafekeng.* It is the site of the famous evolutionist discovery of the baboon-like "Taung child" (*Australopithecus africanus*) "ape-man" skull in 1924. Until 1961 the town was the administrative capital of the Bechuanaland Protectorate, the only "capital" in the world—which was located *outside* of the country it governed! Bechuanaland (now *Botswana)* was, of course, only made a British "Protectorate" in order to "protect" it from the British fear of the Boers' *possible* expansion northwards.

[107] —later promoted to *General* and then *Lord* Baden-Powell.

mighty British army in the early stages of this, the SECOND ANGLO-BOER WAR, which the Boers themselves referred to as their TWEEDE VRYHEIDSOORLOG ("Second War of Freedom").

In what became known as "Black Week" in Britain, Major-General Sir William Penn-Symons (1843-1899) marched a column of well over 4,000 troops up to Dundee in the NATAL midlands; however, he was surprised and routed by the Boers. He only succeeded in getting himself killed. An inordinate number of Irish volunteers fought on the side of the Boers and clashed in battle with the Irish imperial troops. This conflict led to the penning of a ditty which described the strange scene:

"On the mountain side the battle raged, there was no stop or stay;

McKin captured Private Burke and Ensign Michael Shea,

Fitzgerald got Fitzpatrick, Brannigan found O'Rourke;

Finnigan took a man named Fay and a couple of lads from Cork.

Suddenly they heard McManus shout, 'Hands up or I'll run you through;'

He thought he had a Yorkshire 'Tyke'—'twas Corporal Donaghue!

McGarry took O'Leary, O'Brien got McNamee,

That's how the 'English fought the Dutch' at the Battle of Dundee!"

Thereafter, the rather obtuse Natal commander Sir George Stuart White (1835-1912) managed to get his force bottled-up in Ladysmith after taking a staggering 1,200 casualties. The Boers then put the two other British garrisons under siege. However, in this action, Boer ideology over-rode sensible military strategy. In the minds of the Boers, the fact that Mafeking had been used as a supply depot for the Jameson Raid and the fact that the despised Cecil Rhodes was trapped—along with "his" diamonds—in Kimberley, seemed reason enough to maintain those sieges. Since the Boers had already proven themselves to be far superior to the British in open warfare on the South African veld, *that* was where their main efforts should have been concentrated. Instead, like their defeated black foes before them, the Boers now faced well-armed white men entrenched behind good fortifications—a defensive battle-ground which suited the *British;* for the moment.

Now, when a hero was needed, a prominent Boer arose to the challenge. He was a man of humble *Trekboer* parentage. His mother and father had trekked initially as far as Winburg in the ORANGE FREE STATE, where he was born, before they finally settled in Lichtenburg, in the TRANSVAAL. This *rising star* had served with distinction as a junior officer at Majuba, and was then promoted to the rank of Commandant. He had gained *local* prominence by helping to capture the Jameson Raiders. He then gained *international* fame through a series of strategically brilliant military victories against the British when the SECOND ANGLO-BOER WAR broke out, towards the end of 1899. This man's name was Jacobus "Koos" Herculaas De la Rey; now distinguished as a *General*. He was of the same blood-line as Erika Roux—born "Delarey"—a son of Erika's great-uncle Sarel's nephew, and thus he was a cousin of Erika through her father Christiaan. He was imbued with the same warrior spirit as was that Great Trek leader; but the main difference between those two men, was that General Koos De la Rey knew how to motivate men not only by personal example, but also by his refined skills at diplomacy and well-honed insight. He had gained his political acumen as a member of the Volksraad, and his military expertise as an officer in the *veld*. But now, history and destiny called on De la Rey—immortality beckoned unto him; but he would first have to confront the might of the BRITISH EMPIRE on the field of battle: where he would emerge triumphant, again and again. General De la Rey started by inflicting heavy casualties on Lord Methuen's[108] forces near *Modder* ("muddy") River, at the Battles of *Graspan*[109] and Magersfontein.[110]

---

[108] Paul Sanford (1845-1932), 3rd Baron of Methuen.

[109] ("grassy pan"); a *pan* is "a shallow basin or depression; full only after recent rain."

[110] Probably an English corruption of the Afrikaans, *Ma'erfontein* ("meager springs").

However, General De La Rey had a "secret weapon," of sorts: Nicholaas Pieter Johannes Janse "Siener" ("seer" or "prophet") van Rensburg (1864-1926). Van Rensburg had a bushy black beard and piercing blue eyes, and though he was a man small in stature, he was mighty in spirit. The only book he ever read was his Bible: for he believed that other books or newspapers were worldly things and did not spiritually enhance a person. Although he was brought up on a farm, he was not able to bear the sight of an animal being slaughtered, and he forswore all forms of violence. Despite this, he rode with the Boer commando of General De la Rey throughout the war, and was always on the frontlines—but never once carried a rifle, or fired a shot. It was said that his general too, never personally fired a shot at his enemy.

Time and again, Siener van Rensburg would warn his beloved General De la Rey of the approach of enemy forces, and thus enable their Lichtenburg commando to make good their escape. Van Rensburg was constantly given to "disturbing visions" and would often prophesy concerning the outcome of battles—and he was *never once* proved *wrong* in his predictions. The visions seemed to exhaust and trouble him; yet he resignedly accepted his lot as a prophet of the Lord. He was much revered, and a prophet "*not without honor in his own country.*" So confident were the ordinary men of the commando, as was General De la Rey himself, in the accuracy of "Seer" van Rensburg's predictions that they often did not even bother to post sentries, if Siener had told them that his vision revealed that no enemy troops were coming that particular night!

In the early stages of the SECOND ANGLO-BOER WAR, when no-one (except this seer) could have predicted that the British would employ such barbaric methods, he saw a vision of his commando entering caves beyond Pretoria. Behind them came great crowds of Boer women and children, fleeing from their burning houses. He saw great devastation and misery: the destruction of his Boer nation. This chilling prophecy came to fruition through the British "scorched earth" policy of destroying Boer crops, farms, and homesteads in the latter stages of the war.

General De la Rey himself was deeply religious, and inclined towards the psychic, with an active, shrewd and inquiring mind. He firmly believed that God would guide and direct him in every facet of his life. He also possessed the gift of discernment; of being able to sum up a man's qualities after only a short period of contact or conversation with him. His ability to "smell out" cowards or potential traitors also insured the security of his forces. Popular and widely respected, the general was a shining example to his men in battle; fearless, yet considerate and even gentle. They described him variously as "a tough patriot," "a prince among men," and "the Lion of the Western Transvaal." Although ruthless when he had to be, De la Rey would not tolerate the mistreatment of prisoners. He had opposed the war until it became inevitable; but when it came, he fought valiantly—and he fought far longer than many of those who had originally clamored for it.

De la Rey would soon meet a like-minded man in battle, an honorable adversary, who oddly, would eventually become a life-long friend: the British general Lord Methuen. Siener van Rensburg had predicted their first clash, at Tweebosch. He said: "I see a red bull (a British general) coming from the direction of Vryburg ("Freetown"). His horns are pointing forwards. He is eager to fight. But when he arrives at Barberspan, his horns hang lower. His determination is failing, and he begins to feel discouraged. But it will go even worse with him, because when he arrives at the Harts River, he will be completely de-horned. He will be unable to butt. He must be disarmed then." Siener also "saw" the Boers strolling between the British guns and wagons there, and was thus convinced of a coming victory.

The battle at Tweebosch soon followed. General De la Rey's veterans confidently charged the British infantry and their convoy, firing from the saddle. Lord Methuen's force was overwhelmed and the British general himself was wounded and captured; but General De la Rey graciously had him transferred to a *British* hospital—despite the fact that Lord Methuen himself had given the orders to burn to the ground De la Rey's own family farm! Methuen, who was himself only reluctantly following British Army High Command orders in destroying farms, sent

De la Rey a gift from his sick-bed, and a handwritten note reading: "From a general, to a very brave general." Lady Methuen also wrote to General De la Rey, to thank him for his chivalry towards her husband on the battlefield.

A brilliant military tactician, De la Rey soon realized that the British had made a habit of shelling hilltops before advancing, in reaction to the Boers' preference for the high ground. So he shrewdly entrenched his commandos at the *bases* of those *koppies,* and allowed the enemy to waste their cannon-shells on the empty hilltops. Then, the Boer commandos would open fire and decimate the British ranks as they advanced confidently, but ignorantly, towards De la Rey's hidden positions! Time and again, he outmaneuvered his opponents, and his fame as a fearless frontline general spread far and wide.

[General De la Rey and Siener van Rensburg remained in close contact long after the war ended, and sadly, the "Seer" also accurately predicted the date and even the circumstances of General De la Rey's own demise. He had a vision of the general "returning home bareheaded, without his hat" and "in a carriage adorned with flowers" while a "black cloud with the number 15 on it, poured blood." The great general was shot dead at a police roadblock, apparently accidentally, 12 years after the end of the Boer War, on the *15th* of September 1914 (even the digits in 1914 add up to *15).* The distraught policeman who fired the fatal shot had thought that the general's car belonged to the criminal Foster Gang, which was on the run from the police. The general's hat had blown off his head shortly before the shooting, exactly as the "Seer" had predicted!

Another British military admirer of General De la Rey once presented De la Rey's daughter, Polly with a glowing assessment of her father's great and noble character:

"How does a man come to be a gallant gentleman? I have met men of all races, and of all classes who have merited the description, but their number is not great. It is not education, it is not breeding. It is not civilization, it just happens, like genius. Education, breeding, civilization, all these increase the coverage of what is called culture, but they do not increase the number of geniuses nor of gallant gentlemen in the world. These are, I think, born, not made. Old General Koos De la

Rey was one of them. He was a Boer of the Backveld, but the soul in him could not be excelled by any product of Eton or Balliol.[111] Perhaps the open veld—the sun, the moon and the stars, with an occasional war thrown in to bring the pupil down to earth again, are as good schoolmasters as any that civilization can offer if only they have the right material to work on. In General De la Rey's case, the material was there, and no education could have improved it, in fact, it might have spoiled it! As a coat of varnish might spoil a sword blade, or the barrel of a rifle. I have often wished that some great painter could have painted him, some Sargent or Frans Hals,[112] who would have brought out the lovable character in that stern old face. There are certain portraits of him exhibited at Wembley. These may be reproductions of his features, but they no more resemble the man himself than "Marseillaise" on a penny whistle resembles the *Battle Hymn of the Republic.* No one has ever written an appreciation of De la Rey. Those who knew him intimately were not the sort who could write."]

Lord Methuen could claim a nominal, hollow "victory"—of minor importance and with costly casualties—at *Graspan.* He wiped out, nearly entirely, the small Scandinavian volunteer contingent fighting for the Boers under De la Rey's aging, once-formidable, but now rather inept co-commander General Piet Cronje. De la Rey had little respect for Cronje after these battles, and his poor opinion of Cronje would be vindicated within a few months, when Cronje would *surrender* to British forces. De la Rey's own brother was mortally wounded in the fighting, but the indomitable general was not distracted even by casualties that touched his own family. His single-mindedness

---

[111] BALLIOL (founded 1263) is one of the constituent colleges of OXFORD UNIVERSITY; named after John I., de Balliol (1208-1268), King of the Scots; ancestor of Robert I., "the Bruce" (1274-1329). ETON IS KING'S COLLEGE OF OUR LADY OF ETON BESIDE WINDSOR, (founded in 1440 by King Henry VI.).

[112] —Frans Hals (c.1580–1666), Dutch "Golden Age" painter, an exceptional portraiture artist; presumably John Singer Sargent (1856–1925), born in Italy of American parents, the best portrait artist of his era. De la Rey is revered by Afrikaners to this day.

drove him on to the only goal: victory. He would not hesitate to take his *sjambok*[113] to the backside of any Boer fighter wavering in his duties.

Lord Methuen himself, two years later, would as predicted, be wounded and captured by General De la Rey's Lichtenburg Commando. At Magersfontein, British Major-General A. J. Wauchope (1846-1899) was killed, as was as a large part of his elite HIGH-LAND BRIGADE. General Wauchope was buried on the battlefield, but in a curious English misunderstanding of Afrikaans place-names, a monument to him was later erected at *Matjiesfontein* ("Little mats springs"[114])—hundreds of miles away!

---

[113] —a short, stiff whip; pronounced, *shum-bok*. Originally made from thick rhino, hippo, or giraffe hide.

[114] —so named for the mats made from reeds growing there. A health resort and leisure retreat.

Chapter Twenty-five

Erika Roux soon learned about her "long-lost" relative General De la Rey's military victories. She too was born "Delarey," back in the Cape in 1820. Naturally, her son, Joshua Roux (the young warrior-turned-businessman) also heard of his valiant kinsman's exploits. Joshua was now married and had children of his own and lived on the goldfields of Johannesburg. Now nearly 80 years old, Erika had survived many hardships and heartaches: the physical rigors of the Great Trek, the killing of her great-uncle Sarel before her eyes by the Xhosa, the death of her father, the murder of her two children by Kaffirs, the subsequent abandonment of their homestead and trek to what would become their farm on the TRANSVAAL Lowveld, and then the departure of Joshua: her only living child.

Now, sadly, she faced losing her beloved Jan: who, at the ripe old age of 85, had begun to slowly fade away. Erika's robust husband had, for the first time in his long and arduous life, begun to complain of tiredness, and then chest pains. Then, he could no longer ride his horse or hunt: as he had done ever since they first arrived in the eastern Lowveld over 4 decades earlier. Now, his tired old eyes were too dim to read even his beloved Bible, and so Erika, whose eyesight was still surprisingly good, would read passages to him in the evenings. Though Joshua would occasionally bring his family down from "Jo'burg" to the old family farm for a visit, Erika had not heard from him since his last. So she wrote a carefully worded letter to her son, advising him of his aging father's poor health. She reminded him of the fact that most of the area around the family farm had recently been declared the SABIE GAME RESERVE (later to be expanded and renamed KRUGER NATIONAL PARK) and was, therefore, a good place to invest in land. It was also perhaps a better—and safer place—than the goldfields, to bring up her two grandchildren; especially considering the turmoil in Johannesburg caused by the recent outbreak of hostilities with the British. When the Indian *smous* ("traveling merchant") trader, who called at their farm every few months, arrived timeously, Erika asked him if he would be kind enough to deliver her letter to Lydenburg. From there the mail departed weekly by train, from the new depot, *en route* to Johannesburg.

When the letter arrived at the palatial home that Joshua had built at *Doornfontein* ("thorny springs") in Johannesburg, he was sitting at his desk pondering his latest business deal. Joshua had left the family farm, forever—or so he had thought at the time—a few years after the Majuba campaign. Things had gone well for him in Johannesburg. At the time of his arrival, Jo'burg was merely a sprawling shanty-town. However, the discovery of the incredibly rich gold reef had presented him with a "golden" opportunity to enrich himself by starting up a private security company. The new city and the mines themselves were plagued by theft and other vices. It sometimes seemed to Joshua as if all the scoundrels and charlatans in the entire world had made their way to the "Golden City"—to seek their fortune (by means fair or foul).

Before long, his original, small team of Zulu night-watchmen had grown into a veritable army of security guards, which he ran with military discipline and precision. And so, his services were greatly in demand by the neighboring *Randlords:* who needed reliable watchmen to guard their enormous investments. Joshua chose only Zulus for this kind of work. He found Zulus to be more reliable—and more *intimidating* to criminals, than the less-formidable members of the many other black tribes who had streamed to the goldfields, in search of "easy money." His guards were popularly known as *Machingalaans:* a malapropism of the order *Marsjeer in lyn!* ("March in line!")—a command regularly bellowed by the exasperated white corporals during the training of new Zulu recruits.

Communication with these guards and the black mine-workers was carried out in what came to be known as *Fanagalo:* a conglomerate lingo in which most of the nouns were English, the verbs in Zulu, and shamefully, the swear-words in Afrikaans.

It was believed that if *Fanagalo* was spoken loudly enough—and with much arm-waving—almost anyone could understand it! Soon, J. R. SECURITY SERVICES held a virtual monopoly on security contracts with most of the large gold mines—and the money flowed in rapidly.

The former-hunter, once wagon-driver, then Zulu-fighter, now ex-Brit-fighter Joshua Roux was now a wealthy businessman in his own right. His marriage to the beautiful socialite daughter of a prominent "Anglicized-Afrikaner" Randlord had merely increased his good fortune and high-society acceptance. Their lavish wedding made it into the social pages of the many newspapers and journals springing up in the big boom-town—each sporting photographs of the handsome, new couple, with lavish commentary; the headlines reading: *"Meneer & Mevrou Joshua en Angela Roux."* Their happy marriage was soon blessed with a pigeon-pair of angelic-looking twins; James and Julia, and Joshua Roux considered himself a most fortunate man (considering his humble beginnings as a "backveld" farm boy).

But war-clouds had then darkened the bright Witwatersrand horizon, and the growing population of the new city was soon split down the middle. The Afrikaners were firmly behind their President Paul Kruger; while the English-speakers mainly supported the British cause. But not all English-speakers rallied to the English side: including a certain Irishman by the name of Sean O'Connor—who had recently arrived from an Ireland that was itself riven by much anti-English sentiment after centuries of oppression. Sean had landed in Durban with the romantic idea of making his fortune by panning for gold in Barberton and Pilgrim's Rest, but when those gold deposits proved to be little more than a "flash in the pan" themselves, he had made his way to the recently discovered Reef in Johannesburg. Johannesburg was originally the mining "digs" called *Ferreira's Camp*[115] on the farm *Randjieslaagte* ("ridged-lowland").

---

[115] The camp site is now the small suburb of Ferreirastown; named after an early digger: a Boer (of Portuguese descent) "Colonel" Ignatius Phillip Ferreira (1840-1921) who had *assumed* "command" of the dig. *Ferreira* is the Portuguese word for "blacksmith."

[Much later research showed that the naming of Johannesburg could have been a shrewd ploy by ZAR President Johannes Paulus ("Paul") Kruger to reciprocate his high honor of being awarded the KING JOÃO[116] KNIGHTLY ORDER OF THE IMMACULATE CONCEPTION by the Portuguese—without the national recognition to Portugal being detected by the ever-vigilant British. Kruger reputedly did so by "letting it be known" that the town was named after its surveyors! The ZAR had, in their war "settlement" with the British, after defeating them at Majuba, acquiesced to the British "condition for peace" that the Boers were not allowed to make any treaties with any neighbor "to the east or to the west"—without Britain's permission. This would of course, have excluded treaties with both Portugal and Germany, who both had colonies in Southern Africa at this time, and were thus "hostile" and "competing nations," in the British mind. The Portuguese concluded a clandestine agreement with the ZAR to build a railway to their port at Delagoa Bay, thus by-passing the British-held ports in NATAL and the CAPE COLONY; and Germany itself, of course, made no secret of their animosity towards Britain, supplying arms to the Boer republic (as did republican France) to fight against Britain in the forthcoming TWEEDE VRYHEIDSOORLOG ("SECOND FREEDOM WAR."[117])]

However, the burly, bearded Irishman sadly discovered that the days of the happy-go-lucky prospector were already long gone. The only work available to Sean was as a shift-foreman, deep in the bowels of the earth at one of the big mines owned by the Randlords. He had eventually sought alternative employment as a bouncer at one of the many raucous taverns. His enthusiastic services in this capacity, coupled with his irrepressible good humor and seemingly cast-iron physique, soon got Sean O'Connor noticed by some of the many sleazy brothel-owners; but he flatly refused to get involved in their activities as a "pimp"—despite lucrative offers. His Catholic upbringing in rural southern Ireland allowed him to unashamedly bash deserving heads together, but not to market *vice* and *immorality*.

---

[116] Portuguese for Johannes/Johan/John.
[117] For more details, see **Appendix B**.

At that stage, the fast-growing city of Johannesburg was a "den of iniquity" with fortune-seekers from all over the world expecting to find the streets paved with gold; but it was in fact, a place of many *broken dreams*. There was an extreme imbalance between the numbers of men and women, and to remedy this, "ladies of the night" were soon brought there in droves by an unscrupulous "mafia" of foreigners who beguiled simple, but pretty girls from all over Europe—and even America—to come and "work" there. "Protection rackets" were rife, and it seemed almost impossible to do honest business in a town whose sole attraction was the prospect of making "fast money" (regardless of *how)*. It was even rumored that the infamous "Jack the Ripper" had fled to Johannesburg as the police net closed around him in London after his bloody killing-spree in Britain's foggy capital—and that he continued to carry out his diabolical activities unnoticed, in a town where violent death at the hands of criminals, sadly, was an everyday occurrence. Besides this moral squalor, there was also an acute shortage of good accommodation, and, therefore, "slum-lords" were profiteering shamelessly; renting out bare tin shacks at exorbitant rates. After some deaths from cold were reported during the bitter Highveld winter months, a by-law was enforced whereby landlords were obliged to provide "a stove for heating and cooking in every dwelling."[118]

The Calvinistic President Kruger was understandably *horrified* at this influx of undesirables to his rustic Boer republic, and labored manfully to curtail their nefarious activities; but with little success. When the British eventually "inherited" this brazen new city by virtue of their very expensive "victory" in the Second Anglo-Boer War, even Lord Alfred Milner was aghast at the prospect of foreign white prostitutes entertaining the growing number of affluent black African clients. *Lord Milner himself* passed laws to prevent such scandalous racial intermingling. In this at least, he had the firm support of his new

---

[118] A century later, this mandate was still in force in the TRANSVAAL, despite the advent of modern, effective electric home heating.

Boer "subjects"—who considered such abominations to be a dangerous threat: one which would undermine the very moral fiber and foundation of their beloved country. Therefore, the *British government* itself, of its own accord, *institutionalized* the racial segregation laws of South Africa, including those laws prohibiting cross-racial sexual relations.[119] In so doing, the British reinforced the moral and religious standards long practiced by the Calvinistic Dutch settlers who had preceded them.

Joshua Roux first noticed the big, red-haired Irishman while passing by a tavern—when a drunken troublemaker had unexpectedly *flown* through the doorway, propelled by O'Connor, and landed in the dust at Joshua's feet. Noting the consummate ease with which the heavily built drunkard had been raised and then heaved through the air, Joshua impulsively offered Sean O'Connor a job as one of his security managers. The Irish on the goldfields were, as seems usual for Irishmen, split down the middle in regard to their support for either the republican Boers or the imperialistic British. Though some Protestant Irish rallied to the Anglo-British cause, perhaps more sympathized with their Afrikaner brothers on the veld; and many Irish joined the Boer commandos to confront their mutual "olde enemy." After the war, a monument to these valiant *Sons of Erin* was erected by their grateful Boer allies on a prominent hill overlooking the city. But Sean Seamus O'Connor had no such doubts about where *his* loyalties lay, and he took particular delight in ejecting inebriated English "toffs and dandies" from his professional domain, in the rough-and-tumble tavern where he was employed. However, when the well-dressed Afrikaner stopped and asked him if he would like to hire on as security manager with his company, Sean *did not even hesitate.* The likable, hardworking Irishman soon gained his new employer's confidence and trust, and they became firm friends.

---

[119] This was later to become known as the "Immorality Act."

Joshua Roux read his mother's letter again, and then sat with his head in his hands. It had been almost a year since he had last visited his old parents on their farm 300 miles away. He had been so pre-occupied with running his business, making money, and with the social whirl (which his wife so enjoyed), that he had almost forgotten about them.

Over and above those business and social distractions, there was also now the question of the war. It did initially seem to be going well for the Boers, with one victory after another being reported almost daily in the newspapers. But Joshua well remembered the determination and resilience of the British, from his days as a teenager when he had been drawn inadvertently into their war against the mighty Zulu nation. Despite their initial setbacks, the British had re-grouped, re-organized and re-armed, and then returned to completely destroy their foe. Joshua had no doubt whatsoever that they would do the same in this war, against his own Boer people. Their Victorian pride, still smarting from the bloody nose they had received at Majuba almost 20 years earlier, would not allow the British to be beaten again by "a rabble of farmers." The first signs of the nasty turn that had been taken, was at the Battle of *Elandslaagte*,[120] when British lancers galloped after and skewered fleeing Boers. Joshua knew that the British would simply send out more and more re-enforcements and materials of war until, by sheer weight of arms, they would eventually and inevitably crush his people—of this Joshua was certain.

Joshua had to make some big decisions—and fast. Already, he had noticed that production at the gold mines was slowing down. Disrupted supply-lines, civil unrest, and political insta-bility were beginning to take their toll. Sooner or later, those lucrative contracts, which he had long taken for granted, would start drying up—and the likelihood of a *Boer* regaining them

---

[120] "Eland* lowlands."

*Eland is a species of antelope, amongst the heaviest (up to 1700lb.) known; males become "blue bulls."

again soon after the war, in a new, British-dominated economy, was rather slim. So Joshua Roux instructed his coachman to drive him up to the prestigious *Rand Club,* and there, he made a deal. He found a British buyer for his security company (which was not too difficult, as he had previously been made several handsome offers for his lucrative business), and left with a very substantial check, which he immediately cashed for a fortune in gold Kruger Rands at the bank. When Joshua got home that evening, his unsuspecting wife Angela was waiting to tell him about the latest round of tea-parties she had attended and the ball she wanted to plan. Their two young children were already peacefully asleep, having been bathed and fed by the servants. But life was about to change dramatically for the Roux family.

Chapter Twenty-six

What the British may have lacked in imagination in battle on the veld of South Africa, they made up for in their grasp of the bigger strategic picture. Kimberley was mainly of *symbolic* importance *to the Boers,* primarily because they were still disgruntled about having been forced out of their diamond fields by British "annexation," 3 decades earlier; secondarily because Kimberley had become the stronghold of Cecil Rhodes himself: that powerful British personality whom they held in utter contempt. However, *the British* realized that the town held a far greater *strategic* importance. British troops and war supplies were now pouring into Cape Town—making the merchants there rich, in the process—and these troops (and the necessary supplies) had, somehow, to be transported up country to confront the Boers. The obvious and best way, of course, was by rail, and that route *ran right through Kimberley.* So the Boer strangle-hold siege on Kimberley *had* to be relieved.

The siege would last about 4 months and would bring out both the best and worst in Cecil Rhodes' character. Not one to sit around and bemoan his fate, Rhodes energetically set about organizing the defenses of the town: He placed the workshops of his DE BEERS company at the military's disposal, established soup-kitchens for the inhabitants, and generally irritated the garrison commander, Lieutenant-Colonel Robert George Kekewich (1854-1914). Rhodes got under the skin of the military commander due to Rhodes' habit of issuing his own orders (and thus overriding the orders Kekewich had given), liaising with the relieving force, and—if he felt his autocracy was being resisted—*even threatening to hand the town over to the Boers!* When the defenders found their own artillery outranged by the Boers' cannons, Rhodes oversaw the construction, in his company's workshops—from scratch—of a better cannon, with 28-pound shells. It was dubbed the "Long Cecil." The wife of the mayor of Kimberley had the privilege of pulling the lanyard to fire Long Cecil's first answering shot at the besieging Boers. However, the Boers soon negated the effects of this innovation by sending for one of *their* "Long Tom" cannons; which had a unprecedented, very-accurate range of well over 7 miles. Ironically, one of the first shells fired by the newly deployed "Long Tom" crashed through the roof of the hotel and *killed the engineer who had built the British "Long Cecil" cannon!* When the besieging Boers heard of this, they naturally assumed "Divine Intervention" on their behalf—again—and who could disagree? Even the cynical Cecil John Rhodes may have briefly mulled that thought over in his mind.

In Ladysmith, a similar situation prevailed. Completely surrounded, the defenders mounted numerous sorties to spike the Boer artillery, which was regularly shelling the town, causing numerous civilian, as well as military casualties. In a quirk of the Boer character, they noted with indignation that the British officers were playing a game of cricket on the common ("public greens"), *on a Sunday!* The outraged Boer commandant ordered a shell fired at them, sending the batsmen and fielders scurrying for cover. It did not seem to occur to the Boers that *shelling the enemy* "on the the Lord's Day" was arguably *more sinful* than playing a game of cricket! Despite their somewhat "holier than thou" attitude, Boer gunners regularly used the church steeple as a ranging-point, and the church soon showed the damaging effect of their shells. When the British actually managed to damage the muzzle and steal the breech-block of a Boer "Long Tom" cannon in a daring raid, the Boers sent the artillery-piece to Pretoria for repair, where the long barrel was *trimmed shorter* and jokingly renamed, "The Jew!"

At one stage, the encircling Boers tried to dam the nearby river in an attempt to flood the town, but were not successful, due to heavy rains, which washed away their sandbags. Strangely enough, a semi-neutral "Tin Town" was established on the outskirts of Ladysmith, where Boer and *Brit* civilians mingled freely. Well south of the town, the new British Commander-in-Chief, General Sir Redvers Buller, VC (hero of the Zulu Wars), was fast earning his sobriquet of Sir "Reverse"

Buller. In his attempts to cross the Tugela River, his troops were thrown back, time and again, by the well-entrenched Boers: who were led brilliantly by General Louis Botha[121]—inflicting heavy losses on Buller's forces. In a number of areas, the Boers had ingeniously, before battle, marked out their fields of fire with white stones to indicate ranges, and were thus able to decimate the exposed British forces with accurate, long-range rifle and artillery fire. One of the many futile attempts to relieve Ladysmith would lead to an infamous British defeat at the vicious Battle of *Spionkop* ("Spy Hill"). The British could easily have by-passed Spionkop (as they were advised to do by colonial officers), but a bloody-minded determination to clear any Boers off high ground led to their severe losses there.[122]

The Battle of Colenso, also *en route* to Ladysmith in mid-December, sadly, claimed the lives of many Irishmen of the ROYAL INNISKILLING FUSILIERS.[123] The members of the FIFTH IRISH BRIGADE of Maj.-Gen. Arthur Fitzroy Hart-Synnot (1844-1910) took heavy casualties in their ferocious assaults on Hart's Hill (also called, *Inniskilling Hill);* including their assault unit's commanding officer, Lieut.-Col. Thomas Martin Gerard Thackeray (1849-1900), who was killed in their first attack. A second attempt led to the death of their second-in-command Major Francis Alexander Sanders (1855-1900). Hart himself was variously known as a "dangerous lunatic" or by his men as "General No-Bobs" for his habit of refusing to duck, even under heavy fire.

---

[121] —later, Prime Minister of the TRANSVAAL (1907); then the first Prime Minister of the UNION OF SOUTH AFRICA (1910). He later also led the South African "invasion" of German South West Africa, during World War I (1914-18)—which diminished his popularity.

[122] So heavy were the losses of the men, particularly from Liverpool, that the grieving inhabitants "back home" in Liverpool named their soccer stand, "The Kop" (after Spion*kop*), in their memory. Many modern Liverpudlians are unaware of this fact.

[123] *Inniskilling* is Irish for "Island of Kathleen;" originally *Innis Cethlen;* Cethlen was the wife of Balor (who is considered to have been a *mythical* king of Ireland). *Fusiliers* were "British regiments of soldiers originally armed with *fusils* (light flintlock rifles)." The modern town, on Loch Erne, which is home to this regiment, is called Enniskillen, in County Fermanagh.

In all, the Royal Inniskilling Fusiliers lost *1/3 of their enlisted men* and *nearly 3/4* of their officer strength, in this single engagement. The severe losses among the officers' ranks was iron-clad evidence that Boer snipers deliberately attempted to "pick off" any officers, especially those who "led from the front." The dry dongas below were soon filled with the corpses of those courageous Irishmen who died fighting for the English queen (the dongas were later merely filled in with dirt to form their final resting place). Upon hearing of these terrible losses, Victoria Regina spoke sadly of the demise of "my brave Irish."

When that rather insignificant-looking hill was finally taken, most of the surviving Boers had already fled—and the Irish were surprised to learn that when they "captured" the remaining Boers with their rifles protruding from the stone *sangars* ("bunkers")—they only took "hats" and "sticks" as prisoners! The British were equally surprised to discover that there were a number of dead *female* Boer combatants in the overrun trenches around Colenso and Ladysmith. A war correspondent, who would later become Prime Minister of GREAT BRITAIN—and who would one day be considered by many to be "one of the greatest Englishmen who ever lived"—was captured, near Ladysmith, and imprisoned by the Boers after they successfully ambushed an "armored" locomotive, dubbed "Hairy Mary"—due to its odd-looking *hessian cladding* (a heavy, bullet-proof "chain mail" made of very thick rope). Their plucky young captive, *Winston Spencer Churchill* (1874-1965) managed to escape to neutral Mozambique, and he eventually made his way back to the front.

On Christmas Day, 1899, the Boers lobbed a single "Long Tom" shell into the town of Ladysmith. When it did not explode, the soldiers carefully opened it only to discover a *plum pudding* wrapped in a note which read: "With the Compliments of the Season!" Although the SECOND ANGLO-BOER WAR was later called "the last gentleman's war," the fighting was vicious, and the loss of life, limb and property, was severe.

In Mafeking, things were going little better for the besieged British. Colonel Robert Baden-Powell soon devised the notion of using young boys as messengers and scouts, and thus was born the enduring BOY SCOUT movement (formally founded in 1908). Joseph Rudyard Kipling[124] (1865-1936), the "unofficial" *poet laureate* of England, (who wrote of the black man being "the white man's burden") was also trapped within the town of Mafeking. Apparently, Kipling and Baden-Powell collaborated in composing an eloquent 1000-word heliographed[125] message, politely advising the besieging Boers that their efforts would ultimately, be futile. The Boers' heliographed reply was simple and to the point: "Come out and fight!"

The British actually employed the male, black citizens of Mafeking, quite extensively, as armed guards. It had been a popular *myth* that there was a tacit agreement between the white antagonists that this was to be a "white man's war." However, that simply was not true—both sides made use of blacks; though the *British* forces employed *far more*. Up to 100,000 blacks took a direct part in the war on the side of the Imperialists, whereas only about one-tenth of that number were used by the Boers. Furthermore, the Boers did *not* employ the blacks "to do their *fighting* for them;" rather, the Boers utilized the blacks in *non-military* support roles such as servants (laborers, janitors, food service), drivers, couriers, etc. In only a very few instances did the Boers arm their black assistants— but the *British* had no such qualms about arming black auxiliaries and sending them into battle to die. In fact, in the closing stages of the war, the British would use, rather extensively, companies of well-armed blacks to man the thousands of block-

---

[124] Kipling was *offered* the office of poet *laureate,* as well as the ORDER OF MERIT AND KNIGHTHOOD—but *turned it down; refusing* all such pretentious honors. In 1907 he received the NOBEL PRIZE for literature. Kipling himself wrote numerous poems expressing the very same racial sentiments the Boers held. See **Appendix C**.

Another Englishman, the famous author Sir Arthur Conan Doyle, wrote an impressive description of the Boer character, based upon his personal experience as a medic during the BOER WAR. See **Appendix D**.

[125] A method of transmitting messages by reflecting sunlight; which was used extensively by both sides in this war.

houses which the CROWN was to erect across the countryside, in a largely futile effort to contain the free-ranging commandos.

As the war dragged on, with no sign that the vastly outnumbered Boer commandos were considering *throwing in the towel,* the British made increasing use of armed blacks, turning them against their own countrymen. The British used these well-armed blacks as scouts—and as *guerrillas* to raid, burn and destroy *undefended* Boer farms and crops, to steal Boer cattle, and "escort" Boer women and children (often after robbing and raping them) into British concentration camps (which soon began to mushroom on the veld). Tales of innumerable atrocities against non-combatant white Afrikaners, and the violation and humiliation of their womenfolk and daughters at the hands of these blacks, in the service (and on the payroll) of the British army, began to filter through to the commandos in the field—and Boer forces thus sometimes summarily executed any armed blacks that were captured. It was said that the British told the blacks that if the Boers won the war, they would "re-introduce" slavery but that if the British won, blacks would be free to take the Boer farms, and the Boer women as their wives. The seed of hate that had first been sown in the consciousness of white Africans by the brutality of black Africans against the women and children of the pioneering white farmers way back in the late 1700's on the eastern frontier—and then once again in the 1800's on the "Great Trek" to Boer independence—was now being watered anew by their bitter tears from similar abuse in the dawn of the 20th Century.

Another myth of the SECOND ANGLO-BOER WAR, which had no firm basis in truth, was the assumption that British Lee-Metford and Lee-Enfield rifles were inferior to the German Mausers of the Boer forces, and that this *alleged* "inferior weaponry" accounted for the large disparity in battle fatalities between the two armies. Both were bolt-action rifles firing cartridges from a magazine. The British rifle's magazine was detachable, and carried up to ten rounds, while the Boer rifle had a fixed magazine, and was clip-loaded with five rounds, besides the round in the chamber, in both cases. The British rifle's bolt action was short and smooth, the Boer's long and rugged.   In terms of crispness of trigger-action or battle reliability, both the German and British rifles were more-or-less equal. Both cartridges were of the new, smokeless variety, both fired a bullet of similar size, velocity, and ballistic efficiency, and both were capable of inflicting severe wounds, even at long range. The British did encounter some problems in re-setting their sights when the change-over to the new Enfield-rifled barrel came about, but this was soon remedied.

However, the real difference was in human marksmanship. Many of the Boers had grown up hunting and shooting on the veld, whereas most British shooting-practice was restricted to firing at stationary, upright targets on formal shooting ranges. By the closing stages of that war, almost as many Boers were carrying captured *British* rifles as German ones.   In fact, some Boers even *preferred* the larger magazine-capacity of the British rifle. By then, the .303-inch (7.7mm.) British ammunition was also more easily obtainable, sometimes by simply walking along behind a British column, and picking up rounds that fell out of the *bandoleers* of the mounted British troops!

A certain amount of controversy (another myth) was also caused by the *alleged* British use of so-called "dum-dum"[126] bullets, after a few cases *seemingly* thus-marked were captured by the Boers. In fact, these cases of *standard* cartridges had merely been manufactured in a British ammunition factory in *Dum-Dum, India* (a city in West Bengal)—and were not the expanding, fragmenting bullets which the British *had* used against the "Whirling Dervishes," in the desert at Omdurman, just a few years earlier. There were however, a few recorded instances of individual soldiers, *on both sides,* filing off the tips of their bullets and scoring them.

---

[126] *Dum-dum* bullets were those either manufactured or "improvised" to be blunt-nosed, hollow-pointed, or scored on the end, so that they would expand or split apart upon impact, causing even greater wounds and thus having greater stopping power. Dum-dum bullets have since been banned for military use by general international conventions.

Another controversy which circulated claiming that the Boers used "poisoned bullets" also turned out to be *false*—the green tinge on some recovered Boer copper-jacketed (7mm.) bullets was merely *verdigris* corrosion (copper discoloration) from poor storage in humid caves or from close contact with leather bandoleers (and British bullets no doubt, if in the climate long enough, looked the same).

Regarding artillery, the Boers had fine, but few, long-range Creusot "Long Tom" cannons (from France), and shorter-range cannons (from Krupps of Germany), which fired high-explosive shells. The "State Artillery" was the only formal, uniformed corps in the Boer army. The British utilized myriad light field pieces, including 20 rapid-firing *Pom-Poms*[127] (1-pounder Maxim-Nordenfield cannons which could hurl a respectable 30 rounds a minute) and some heavy, converted naval guns. In the field, the British artillery eventually proved superior, due to their greater numbers, and much longer tradition of gunnery training.

Boer commandos had also long been adept at fire-and-movement, hit-and-run tactics and the prowess of their veld marksmen was already legendary *generations before* this war started. The Boers thought nothing of merely holding a defensive position just long enough to inflict casualties on the invading British forces, only to prudently retreat at the last moment and thus live to fight another day. The Boers were not at all keen to face British bayonet charges, however—a tactic which their opponents eventually learned to exploit; but at the risk of taking heavy gunshot casualties themselves. The Boer fighters were experts at fieldcraft, and were very much at home on the vast, rugged South

---

[127] Pom-Poms was a nickname given to them due to the sound they made and also due to the fact that they were used extensively by the *Poms. Poms* (or *Pommys)* was a nickname for the English (still used by Australians); it was apparently *originally* an acronym applied to those British convicts sent to Australia: P.O.M.: "Prisoners of (His/Her) Majesty" or P.O.M.(E.) "Prisoners of Mother (England)." Another, rather contrived origin is reputed to be a linking of rosy *pome*granate cheeks (on pale new English immigrants) to a money-*grant* they received; then extrapolated to a *pome-grant,* and thus "Pome" or *Pommy.*

African veld. They were highly mobile, knew the terrain, camped in the open, and drew their supplies from wherever they could. If they could not raid a British camp or column for ammunition as well as food, they had to rely on the crops and livestock of their own farms, being run mainly by their womenfolk, or by bagging fowl or game.

The British forces mostly moved in long, slow, cumbersome columns, and often attacked across open ground on a broad front, exposing their men to withering, long-range fire. When the British eventually began employing small mounted "commandos" of their own, often comprised of colonials, they met with more success than did the slow columns. The Boers—other than their modern artillery corps—seldom wore formal uniforms and fought mostly in drab civilian clothes and soft-brimmed hats. The British army, having finally and wisely dispensed with their conspicuous red coats with white helmets, belts and pouches—a carry-over from the Napoléonic wars a century earlier—now wore *khaki* uniforms and good, lightweight *tan* helmets. Thus, the Boers nicknamed the British troops, "Khakis" (since they no longer wore "red coats"). They also dubbed the British foot soldiers, "Tommies"—in stereo-type of a legendary British *foot-slogger* ("infantry"), *Tommy Atkins*:[128] since the numbers of British troops were so overwhelming, they seemed to be everywhere at the same time.

As time went by and their own clothing became increasingly tattered, the Boers were sometimes obliged to wear captured British uniforms, but at the risk of being shot in error by their own

---

[128] It seems the nickname developed due to the fact that in 1815, rather illiterate British recruits filled out a certain form which had "Private Tommy Atkins" as an example on how to fill out the form; this example was later "promoted" to sergeant when he was able to actually sign his name instead of making a mark. Rudyard Kipling wrote a poem in 1892 titled, "Tommy (Atkins)." Later, the nickname was popularized by the British Commander-in-Chief, the Duke of Wellington, in 1843. Welllington had been asked what name he thought typified the average British footsoldier. He re-membered from his first campaign in the Low Countries (in the 1790s) a badly wounded, but stoical, soldier whose name was "Thomas Atkins." See **Appendix C**.

men, or executed as spies by the enemy. On one occasion, a Boer commando surprised a British patrol which was disrobed and washing in a stream near Ladysmith. They disarmed the "Tommies," stole their uniforms, and sent them back to camp in their underwear! That embarrassing incident caused that stream to thereafter become hilariously known as the *Onderbroekspruit* ("Underpants Creek")!

The Boers rode mostly on their tough, willing *Boerperds,* and the British rode a variety of equine mounts, many of them imported from Argentina. An enduring legacy of these South American horses is found in the colorful *cosmos* flowers *(Bidens formosa)* that now grow alongside any road that British cavalry had traversed during the war; the seeds were scattered in the dung produced by the South American feed imported with those Argentine horses. The Boers were generally considered to be superior horsemen to the British on the challenging African veld, and were sometimes literally in the saddle for weeks on end. It is estimated that as many as 400,000 horses died during that war, and probably at least twice that many oxen—after having worked hard under miserable conditions, both horse and ox inevitably ended their sad existence serving as meat rations for the troops and hungry civilians. In an attempt to make the horse-meat psychologically less repulsive, the equine delicacy was called *cheval* (which is merely French for "horse").

The systems of recruitment and command were, however, very different between the two armies. The British "class" system was still very much in force in Victorian England, and their army's commissioned officers were invariably from the *upper classes*. Most had been through military academy training, but this did not always adequately prepare them for the vastly varying conditions and rugged veld of South Africa, or for the fast-changing face of modern warfare. Their non-commissioned officers, the corporals and sergeants (known to be the backbone of any army) were generally hardy individuals who had worked their way up through the ranks. With only a few notable exceptions, they seldom rose to the ranks of the commissioned officers. They were the imposers of discipline, and were responsible for the carrying-out of battlefield orders from the higher command. The enlisted men were mostly from the *lowest rungs* of the British "social ladder;" many having been recruited in the pubs, jails, and sometimes even the gutters of England, Scotland, Wales, and Ireland. The army guaranteed them food, a uniform, and the "Queen's shilling," but not much else. The annals of British military history seldom mention the names of private soldiers—again with a few notable exceptions—the assumption being that whatever battle honors they did achieve, were, in any case, merely the result of following the orders given to them by their officers. The British *Tommie* himself was seen, by the Boers, as a brave (though sometimes seemingly suicidal) individual; but the Boers often viewed the actions of the British officers as *idiotic*. While Boer knowledge of the terrain was excellent, British campaign maps were woefully inadequate, and more than once, the British officers used an outdated *high school atlas* to plan a major operation! All told, the British army in South Africa eventually fielded about 450,000 white combatants, against only about a tenth of that number of Boers.

The Boer army, in contrast, was made up mostly of enthusiastic volunteers, although commando service was also a duty, and quite often grandfather, father and son, all from the same family, were called up. They were usually expected to report with *their own* horse, saddle, blanket, eight days of rations, and a rifle (if they had one suitable for the purpose). As a Boer general once eloquently stated, in an effort to encourage his disheartened men: "These Tommies are serving a queen that most of them have never seen, and are fighting in a hostile land thousands of miles from their homes. You, on the other hand, are fighting on *your own* land, in defense of *your own* farms, women and children."

Boer officers were *elected,* and commando ranks were generally restricted to a *veld-kornet*[129] and a commandant. A commandant who did not perform satisfactorily to his own men's expectations could easily find himself reduced to being an ordinary soldier again, within his own commando. The commandants themselves were in turn, under the direction of a general.

---

[129] "Field Cornet;" a type of Lieutenant, Captain or Major, usually a Boer commando cavalry officer.

Commando units were mostly comprised of citizens from the same town or district, and vied with other commandos for battle successes against the British. Boers were also free to leave and join *other* commando units at will.

There were also many foreign volunteers (and a few unpaid "mercenaries") in the Boer forces, including a large Irish contingent, led by American Colonel John Y. Filimore Blake (1856-1907), and his second-in-command, Irishman Major John McBride (1865-1916). Although McBride survived the ANGLO-BOER WAR, he would eventually be executed by a British firing squad during the Irish "Easter Rebellion" of 1916. Other individual mercenaries or groups hailed from France, Germany, Holland, Russia, Scandinavia, Scotland, the United States, and various other nations. Tragically, the small Scandinavian contingent was annihilated in the early stages of the war, at Magersfontein, when Lord Methuen's HIGHLAND BRIGADE perforated them with bayonets. A second "Irish Brigade" was then formed to accommodate the large numbers of foreign volunteers, under an Australian, Colonel Arthur Alfred Lynch (1861-1934). This Irish Brigade also included 200 "Italian Scouts." A "German Brigade" fought under Colonel Adolf Friedrich Schiel (1858-1903), who played a role in setting up the only uniformed Boer corps, the *Staatsartillerie* ("State Artillery"). Another notable German volunteer was Ferdinand Adolf August Heinrich ("Harra") von Zeppelin[130] (1838-1917).

However, after a number of setbacks, *all* foreign volunteers were reorganized to serve under General De La Rey. Many of these brave, selfless men would be counted among the *Bittereinders*—fighting to the "bitter end" of the war. A Polish Jew was on the Boer general staff, and a Russian Jew fought with the Cape rebels. A Frenchman named Count Georges de Villebois-Mareuil (1847-1900), actually fought as a Boer general. Villebois-Mareuil, a former-FRENCH FOREIGN LEGIONNAIRE, was killed in action at *Boshof* ("Forest Hall"), fighting for Boer

---

[130] Graf ("Count") Zeppelin would later become famous as the designer of the dirigible airship that bombed London in the FIRST WORLD WAR (1914-18).

freedom. He was buried by his honorable foe, British Lord Methuen, with full military honors, attended by a guard of 1,500 Loyal North Lancashires.

A few Boer women also rode with their men into battle, and the odd general was known to be accompanied by his entire household, following after him in wagons. In contrast to the British, who, like the Romans before them, would often delay engaging with the enemy until after they had "finished their breakfast," the Boers mostly ate "on the run" or in the saddle (and did not stop periodically, and thus predictably, for "scheduled" meals). The Boers also slept in the open, whenever time and circumstances dictated; thus, they were not slowed down by the constant need to erect and then dismantle large tented camps, or load and unload cumbersome carts and wagons with such equipment. Thus, the Boers were more flexible and practical; whereas the British were more rigid and concerned with their peculiar perception of traditional etiquette.[131]

The SECOND ANGLO-BOER WAR or *TWEEDE VRYHEIDSOORLOG* ("Second Freedom War"), as the Boers themselves consistently called it, had thus ushered in a new, more-*mobile* type of modern warfare.

---

[131] This same mind-set, in the early stages of the FRENCH AND INDIAN WAR, would hinder the British and Americans, who were accustomed to fighting in *the British method*. The British notion of a "fair fight" was: both forces lining up, fully exposed in the middle of a field—taking turns shooting at each other, "like gentleman." However, the Indians, who were recruited by the French, fought from behind rocks and trees; while the British and Americans fought in the traditional *British manner*. It was only after General Edward Braddock was shot (at the beginning of the war, 1755) and George Washington took command—and told his men to take cover and "fight fire with fire" (fight as the *Indians* fought)—that the day was saved and the Colonials began to win. The British later, in the AMERICAN REVOLUTIONARY WAR, hired the Indians (with promises similar to those given to the blacks in the ANGLO-BOER WAR) to fight against the Americans. The *Brits* also acted similarly in Central Africa, pitting tribe against local tribe.

Chapter Twenty-seven

When Joshua Roux told his wife Angela that he had just sold his profitable security business, "lock, stock and barrel" to a British Randlord, she was *horrified*. The sight of many hundred solid-gold *Kruger Rands* in the sturdy trunk, which Joshua opened with a flourish, did little to mollify her. She was somewhat relieved, however, by his reassurance that they would retain their house; but then he again dashed her hopes of "life as normal" when he told her that he was going to lease out the mansion, and that they were moving to the Lowveld to see out the war. "The British are coming. I have no doubt about that," Joshua announced. "So I have asked Sean O'Connor to stay on here and make the best deal he can, by leasing the house to the British army's high command, which will no doubt be looking for headquarters and suitable accommodation for their upper echelons. They will probably commandeer the house for their own use anyway, so we might as well try to rent it to them first."

Joshua then prudently made arrangements to have his fine race horses secreted out of Johannesburg and stabled at a safe distance from that city for the duration of the looming war; to keep them beyond the rapacious eyes of the advancing British cavalry, to prevent losing them. One of Joshua's friends was a neutral English rancher who had stables of his own, situated in the countryside, about midway between Johannesburg and Pretoria. Joshua paid him quite generously to discreetly board his considerable equine investment. Had Joshua known anyone who had previously offered to buy his fine beasts (as with his business), he might have sold them outright; but alas, there had been no such offer. However, time did not allow him to find a buyer of such luxuries at a reasonable price, so he decided to stash them where he thought they would be safe.

Not one to waste too much time bemoaning her fate, Angela was up early the following morning, ordering the servants about, packing away her best linen and ornaments, and locking away favorite pieces of furniture into a storeroom. By the end of that week, they were ready to take the train to Lydenburg. Their twins, James and Julia, were of course, very excited. They dashed about, collecting their toys and books, and chattering excitedly about all the horse-riding and exploring they were going to do on *Ouma* and *Oupa's* ("grandma" and "grandpa's") farm. They both spoke English equally as well as they did Afrikaans. Angela had made sure that they had been enrolled in a dual-language primary school, as she believed strongly that they needed a classical and western education, since English was now a world language, which contrasted to the tongue of their ancestors, the parochial Afrikaans (which was part of their heritage). However, though the Roux twins were educated and brought up as *Anglicized-Afrikaners,* their father always addressed them in his mother tongue. He also regaled them (in Afrikaans) with his tales of the *Great Trek,* the battles against the black tribes, and the history, folklore, and legends of his Boer people. Sadly, at a time in South African history when the distinction between Afrikaans and English-speaking white Africans was slowly becoming less distinct, the war once again starkly re-drew the lines of division. Sean O'Connor accompanied the Roux family to Johannesburg train station, helped to load their many, heavy trunks onto the luggage coach, and then assisted them with their hand-luggage into their first-class compartment. He then ordered the coachman to take him back to the mansion, where he would await the coming of the British.

The train journey to the eastern TRANSVAAL first took them slowly out of the sprawling suburbs of "the Golden City," then the wheezing steam engine gradually gathered speed as they passed the fast-growing industrial towns of the bleak East Rand. Soon they were traveling over the grassy Highveld plains, and the children hung out of the compartment window, pointing out to each other distant herds of *blesbok* and *wildebeest.* Angela Roux sat silently, staring out of the open window. Her husband tried to cheer her up by telling her rather unconvincingly that the war was unlikely to last very long, and that all the bellicose pronouncements and militaristic attitudes of the Boer forces would no doubt soon evaporate when the harsh reality of war with the mighty BRITISH EMPIRE finally struck home.

Secretly, however, Joshua Roux *was hoping* that the Boer commandos would give the *Brits* a good thrashing; but down deep in his heart, he knew that their republican cause was ultimately doomed. As he left their mansion, he had looked at himself in the long hall mirror—and had noticed a slightly paunchy and pallid man in his early 40's looking back at him; with the stresses of business and city life already etched on his yet, still-handsome face, his light-brown hair now graying at the temples. Gone were his ruddy tan and the clear eyes of his youth, which he had spent hunting on the Lowveld, then in the fire of battle. Those features were now replaced by a somewhat care-worn and even slightly cynical look. Reminiscing and reflecting upon these things, Joshua Roux vowed silently to take better care of his health from then on. Looking around the train cabin, he glanced at the sturdy, locked chest full of Kruger Rands under the padded dark-green leather compartment seat, and took his wife's hand. Joshua looked into her beautiful blue eyes, but the tears that he saw brimming there, raised a lump in his throat.

Chapter Twenty-eight

After their initial resounding victories in the opening battles of the war on both fronts, and their "successes" in bottling-up British forces in Ladysmith in NATAL, and in Kimberley and Mafeking in CAPE COLONY, the Boer forces were elated—but despite their many victories the Boer hopes of forcing Britain into negotiations were but *pipe dreams*.

General De la Rey's marksmen at Graspan had decimated the British Naval Brigade. At the Battle of Magersfontein they had inflicted over 1,000 casualties on the Guards and the elite Highland Brigades (the British Empire's finest troops). Boer casualties were less than 1/5 of that, but their much lower overall numbers meant that even these losses were keenly felt.

General Sir William Forbes Gatacre (1843-1906) had failed dismally in his attempts to dislodge the Orange Free State forces from the *Stormberg* ("Storm Mountain") on December 8, 1899 —and the Boers captured 696 British soldiers. By this time, the Boers had already captured *several thousand* British troops, which fact presented a problem in itself: What to do with them? They were initially held in camps in the TRANSVAAL, near Pretoria, and were generally well treated.

[However, as the war progressed and the number of prisoners *grew* (and the Boers' meager supplies were *diminishing),* the Boers would, inevitably, have to begin releasing them.]

In NATAL, General Redvers Buller was making suicidal frontal assaults on General Louis Botha's well-entrenched forces on the north bank of the Tugela River. Buller's forces were pinned down in the open, suffering badly from sunburn, dehydration, and of course, well-placed Mauser bullets. British casualties amounted to about 1,100, while the Boers sustained only 40. The nickname *Rooinek* ("red-neck") was also soon applied by the Boers to the *Tommies,* on account of their sun-burned necks. Those Celts in the British forces who were wearing kilts had also been badly sun-burnt on the backs of their legs while they lay prone and helpless under the Boers' devastating artillery barrage and witheringly accurate long-range rifle-fire. Some hapless British soldiers even unwittingly took cover behind the small, "pre-marked" white stone range-finders!

Lieutenant Frederick ("Freddie") Hugh Sherston Roberts (1872-1899) was killed trying valiantly to save British guns at Colenso. When news of the death of his only surviving son reached him in London, the retired father of the fallen officer, Field-Marshal Lord Frederick Sleigh Roberts (1832-1914), an aging but highly experienced campaigner, immediately offered his services to the BRITISH CROWN. This personal tragedy for Lord Roberts would become one of the few instances of both a father and son both being awarded the "Victoria Cross" (VC) in the same conflict. Gen. Buller recommended Freddie Roberts for the VC. This was highly irregular, for the British, as a rule, only awarded a VC to a wounded soldier, if he was "very likely to survive;" however, Roberts was *mortally* wounded (though he survived for 2 days). *Very rarely* was the VC awarded *post-humously*. However, it seems that Roberts must have been a man after Buller's own heart. Buller's most redeeming quality was that he was himself an extraordinarily brave man and would not have asked any of his men to do anything which he was not prepared to do himself. Buller had given an order to *save the guns* "at all costs." Roberts was mortally wounded by a shell while selflessly obeying those orders: while "laughing and twirling his riding-crop" as he galloped towards the abandoned guns under heavy Boer artillery and rifle fire.

"Black Week" for the British forces in South Africa saw General Buller retain his command in NATAL, despite a public outcry *back home* at his glaring inability to made any significant headway against "a rabble of farmers," as the British press consistently referred to the Boer combatants. The most powerful nation on earth had confidently attacked one of the smallest nations in existence, yet was itself now suffering staggering numbers of casualties, and was being forced into humiliating surrenders on a scale not seen for over a century.

But, by now, the mood had changed dramatically in Britain. Initially the British attitude was that Britain would merely have to "punish" a handful of *rebellious* Boers in a *minor* colonial campaign—and many had even feared that the Boers "would not even fight." However, those delusions now gave way to the sobering realization that this was a *real*, full-scale war.[132] The fearful losses which their forces had already sustained served not only to reconfirm this sober realization, but it actually gave the British a greater sense of purpose—and a renewed determination *to crush* these "upstart Boer republics."

Patriotic fervor soon reached fever-pitch, and Lord Roberts was appointed as the new British Commander-in-Chief, with Lord Horatio Herbert Kitchener (1850-1916)—fresh from his victory at Omdurman (North Africa), of "dum-dum" infamy—as his new Chief of Staff. Although neither of these new appointments had General Buller's experience of fighting in South African conditions, the British government and the British public had every confidence in their new field commanders. Already, their subjects throughout their far-flung empire were rallying to the British cause: Volunteers from Australia, New Zealand, and Canada would soon join their forces on the harsh South African veld. As time went by, it became obvious that these new and highly mobile colonial units—and the "Australian" Bushveldt Carbineers in particular—would be rather more successful than their Imperial counterparts in fighting the Boers on their own terms. Like the Boers themselves, the men of these British colonial units had mostly led a rural existence (under similar circumstances, such as in the formidable *Australian Outback)*, and many were thus natural marksmen and horsemen. Of course, the Boers saw these men as "betrayers" in a sense: since the Afrikaners had no quarrel with any of those other countries. Understandably, *bad feelings* were generated, within the Boer consciousness, by these other nations *volunteering* to fight

---

[132] If the British had taken the trouble to read the Scriptural caution (in their own English Bible; I Kings 20:11) of not boasting while putting *on* one's armor, but while taking it *off*—the British may have been more circumspect and not so overconfident.

against the Boers. The Boers were not aggressors—they were a peaceful, independent, white, Christian nation fighting only to defend what was theirs. Yet these volunteers chose to fight on the side of imperialist Britain. Bad feelings toward these other nations would linger in the Afrikaner mind long into the future.

One of these volunteers was an English-born and educated "Aussie" *outback* cattleman, horse-breaker, *raconteur* ("storyteller"), and poet named Harry "the Breaker" Harbord Morant (1864-1902)—who claimed to be the bastard son of a British admiral. Morant would gain notoriety for allegedly *murdering* civilians (including a "whistleblower" German missionary) and for *executing* Boer prisoners. When Morant landed in South Africa, he stayed for about a week at Cape Town's prestigious MOUNT NELSON HOTEL, but skipped out without paying his bill. Shamefully, even some Cape Afrikaners joined Morant's mounted unit. These *volksveraaiers* ("folk-betrayers") were despised by both sides, and particularly by Morant, who suspected that they might be Boer spies. "The Breaker" (along with one of his compatriots) was later executed *by the British,* apparently under diplomatic pressure from Germany, after a "show trial."

Morant claimed throughout his court-martial trial that he was "just following orders"—but he was unable to produce any *written* orders to substantiate this claim. When asked by the prosecution, "under which rule," was he permitted to execute prisoners, Morant glibly replied: "We got 'em, and we shot 'em, under 'Rule 303'..." (referring of course, to the .303 caliber of the British army-issue rifle). The defiant Morant protested his "innocence of war crimes" to the end. He also curtly admonished the soldiers serving in the firing-squad as they were about to execute him, to, "Shoot straight, ye' bastards!".

His tombstone in Pretoria bore the epitaph:

"And a man's foes shall be they of his own household." (Matthew, Ch. 10 v.36)

This epitaph, apparently, was *not* of *his own* choosing: for before he was executed Morant was offered the services of a priest, but he sharply refused any such spiritual counsel, defiantly declaring, "I am a pagan."

[Another epitaph, apparently misinterpreted, also appeared on the grave: *"He that loseth his life shall find it."* The actual quote of Jesus Christ (Matthew 10:39) reads: "He that findeth his life shall lose it; and he that loseth his life *for My sake* shall find it." This is expanded in Matthew 16:25-26: "For whosoever will save his life shall lose it: and whosoever will lose his life for *My sake* shall find it. *For what is a man profited, if he shall gain the whole world, and lose his own soul? Or what shall a man give in exchange for his soul?*"

Profound words indeed. More appropriate verses for Morant's tombstone might have been:

"The ungodly *are* not so: but *are* like the chaff which the wind driveth away." (Psalm 1:4)

"...for all they that take the sword shall perish with the sword." (Matthew 26:52) or

"Be not deceived; God is not mocked: for whatsoever a man soweth, that shall he also reap. For he that soweth to his flesh shall of the flesh reap corruption; but he that soweth to the Spirit shall of the Spirit reap life everlasting." (Galatians 6:7,8)

In other words: If more people lived their lives in the light of eternity, perhaps fewer people would violate the rights of others (both on personal and national levels).]

Morant's "commanding officer" was Captain Alfred "Bulala" Taylor (1862-1941)—ostensibly the man who *should have* taken responsibility for the nefarious actions of his mainly Australian, British colonial unit, the "Bushveldt Carbineers." However, in reality, Taylor was somewhat of a *doppelganger* ("split-personality"). He was in fact a Dublin-born British intelligence officer, and Native Commissioner for the *Spelonken* ("caves") area of the *Soutpansberg* ("Salt-pans mountains"). He gained his African nickname of *Bulala* ("kill") for his heavy-handed methods of dealing with both black and white civilians—and Boer captives. Taylor judiciously resigned his commission *the very day* he was arrested with Morant for *war crimes.* After some apparent collusion with (or behind-the-scenes interference from) Lord Kitchener, Taylor was deemed a "civilian" by the time the matter came to trial by court-martial. He thus "walked free," and later made his way to Rhodesia (as it was called in those days), taking with him a *huge haul* of livestock, wagons and valuable possessions which had been "confiscated" from black kraals and from Boers who had surrendered to the British forces.

Despite their stunning early setbacks, British forces would soon be advancing on all fronts and then (as Joshua Roux had predicted) it would be just a matter of time before the Boers were overwhelmed. A merciless guerrilla war of attrition then ensued and though the *Hensoppers* ("hands-uppers"), as they were called, surrendered, the *Bittereinders* ("bitter-enders") maintained operations until the final moments of that detestable conflict.

Chapter Twenty-nine

Joshua Roux and his family disembarked from their train in Lydenburg, and Joshua's first stop was at the Landdrost's office, where he surprised that gentleman by offering payment in gold Kruger Rands for the yet-uninhabited 8,000 morgen parcel of land alongside his father's farm below the Sabie Ridge. With those title deeds and a substantial portion of his gold coins stashed in a safety-deposit box at the elderly Hiram Goldberg's bank, Joshua then hired a comfortable coach and a wagon to transport his family and their luggage down to the Lowveld. The two children, whose last visit to their grandparents' farm had been nearly a year ago, delighted in competing with each other to identify the various antelope species, which they spied on their bumpy journey down the escarpment road. That road would soon be named "Long Tom Pass," after a Boer gun-emplacement. They occasionally pulled over against the rocky cutting to allow some riders to pass (so narrow was the path) and they briefly greeted each other and exchanged quick pleasantries. As a result of these chance encounters, news of the quiet arrival of the legendary *hero of Majuba* soon spread throughout the district. As they finally approached the stone farmhouse on the little stream near the Sabie River, Joshua had expected to see his old parents standing on the stoep, but there was no sign of them. It was only as he helped his wife down from the coach that his mother Erika emerged from inside the humble cottage to greet them. The twins ran joyfully towards her, but the deep sadness etched on the face of their grandmother stopped them in their tracks.

"Dis jou Oupa—hy kannie langer uithou nie." Erika Roux announced quietly that their grandpa, Joshua's father, was dying, and could not hold out much longer. Jan Roux had been suffering from chest-pains and fatigue for some weeks, and just two days earlier, he had suddenly weakened and taken to his bed. Erika had stayed at his bedside, hoping and praying that her man would somehow miraculously recover, but his 85 hard years had finally

taken their toll on his once-sturdy frame. He opened his eyes when his son and daughter-in-law, and his two young grandchildren entered the darkened bedroom, but was too weak to speak to them. His big hands, once strong enough to trek and fight and farm, were now bony and feeble. His once-striking blue eyes were dull and short-sighted, and his once-handsome face, now thin and drawn. Angela and the twins went out and sat on the bench on the stoep while their luggage was being unloaded, and the empty coach and wagon soon departed for Lydenburg. Joshua and Erika remained at Jan Roux's bedside and Joshua told his parents that he had purchased the big tract of land alongside theirs. The old man smiled at the news, and when he finally gathered the strength to speak, said: *"Pas jou Ma goed op, seun. En jy moet nie in die oorlog teen die Engelse betrokke raak nie. Dit is een geveg wat ons nie kan wen nie."* Jan thus told his son to look after his mother, and not to get involved in the war against the English, as this was one fight that they could not win. Then the old trekker closed his tired eyes for the last time, and within the hour, Jan Roux's spirit had moved on.

Joshua Roux's arms and back ached as he wielded the pick that he was using to dig his father's grave on the koppie overlooking the farmhouse. The tangled roots of the spreading thorn tree were making his unpleasant task even more difficult, and he quietly decried his own lack of physical fitness. Almost two decades of comfortable living in the *Golden City* had robbed him of his vigor and vitality, and the blisters on his hands now stung as much as the tears in his eyes and the pain in his heart. Finally, he reckoned that the hole was deep enough to thwart the hyenas, and he leaned the pick against the tree, alongside the shovel. Walking back down the slope to the farmhouse, he wiped the sweat from his brow with his shirt-sleeves. It was mid-summer on the Lowveld, and the humid heat penetrated even the shade of the stoep. He sat down heavily on the old *riempie-bench*, breathing hard. Looking down, he realized the bench was one he had watched his father build from scratch—then with solemn respect, he realized that most everything on the homestead, his father had built. He then reminisced a little, and regretted having stayed away for so long. How he would miss *die ou man, sy geliefde ou vader!* ("the old man, his beloved old father!").

Joshua was still sitting, resting in the shade, while wondering how he was going to carry his father's corpse up the koppie, when he saw 4 riders approaching. They were Boer commandos, their Mauser rifles and cartridge-filled bandoleers slung over their shoulders. They had soon dismounted and tied their sweating ponies to the rail of the stoep. They introduced themselves as Lowveld farmers who were on their way to join up with the local commando. They informed him that the commando's commandant had recently been killed by a British bullet and they wanted Joshua to take his place. They were aware of Joshua's reputation as a marksman, and knew of his experience in fighting the *Tommies* at Majuba two decades earlier. They pleaded with Joshua to join them and lead them against the approaching British army.

Just then, Angela and Erika emerged from the kitchen, and offered tea and coffee to the new arrivals. They apologized for not having any fresh rusks to offer the men, but explained that things in the household were not as they should be, due to the recent death of Meneer Jan Roux. The men rose, hats in hand, and offered their sincere condolences to the family for their great loss, and also their apologies for the poor timing of their visit. Joshua replied that their visit was indeed Providential, and asked if they would be kind enough to assist him in the solemn task at hand; that of helping him to place his father's remains within the crude coffin Joshua had fashioned from some planks, and then help him carry it up the hill to the grave he had freshly prepared. They empathetically expressed that they would be most willing to assist him in the unpleasant task. Somberly, they completed the short, mournful trek—and very soon thereafter Joshua had shoveled the big pile of red earth back into the grave over his father's casket. Erika sobbed heavingly while a grieving Angela and the twins watched silently. As if in sympathy, a distant jackal howled a mournful bushveld dirge.

When the men later asked concerning the smaller hole which was dug alongside his father's grave, Joshua replied that it was for his late father's favorite old dog, which was now itself dying from tick-bite fever. Joshua had lied—for the first time in his life—for he planned to bury his chest of remaining gold coins there next to his father's grave. As the men were preparing to leave they promised that they would return in a week or two with their commando; at which time they hoped that Joshua would then see fit to lead them against the British. Time was of the essence, they asserted, since the British were already beginning to send scouts, skirmishing patrols, and *sapper*[133] demolition-engineers into the Lowveld, endeavoring to sabotage the Boers' last rail-link to the east coast and the neutral Portuguese port at Delagoa Bay. They were then quickly on their way, after again offering their most sincere condolences.

Angela Roux, having grown up in the city of Pretoria, and having then lived in town in Johannesburg, knew *virtually nothing* about farm life. On their infrequent visits to Joshua's old parents on the farm, she had generally managed to avoid dirtying her pale, soft hands. She had helped willingly enough with the domestic chores in the farm kitchen—and had once even deigned to milk a cow—but if the truth be told, she had always looked forward to getting back to their comfortable, newly electrified and luxurious mansion in Johannesburg (where the *servants* saw to the house-work, and their chef did most of the cooking). The prospect of having to take over the rustic household from the elderly Erika, was a daunting and distasteful obligation to Angela. Nonetheless, she threw herself into the task, and tried bravely to stop herself from gagging when she had to squeeze out droppings from a buck colon to use the entrails for sausage casings or when she had to wash *feces* from the fresh eggs provided by the chickens in the

---

[133] As in "*sapping* the strength" of a building/bridge's foundations, by undermining/explosion. An official term used by the military for specialist demolition and engineering troops, or even for mine-*clearing* units (a highly skilled and hazardous military specialization). Undermining of walls was commonly employed in sieges of cities in ancient times—including the siege of Jerusalem.

henhouse. The old iron "donkey-boiler"[134] behind the cottage, which supplied the hot water to the bathtub, had to be *constantly fed* with firewood, which the children collected. Water was collected in buckets from the little stream near the house, and more than once, Angela had to repulsively *strain out tadpoles* before filling the kettle for tea. The raw, bloody meat was sometimes still warm, as, most often, the buck was newly shot and quickly skinned by the knife held deftly in Joshua's capable hands. This was a particular horror for Angela: since there was no refrigeration (unlike their mansion in Johannesburg), all meat had to be *immediately* pickled, smoked, or salted and dried. Vegetables and fruit, which used to be delivered to her front door in Johannesburg by the Indian market gardener, now had to be dug up in the vegetable patch or picked from the orchard alongside the farmhouse.

For his part, Joshua set out quite early most mornings, after overseeing the children's feeding of the farm animals. He would take one of the horses, and generally did not return until he had shot a buck. He then skinned and quartered it, or sliced up the meat for *biltong* and dried-sausage making. He chopped firewood and timber and fixed the railings around the *kraal*. Soon, the paunch that he had developed in the city, began to shrink, while the color returned to his pallid face.

It had been well over a month since his father had died, and the commando members, who had visited him the day he buried his father, had not yet returned. Joshua was beginning to wonder if, after meeting him, they had changed their minds about wanting him to lead them. Maybe, he thought, they were wholly unimpressed (with the aging, out of shape, city-slicker); maybe they thought that he was perhaps, no longer the legendary hero of Majuba of whom they had heard so many amazing stories. Clearly, he was not that same, fierce, young warrior who had survived the massacre at Isandlwana, who fought bravely in the desperate defense of Rorke's Drift against the Zulus, and who had then scaled the slopes of Majuba Moun-

---

[134] A crude metal device, a barrel/boiler mounted above a semi-open fire, working away quietly and not requiring much attention, other than "fodder" (wood); rather like a *donkey working a mill.*

tain, demonstrating his extraordinary marksmanship and nerves of steel, inflicting severe casualties upon the British.

Despite his curiosity over why the commando had not returned, Joshua also remembered his father's dying request, that his only son should not involve himself in the war against the British: a war that could not be won. With this in mind, Joshua was somewhat relieved that they had not returned. Nonetheless, as he got physically fitter, and the blood again began to race in his veins when he galloped after and shot a *rooihartbees* ("red hartebeest"), his thoughts returned to that first, short war against the British. His superb shooting skills had not suffered any diminishment over the years. When he practiced with the old Martini-Henry that he had used at Majuba (which had then been left behind on the farm when he moved to the goldfields) he still regularly found his mark at 400 paces.

Angela watched her husband from the stoep of the farmhouse. There was a spring in his step that she had not seen since shortly after their courting days. The new fire in his eyes reminded her of the Joshua she had married more than a decade earlier; before he had gained the monopoly of security contracts on *all* the big goldmines—back then, when he was still hungry for success. Financial success had certainly come to him, through his vision, hard work and perseverance. She remembered the day that he had come home to proudly tell her that he had gained membership to the prestigious *Rand Club*—and from then on most of his business deals would be done in their wood-paneled, cigar-smoke-filled boardrooms. She remembered how he had carried her effortlessly over the threshold of the brand new, Herbert Baker-designed[135] mansion which he had built for them in Doornfontein, on Terrace Road, alongside some wealthy Randlords.

Angela herself had been so very proud of her dynamic husband, whose name was whispered at gala dinners as the fighter

---

[135] Herbert Baker (1862-1946) had designed many of the palatial buildings in the Cape, which Cecil Rhodes himself had ordered built. After Baker moved to Johannesburg he was commissioned to design all the best mansions and civic buildings there.

who had felled myriad soldiers in the First Anglo-Boer War, including a British general: a feat for which he modestly refused to accept personal credit, asserting that he had fought alongside many other good Boer sharpshooters, any one of whom may have taken that fatal shot. Angela herself, as Mevrou Roux, had been indescribably elated to welcome the elite of Johannesburg society to their fine mansion, to be served by her *white* servants in their smart uniforms. When the Roux's raced their thorough-bred horses at the new race track in *Turffontein* ("Turf springs"), she would eagerly take her place in the winner's circle alongside her husband—and gracefully accept the accolades heaped upon them. Angela was, in those earlier days resplendent in the os-trich-feathered fashions of the day and Joshua in his *tux and tails,* doffing his top-hat to the mayoress. When their delightful twins were born, she knew that her happiness was complete.

However, now, as *she* sat on the old homemade *riempie-bench*[136] on the stoep of the humble stone farmhouse, she won-dered how her wonderful dream-life had evaporated so suddenly. "Damn those British," she thought—"those gold-greedy imperial-ists! Had not old man President Kruger himself said that it was not political concessions to the *uitlanders* that the British wanted...? but that the British actually wanted the Boer's *entire country*—and its rich goldmines?" How right he had been. Further, Joshua and Angela discovered that their *very own* neighbor on Terrace Road, a fabulously wealthy Jewish financier, who had dined with them at the Roux's own table, was *also* now rumored to be colluding with the British to gobble up a Boer gold mine or two after the war!

Angela then mechanically stood up, bent over to pick up the old basket next to the bench, and walked emotionlessly over to the henhouse to collect fresh eggs for their breakfast, as she surrendered to reality.

---

[136] *Riempies* ("little reins") are thin rawhide strips, which were laced to form a strong, criss-cross lattice on a bench-frame. These were also woven into long whips to crack above trek-oxen.

Chapter Thirty

General "Reverse" Buller did eventually force his way through to relieve Ladysmith—but at the cost of terrible losses to his own troops. At the vicious Battle of Spionkop, almost within sight of the town, his men were badly mauled again. In fact, so often was the imbalance in the losses between Boer and Brit—that (as at Spionkop) many a clash was truly more of a *massacre,* than a battle.

Perhaps this partially accounted for some of the rather dastardly British conduct during the latter stages of the war: Being unable to beat the Boers, in open battle on the veld, and suffering such heavy losses at the hands of "a rabble of farmers" —some of the less-principled British commanders then resorted to barbaric forms of *revenge.* These extremely "ungentlemanly" forms of revenge which the British exacted against the Boers included: their infamous "razed-earth" policy, their "starvation-camps," and their use of the local black population to loot, terrorize, violate, and humiliate the undefended civilian Boer women and children on their own farms.

Having breasted the towering Spionkop in the misty darkness, the British dug in; but sunrise revealed that they were not on the actual summit of the hill, but merely on a plateau somewhat below it. The Boers soon realized this, and then poured accurate rifle and artillery fire into the shallow, misaligned British trenches from a nearby hill. The carnage was horrific, and more British soldiers died in that small area of about one acre, than in many major battles fought during Britain's long and illustrious military history.[137] Most of the British dead were later found to have been shot clean through

---

[137] One dead trooper's mother later made the long journey from England to plant a tree next to her son's grave on the plateau. That lonely tree still stood a century later, despite having been struck by lightning more than once.

the head (so accurate was the Boer sniper fire) or torn apart by shell fragments. There were so many British dead in one of their long, shallow trenches, that the burial detail needed merely to fill in the trench—already filled with corpses—to provide their final resting place.

Again, the veld commandos were encouraged by their success against the imperialist invaders. But the tide of war was about to turn against the Boers.

Just weeks before General Buller relieved Ladysmith, cavalry Lieut.-Gen. John Denton Pinkstone French[138] (1852-1925) had succeeded in delivering besieged Kimberley. Two days before that—significantly, on the anniversary of the Battle of Majuba—Lord Kitchener had gained a costly victory over the elderly Boer General Piet Cronje at *Paardeberg* ("Horse Mountain"), capturing about 4,000 Boer combatants. Elated British troops even etched "Remember Majuba, Johnny Boer!" on the wall of a ruined Boer farmhouse.

Despite his bungling in the early stages of the battle, Kitchener had gained an advantage by making innovative use of observation balloons at Paardeberg, and thus, it was rather easy for the British to locate Boer troop movements. General De Wet extended a lifeline to Cronje by opening up a corridor for an orderly withdrawl, and after Kitchener's artillery had decimated the corralled Boer horses, De Wet offered to send more mounts. However, the aged Cronje, who still thought and acted in the "old way" (and had even *formed a laager* to "resist" the British) procrastinated, and in the end, the Boer forces were easily trapped by Lords Kitchener and Roberts. The usual mobility of the Boer forces was compromised by their own extensive use of trenches. The presence of many civilians had also slowed down the Boer forces at a time when a quick retreat was necessary (since, at times, many now-homeless women and children tagged along with the Boer troops).

The British public now had two reasons to be hysterical with joy—the news of the lifting of all 3 sieges and, *finally,* a

---

[138] Earl of Ypres, later Lord Field Marshal.

major victory! Their celebrations knew no bounds as newspapers announced, rather prematurely, "Johnny Boer's last grip has been loosened!" In fact, the *hysterical* antics the British public exhibited in their celebration of the lifting of the siege of Mafeking gave rise to a new expression, "to Maffick!"

Cronje's humiliating surrender at the Battle of *Paardeberg*, especially with so many men, was a particularly heavy blow to the Boers, and it was their first major defeat of the bloody war.[139] In that surrender, in one fell swoop, the Boers had lost over 10 percent of all their fighting men.

The Boer army's own "western front" had basically collapsed, and Lord Roberts was soon marching into their Free State capital, Bloemfontein. The British began to believe—*incorrectly,* as it turned out—that victory was now close within their grasp. But the Boers were *far from finished;* they still had most of their men in the veld, and were keen to fight on. The British, rather prematurely, offered an amnesty, but only a few Boers responded: handing in rifles, which, for the most part, were obsolete, Martini-Henry rifles (with British-military insignias stamped into them)—relics of the FIRST ANGLO-BOER WAR, which had been fought *20 years* earlier! The British forces then marched on Pretoria, their troops loudly singing, "We are Mar-ching to Pre-tor-ia! Brit-ann-ia Ru-les the Wa-ves,"[140] as they tromped along.

Thus, both Boer capitals were now in enemy hands and the British anticipated an early Boer surrender. But the highly mobile Boer commandos ignored these losses as the war was about to enter a new, guerrilla phase—one which would cruelly devastate the embattled country.

---

[139] Sadly enough, in later years, the aging Cronje toured with a "Wild West"-type show; and in the climax of this show—day-after-day—Cronje shamefully re-enacted his own humiliating surrender to the British.

[140] Oddly enough, this became a marching-song for later generations of both young Afrikaans and English-speaking conscripts in the future SOUTH AFRICAN UNION DEFENSE FORCE. English speakers are often called *rooinekke* ("rednecks") to this day.

On March 17, 1900, the presidents of the two Boer republics held a *Krygsraad* ("council of war") and an ailing President Kruger made an impassioned appeal to "God's chosen people" not to lose heart. President Marthinus Theunis Steyn (1857-1916) of the ORANGE FREE STATE—which was, of course, no longer "free"—pointed out correctly, that there was much *international sympathy* for the Boers; but once again, any expectations of "help from abroad" were *pipe dreams*. It was up to the individual men and women to defend their embattled Boer nation.

The FREE STATE's new Commandant-General Christiaan Rudolf De Wet (1854-1922), a brilliant tactician, and a man who would become the favorite of foreign supporters of the Boer's republican cause (due to his uncanny ability to slip through the British cordons time and again), proposed 10 days of leave for the commandos to visit their families. With Gideon-like wisdom, he reckoned that those who returned to fight, after being refreshed, would be the best men, who were truly dedicated—and those who did not return, would be no real loss to the commandos.

Generals De Wet and De la Rey would now *take the war to the British* in a different way. When Mafeking was relieved by the British in the second week of May, the Boers had finally learned the folly of tying up their own, very limited numbers in futile sieges against strategically unimportant towns. Lord Roberts had by now crossed the muddy Orange River with *70,000 troops* and about *180 artillery pieces!* Counting Buller's cumbersome force in NATAL, which was also finally on the move, combined with Roberts' force, the Boers, only 30,000 strong, would have to face around *100,000 British troops*—with *thousands* of British reinforcements arriving constantly at both Durban and Cape Town. Therefore, Boer commandos commenced this new phase of warfare by blowing up railways and bridges, and by attacking British convoys and supply lines.

By the time Johannesburg surrendered to British forces at the end of May, Joshua Roux and his family had already been on their farm in the Lowveld for two months—and the Lowveld Commando had *still* not returned to recruit him. Joshua assumed that they had changed their minds and that he would be able to honor his father's dying wish that he stay out of this unwinnable war. However, unfortunately, that assumption was soon proved false. When the British forces triumphantly entered Pretoria, on June 5, President Paul Kruger had already fled to avoid capture and humiliation and arrived unexpectedly by train in the eastern Transvaal. In the interim, Gen. Christiaan De Wet had managed to capture 500 Imperial Yeomen (The Queen's elite Royal Guard). Gen. Louis Botha had mustered 6,000 men and 23 cannons, and was ready to fight on. There was also a new rising military star, General Jan Christiaan Smuts (1870-1950), who was busy raiding into the Cape Colony. The combined forces of Generals De Wet, Botha, Smuts, and the inspirational "Koos" De la Rey—with their guerrilla tactics, would make British lives a *living hell* in South Africa for the rest of that year. British Lord Kitchener then used 30,000 men in a giant "sandwich" to try and trap Gen. De Wet, but failed to pin him down—as he would fail on numerous other occasions. A little-known fact is that, ironically, De Wet's men had allowed to slip through *their* hands, an individual who would have been a most extraordinary captive: After having ambushed a British train, the Boers simply *watched* as a single horseman leaped from one of the open livestock wagons, and galloped off into the night—that horseman was none other than Lord Horatio Kitchener himself!

Finally, the Lowveld Commando, over 100 strong, rode up and camped on Joshua Roux's farm—and waited for his answer concerning whether or not he would accept their offer for him to lead them into battle. Joshua battled within himself the mixed emotions which pulled at his heart, and the conflicting arguments which he played over in his mind. He wanted to stay out of a war in which he stood to lose everything, after having struggled so long and hard to make something of himself. He did not want to jeopardize his family, leaving them bereaved if he should die in battle. He also wanted to fulfill his dying father's last request. However, he was also somewhat relieved when the soldiers did return: for part of him *did* want to *fight* the British: to *expel* those who had once again *invaded* the Afrikaner's sovereign Boer nation with the plan to steal it.

Joshua Roux sat on the "dog's tombstone" alongside his father Jan's fresh grave, and stared out over the cooking fires of the commando camped near his farmhouse. In his mind, he wanted to remain with his family, and to heed his father's advice to stay out of the unwinnable war against the British. But in his heart his warrior's spirit (forged with fire and blood on the battlefield as a young man) stirred within him, filling him with the desire to fulfill his Biblical name and once again be a *deliverer* of his people. The men camped below him were no different from him—apart from his wealth (much of it now buried below where he sat). They too, had wives and children on their humble farms in the Lowveld. They also realized that they were now fighting a deadly guerrilla war of attrition against the invaders, and could expect no quarter in battle, or clemency if captured.

It was rumored that the British intended to deport Boer captives to far-off lands, and had begun *burning* the farms and *demolishing* the homes of those *Bittereinders* who wanted to fight on. This reprehensible, British, terrorist tactic effectively destroyed the Boer commandos' main sources of food and supplies. However, the British treatment of Boer *Hensoppers* who had surrendered early-on was comparatively fairly good. Therefore, many war-weary, naïve Boer *Bittereinders* thought that surrender conditions for them, later in the war, would be the same. Many were already assembling at train depots with their families, with whom they imagined they would be interned in the "concentration camps." These tented concentration camps were now springing up like patches of white mushrooms across the veld.

It was a hard choice, but Joshua Roux could not countenance himself surrendering meekly to the British, without even having fired a single shot in defense of his homeland. He then saw a young *veld-kornet* (a Boer "coronet" or "lieutenant") making his way up the koppie towards him, carrying one of the new Mauser magazine rifles.

"Meneer Roux," the man addressed him, *"miskien as u 'n skoot probeer met die Mauser, sal dit help om jou gedagtes oor die oorlog te laat fokus."* ("Mr. Roux, perhaps if you try a shot with the Mauser, it might help you to focus your thoughts, about the war.") Joshua took the cocked rifle from the young *veld-kornet's* outstretched hand, leaned it in the crook of the tree alongside his father's grave, raised the rear sight to its maximum and took a bead on a prominent white rock (roughly about the same size as a Tommie's helmet) almost half-a-mile away. His shot shattered the rock. He handed back the Mauser, and then noticed that all the men in the camp below had fallen silent, and were looking up at him. *"Dis 'n goeie geweer!"* Joshua declared. ("This is a good rifle!") A cheer went up from the men below, and when Joshua Roux walked into the cottage at sunset, his wife knew that he had finally made up his mind—he would indeed lead the commando against the British.

They rode out at sunrise the next morning, Joshua having assured his tearful wife and silent mother that his commando had orders only to operate within their own district, and that he would try to make regular visits back to them on the farm. Young James Roux thought his father very brave and valiant, riding off to war at the head of his commando, and shook his father's hand good-bye, manfully. But little Julia wept bitterly, and clung to her daddy's arm, before being led away by her mother. When the dust from the horses' hooves had settled, Erika Roux walked slowly up the koppie to her husband's grave, and in a silent prayer asked the Good Lord to watch over their headstrong son.

Chapter Thirty-one

It was only 10 days after Joshua Roux had left the farm, leading the Lowveld Commando into battle against the encroaching enemy, that a British patrol arrived outside the stone farmhouse. Accompanying the 10 *Tommies* were as many armed, mounted blacks. The Roux's big tan Boerboel, unaccustomed to the scent of the black men, approached the nearest black trooper and bared his fangs threateningly. The soldier matter-of-factly cocked his rifle and shot the dog. The shrill screams of the two children were drowned out by the British corporal loudly announcing, in English, in a mechanical tone, Her Majesty's Eviction Notice and Arrest Order. As he broadcasted this outrage he indifferently ignored the angry glares and astonished expressions of Erika Roux and her distraught daughter-in-law. The terms of the Order, signed by Lord Kitchener himself, stipulated that:

1. *All* of the buildings on the Roux family's farm are to be *destroyed*—for having harbored combatants;

2. *All* of the Roux family's field and orchard crops and all of their livestock are to be *confiscated*[141]—for having supplied the commandos with food;

3. *All* of the fruit trees in the orchard on the Roux family's farm are to be *chopped down, the stumps thereof poisoned and the fields burned*—to prevent the commandos from obtaining food in the future; and

4. The women and children on the Roux family farm are to be escorted to the nearest concentration camp—for their own safety.

Obviously, British intelligence sources were good. The corporal then folded the document and tucked it back into the breast-pocket of his khaki tunic, before ordering his men to carry out the instructions. The soldiers immediately began rounding up the red Afrikander oxen and cows, and catching the

---

[141] —which would then be fed to the very *British* troops (and their black recruits) who were fighting against the Boers.

poultry, laughing when one of the chickens made a dash for the open, but was stopped dead by a large stone thrown at it. Others stripped what fruit hung in the little orchard, and then began chopping down the trees and anointing the stumps thereof with a virulent poison. Three soldiers barged roughly past the proud old Boer lady standing defiantly in her doorway, and began rummaging through the trunks and homemade cupboards, pocketing any valuable items they came across.

When Angela Roux rounded on the corporal and began berating him in perfect English about the behavior of his men, the surprised soldier took her aside and explained in his Cockney accent: "Sorry missus, but we'ze jus' followin' orders. The Lowveld Commando, led by your 'usband, blew up a railway bridge jus' behind ol' man Kruger's train, an' then shot up a British unit tryin' to repair it. So the men feel a bit strongly— like, an' you cain't really blame 'em!"

He then turned away and began to supervise the blacks as they loaded up onto *the Roux's own* battered oxwagon, sundry items, which the British soldiers considered useful to the Crown; such as: the Roux's blankets and bedding, shovels and buckets, fire-irons and pots, food, and dried meats. At the same time others of the black troops harnessed a team of Erika Roux's oxen. On the corporal's orders, the two women hastily packed two small trunks with warm clothing and some toiletries, and then stood waiting and watching. The twins hid behind their mother's skirt: little Julia clutching her favorite doll (which she was fortunate enough to grab and which the soldiers "graciously" allowed her to keep); young James watching intently as two *Tommies* carried a small, but obviously heavy wooden box marked "Explosives-Demolition." They carried the crate into the cottage and placed it alongside the stone hearth. The corporal then ordered Erika, Angela, and the twins onto the wagon, but little James lingered and continued to watch the surreal event with wide, expressionless eyes. The soldiers then lit the corner of the thatched roof of the cottage with a brand from the fireplace. The flame soon took, and within minutes, the roof was ablaze. The corporal finally lifted young James Roux onto the wagon, and ordered the black soldier standing at the head of the inspanned oxen to lead them off. When they were about a hundred yards from the cottage, the blazing thatch collapsed, and a minute or two later, a deafening explosion rent the air—and each of the Roux family jumped in their seats. Erika Roux looked back as the pieces of the house flew in all directions: the thick beams, which her late husband had hewn from the riverine forest 4 decades earlier, shattered into splinters and the heavy stones which he had dragged down from the hills (and then painstakingly stacked to form the walls of their cottage), showered down in pieces all over what was once their yard. In answer to Angela's anxiously whispered query as to the whereabouts of her husband's old firearms and cutlass, Erika quietly replied that, before his departure, Joshua had wrapped them in oilcloths, and buried them a safe distance from the cottage.

The British corporal, fearing that any Boer commando in the vicinity may have heard the explosion and then headed in that direction to investigate, quickly dismounted and ran to the top of the koppie nearest the farmhouse to gain a better view of the surrounding bushveld. Seeing nothing, he then decided to take the opportunity to relieve himself on the small, carefully etched tombstone of the dear old, departed "dog" named Cecil, "who loved to dig in holes" according to the Afrikaans inscription: *"Hy het baie gehou om in gate te grouw."* Adjusting the fly of his trousers, the Tommie quickly made his way back down the hill, passing the shattered, smoldering ruins of old Erika Roux's home and the burning fields; barely giving the scene of their crime a second glance. Little did Corporal "Tommy Atkins" know of course, that he had just urinated on a small fortune in Kruger Rands.

On the bumpy wagon journey to the nearest rail junction, Angela Roux was inconsolable. Her sobs eventually prompted her young son to put his arm around his mother's heaving shoulders, and peck her tenderly on a tear-stained cheek. Little Julia sat on Ouma Erika's lap, and snuggled under her grandmother's knitted shawl against the winter chill. During their search, the black soldiers had found a jug of citrus brandy in the shed alongside the small orange orchard, and they now surreptitiously passed it among themselves, being careful not to be noticed by the British corporal. Soon, the one who had managed to consume the most began leering at Angela Roux, and when he maneuvered his mount closer to the wagon and reached out to feel the silky blond hair cascading from under her bonnet, she gave his horse a sharp slap on its rump, whereupon it started, and threw the inebriated rider into a nearby donga! The twins laughed gaily at this sight—and for a brief moment—forgot that they were on their way to a *prison camp*.

President Paul Kruger, having fled Pretoria by train, on May 30, 1900, to avoid capture by the British, sat disconsolately in his railway carriage, looking at a map of his beloved country. His adjutant, using a *red* pencil, had shaded-in those areas which were now ostensibly under *enemy* control. Cecil Rhodes' imperialist dream of *painting the map red* "from Cape to Cairo" appeared to be fast becoming a reality. Other than Portuguese Mozambique, for which Kruger was now heading, and German South West Africa, the map directly to the north of the SOUTH AFRICAN REPUBLIC, was entirely red. To the south NATAL, and of course the EASTERN and WESTERN CAPES, had been taken over by the British long ago. Now, the gold-rich TRANSVAAL and the ORANGE FREE STATE (which itself had substantial gold deposits) had also largely been shaded in with the red pencil.

The old president, with a sigh, put the map aside and looked out of the carriage window. He waved sadly to Joshua Roux and his men, who were riding alongside the train. They raised their hats in salute and cheered him, but their smiles were weak and strained. The Lowveld Commando now saw action on an almost-daily basis. Their old president too, had been forced to leave his beloved wife behind, and like them, he was now adrift on the veld, playing cat-and-mouse with the rapidly advancing British. A new strategy of raiding into the CAPE COLONY in the hope of arousing a Boer uprising there and diverting the British forces, although fairly successful, was not decisive, and Louis Botha's sally into NATAL had also been turned back. General

Botha had actually met with Lord Kitchener in Middelburg on February 28, but they could not come to an agreement; so the war dragged on.

As the president's train headed slowly east across the plains of the Highveld towards Delagoa Bay, he had seen the women and children of his *volk* ("people") already gathering at the railway sidings in anticipation of the British army's arrival. They waved bravely to their fleeing president, and his rheumy old eyes filled with tears at the sight. Kruger wondered now if his decision to resist the might of the BRITISH EMPIRE had been a wise one. When the British were closing in on the Witwatersrand, he had seriously considered the prospect of surrender, to save the precious lives of his volk. But President Steyn of the ORANGE FREE STATE (their faithful allies) had been furious at the suggestion. Having been drawn into the war by the TRANSVAAL, he and his people had made heavy sacrifices for the republican cause, and Steyn believed that the Transvaalers should not be so hasty as to consider surrender when the advancing enemy reached their borders.

The last formal battle of the war had taken place east of Pretoria at Diamond Hill—or *Donkerhoek* ("Dark Corner") as the Boers called it—where General Louis Botha had managed to hold up the British advance, but had then withdrawn just in time. Now, Generals De la Rey, De Wet and Smuts were ranging far and wide across the veld, attacking their enemy in a series of lightning raids. Joshua Roux's Lowveld Commando, which now escorted the presidential train, was just one of scores of such commando units: who were like so many tiny Boer terriers snapping at the heels of the big British bulldog. They darted in, bit hard on any exposed portion— and then quickly retreated as the lumbering, angry British army turned to face them.

The British then accelerated their barbaric "scorched earth" policy of burning Boer farms to deprive the commandos of supplies. The British also were busily engaged in a new and very costly, labor-intensive military enterprise: the construction of *thousands* of "blockhouses," which also had fences of barbed wire strung between them. In an effort to end the war, the British used these structures in their attempt to "corral" and *drive* the commandos into them; to capture them like herds of wild game. Flying columns of cavalry and mounted infantry, made up of British and Colonial units, now tried to challenge the Boers at their own game—and were having some, limited success.

As the presidential train progressed eastwards, keeping just ahead of the British demolition *sapper* engineers, the heartbroken "Oom Paul" Kruger slowly and reluctantly headed towards exile from his beloved country and his grieving Volk. At various stops along the way, arms and ammunition were allegedly offloaded and stashed for use by the Bittereinder commandos still holding out, and even a temporary "government in exile" was set up in the new Lowveld town of *Nelspruit* ("Nel's creek"), to see to the administration of the fast-collapsing Boer republic. It was also widely rumored that a huge fortune in solid-gold coins was hidden with great secrecy in various caves in the eastern TRANSVAAL, to fund an anticipated drawn-out resistance struggle. These so-called "Kruger Millions" were never again spoken of and have never been discovered. President Kruger eventually made his way safely to Delagoa Bay, and onto a warship, the cruiser "De Gelderland,"[142] which had been sent by the Dutch Queen Emma of Nassau (1858-1934), which then whisked him off to Europe. But the Boers fought on.

When Joshua Roux decided that the exhausted men of his commando needed a break from the fighting, he had sent them back to their farms, with orders to re-assemble at his farm after 10 days. When Joshua, who was riding alone, cleared the Sabie Ridge overlooking his mother's farmhouse, his heart sank. The stone cottage that his father had built lay in ruins, there was no sign of his mother and his family, their livestock was gone, the crops had been burned and the citrus orchard had been chopped

---

[142] "The Gelderland" (a province in the Netherlands). This was one of the rare occasions in which the Boers ever received "help from abroad."

down. Joshua was outraged and thought to himself that the British themselves, being quite familiar with the Bible, should have known that God forbade His people to carry out such evil deeds—even against their enemies (Deuteronomy 20:19,20). How much more shameful were such British war crimes—when committed against their own cousins! In their lustful greed, the *great missionary nation of the world,* violated the commands written in the very Word of God, which they sought to teach to *other,* "less-civilized" peoples.

The skull of the faithful Boerboel, which the black soldier had shot, had been picked clean by scavengers and lay near the stoep. Joshua Roux sat on the koppie alongside his father's grave, overlooking their ruined farm, and wept silent tears. His father had been right—he should have stayed out of this "unwinnable war" with the British. But, he reasoned to himself, even if he had not fought himself, their fate may have been the same: for there is no way he would have refused sharing food and supplies with the Boer commandos when they were in need.

Chapter Thirty-two

When the remaining members of the Lowveld Commando began drifting in to their commandant's farm after their short leave, they found Joshua camped in the ruins of his mother's cottage. He had managed to shoot a bushbuck and had smoked some of the meat, so his stomach had been filled, but his soul was desolate, and it showed. He looked gaunt. The weight he had put on during his years on the goldfields had long since been shed; but now he looked ragged. His thick hair was wild, and his beard, which had grown long in the months on commando, was unkempt. His clothing, like all of theirs, was tattered by the thorns, and his *velskoene* ("raw-hide shoes") had worn through from rubbing on the stirrups. Of the hundred-or-so original members of his commando, less than 60 now sat silently around him. They had lost 20 men to British bullets, and equally as many again had decided to surrender at the railway sidings, after finding their farms in ruins, and their own families gone. Joshua Roux now looked into the faces of his men, their hollow eyes haunted by their losses and hardships. He saw farm boys in their teens, sitting alongside their fathers, and grizzled old men. All had one thing in common—they had lost everything.

"Wat sê julle, manne?" Joshua asked. ("What do you say, men?") "Do we surrender to the *Tommies* and go and join our womenfolk in the camps, or do we fight on?" A murmur went through the assembled Boers, and one man stepped forward. His name was Jonathan Du Plessis and he explained that he had dared to sneak up to the barbed-wire fence of the concentration camp near Barberton, where he had heard that his wife and family were interned. It was the dead of night, but he had managed to attract the attention of a man relieving himself near the fence. The old man, whom he recognized as one of the farmers from his district, had then told him that his own elderly wife and his young grandchild had died of cholera soon after

arriving there; due to the poor sanitation in the camp. The farmer had heard that there were as many as 40 such prison camps now, confining well over 100,000 Boer civilians, and that there had been *many* deaths. When asked if he knew of Mevrou Marie Du Plessis, the farmer had replied, sadly, that she was no more. What of his young son, a devastated Du Plessis had then asked? The farmer shook his head, and had then hurried back to his tent, because a *Tommie* guard was approaching.

On his journey back to meet up with his commando at Olifantshoek, Jonathan Du Plessis had passed many farms— all of them desolate and in ruins. Then he had come across a Boer woman and her teenage daughter, sitting under a tree in the veld, their clothes torn, their faces dirty and bruised. They told him that a patrol of armed and mounted blacks, recruited by the British, had intercepted them as they were making their way on foot to hand themselves over at one of the concentration camps. The woman and her daughter had been raped by the blacks and their meager possessions stolen. The patrol had then abandoned them in the veld to die; where Du Plessis had found them.

In the absolute silence of the seated commando, Jonathan Du Plessis went on to explain that he had given the famished woman and her daughter his last bag of biltong, which they devoured, and he had then escorted them as close to one of the railway sidings as he dared, before riding off. As far as he knew, his own small family was now dead, his farm was ruined, and he thus had nothing left to lose. Du Plessis wanted to fight on, he wanted the commando to attack the damned British devils wherever they could. At this pronouncement, a faint cheer went up from the ragged men of the Lowveld Commando and they had soon saddled up their gaunt ponies, redistributed their remaining ammunition and meager food supplies evenly between them, and prepared to ride out. By now, quite a few of the Boers of that commando were carrying British .303 Lee-Enfield rifles; for which it was now much easier to obtain cartridges—which they "borrowed" from the *Tommies* themselves. It seemed appropriate, thought

Joshua Roux, that the *Tommies* might now be killed with their own bullets, fired from rifles made in England.

When the Lowveld Commando crested the Sabie Ridge, and then rode steadily across the bushveld to attack one of the British blockhouses now spanning the countryside, they passed a ruined farmhouse close to the track. A few chickens were scratching in the dust of the farmyard, and then one of Joshua's men noticed a black face peering fearfully at them from behind one of the shattered walls. On investigating, they found a family of 6 blacks inhabiting the ruins. They had fashioned a shelter from some of the pieces of corrugated roof sheeting lying about, and when questioned in their own language by one of the Boers who could speak the lingo, they revealed that they had been given permission by the British patrol who had demolished it, to "take over" the "abandoned" farm, since two of their adult brothers had helped the *Tommies* to "round up the cattle." Some outraged men of the commando wanted to execute the blacks then-and-there, but their commandant had a better idea. He calmly ordered the blacks to bundle up a few short lengths of wood and clumps of grass in some pieces of cloth. He then made them walk about 50 yards ahead of the commando, with rifles trained on them lest they should try to flee. This procession then approached the nearest blockhouse manned by black "British-auxiliary" troops.

When Auxiliary-Corporal Ziva Gomelo peered out of the rifle-slot of the blockhouse, he saw approaching 6 members of his own family, bearing bundles of what he assumed was food. The British army rations that he and his section had been issued were sparse, and although the tinned "bully-beef" was nutritious and kept well, the hard biscuits were tasteless and stale. He noticed his wife walking to the fore with a bundle on her head, and he quickly descended the steps inside the blockhouse to open the iron door. If she had brought some home-brewed sorghum beer with her, she would be most welcome to stay the night, and "comfort" him downstairs on his cot. All 7 members of his section now walked out to meet the arrivals, their Lee-Enfield rifles slung carelessly over their shoulders. It was only when their corporal fell backwards, shot through the head, that the other black soldiers realized that they were under attack by Boers. The crackle of rifle shots from the nearby copse of trees caused the bundle-carrying civilians to throw themselves prone on the ground, and not one of the black soldiers made it back to the safety of the block-house. Soon, the shocked civilians had fled back towards "their" farm, and then Joshua Roux's men swiftly stripped the blockhouse of any ammunition and tinned food they could find. The section manning the next British blockhouse only a mile away frantically tried to use their newly installed telephone to call their comrades, but the line had been cut. So they signaled with a mirror to the small fort at the nearest railway junction who may also have heard the shots, and a platoon of 30 mounted *Tommies* soon set out in determined pursuit of the Lowveld Commando; unaware that they were up against 60 battle-hardened Boers. Joshua Roux and his men then laid an ambush for the British, and when the detachment rode through a narrow gap between two koppies, they mowed them down with accurate rifle fire from the rocks above.

"Bloody *rockspiders!*" shouted the British sergeant angrily as his horse suddenly crumpled under him, and he sprawled in the dust, the last of his men to fall. When he felt a Boer *velskoen* tramp hard on his outstretched arm as he scrambled on his knees towards his fallen rifle, he knew that they had something in mind for him, other than a bullet. *"Staan op, Tommie!"* bellowed their commandant, a big man with wild brown hair and an unkempt beard, his fierce green eyes glowering under the brim of his hat. The sergeant rose slowly to his feet, hands raised in the air, and was soon surrounded by grim-faced Boers. He looked about him and noted that they were all ragged and gaunt, and that quite a few of them were carrying British rifles. In perfect English, Joshua Roux then informed the sergeant that they would let him live, on the condition that he delivered a message to the commander of the British concentration camp near Barberton. He was to tell Mevrou Angela Roux that her husband sent his best regards, and that he hoped that she, their children and his mother Erika, were well. Further, he was to pass on the best wishes of all the men in the Lowveld Commando to any of their relatives still surviving in the camp.

"What is your name, Sergeant?" Joshua asked. On hearing that his name was Wilson, the men of the commando then assured Sergeant Wilson that they would definitely come and "get him" if he did not deliver their messages to their families. He promised to do so and they stood and watched him ride off in the direction of Barberton, on one of his platoon's surviving horses; but without his rifle, of course. When the galloping Sergeant Wilson had disappeared over a ridge, the rest of the men of the Lowveld Commando began hurriedly stripping the khaki tunics, bandoleers and hobnailed boots from the bodies of the dead British soldiers, and putting on themselves whatever happened to fit reasonably well. Soon, the commando rode out, after having pulled the 29 stripped bodies into a neat row alongside the dusty track; where the corpses would await the eventual arrival of a British burial party. Now, about half of Joshua's men were wearing British tunics, but he warned them to remove any insignia (and to take no British helmets) to prevent their being shot as spies if captured by the British—and to prevent their being mistaken for Tommies and ambushed by another Boer commando.

When Sergeant Wilson dutifully reported to the commander of the sprawling, tented concentration-camp in the veld near Barberton, the first thing that struck him about the place was the stench of death. He saw a burial-party on the outskirts of the camp, lowering numerous tiny wooden coffins into graves alongside rows of scores of white crosses and mounds of fresh earth of those already buried. Major Woods, a greying, kindly looking man from the Medical Corps was temporarily in charge of the camp. He looked tired and drawn, and bemoaned the fact that he had not been able to keep the death-rate in the camp from rising; due to the poor quality and meager supplies of the food rations for the prisoners, and the lack of even basic medical equipment and disinfectants. The major hardly heard the sergeant explaining that his platoon had been wiped out that morning, and that he had a message for him. The major was distracted by the entrance to his field hospital of a well-dressed Englishwoman. In her strong Cornish accent, she berated Major Woods about the location of the field toilets too close to the creek that supplied a trickle of muddy water to the camp. This single, easily correctable mistake was greatly responsible for the poor health (and deaths) of even the sturdiest of the Boer women and children; who were now suffering badly from dysentery.

"How many children have you buried this week, Major Woods?" Emily Hobhouse (1860-1926) demanded to know. The harried major replied that it was 30 that week; up from just over 20 the previous week. "Outrageous! You should be ashamed of yourself!" she chided. "I am going to make a full report on the appalling conditions in these 'death-camps,' to the newspapers, and *especially* to the BRITISH PARLIAMENT when I get back to London, and you can rest assured that *your* name will be prominent on my list of culpable camp-commanders, Major Woods!" With that, she stomped out of the reeking field hospital in a huff. When Sergeant Wilson next saw her, she was carrying a crate of bread-loaves past the doorway, on her way down to the long lines of tents, followed by a number of orderlies bearing more crates.

A few rows of benches had hastily been formed into an outdoor school in anticipation of Emily Hobhouse's visit, and some of the stronger children were attending rudimentary classes, but Emily soon noticed that the medium of instruction was English only. One child sat with a sign reading "donkey" hanging around his neck. She asked a Boer mother observing the instruction what the meaning of the sign was. The mother told her that the Afrikaans phrase for "many thanks" was *baie dankie;* which sounded rather like "buy a donkey" to the Anglo ear. Therefore, the English orderly now in charge of the "educational" classes had adopted the sign as an insulting *punishment* for any Boer child who dared to speak in Afrikaans within his earshot.

The major sat with his head in his hands and his elbows propped on his cluttered desk. Before him were long, alphabetical lists of the inmates of the camp, many of whose names had already been scratched out by the medical orderlies assigned the task of burying the dead; the date of death of the deceased was scrawled next to each name. "What was that name you asked for, Sergeant?" the major asked in a tired voice, as he fitted his wire-rimmed reading-glasses over his nose, and peered over the lists. "Roux, Major. Missus Angela Roux, her mother-in-law Erika, and some kids," Sergeant Wilson replied hopefully.

Major Woods scanned the lists, then stopped, and looked up over his glasses. "Sorry, Sergeant, but the Roux twins were both buried last week. Here are their names right here: James and Julia Roux, twins aged 8—in the same coffin, by the way. It's the dysentery, you see. Kills the youngsters in just a week or so. I remember them now, well-spoken, well-educated kids. Must have come from a good home. Angela Roux, their mother, is still alive—but just barely. Quite the classy lady, that one. And the old girl, her mother-in-law, Erika, too. Tough old bird, she is. Came barging in here just the other day, now that I recall. Wanted something to calm her daughter, who was absolutely hysterical about the deaths of her twins. Couldn't help her, of course. All the medicine is going to the troops. They still seem to be getting quite a pasting from Johnny Boer, eh? And this despite old Lord Kitchener's *infamously expensive* blockhouse scheme! Did you say that your *entire* platoon was wiped out, Sergeant? Damned shame. I do wish the Boers would call it quits now; there's no disgrace in surrender, once you realize you are up against a superior. The Boers are being shipped off to Ceylon and St. Helena Island if they're captured now, poor blighters."

With that, the major rose, and hurried off in the direction taken by Emily Hobhouse, calling back over his shoulder that Sergeant Wilson was welcome to deliver his message personally, to tent number 243, row D. By the time the major got past the coffin-makers and the latrines, he was feeling quite ill himself.

Sergeant Wilson walked slowly down the long rows of sun-bleached white bell-shaped tents, searching for D-243. Here and there, he saw emaciated Boer women, and the occasional old man, sitting disconsolately in the winter sunshine. The rest of them seemed to be lying in the tents, obviously too weak to move. The stench that he had smelt in the field hospital was here, too. He saw a few children sitting on the ground; thin and drawn, and they looked back at him with dull, hollow eyes. Nearby, a pretty young Boer mother sat rocking her dead baby in her arms, weeping inconsolably. One old man slowly came up to him, and grasped his arm with bony fingers. He asked in his broken English if the commandos were still fighting in the veld. Sergeant Wilson replied that they indeed were; whereupon the old man smiled a toothless grin, and then turned away, his thin shoulders suddenly squaring up and a little spring noticeable in his step.

Finally, Wilson came to the correct tent and peered into the dark interior. A young woman, her wavy blond hair spread out on the pillow, lay on the cot. Beside her was a chamber pot full of vomit, a battered tin plate of stale bread-crusts, and a mug of cloudy water. Wilson could see that she was dying; her jaundiced skin stretched as thin as parchment on her prominent cheek-bones. A much older woman, who appeared to be in somewhat better health, rose slowly and then emerged from the odoriferous tent and asked him what he wanted.

Taking off his helmet, Sergeant Wilson told Erika Roux that he had a message from her son. The younger woman on the bed opened her eyes and tried to sit up, but was too weak. "He said to give you his regards, Mevrou, you and Missus Angela Roux, and the...." His voice tailed off as he realized that it was now pointless to mention their children. "He also said that the men of Joshua Roux's commando want to send their best wishes to their own families here, and that they themselves are all well." He had added that last bit of information, thinking it appropriate, despite the tired and tattered commando he had seen after the ambush. Mevrou Erika Roux thanked him for the message and informed him that she would pass the word along to the other appropriate families—those that were still alive. She then went back inside the tent to console her daughter-in-law, who was now sobbing quietly into her pillow.

When they had first arrived at the Barberton concentration camp, Angela Roux had determinedly set about trying to improve the living conditions of the inmates, and those of the many children, in particular. She had organized games and an open-air school for the children, and conducted many of the lessons herself. She had become involved in the field-kitchens, trying to eke out as much goodness as possible from the low-grade greens and other withered (and even rotting) vegetables provided by the British for the Boers in the camps. She used what parts of the vegetables she could salvage, and made nutritious broths—stews were not an option, since they were given no fresh meat. She had even complained bitterly to the camp-commander, Major Woods, about some of his men watering their horses in the same tiny stream that provided drinking-water for the camp: as the horses' hooves and droppings polluted their only supply of water. Angela Roux and her old mother-in-law Erika had become familiar, dignified figures around the sprawling camp. These two Boer Florence Nightingales visited the sick, dressed sores on inmates (who were *turned away* by the ill-equipped field hospital), and generally helped to keep spirits up by words of encouragement and pitching in to help wherever help was needed.

But when *her own* beloved twins had fallen gravely ill with the epidemics now ravaging the camp, Angela's brave face had swiftly crumbled and as she held their wasted young frames to her bosom, her heart had failed her. When little Julia—and then James one day later—had died in her arms, she was inconsolable. Once their emaciated young bodies were buried in the same coffin—on her insistence—she herself began to fade away. She stayed in her cot, refusing to eat even the crusts of bread that Erika occasionally managed to scavenge for her at the kitchens. Erika Roux had longed for news of her son Joshua, hoping that any confirmation that he was still alive, somewhere on the veld, would give Angela some hope and a reason to live, knowing that her husband was safe. But no such encouragement had come—until now—and Erika feared that the welcome news had come *too late*. Angela Roux was too far gone.

Having delivered his message, Sergeant Wilson galloped hard away as the gates of the death-camp swung shut behind him, and he hoped that as he rode, the wind would clear that dreadful stench from his uniform and he breathed deeply to cleanse his nostrils. He had not gone more than a few miles along the narrow track towards his unit's headquarters at the rail junction, when a group of Boers stepped out from behind some trees, rifles leveled. He reined-in his sweating horse.

"Did you deliver the message, Sergeant Wilson?" Commandant Joshua Roux asked gruffly through his tangled beard. Sergeant Wilson replied that he had indeed. "And to whom did you deliver it?" he was then asked. Wilson told him that he had delivered it to Mevrou Erika Roux in person, and that she looked well. The Boers had by then crowded around the nervous sergeant, and listened intently as he spoke. When Joshua asked how his wife and children were, Sergeant Wilson looked at the ground, and replied that Missus Angela Roux did not look at all well, and that he had not seen the two children. Their commandant then turned away, but the other men pressed closer, demanding to know if Wilson had come across anyone by this-or-that name, or if he had seen a particular person fitting this-or-that description? Wilson had to reply apologetically in the negative to all their anxious questions, by telling them that he was unable to remember any names, but that Erika Roux had promised to pass the word on to the other families. When the Boers finally realized that he could tell them nothing more about their families, the British sergeant asked if he could now get back to his own unit. The Boers then stood aside to let him through, and he noted that many of them were now wearing the uniforms of the dead men from his own platoon; some tunics bearing blood-stained bullet holes; others just splatter. With a stifled sigh of relief, Sergeant Wilson rode off. When he finally got back to his own unit's headquarters, Wilson was astounded that no-one, not even his commanding officer, seemed particularly interested in his story—other than noting that he no longer had his rifle and that he was the sole survivor from his platoon. It was only then that Sergeant Wilson heard the news that seemed to be occupying everyone's attention. Queen Victoria had died, and the *entire* BRITISH EMPIRE was in mourning.

At another concentration camp, near the hamlet of Bethulie, the Boer women interned there watched in despair as the burials of their children inexorably rose to almost 30 per day. Yet they held fast to the promise of God in Matthew 10, verses 26-31:

"Fear them not therefore: for there is nothing covered, that shall not be revealed; and hid, that shall not be known. What I tell you in darkness, that speak ye in light: and what ye hear in the ear, that preach ye upon the house-tops. And fear not them which kill the body, but are not able to kill the soul: but rather fear him which is able to destroy both body and soul in hell. Are not two sparrows sold for a farthing? And one of them will not fall on the ground without your Father (knowing). But the very hairs of your head are all numbered. Fear ye not therefore, ye are of more value than many sparrows."

[Sometime after the end of the war, the surviving women of that camp (in which 1,800 civilians, mainly children, had perished) approached the widow of former-President Steyn of the ORANGE FREE STATE, and requested her influence in ensuring that the smallest coin minted in the country would bear the impression of two *mossies* ("sparrows"). This was duly carried out, and the tradition maintained until a new, black government came into power over 90 years after that devastating war, whereupon that minting was discontinued.]

Of the 116,000 Boer civilians interned by the British in concentration camps, an estimated *27,000* died—nearly 1 out of 4—most of them children, and mainly of diseases like cholera, measles and dysentery; but many also from malnutrition. Lord Kitchener had set *two distinct* "grades" of food rations for the prisoners; both of them poor—but the *poorest one* was for those families whose men had refused to surrender. It was a malicious, calculated, slow starvation.

The seed of hate had thus been sown, once again, in ground fertilized with Boer blood, watered by Boer tears. Emily

Hobhouse duly reported the dismal camp conditions and mass mortalities to a horrified British public and to a *noticeably less-sympathetic* BRITISH PARLIAMENT. The fate of the many black and colored servants of the Boers interned in separate British concentration camps was equally dire and also resulted in many mortalities. It is doubtful any of *these* blacks or coloreds appreciated the British "liberating them" *from the Boers*. It is not recorded if that blessed Cornish "angel of mercy" ever visited any of those "black" camps. Her concern for the plight of the Boer women and children earned Emily Hobhouse an enduring place in the hearts of the Boers—she was buried at the foot of *die Vrouemonument* ("the Women's Memorial") in Bloemfontein and, a few decades later, a new vessel in the South African navy was named in her honor.[143]

---

[143] However, when the "New Regime," the first *black* South African government—under the Xhosa-dominated AFRICAN NATIONAL CONGRESS (ANC)—came to power, the vessel lovingly named after that feminine symbol of compassion was callously and militantly renamed *Mkhonto* ("spear"). This simple act should have been a harbinger of the real intentions of this "new government" which was hailed by Western *liberals* as a champion of "peace" and "democracy."

Chapter Thirty-three

By 1902, the British had erected *18,000* blockhouses (spaced about a mile apart), which were manned by sentries, ever on the look out, and tens of thousands of troops (many of them black). These blockhouses penned in the Boers, restricting their movement, and also guarded strategic areas, such as rail junctions and bridges, river-fords and towns. Some of these blockhouses were built from *pre-fabricated iron, shipped over from England.* Others were built from local stone—and a century later, many still stood as silent sentinels on the veld; enduring symbols of an empire on which the sun did, finally, set.[144] Local blacks also informed the British of any movements of Boer commandos—for the reward they would receive (either money or the coveted Boer cattle).

However, at the dawn of the 20th Century, Britain was still at the peak of her powers. Hundreds of thousands of imperial troops now ranged far and wide across the rugged South African veld, mounting massive sweeps to drive the remaining *Bittereinder* Boer commandos into the *thousands of miles* of barbed wire stretched between the blockhouses. But the rewards from such a hugely expensive operation were paltry. Less than 4,000 Boers were flushed and trapped by this method, roughly 1 single Boer commando member for every 4 or 5 blockhouses! The legendary General De la Rey showed that he was still unbowed however, by routing, and then capturing British General Lord Methuen at *Tweebosch* ("Two bushes"). General De Wet continued to elude all attempts to corner him, Generals Jan Smuts and Louis Botha

---

[144] Rudyard Kipling himself wrote a moving, yet unflattering poem, titled, "Recessional." It lamented the deteriorating state of the British Empire and hearkened to God's ancient people to return their eyes to Him. His poem did not curry him much favor with the Royalty. He wrote it for Queen Victoria's DIAMOND JUBILEE, in 1897. See **Appendix C.**

raided into the CAPE COLONY and NATAL respectively, and Commandant Joshua Roux and his men became the scourge of the Lowveld. By this time, however, the Boer commandos still in the veld were starving, ragged, and low on ammunition. What game they could shoot and eat, they did. What enemy uniforms they could capture, they wore. What cartridges they could steal from the British—they fired back at them.

Conditions in the concentration camps had been improved somewhat, thanks to Emily Hobhouse and the recommendations of the FAWCETT COMMISSION, despite Lord Kitchener and the British War Office's attempts to cover up the huge numbers of Boer civilian mortalities.

In Johannesburg, Sean O'Connor had been waiting patiently at the Roux mansion for the arrival of the "olde enemy"—and arrive they eventually did. As his wise boss had predicted, most of the gold mines had ground to a halt, and Joshua Roux had thus fortunately also been proved correct in his subsequent decision to sell-off his big security business to a British entrepreneur while it was still worth a fortune. When the immaculately uniformed and high-ranking adjutant rode up to the palatial Doornfontein mansion to proclaim it the new auxiliary headquarters of the British High-Command, and a residence for their top echelons, the hulking red-haired Irishman in the front doorway simply unfurled a document that his employer had drafted, and proffered it to the British officer. It was a lease-contract for the property, outlining the terms, conditions and the rental amount, which was substantial. The British officer adjusted his monocle, then perused the formal contract with a raised eyebrow, but eventually signed it on behalf of his superiors.

His work there being done, Sean O'Connor tucked a copy of the lease into his pocket, then rode down to the livestock auction yard, and purchased two sturdy mules, which were saddled with an exorbitant price by that stage of the war. Inflation had run rampant, paper money had lost much of its face-value and even basic essentials were now very expensive. Good, fresh food was hard to come by, due to the British Army's callous destruction of the Boer farms and their devastation of the agricultural economy. Sean then led the mules to a hardware store and had soon loaded them with picks and shovels, pots and pans and all the other accoutrements of a gold-panning prospector. His next destination was the railway station, where he had his own horse, the two mules and his "mining equipment" loaded onto a train departing for the eastern TRANSVAAL.

A fellow passenger, a young Jewish lawyer by the name of Sam Goldberg, informed Sean that he was heading for the growing Lowveld town of *Nelspruit* ("Nel's creek"), to establish a legal practice there. He also informed Sean that he had an *Irish* partner by the name of McGinty, who was on the same train, hunting up some libations. *Nelspruit* itself briefly held the honor of being the temporary "capital" of the Republic—as the seat of the *displaced* Boer government. Sam had recently qualified as an attorney, and *en route* to Nelspruit, he planned to visit his older brother, who had recently taken over the bank in Lydenburg from their father, the late Hiram Goldberg. McGinty himself eventually appeared from the dining car clutching two bottles of *Tullamore Dew*, and after being introduced to his countryman, Sean O'Connor, McGinty graciously presented him with one of the bottles.

Their concern at the prospect of their train being derailed by an attack by the dreaded Lowveld Commando soon vanished along with the whiskey. There was nary a drop left in the bottles by the time the train arrived in Lydenburg, and it was some time before the three men even realized that the train had stopped! When Sean eventually disembarked, the 4 British sentries guarding the station platform hardly noticed the rather unsteady, jovial Irish prospector leading his laden mules—dubbed *Jack* and *Jenny*— through their security cordon. Within that week, "gold-panner" Sean O'Connor had reached the abandoned Roux farm on the Sabie River, by following the directions his employer had dictated to him before leaving Johannesburg.

The Lowveld Commando had ranged far and wide on the Lowveld, sabotaging railway lines, destroying bridges, ambushing British engineering corps or armed patrols, and generally making life miserable for their invading enemy. The Boer commandos lived off the land, drank from streams and slept in the open. But time and space were both running out for the *Bittereinder* commandos still operating in the veld, and it was not long before the blockhouses and barbed-wire barriers began to severely restrict their freedom of movement.

Joshua once again gave his exhausted fighters 10 days of well-earned leave, although most of them now had nowhere to go; their farms having been razed by the British. Thus it was with a remnant of about 30 gaunt men mounted on bony *Boerperds* that Joshua Roux again rode up to his own, devastated family farm at Olifantshoek. As the depleted commando cautiously approached the ruined farmhouse, they were surprised to see a canvas awning stretched between the shattered stone walls, and smoke from a cooking-fire rising up. Grazing peacefully nearby was a hobbled horse and two mules, which pricked their ears towards the approaching mounted men. The commandos slipped off their ponies, and stealthily surrounded the farmyard, approaching with rifles cocked, assuming that the farm had been taken over by blacks. The sound of someone singing "When Irish Eyes are Smiling" in a low voice, and the delicious aroma of frying bacon and beans, wafted from the ruins. Peering around a corner of one of the tumbled walls, Joshua Roux saw the hulking shape of his former Jo'burg security manager sitting on a rock and preparing his breakfast, which was sizzling in an iron pan.

When Sean O'Connor looked up from his cooking and saw the rifle barrel pointed at him from behind the ruined wall, he rose slowly, hands in the air, and proclaimed in a loud voice: "Sure, 'tis no good robbing me yet! I haven't found a damned penny-worth of gold in this God-forsaken river!" To the big Irishman's unbridled delight, the laugh that resounded among the ruin was the unmistakable one of his employer, Joshua Roux—who then found himself clamped in a rib-crushing bearhug. The men of the commando were soon crowded around the laughing pair, enviously eying Sean's fine breakfast. Noticing their condition, he quickly rummaged in one of his sacks, and then triumphantly held aloft a leg of smoked pork, which he proceeded to cut into many cubes, to be added to a big pot of beans, spiced with onions, which before long was brought to a seething boil and its hearty aroma set the weary, hungered patriots' mouths to watering. It was the famished commando's first solid meal in a week, since they had last caught a few scrawny chickens on the outskirts of a British transport camp. After they had all eaten, taking Joshua aside, Sean proudly produced the signed lease-agreement for Joshua's house in Johannesburg, and Joshua gave the big Irishman a hearty, approving grin and a proud pat on the back. Their talk soon turned to the war with the British. Within a few hours, the Lowveld Commando set out again, but this time, they were followed by an Irishman proudly bearing a captured English rifle, and leading two laden mules behind his own horse. He was quietly singing an old ballad that told of battling the English in his far-away homeland.

But Sean O'Connor did not get much of a chance to savor the sweet taste of fighting against his traditional enemy. Just a few weeks after having joined up with the Lowveld Commando, having participated in only a few short, sharp, minor skirmishes with British patrols, and having assisted in the blowing-up of two nearby rail bridges, Sean awoke one morning to the deafening sound of artillery shells bursting close to their temporary camp in a small *kloof* ("gorge or cleft") between two koppies. The sleeping commando had been spotted by a black herder, and he had duly reported their presence to the nearest British camp, in anticipation of a reward. Under the cover of darkness, two platoons of mounted infantry and a team of gunners had taken up positions around the kloof, and at first light, opened up with an artillery barrage, lobbing high-explosive *lyddite* shells into the kloof. Shrapnel fragments whined through the air, and British bullets buzzed and hissed over the heads of the prone commando. Joshua Roux hastily deployed his 30 men in a defensive ring among the surrounding boulders, and they began to answer the British fire with accurate shots at any tan helmet they saw silhouetted against the skyline. But as the enemy spotters on the koppies above them directed the cannon-fire closer and closer to their position, the Boers began to take casualties. The first man to be killed by a flying chunk of hot shrapnel was Jonathan Du Plessis. Then Manie Wagner and Buks Botha died, blown apart by a shell. Sean took a bead on a Tommie who unwisely stood up to see if the exploding shells were having the desired effect, and his shot was true. Joshua, lying alongside the Irishman, slapped him on the back in congratulations at his first clean kill, but the expression on his face was one of grave concern. They were surrounded, and if they lay where they were, they would soon be torn apart by the increasingly accurate shell-fire.

For the very first time in his 25 years of on-and-off soldiering, Joshua Roux contemplated the prospect of surrender. When he saw Drikus Coetzee, one of his bravest men, shot through the head as he peered up at the Tommies on the koppie directly above them, he made up his mind. Hauling out his white handkerchief, he knotted one corner onto the ramrod of his rifle, and waved it above the boulder behind which he was sheltering. He then heard an English voice shouting out the command to cease fire, and a few more sporadic shots later, the firing from above stopped, and the scrape of many hobnailed boots could then be heard approaching fast over the rocky ground.

When the surviving men of the Lowveld Commando stood slowly up from their hidden positions among the boulders, with their hands raised, they were approached by a detachment of Tommies with fixed bayonets. At their front was a familiar face—that of Sergeant Wilson. When one of the younger Tommies prodded Joshua Roux in the chest with the point of his bayonet, the sergeant ordered him to desist. Further, the Tommies were not at all pleased to hear the Irish brogue of Sean O'Connor when he protested at being shoved around by *Brits* half his size. The big Irishman then ordered the Tommies to catch his mules, which had fled, and to make sure that *Jack* and *Jenny* got castor-oil weekly, for their constipation! Thereafter, the men of that legendary commando were generally well-treated by their British captors, considering all the mayhem they had caused on the Lowveld over the past year. Any hopes they may have harbored about being interned with their families at the concentration camp near Barberton were soon dashed, however, when they were loaded onto a heavily guarded train which took them to the busy port of Durban (about 600 miles away by the rail of the day).

It was the first time that many of the Boers had ever seen the ocean. There, they were joined by hundreds of other Boer prisoners of war, and put on a steamship, which soon set sail for the remote island of St. Helena. On the long sea voyage, their despair grew in proportion to the distance they sailed away from the beloved land of their birth, away from their devastated farms and their few surviving family members. It was left to the irrepressible Sean O'Connor to try and cheer up the disconsolate men of the now-defunct Lowveld Commando, with his quirky Irish ballads and poems, theatrically delivered in his booming voice above the roaring of the waves and the howling gales of the cold Atlantic. The Lowveld Commando, led by their indomitable commandant Joshua Roux, had been among the last of such units still maintaining operations against the British army on the South African veld by the early months of 1902. Only a few other *hold-outs* had remained, led by die-hard Boer generals like "Koos" Herculaas De la Rey, Christiaan De Wet, Louis Botha and Jan Smuts—all of them brilliant military tacticians, and fearless leaders of brave men.

Chapter Thirty-four

But the time to talk of surrender and peace had finally come, and in April 1902, the Boer generals came off the field of battle, and up to the conference table, for "talks about talks." Many of the *Bittereinders* still talked of fighting on, but overall the Boer Volk were weary of war. Their *civilian* losses far outweighed those of their military. The Boer commandos lost almost 8,000 men: around 5,000 in action and another 3,000 from war wounds. Shockingly and reprehensibly, almost 28,000 civilians died in the concentration camps—mostly women and children! Thus, 12% of South Africa's white population died as a result of this unjust war. On the other hand, the British lost around 22,000 men: about 8,000 in action and another 14,000 from disease and war wounds. Additionally, around 20,000 blacks died in the war fighting *for Britain,* or perished in their foul concentration camps. In cold monetary terms, the direct cost of the war for Britain was estimated at £220,000,000[145]—enough to bankrupt any country less wealthy than Great Britain.

In material terms, the Boers lost their entire livelihood: Their houses and barns were demolished; most all their personal house-

---

[145] —about £5,147,000,000 or $10,293,000,000 in today's currency. This included the money Britain paid to "reimburse" the Boers for their demolished farms: 63,000 claimants—£3,000,000 (£70,200,000 or $140,400,000 in today's currency)—a mere pittance of £48 per person (£1,114 or $2,228 in today's currency): which must have been more of an insult than a blessing. Vineyards and orchards take years to establish and the loss of these staples of life to a farmer is hard to estimate, let alone compensate; though money can be given for new seedlings and labor, money cannot compensate for the 5-10 years it takes to re-establish. The war *cost* to Britain also *included* the £30,000,000 (£700,000,000 or $1,400,000,000 in today's currency) Britain spent to build new railways, and the enormous cost of establishing thousands of blockhouses to restrict the movement of Boer commandos.

hold possessions were stolen or destroyed; their farm equipment, transport wagons, and household food was stolen; their crops, the fruit of their orchards and vineyards, and their poultry, livestock, and horses were all stolen by the British army and the blacks (and their trees and grapevines cut down). Of course, the Boer's gold and diamond mines were also stolen by the British (since gaining possession thereof was the *real* reason for the war). Their mines, industries and businesses, farms and orchards had lost years of production while the blacks and British had ravaged their country and feasted on their livestock. The Boers also suffered the cost of the physical damage to their country's infrastructure, towns and civic buildings due to the war, as well as the cost of munitions for a war forced upon them by the British invaders.

The psychological cost to the Boer *people,* the *Afrikaner Volk,* of both republics of the Boer nation, was immeasurable: They had lost their national independence and their personal freedom. Many of the Boers' children and wives had died slow, miserable deaths from starvation and disease in the camps (and hostile strangers, both black and white, had violated their unprotected womenfolk). Many of the Boer men had been shipped off to distant lands. Of course, many Boers (men and women) had also died in agony in battle (and some even *after* their surrender, at the hands of unprincipled war criminals like "Breaker" Morant). Many dignified old men and innocent young boys also died in the camps.[146]

It was a much-depleted and war-weary Boer Volk that contemplated their future under Imperial British rule. The Imperialists' terms for peace were *remarkably lenient;* considering that their own mighty army had been severely punished, by a mere "rabble of farmers" (as the British press consistently referred to the Boers) in the war in South Africa—as Rudyard Kipling put it, the British

---

[146] In light of all that the Boers suffered in this unprovoked war, how the British could have thought that £48 per person was "just compensation," was beyond rational understanding. A whole generation of "poor whites" resulted from this unprovoked British invasion and aggression.

army was taught "no end of a lesson"[147] on the veld. Acceptance by the Boers of the sovereignty of the IMPERIAL CROWN was *paramount* in the British mind, with self-rule vaguely promised, "when circumstances permitted." Amnesty was extended to perpetrators of all acts of war "committed in good faith" and only the leaders of the Cape rebels ("the undesirables" as they were called) would be punished by losing their own voting rights; though they were not given any prison sentence. The Dutch language—now essentially *Suid Afrikaans*—would be allowed in courts and in schools. There would be no punitive property taxes imposed upon the Boers. Britain even made limited funds available for agricultural reconstruction, and especially for the purchase of livestock.

Whether these "generous" peace terms offered by the British, at *Die Vrede van Vereeniging* ("The Peace of the Union") were a reflection of a *new* Anglo "humanitarian spirit," or whether they were due to the assuaging of Britain's *national* "guilty conscience," was hard to say. This document was eventually formally signed at "Melrose House," a magnificent mansion in Pretoria, on 31 May, 1902. The mansion had been "requisitioned" by the British Army as a headquarters during the war. The town of Vereeniging,[148] was itself established largely by the Russian-born, Jewish entrepreneur Sammy Marks,[149] friend of Paul Kruger. Marks had become the owner of the first officially approved distillery in the Boer republic. Vereeniging itself would soon grow into a mighty industrial *behemoth*. Lord Milner, despite declaring, "We are all friends now," was unable to persuade Generals De la Rey, Botha, and Smuts (still jaded from their unaltered perception of Milner as an *unrepentant* "Boer-hater") to serve on the new

---

[147] In "The Lesson," in his, <u>The Five Nations</u> (1899-1902).

[148] —now a city in the *Gauteng* province; Gauteng (in the Sotho/Tswana language) means, "Place of Gold."

[149] —(originally, Marx). He arrived in 1869 and his cousin, Isaac Lewis (originally Levins) followed shortly and they founded the partnership of LEWIS & MARKS, LTD. They had close ties with "Barney Barnato" (Barnett Isaacs). Barney and his brother later traveled to London to form BARNATO BROTHERS, LTD.

TRANSVAAL LEGISLATIVE COUNCIL. Milner remedied even this embarrassment to his own advantage by installing his "kindergarten" of young Oxford graduates as a foundation for efficient governance and the immediate post-war civil administration of the devastated economy.

First priority for the post-war British government was to *get the gold mines open and operating again* as wealth generators (which itself seemed to reinforce the fact that BRITAIN had instigated and waged the war to steal the gold and diamond mines). In order to get the mines up and running and producing, the CROWN imported around 60,000 indentured *Chinese* laborers (due to the difficulty in recruiting black labor for the same low wages). The black tribesmen had initially been lured to the goldfields in large numbers by the prospect of wealth, but many had since left the *Golden City* during the war years. Although rather unpopular, these Oriental "coolies" proved to be much harder workers, and the streams of gold were soon flowing again.[150]

Lord Milner, however, reneged on his promise to place South African Dutch on an equal footing with the English language and government schools were instructed to *strongly discourage* their students from speaking Afrikaans and to teach their pupils *only in English*. Both Afrikaans and English-speaking citizens of this new, 20th-Century South Africa were nonetheless re-united in their belief that it had been a white man's war, and that this was a white man's country. Black South African citizens' political aspirations were largely side-lined, eventually giving rise to various, disparate and separate black African and Indian political movements; the latter championed by a young lawyer by the name of Mohandas Karamchand ("Mahatma") Gandhi (1869-1948), who had organized a corps of volunteer Indian stretcher-bearers during the war.

The British had also brought by ship to NATAL a large number of Hindus, a few decades earlier, to work the sugar-cane fields now spreading lushly over the hillsides; again because many black

---

[150] See **Appendix E.**

men appeared to detest manual labor: even though it meant being paid and bettering themselves. In their tribal system, women did virtually *all* the work (and still do!), while the men were seemingly content to lie around preserving their energies for cattle-thieving or procreation. Following in the immigrational wake of the Hindus were mostly Muslim merchants, and soon enough, NATAL—and particularly the town of Durban—had a flourishing Muslim community, in addition to its Indian neighborhoods. Each of these imported foreign race-groups brought with them their own religion and culture, which were then introduced into South Africa's Christian, Anglo-Dutch society. In the century that lay ahead, these Indians would be subjected to the *same* government legislation restricting their movements and political activities as would the blacks; but *they* set about making a good life for themselves as an ethnic minority with their innate intelligence, determination to succeed, their vigor, and hard work.

The burgeoning numbers of blacks now largely languished in their tribal homelands. The British then found a way of forcing them back into the labor market (to some degree) by *legislating* the *imposition* of such things as a "Hut Tax"—which could only be paid in *cash* (not in pumpkins, or goats). Black men were fond of having many wives (and still are), each with her own hut, so this law was, of course, extremely unpopular. The enterprising, new, immigrant Indian community however, forged ahead, and within merely a generation or two, were among the wealthiest of citizens, per-capita, of their adopted country. As was the case, in most African contexts, the blacks soon came to *resent* the Indians, being jealous of their successes (in much the same way that the blacks harbored these feelings against the *equally* hard-working, law-abiding, skilled, and successful whites). Whenever an opportunity or an "excuse" arose, the blacks ransacked Indian-owned shops, destroyed their homes, raped their wives and daughters, and brutally murdered the men and their sons.

But the perceptive Indians of South Africa soon learned how to insure their own peoples' survival—by becoming involved in racial politics on the side of the "oppressed black masses"—thus trying to appease the blacks by appearing to be their "friends" who *sympathized* with them: so that the blacks would vent their jealous frustration and wanton rage on someone else (that is, on the *whites).*[151]   However, ironically, usually by their own choice, the Indians lived socially similar to the white communities (not similar to the blacks—from whom they also mainly *chose* to live segregated); while retaining their own Indian culture.

> [In the later, *black*-ruled South Africa, Indians held many of the "deputy" administrative posts, and they were then essentially, the "brains" behind the *brawn*. Though originally imported for manual labor, they proved themselves intelligent and industrious, and soon occupied "white collar" positions; thus, very few still worked in the fields for which they were originally imported.]

---

[151] While it may have seemed pragmatic at the time, it was a rather *ill-conceived* plan: for such confederation could only offer "protection" *for as long* as the "common enemy" (the "oppressive" white man) *actually existed*. Some *less*-near-sighted Indians astutely realized that once the whites were destroyed or driven out, the blacks would again turn on the Indians (for the same reasons that they attacked the whites). Such xenophobic "riots," looting, violence, and mayhem (which the blacks perpetrated against even the Indians, their "allies") would break out, from time to time; most notably in 1949, and again in 2008.

Chapter Thirty-five

It was after almost a full year of imprisonment on the remote Island of St. Helena—where Napoléon Bonaparte's "prison cottage" still stood—that the prison transport ship, on which Joshua Roux and Sean O'Connor stood watching the horizon, finally steamed into Table Bay. The ship did not go directly to Cape Town harbor, but stopped briefly at *Robbeneiland* ("Robben Island"), about 4 miles off the coast of Cape Town. The two men had been obliged, much against their wills, to take an *oath of allegiance* to the CROWN, before being released to make the long sea-voyage home, compliments of His Majesty, King Edward VII. of England (1841-1910).

The two men gazed longingly at the South African mainland, and it seemed to Joshua, especially, that it was now so close that he could actually smell it, and almost reach out and touch his beloved homeland. Table Mountain loomed over the city and the bay, its table cloth of cloud swirling evocatively. Joshua was anxious to get ashore after having been separated from his family for so long, with no word from them. They walked down the gangplank onto the wharf, and every prisoner was then unceremoniously dusted with carbolic-powder disinfectant as they stepped ashore. Despite the acrid powder on their hair and clothes, they were elated at now being so very close to becoming free men once again.

However, that moment was shattered when an *aparatnik* ("attaché") from the British Governor's Office barked out, "Roux...? Commandant Joshua Roux...?" *"Ja, ek is Joshua Roux"* ("Yes, I am Joshua Roux"), he replied—not being in the mood for British bureaucratic nonsense, he chose to respond in *Afrikaans*. "I am Lieutenant Nigel Blythe, of the RETURNED BOER PRISONER PROCESSING BOARD. Please follow me," the man curtly ordered, and stiffly spun on his heels and walked away at a quick pace. He then stopped abruptly, turned around, and noticing that Joshua had not begun moving, reiterated mechanically, but more forcefully, "I *said,* follow me." Joshua and Sean looked at each other as if to say, "Oh brother, what is this all about...?"

Sean O'Connor (known to his *captors* as, "Phil' McAvity!") called loudly after him, "If it's de-fleaing you're wanting us for, we've been done already, thank you very much! But if it's for a stiff whiskey to welcome us home, lead on, Blythe Spirit!" The back of Lieut. Blythe's neck turned noticeably redder, but he continued on his march towards the squat administration block a short distance from the wharf, with Joshua and Sean now ambling along behind him. Blythe took them through a maze of doors until they arrived at a certain office in a government building of "His Majesty, King Edward VII." (it said so on the door). Once inside, Lieut. Blythe remained aloof, without making any eye contact and without speaking a word, while he rummaged through various filing cabinets. Finally, he pulled out a small package wrapped in brown paper and tied with white string. Lieut. Blythe, without ceremony, handed the package to Joshua and curtly said, "This is for you. Good day," and then looked toward the door, and then back at Joshua. After pausing for a moment, Joshua, taking off his hat, declared, *"Baie dankie. Bly te kenne, Lieutenant Blythe. Goeiedag!"* ("Thank you very much. It was a pleasure to meet you, Lieutenant Blythe. Good day!") "If this stiff Brit doesn't have any manners," Joshua thought to himself, "then I shall teach him how a gentleman behaves." With that, Joshua and Sean left the government building.

Outside, Joshua leaned against the wall, in the shade, and opened the mysterious package. To his surprise, Joshua found within a smaller package, and a personal, handwritten letter *from General Jacobus "Koos" Herculaas De la Rey!* Stunned, he opened the letter, and read out loud for Sean's benefit.

"My Dear Commandant Joshua Roux,

"Some time ago I received a letter from your dear mother Erika, reminding me that she is the daughter of Christiaan Delarey, who was a nephew of my late great-uncle Oom Sarel Delarey and inquiring as to your whereabouts. It seemed that she had not heard from you since last receiving a message while she was still incarcerated at the Barberton concentration camp, from which she posted her letter. I thus made inquiries and learned that you had been captured and transported to St. Helena. Unfortunately, I was unable to pass on this news to your dear mother, as I was by then very involved in the signing of the peace agreement with the invaders. However, I have recently learned that you have already boarded a ship and are now well on your way homeward on your return to our beloved South Africa. As I write this letter, I am already in *Kaapstad,* soon to board ship myself. Generals De Wet and Botha are accompanying me to England and Europe (after which we shall also travel to the United States of America) in the hopes of raising funds for our impoverished people who have suffered so much during this awful war, many families having lost everything.

"I have only briefly stopped here in *Cape Town* and had very much wanted to finally meet you; however, my ship departs in a few days and I hear that you are still at sea after having enjoyed your 'vacation' on that beautiful Isle. I so wanted to spend some time with you. Your bravery did not go unnoticed and I heard of your many exploits and thank you for all that you did and all that you sacrificed in fighting for our people and protecting our President. I wish I had more time to write a more detailed letter, but there are many things that require my attention.

"Please accept this small stipend, as a gift from your grateful cousin. I know you will be penniless upon release from prison and your home is far from Cape Town. I trust that this small sum will provide you with means for food and transportation and other necessities until you are back home. My prayers are with you and our Volk, as we try to put our lives back together. Give my regards to your mother. God bless, and stay strong. Your cousin, Koos De la Rey."

Joshua was stunned and as he opened the smaller package, he discovered £5.[152] Sean, with his mouth agape, was speechless (which was a rare event for this lively, talkative Irishman). Joshua, with a new spring in his step, thanks to the personal letter from his famous cousin, General De la Rey, and thanks to this kind sum of money provided Providentially by him, then led Sean back to the wharf, where a trestle table had been set up. A sergeant, after checking off each man's name from the prisoner-roll, handed to each man a pack of British army rations, a brown suit, and a pair of sturdy shoes. It was fairly obvious from their appearance that the suits and shoes had been collected by some charitable organization. Sean leaned forward, and requested a suit in Extra Large, and a pair of Size 12 shoes. The British quartermaster-sergeant bellowed back, "They only come in *two* sizes: *too* small, and *too* large!" Obviously amused by his own joke, the sergeant then ordered them: "Move along then! 'Aven't got all bleedin' day!"

Soon enough the men, duly "processed," re-boarded their ship, and it steamed the few miles into Cape Town harbor itself. As their ship nudged up against the dock, another ship sailed slowly by, heading out to sea. At the rail of that ship stood an imposing gentleman with a full beard, dressed in a dark suit. It was none other than General Koos De la Rey! A delighted Joshua shouted out, *"Dankie, Generaal!"* and that gentleman smiled broadly and waved his top hat. Alongside him stood Generals Christiaan De Wet and Louis Botha. Their ship soon steamed out of sight. It seemed ironic, thought Sean, that these two brave, battle-scarred Boer commanders (used to charging on their *Boerperds)* should catch first sight ever of the other (on the sea), in peace-time: as one was returning home from imprisonment abroad, and while the other was sailing abroad to raise funds for the rehabilitation of their Boer Volk, devastated by war.

---

[152] £117 or $235 in today's currency. While this does not seem that much to us today, in 1902, it was substantial. Travel and food were much less expensive. It was equivalent to about 2-3 month's wages for an artisan of that time in history.

Joshua and Sean savored the moment and having at long last stepped onto Afrikaner soil, they both breathed a deep sigh of relief. They took the opportunity to make a short tour of the town, gratefully taking in the exciting sights and smells of the "Mother City," and had soon made their way to the imposing old castle. They climbed the ramparts, and looked out over the bustling town, unaware that they were standing on the very spot where, almost exactly 250 years earlier, Jan van Riebeeck and his wife Maria had stood, surveying the carts of hippo meat being trundled up to the big gates. The two men then looked up at the slopes of Table Mountain (where Tipa the Strandloper had once hunted); those slopes were now dotted with prosperous, well-landscaped suburbs. Fine new mansions had sprung up all over Cape Town (built with war-profits).

Eventually, the two made their way down to the station to purchase train tickets. The duo then began their long rail journey across the semi-arid, but beautiful Karoo, and the rolling, grassy plains of the FREE STATE, back to Johannesburg. The two men sat staring out of the rattling window of the second-class coach, their simple meal of tinned bully-beef, bread, and cheese spread between them. Deep in thought, Joshua wondered what awaited him concerning the fate of his family. "Well, if things have started out this well, thanks to my dear cousin, then maybe everything else will be just as blessed," Joshua thought to himself. Sean, on the other hand, amused himself by tossing the stale army biscuits to the *picannins* ("black boy-children") running alongside the train, and adding up, in his mind, his estimate of the enormous sum of money the British must have spent to build the hundreds of blockhouses that they passed; there was one at every crossing, bridge and rail-junction!

After reaching the Johannesburg train station, which was as far as their tickets would take them, they then made their way on foot towards Pretoria, and stopped at "Halfway House" (a mail-coach staging post halfway between Johannesburg and Pretoria). There, Joshua visited the isolated stables of his English friend (where he had "hidden" his racehorses just before the war) to secure mounts for himself and Sean. However, he was infuriated to discover that his plan had been thwarted (he was of course, also out the significant sum of money he had paid in advance to board them) and that his horses had *not* been safely hidden from the rapacious eyes of the British army. The Englishman apologetically informed Joshua that shortly before the end of the war, a black stable hand had led the British cavalry quartermasters to the remote farm (after being promised a reward if his information about "the rich Boer's horses" was true). Upon finding the horses, the British cavalry quartermasters "requisitioned" them for some of their senior officers. Since Joshua's English friend had no "bill of sale" proving that the horses were his, the British declared them to be "rebel property" and thus, were claimed by the CROWN. Thus, Joshua's fine racehorses had ended their days under who knows what horrid conditions, on some far-off battlefield; as had so many other hundreds of thousands of horses in that cruel war. Nonetheless, Joshua warmly shook the hand of his English friend, though Sean (not caring for Englishmen of any stripe), never even looked in the Englishman's direction and pretended not to hear the conversation.

From there, Joshua and Sean plodded on, to Pretoria, where he went in search of Angela and his twins at the home of her father. Sadly, the new owners of the house told him that the widowed old man had passed away; that they had bought the house from the executors of the late Meneer Maynard's estate, and that they knew nothing of his daughter Angela.

A bewildered Joshua, with his stout Irish companion, then returned to Johannesburg, after Sean succeeded in securing for them a ride (by hitch-hiking) on a kindly trader's wagon. Joshua then re-took possession of his own home in Doornfontein from the British Army, and collected a substantial rent check—redeemable only at the War Office in London! Joshua then visited the Rand Club, where he was recognized and welcomed by a surprised doorman. Joshua soon arranged for a wealthy British immigrant tenant to lease the mansion. He also used the Club's new Bell-telephone to arrange a money-draft, wired to him from the bank in Lydenburg; after having assured the banker—the son of the late Hiram Goldberg (the original proprietor of the bank)—that there was more than enough security for the draft, safely locked within the bank's own vault (which Joshua had deposited there when he purchased the land next to that of his parents). Joshua then used that telegraphed money to purchase a fine, new-fangled and very expensive automobile, a 24-horsepower Daimler-Benz "Phoenix," and after an hour's driving lesson from the American salesman, Joshua and Sean O'Connor drove eastward out of the *Golden City*—in hopeful search of Joshua's family on the Lowveld. Despite the pneumatic Dunlop tires, it was a tiring and bumpy journey on the dusty road alongside the railway tracks, and their supply of extra gasoline was running low by the time they drove in to Barberton to refuel. The owner of the new motor-garage was happy to oblige, and his wife invited them to stay for a meal, but Joshua was anxious to reach the concentration camp, eager for news of his family.

Everywhere around Barberton, Joshua noticed the name, "Stafford Parker, Esq.," emblazoned on various business enterprises, and on the short drive out of Barberton he related to Sean the story of how, as a teenager, he had been offered a job in Pilgrim's Rest by that entrepreneur. However, Joshua purposely neglected to make any mention of his personal encounter with Cockney Liz.

After reaching the abandoned "death-camp" near Barberton, Joshua and Sean were stunned to see the seemingly endless rows of crosses marking a staggering number of graves of those persons who had been interned (and then interred) in that one camp. Methodically, Joshua began reading the stenciled names on the white, wooden crosses. The more names he read the more anxious he became, until he was frantic and literally running up and down the rows of crosses, feverishly reading the names as they blurred by—until he was stopped dead in his tracks, stunned, as if struck by a Cape buffalo. There, before his eyes, appeared the name, "Angela Roux," on one of the generic crosses. Then, Joshua looked one grave over and read *two* names on one cross: "James Roux" and "Julia Roux." Thunderstruck, Joshua, as if in slow motion, collapsed to his knees in despair. As the waves of emotion overcame Joshua, a panting Sean O'Connor finally caught up with him. First, Sean looked at Joshua, then, he looked at the cross bearing the name of Joshua's wife—and then, the cross bearing the names of Joshua's twin children. Sean's heart skipped a beat as he saw these names. Up until then, for Sean, the war had been a bit impersonal; since no one really close to him had perished. But now, upon learning of the deaths of his former employer and closest friend's wife and children, the war struck a lot closer. All throughout their internment on the island of St. Helena, daily, Joshua had talked about his dear family and that it was the thought of them which gave him hope. Now, it seemed as if that hope was dashed. While still bent over, trying to catch his breath, Sean placed his big hand on his friend's shoulder to comfort him. He opened his mouth to say something—anything; but no words would come out. "What does one say in the face of such irremediable loss...?" Sean thought to himself, as he wiped away the tears which had now begun to flow from *his own* eyes.

Sean then remembered the Biblical story of how Job's friends, in the face of his great tragedy, sat with Job for 7 days without saying a word, without even eating—simply *being there* in his time of greatest need. Sean knew he did not have the wisdom to offer any words; but he realized he could simply be there for his best friend in the world. Sean patted Joshua gently on the shoulder as Joshua began to shudder and sob in despair, and the big Irishman found himself having to continually dry the tears from his own cheeks with the shirt sleeve of his other arm. Devastated, Joshua knelt there, stunned, heartbroken, distraught. As he mourned, the sky slowly darkened and it began to drizzle, and he had a moment of *deja vu* to the day he had buried his dear father—and the bitter recollection of his dying father's plea to him not to involve himself in a war with the British, a war they could not win.

It all seemed so surreal. "How is this possible?" he thought to himself, "...they were so young, so full of life, when I left them and went off to war... so young... now gone..." Joshua remained there grieving, for many hours, his thoughts racing uncontrollable through his mind, first in one direction, then in another. Feeling empty and forlorn, Joshua stayed there, on the cold, hard ground next to their simple graves, unable to wrench himself away. It was some time before Joshua actually noticed how unkempt the graves were, and he began to pull handfuls of grass and weeds off at ground level, to make their graves look a little more respectable. He straightened the cross over the grave of his children and brushed the cobwebs off the angles of the crosses. He then plucked a few veld flowers growing among the grass alongside him and placed them in a small bouquet upon the graves. Thankfully, the rain had stopped drizzling and a pair of nesting sparrows then landed nearby, unafraid, and began to sing sweetly as a ray of sunlight broke through the dark clouds, illuminating the white crosses. Joshua then slowly rose, brushed the grass from the legs of his pants and holding his hat between his hands at his belt, with his head bowed, managed to utter a few solemn words, *"The Lord giveth, and the Lord taketh away. Blessed be the Name of the Lord!"* Sean nodded in silent agreement as he patted his friend on the back and thought to himself that he had been right not to try and offer any words of consolation, taking it as a sign from above that Joshua himself had now quoted from the book of Job.

Joshua then, remembering his dear mother, began to studiously re-examine the names on all the crosses marking the graves in that awful place, as a shop-keeper taking inventory. As he walked along the rows of crosses, looking for his mother's name, he would, from time-to-time, see other names he recognized. The names of *Marie Du Plessis* and her infant son *Dawid* buried alongside each other, reminded him of the earlier loss to one of his brave commandos, who was himself killed when they were captured near the end of the war. Though his soul was still tortured, Joshua gained some solace in *not* finding the grave of his old mother there, next to his beloved wife and children—and with but a faint hope in his heart, they set out again towards Olifantshoek, to his parents' family farm which the British had demolished. Though the trip to the abandoned concentration camp seemed like the longest trip Joshua had ever taken, despite the speed of his new-fangled motor car—the trip to Olifantshoek seemed like an eternity. Everything seemed to blur by in slow motion, as Joshua sat in silence, staring numbly at the road ahead of them as they jostled along with Sean at the wheel. Every now and then he would wipe a few tears from his bloodshot eyes. Sean would look over, concerned about his friend, and would say a silent prayer that the Good Lord would see fit to have Joshua's mother still be alive and in good health. Sean then realized that Joshua was not alone in his loss, grief, and bereavement—thousands of other Boer families (as well as all the other nationalities, who had honorably fought with the Boers for their freedom) were daily suffering under similar conditions. When this thought occurred to him, Sean also offered a short prayer that the Great God would touch the lives of *all* His children and be with them in their times of greatest need and comfort them as only He could comfort them. Then, being the rather irreverent, brawny Irishman that he was, Sean also offered a few *imprecatory* prayers aimed carefully at *daardie verdomde Engelse duiwels* ("those damned English devils"). Then, feeling somewhat self-satisfied, and sitting a little higher in his seat, he grasped the steering wheel more purposefully and returned to the thoughts at hand: the task of making their way safely to Olifantshoek, over the rutted track that passed through Pilgrim's Rest.

Joshua suggested that they should pull over and stop at the tavern in Pilgrim's Rest for a quick meal. Though he didn't feel much like eating, he knew that he would need his strength for whatever might lay ahead. He also thought he may try to drown his sorrows a little and slake his dear companion Sean's mighty thirst *en route* to the Sabie River farm.

Somewhat concerned that the "sins of his youth" may come back to haunt him, Joshua took the opportunity to make discreet inquiries with the grizzled barman as to the fate of Cockney Liz. To his immense relief, he was informed that she had left Pilgrim's Rest well over a decade earlier, making her way to Barberton by mail coach, along with Stafford Parker. There, she continued with her cabaret act, at the fine hotel that her benefactor had acquired. This was fortunate for Joshua, for as they were consuming their libations, a slim, pretty, red-haired barmaid with a strong Irish brogue suddenly launched herself at Sean, clung to his neck, and cried copious tears of joy. To the big Irishman's amazement, it was his sister Kerry, who had made the long sea journey—all the way from Galway Bay in Ireland—to Durban, South Africa, in search of her long-lost, fortune-seeking brother. She had scoured the gold-panning camps around Pilgrim's Rest, after having made inquiries at every turn of her journey up from Durban—to no avail—and in despair at not finding him (dead or alive) had ended up working to support herself in that quaint town.

When a beaming Sean introduced a grieving Joshua Roux to Kerry O'Connor, after briefly explaining the tragic news to her, Kerry's immediate attraction to Joshua was obvious—but it would be *many* months before Joshua would be able to see her for the lovely girl that she was: so devastated was he by the realization that he would never again see his dear wife or their darling twins. It was the prospect of being re-united with them that had warmed his heart during the icy winter in the prison camp on the wind-swept island of St. Helena—it was that one thought that had kept him hopeful. Now, though those hopes were dashed, he still clung to one solitary, *frail* thread of hope. Thus, he was anxious to travel to their old farmstead to see if his aged mother had survived the war. But first, the likable Irish rogue sitting alongside Joshua had some explaining to do: for he had written to his sister in Ireland, during his time as a gold-panner and then while he was a bouncer. He had also written while he was a security-manager working for Joshua Roux at J.R. Security Services. Later, finally during his short involvement in the war, upon his capture, he had slipped a brief letter to a sympathetic, passing civilian at a rail siding. However, he had bent the truth *just a wee bit,* as he now explained to his boss and sister.

Kerry O'Connor had been given the impression, in her brother's eloquent, highly embellished letters, that he had *struck it rich* gold-panning the streams of the Transvaal escarpment and that he had then moved to Johannesburg with his *small fortune.* Subsequently, he had further *made it big* in the *Golden City,* where he lived in a *palatial mansion,* and was there served hand-and-foot by many groveling English servants. His doorman *Joshua,* a "rustic Boer," had convinced him to abandon his lavish lifestyle, and to take up arms to assist the Boers against the "olde enemy," England. So Sean had given up everything for that honorable cause, and after virtually single-handedly decimating almost an entire British regiment—with just a little help from his faithful Boer *butler*—he had been captured. However, he had managed to post his last letter (after being captured) to his admiring sister in Ireland. His sister had then regaled the awe-struck inhabitants of her rural village with lurid tales of the *exploits* of "their very own Sean O'Connor," now a "wealthy success-story" turned "war hero" in far-off South Africa!

But then the flow of letters had abruptly stopped, and her brother seemed to have disappeared off the face of the earth: presumably deported—or dead! Of course, Sean's letters were virtually a work of fiction, but his sister had not know that. She had set sail for South Africa in the hope of tracking him down—or at worst, planting a tree next to his lonely grave somewhere in the vast South African veld. Her inquiries were not helped, of course, by the fact that Sean, in his impish manner, had given his British captors a comical, false name, that of "Phil' McAvity!" But now, *here he was,* larger than life, and she could not bring herself to be angry at him; so overjoyed was she to find him alive and in robust good health!

Sean O'Connor, now looking rather shamefaced, generously offered to buy Joshua Roux a drink in his attempts to "break the ice" and *smooth things over*—but then suddenly remembered, "rich man" that he was, he had not a penny, and had to borrow a pound from his former "butler." Sean went on to explain that he could not bring himself to tell the "folks back home" in Ireland that he had found no gold at all, and that he had to resort to working as a bouncer in a bar! However, once he had told the first lie, of course, he was obliged to keep up the pretense by spinning a larger tapestry out of his desperate yarn. Joshua heartily laughed out loud, slapping his clever friend on his broad back, upon hearing his sister Kerry retelling Sean's "African Adventures"—those fantastic tales she had read in her brother's imaginative letters. Of course, Joshua forgave his good friend for relegating him to being his "domestic"—his "rustic Boer doorman!" Sean was worried that his proud Boer friend, and former employer, would take issue with his fabrication; but in truth, good natured as Joshua was—after all that he had been through, it actually felt good to laugh out loud at something so unimportant. Meeting Kerry and hearing the outlandish stories was a Godsend though nothing could heal his heart other than time and God's grace—it at least helped to lift the dark, heavy mood which had hung over him since the life-changing, heart-wrenching discovery they had made at the abandoned "death camp."

It was not very much later that all 3 of them—the 2 men now more than slightly tipsy—were weaving their way down *Long Tom Pass* in the automobile, passing a bottle of whiskey between them, and heading towards the Sabie Ridge. When old Erika Roux saw two drunken men and a girl crammed together on the front seat of a new-fangled automobile, bouncing and swerving down the track towards her half-rebuilt stone cottage, she went inside, and re-emerged with the Cape gun to see them off. She had wrapped the gun in an oil-cloth and buried it (as had Joshua, with their other firearms) just before the Tommies arrived, robbed them, destroyed their farm, and then taken her, Angela and the twins to the concentration camp. After she had finally made it back to their demolished farm (riding on the wagon of a kindly Indian *smous)* she had unearthed the gun; should she ever have need of it. She had taken the few Pounds Sterling which the new British government had offered her in meager "compensation" for the destruction of her farm, and with the generous help of a returning Boer neighbor and his sons, purchased the basics of life, and had begun slowly to restore the demolished cottage. One of those Boer boys, a strapping young lad who had himself barely survived the death-camps, now rode up on his pony to the raucous strangers in the noisy automobile and demanded to know who these drunken trespassers thought they were, coming here to bother poor Tannie Erika.

Erika Roux nearly fell off the stoep when she realized one of the brash intruders was her beloved son. Erika looked still strangely beautiful in her old age, and was obviously overjoyed at the return of her only surviving "child"—as was Joshua, to find his old mother alive and well. He was elated to see her beaming face, she as joyful and relieved at seeing him as he was at seeing her. Joshua wrapped the petite Erika in his big arms and mother and son embraced tenderly for a long while, Erika weeping tears of joy. She then whispered in her son's ear, "...Angela... the twins... do you know...?" Joshua softly interrupted her, and "*Ja, Moeder... ek weet... maar hulle is nou met Pa, en met die Goeie Here, in die hemel...*" ("Yes, Mother... I know... but they are now with Pa and with the Good Lord, in heaven.") "But thankfully," he added, a little more cheerfully, "the Good Lord has seen fit to spare you and me. *Ja,* in Africa, only the strong survive." They embraced a little longer, sharing each other's grief and bitter-sweet joy, while Sean and Kerry stood politely beside the *Phoenix*, waiting to be introduced to Joshua's aged mother.

Soon, Erika was serving Joshua and his two Irish friends some strong *moer* ("ground") coffee to sober them up. She had also fetched them some aromatic, freshly made rusks, which she had baked in a temporary "oven," which she had fashioned from a hollowed-out termite mound and heated with coals. It felt good to Erika to have someone other than herself, to care for again; it gave her a profound sense of purpose.

Within a few weeks, Joshua had helped Sean and Kerry O'Connor build a simple cottage close to his mother's, and the two men then set about rebuilding the devastated Roux farm. Within a few months, Erika had convinced herself that this pretty, green-eyed, flame-haired, hard-working, and delightfully cheery Irish girl (despite some mild differences of opinion concerning the proper ingredients necessary for a good stew) would make a fine daughter-in-law. Erika soon began dropping non-subtle hints to Joshua about his advancing middle-age, and his need to produce an heir to inherit the two farms (and of course, the rest of Joshua's fortune in Kruger Rands, still stashed under the "dog's tombstone"). Kerry O'Connor's considerable charms had not gone totally unnoticed by Joshua, and after, at last, he considered his long period of mourning to be over, he had slowly and awkwardly begun to woo her, his best friend's sister. As life would have it, Joshua was not alone in his interest in the beautiful Kerry: A local entrepreneur, who made it his business to call at the Roux homestead on the pretext of presenting investment opportunities to Joshua, always arrived with an extravagant gift and flowers for the Irish girl. This rankled with Joshua, and so in his own way, he too began to bring her veld flowers, and then one day a tiny, orphaned meerkat whose mother had perished in the claws of an eagle. Not long thereafter, he presented her with a cuddly, fat Boerboel puppy he had acquired for her, which had been born on a neighboring farm (it actually being a blood-relative of his own dog, which had been cruelly slain by the black trooper). However, he need not have worried about Kerry's loyalties: for she had already set her heart on Joshua and *Joshua alone*—and after almost a year at the ranch, she finally accepted his recent, solemn proposal of marriage.

The hulking, beaming Sean O'Connor looked rather awkward, dressed for the first time in his life in *tux and tails,* as best-man at their wedding. Sean had a dual role, of course, as he also had to "give his sister away," to his best friend. The new Mevrou Kerry Kathleen Roux was only mildly disappointed that her wedding night was spent in the Lydenburg Hotel's hastily pre-pared "honeymoon suite," rather than in their own home—how-ever, their proposed new farmhouse had not been built yet! Her handsome new husband, whom she declared had "cleaned up well," presented her with a charming, pure-gold necklace as a wedding gift. Joshua had hired his banker's cousin, who was a jeweler, to craft the necklace from a number of his Kruger Rands which he had withdrawn from the vault at the Lydenburg bank. In honor of his young wife, Joshua Roux renamed the newly extended wildlife ranch *Kerryvale* ("Kerry's valley").

Chapter Thirty-six

The devastating SECOND ANGLO-BOER WAR (or the "Second Freedom War," as the defeated, but unbowed Boers themselves still called it) had set the stage for the building of a totally new UNION OF SOUTH AFRICA, and there would be nearly a century of dizzying progress and Western civilization which would distinguish the new, white African nation. The innovations and improvements were myriad: A vast network of railways to carry mining and agricultural produce was laid; the deepest mines in the world and the busiest harbors in Africa were dug; spectacular bridges spanned gorges; highways and tunnels were carved out of the mountain-sides; huge dams were erected to irrigate the flourishing farms; well-planned towns sprang up; modern cities with soaring sky-scrapers expanded; fine western-style universities, disciplined, uniformed public and private schools were founded; booming factories and lucrative business enterprises were established, and the economy of the country flourished, producing *far more than the rest of the whole of Africa combined.*

SOUTH AFRICA's fledgling UNION DEFENSE FORCE of mainly white troops, in the First World War, would drive the Germans out of Namibia and Central East Africa and fight for the Allies in France. Later, during the Second World War, the *Springboks* (the name by which the members of the South African army were known by their allies) would again drive the Italians *and* Germans (led by their brilliant General Erwin Rommel) out of North Africa, to free their black African neighbors from "colonial oppression." They would also temporarily occupy the island of Madagascar to prevent the Japanese from taking it. The proud

Springboks[153] would, as athletes and sports teams, triumph on the playing-fields of the world, and earn gold medals at the Olympic Games. Boer general-turned-statesman, then Allied Field-Marshall Jan Smuts would become a founding-father of the LEAGUE OF NATIONS (later to become the UNITED NATIONS), and South Africa would take its well-earned seat at that august assembly.

The Afrikaners would finally regain the reins of their government in 1948, and a new REPUBLIC OF SOUTH AFRICA would then be declared, in 1961. The first half of the first verse of the national anthem *Die Stem van Suid-Afrika* ("The Call/Voice of South Afrika") of the new republic would echo its Trekboer pioneer heritage:

"Uit die blou van onse hemel, uit die diepte van ons see; Oor ons ewige gebergdes, waar die krantze antwoord gee; Deur ons vêr verlate vlaktes, met die kreun van ossewa; Ruis die stem van ons geliefde, van ons land Suid-Afrika..."

("Ringing out from our blue heavens, from our deep seas breaking round; Over everlasting mountains where the echoing crags resound; From our plains where creaking wagons cut their trails into the earth; Calls the spirit of our Country, of the land that gave us birth...")

[The above translation is poetic, not literal. This stirringly beautiful anthem was penned by Cornelis Jacob Langenhoven (1873-1932), who was born near Ladismith in the Klein Karoo. A prolific writer of Afrikaans stories and poems, he was instrumental in having Afrikaans replace Dutch in Cape schools in 1914.]

---

[153] From 1903 on, all national sports teams were called *Springboks;* however, after the AFRICAN NATIONAL CONGRESS (ANC) took over (1994), most teams were renamed. Only the twice world-champion rugby team is still called the *Springboks*. Rugby in South Africa was long dominated by white Afrikaners; but this was changed when "racial quota" legislation was introduced. The cricket team was renamed the *Proteas* (implying, "diversity"). The *Protea,* commonly called *Suikerbos* ("Sugarbush"), is a genus of South African flower with myriad and divergent varieties; which was named by Carolus Linnaeus in 1735 after the Greek god *Proteus* (who could change his form at will).

Slowly but steadily, as slowly and steadily as their ox-wagons had traversed the veld, the Afrikaners made the country their own. Afrikaner culture, literature and holidays closely and proudly reflected their trekker heritage and Boer traditions.

However, this proud, white Afrikaner tribe would then commit a fatal political *faux pas,* a "cardinal sin"—in the eyes of a liberal world—which would lead to the dissolution of their independent, Christian republic ruled by white Afrikaners, a mere 30 years after the REPUBLIC OF SOUTH AFRICA had declared its independence. South Africa announced that the long-established and Biblically mandated *separation of the races* was to be their country's "official government policy." They even gave it an official name, calling it: *Apartheid* ("Apartness"). As *damage control,* they would later give it another, more "friendly" name, "Separate Development." They also alienated the friendly coloreds of the Cape (who had served bravely alongside them in two World Wars) by stacking the supreme court bench with those whites who would repeal the voting rights of the colored population.

In 1958, a big, fair-haired, blue-eyed Holland-born Professor of Applied Psychology, Hendrik Frensch Verwoerd (1901-1966), the so-called "architect of Apartheid" (which was actually instituted by British Lord Alfred Milner almost 60 years earlier) became Prime Minister of South Africa. After surviving an earlier attempt on his life, he was assassinated in parliament by a messenger: stabbed to death by an apparently deranged immigrant, Demetrios Tsafendas (1918-1999); who was born of a Greek father and a black Mozambican mother. Tsafendas was "liberated" in 1993 when the multiracial *"GOVERNMENT OF NATIONAL UNITY"* controlled the nation (until the elections of 1994); but having nowhere to go, he remained in the mental institution until he died 6 years later. He was then declared a "Hero of the (black) Nation."

Just a year before the declaration of the Republic, an event occurred at Sharpeville in the TRANSVAAL, in 1960, which would resonate around the world, and forever-after be used as anti-Afrikaner propaganda. A mob of about 6,000 blacks, protesting against a law which compelled them to carry identification-passes allowing them to work in "white" areas, surrounded a police station. The ostensibly "peaceful" demonstration turned ugly when a woman inserted a gasoline-soaked rag into the fuel-receptacle of a police vehicle and then lit it. The resultant explosion panicked the small contingent of besieged policemen (already on edge due to the fact that nine young policemen had recently been hacked and burned to death by a mob near Durban). The commander at Sharpeville ordered his policemen to be ready to shoot, but *only* if the masses broke down the fence; their last line of defense around the police station. When the mob stormed through the fence, firing broke out, and 69 of the rioters were killed. The senior police commander Lt. Colonel Pienaar later told a commission of inquiry into the "Sharpeville Massacre" that: "The Native mentality does not allow for a peaceful demonstration. For them to gather [together], means violence." Although the white Afrikaner, by virtue of their 3 centuries of contact with black Africans, could claim to "know" them better than any other white nation did, a liberal media's spin on these events, led to a world-wide perception that the Afrikaners were *violent* "white supremacists" and thus international sanctions against them were necessary.

To their credit, the white Nationalists *did* allocate many of the most beautiful and fertile regions of the *Afrikaner's own* country (including some of the most scenic coastal areas), for the sole habitation of the various black tribes—and encouraged the traditional black chiefs to rule their own people within those "homelands," much as they always had. The Afrikaners also developed modern infrastructure in the form of roads, reservoirs, hospitals, schools, civic buildings, industries, and even airports for the blacks, *in those semi-independent tribal homelands.* Yet still, the blacks continued to swarm to the "white" areas; *demanding* (and receiving) housing from the white authorities or they established sprawling squatter camps (which soon became squalorous, crime-riddled ghettos) around the peaceful, crime-free, white settlements.

One by one, largely as the result of liberal political machinations, the many black African nations to the north (most of which had *prospered* as European colonies) were given "freedom" as autonomous nations. The European powers turned the reins of their former African colonies over to the natives. However, nearly as quickly as their former European masters pulled out, those countries reverted to anarchy, barbarism, brutality, and chaos, followed by inevitable economic and agricultural collapse, famine and starvation. It would take *billions* of dollars of Western aid to once again stabilize them, and to help feed their burgeoning populations.

The "liberal" Western world would then turn against the SOUTH AFRICAN REPUBLIC, and its proud tribe of *white,* Afrikaans- and English-speaking pioneers. Much of the West also turned a deaf ear to any South Afrikaners' attempts to explain *why* apartheid was a necessary institution to preserve the integrity of their white, Christian African republic. Though no one listened, the Afrikaners explained why Apartheid was mandatory:

- The Afrikaners themselves refused to live or behave like the black Africans;

- It was required to maintain law, order, and safety, and to preserve their Christian civilization;

- It was necessary to preserve the racial integrity of the white Christian hegemony of their Republic (this in itself was certainly no crime, for all nonwhite races demanded the same basic right);

- The Afrikaners refused to be "governed" by the black Africans, who had consistently opposed them; blacks who had supported an imperialistic invader (Britain) against them; blacks whose "moral" standards were far different than their own—and because God had commanded it in His Word; and

 - The Afrikaners refused to allow their independent Republic to revert to barbarism, as all other European colonies in Africa had done, once they succumbed to "black majority rule" (even though their Republics were never really British "colonies"—the Afrikaners had existed autonomously before the British came and stole their nation from them).

However, the *"wind of change"* was sweeping through Africa, as a virulent liberalism was raging through the West. The propaganda of the liberal press and *libertine* Hollywood moguls would hold a monopoly over impressionable minds; the mythical "noble black savage" would be exalted and welcomed with open arms into many European countries (bringing with him a pagan religion, lower standards, and many new vices); rather than enjoying true civilization, the black African seemingly set about to destroy it by corrupting its institutions. Yet despite his apparently irreparable harm to white, Christian civilization, he received (and continues to receive) nothing but praise from the liberal media and Western governments.

On the other hand, the white Africans, the builders of the only true modern civilization in Africa—who brought peace, safety, and prosperity wherever they settled—would be vilified and become the social pariahs of the world. SOUTH AFRICA, which had already seceded from the British Commonwealth of Nations, was soon expelled from the very UNITED NATIONS that it helped to establish. Crippling, *discriminatory* international sanctions would be enforced against SOUTH AFRICA— for their "crime against humanity"[154]—for wanting to preserve what was theirs, by the unflinching practice of their *own*, traditional religious and political beliefs, within the borders of their *own* nation. The white Afrikaners were not guilty of telling *other* nations how they ought to live; nor were they guilty of oppressing other weaker nations around them—their "crime" was desiring to preserve the integrity of their own institutions and their *own* nation.

International demands for "democracy" in the white Afrikaner-ruled nation would grow ever more strident—yet, hypocritically, these same liberals studiously ignored the glaring fact that 90% of black African-ruled countries themselves were *not* democratic, and that *not a single* Arab-ruled African nation was either.

Yet, the white African tribe endured and even prospered, against all these odds, becoming self-sufficient and self-reliant. In co-operation with Israel, they developed a nuclear capability, and also the world's first viable oil-from-coal facility. They were front-runners in many fields, such as: agricultural science, engineering, aeronautics, advanced guidance systems, deep-level mining, wild-life conservation, higher education, and medical research—in fact, the world's first heart transplant was performed in 1967 by Dr. Christiaan Neethling Barnard (1922-2001). The South African *Rand* was considerably stronger than even the U.S. Dollar, and the

---

[154] —which is what the UNITED NATIONS declared Apartheid to be (yet, they have been silent on the ANC's "reverse-racism.").

standard of living of *all* South Africans was easily the highest in Africa—and was among the highest in the world. Yet even within the whites own ranks, there were those (mostly English-speaking or Jewish) who joined militant *black* "liberation movements" and rallied support in the West for these organizations.

The whites of South Africa (abandoned by the rest of the world) then developed the best-equipped and most-modern army in the southern hemisphere: to protect their new Republic's borders against a violent wave of communist-armed and trained "black-liberation" armies building up to their north (also supported by many of the nations of Christendom). Young white men and boys would give their lives in defense of their beloved country, to protect their farms and homes, their parents and siblings, and their wives and children. In the land of their birth (their Afrikaner homeland for over 300 years), they would endure the violent and bloody birth-pangs of "Black Consciousness," then face an internal rising tide of black terrorism—well-armed and encouraged from abroad.

As a result, *anarchy* would soon stalk their once-safe streets and then ravage their productive, peaceful farms, held back only by the efficiency of the centuries-old, rural *commando* units. Black students crying "Freedom before education!" would burn to the ground *their own* schools, civic buildings, clinics, and infrastructure (which the whites had built for them)—and even cut down the avenues of trees, which the whites had planted, calling them "symbols of colonial oppression." They would *burn alive* (utilizing their horrific, diesel-filled, rubber tire "necklaces") even their *own* people suspected of being "collaborators" with the whites. They would brutally murder innocent white civilians; even white teachers and nurses, who had devoted their lives to the service of blacks.

The ANC's (AFRICAN NATIONAL CONGRESS) communist-trained "militant wing" of this "black liberation struggle," was a group called *Mkhonto weSizwe* (MK), meaning, the "Spear of the Nation." This "liberationist" organization would torture and execute *hundreds* of blacks within their own camps, in the "frontline states"

(Angola, Botswana, Mozambique, Namibia, Zambia, and Zimbabwe) who were suspected as "traitors." This declared terrorist group, based to the north of the white republic, planted land-mines on South African farm roads, and detonated limpet-mines and car bombs in towns, indiscriminately killing and maiming innocent *civilians* (both black and white). Yet they never actually confronted the white *army* in South Africa in battle. In the "frontline state" of Angola, most of the real fighting against the whites was done *for* the black "liberation forces" by 50,000 *Cuban* troops, outfitted with *Russian* tanks and Mig fighter-aircraft, which culminated in a stalemate, at the hard-fought Battle of Cuito Cuanivale, in October of 1987. The San-Bushmen of Namibia, the original inhabitants of that desert land (many of whom had acted as trackers for the South African Army), were dispossessed of their allotted homeland there by the incoming black government, as a "punishment" for that *allegiance*. Notably, many moderate *black* Namibian troops *also* fought *alongside* the white troops, against the Marxist-led and Cuban-backed infiltrators from Angola, the Owambo, who now have a majority in the new *Namibian* government.

Yet still, the strongly Calvanistic, Christian white African nation endured; preferring to live as an independent ethnic minority *under virtual siege*—declared an enemy of the world—than to capitulate to a *communist*-backed, black majority rule and turn their backs on their God and their very heritage. The *Apartheid* era itself would last a mere 40 years: one generation —considerably less than the 70 years that the people of Eastern Europe suffered under the heel of *communism*. Yet, the white Afrikaners reasoned, Apartheid was not some *foreign* institution *imposed* upon *some other* nation, as was the case with communism; it was essentially the "House Rules" a sovereign people established to maintain law and order *in their own nation*. The primary reason *Apartheid* was instituted was the absolute refusal of the whites to have blacks living permanently within their towns and suburbs. Seeing how the blacks lived in their own villages—and obeying God's command to "be separate," the Afrikaners legislated Apartheid to preserve the integrity and safety their own nation and people. Further, the Afrikaners,

being a Christian people, would not allow dark-art practicing nonbe-
lievers to live among them; since centuries of missionary efforts, they
argued, had produced no real moral advancement or notable spiritual
change in the majority of the black peoples of South Africa.

Yet the albatross of *infamy* engendered by *"the legacy of
Apartheid"* would forever be dredged up by the incoming ANC
to stigmatize and discriminate against *all* whites—and to then
justify the passing of legislation to dispossess skilled white South
Africans of their jobs, and white farmers of their land, even *2
decades* after the whites *themselves* had abolished the policy of
Apartheid. Hypocritically, the blacks now began to impose similar *discriminatory* legislation against the ethnic-minority whites;
but now that "the tables had been turned," such racial discrimi-
nation was considered to be a *good* thing.[155]

Before the 20th Century drew to a close however, the *status
quo* in the REPUBLIC OF SOUTH AFRICA would change dramatically. An Afrikaner lawyer named F.W. (Frederik Willem) De
Klerk (born 1936), would become President of SOUTH AFRICA
(1989-1994). He was a leader within the conservative circles of
the nation, who had espoused traditional views concerning segregation—however, once he became president he *incomprehensibly*
made a 180° change in his philosophy, and in his first speech, he

---

[155] This duplicity is the *modus operandi* that international commu-
nists have ever employed in their attempts to undermine all sovereign Christian nations. It is alleged that communistic (and thus
atheistic) liberals put the white Christians on a contrived "guilt
trip," by declaring their segregationist attitude and practices to be
"unChristian," and even "immoral." A wedge is thus driven in
among society to weaken it from within (divide and conquer).
Once legislative concessions have been made and all have been
declared, "political equals," then the masses of nonwhites outvote
the white Christians in their own lands. Once the nonwhites hold
the power, the very same "oppressive," discriminatory, "racist"
laws which the liberals declared to be "immoral," are then re-
legislated *against the white Christian minority* in their own land.
Since only the nations of Christendom have stood in the way of
communist world domination, *all* white Christian nations have thus
purposely been weakened, and some destroyed in this fashion.

tried to convince his own people that they should "share power" with the black masses. De Klerk—called by some *'n Volksveraaier* ("a Folk-betrayer")—lifted the ban on the the AFRICAN NATIONAL CONGRESS (which had been considered a terrorist group) and released its leaders from prison. Gullible, liberal whites were beguiled into believing that a democratically elected, black-majority government (composed of those who had objected so violently to being "discriminated against" on the grounds of their race), would be "fair," once elected. These liberal whites were soon rudely awakened to the reality of race once the blacks, upon gaining power, vengefully *re-imposed* many of those very same discriminatory laws against the white minority. Many of those (again, mostly English-speaking or Jewish) liberals left the country soon after coming to this belated realization. A new, rapacious black government *was* swept into power by an overwhelmingly black majority vote. An autocratic black regime then—for the first time ever in Afrikaner history—would begin to rule over, and then *legislate against* the whites in the whites' own country: a country which they had transformed from an untamed wilderness, with their blood, sweat and tears, into a veritable utopia.

Many common blacks would then also begin to take their own brutal, *perceived* "revenge" on those whom they considered their former "oppressors"—*all* white people. During the very first decade of black majority rule, violent black criminals would brutally torture, burn, shoot, and hack to death *thousands* of peaceful, white farmers, savagely violate their wives and daughters, and even brutally murder many of the white peoples' faithful black and colored workers. These rural whites could no longer rely upon the protection of the white commandos—because the ANC had *disarmed* and *outlawed* them as "white supremacist groups." Merciless black criminals, unopposed, would also begin killing innocent white civilians in their own homes, in the towns and in the cities. Yet, not a *single,* black South African politician—nor even a single *white liberal* politician (previously so vocal in condemning the "unjust treatment" of blacks)—would utter a word of protest against, or condemnation of this slaughter of innocent people. Not only was this obviously immoral, it was foolish and even suicidal: for they were allowing the genocide of the Afrikaner Boers—the farmers—the very *food-producers* of their country (the very backbone of the rural areas). But the world—even the *Christian* world—would turn a "blind eye" to the blacks in their "ethnic cleansing" of the white, Christian Afrikaner (and the world continues to turn a blind eye to this day).[156]

Yet, the growing black masses would depend, for their very lives, upon the infrastructure and farms painstakingly built by those hardy white African pioneers: both Boer and British. Sadly, these two European peoples—kinsmen—had been set on a collision path, laid two centuries earlier and then reinforced a century later (by hidden powers): so they would destroy one another. The Boers and the British did not realize that the *real* enemies of their civilization stood impatiently on the sidelines, like hyenas, watching and waiting, for their own chance to grasp the reins of power and divide the spoil.[157]

When the dust finally settled, South Africa would be under the leadership of a wily Xhosa lawyer: who had been jailed for sabotage and for trying to start a "race-war." The name of that Xhosa lawyer was of course, Nelson Rolihlahla[158] Dalibhunga Mandela (born 1918). Mandela's father, Gadla Henry Mphakanyiswa (1880-1928), had 4 wives. Nelson was born to

---

[156] Scripture declares that men will have to answer to God for their indifference (Proverbs 21:13; Matthew 25:41-45; Galatians 6:10; I Timothy 5:8); not to mention *accessory to murder* (by hypocritically and callously doing nothing to stop it).

[157] During South Africa's post-Apartheid war crimes tribunal (the "Truth & Reconciliation Commission," chaired by Archbishop Desmond Tutu) it was revealed that while the white "Apartheid regime" had murdered just over 500 of their (mainly black) political opponents—the ANC "liberation movement" had murdered over 22,000 of *their own* (mainly black) political opponents!

[158] —*Xhosa* for "troublemaker." The last name he was born with is *Madiba,* which is the name of his clan (and he preferred to be called by this last name). His foster's mother's name was "No-England"—which is ironic, since it was the British who were greatly responsible for the political pressure which precipitated his release from prison.

the 3rd wife, Nkosekini Fanny Mphakanyiswa. Nelson Mandela was considered by many to be a "black messiah."[159] He was eventually freed from prison (largely as the result of British interference and pressure from liberals in other Western nations)—despite *still* professing the belief that violence was a legitimate political tool to wrest the government and the nation from the whites. Though Mandela claimed to espouse "democracy" (when it was to his benefit, as a sure means of gaining power in South Africa), he consistently criticized the leaders of western democracies—while his close personal friends included people such as Cuban dictator Fidel Castro, Libya's Muamar Gadaffi, and Palestinian leader Yasir Arafat.

After lengthy "negotiations" to "share power" with the black majority under a new constitution (which was the *only* mandate that 72% of the white electorate had given their leader), De Klerk and his henchmen ignored pleas (as did the mainstream press) from Afrikaners to establish *'n toevlug in die weste,* ("a refuge in the west")—in the historically "white" Western Cape. Afrikaners were demanding *their own* state, or at the very least,

---

[159] More as an "anti-Christ" by many white Christians, partly due to his prisoner number, "4-**666**-4." The number *666* is revealed in Scripture as being the number of the "Beast" (partner of the "Antichrist"), in Revelation 13:18. Modernly, fund-raising music concert organizers are careful to say "four-*double*-six-six-four" (perhaps to avoid the "Mark of the Beast" connotation). The number originated from Nelson Mandela being prisoner number 466 of the year '64. Nelson Mandela's then-wife, Nomzamo Winnie, during the time of her trial for *kidnapping* and for being an *accessory to murder*—had a luxury car, the registration of which was "NWM-**666**-GP." She was convicted, and received a *fine.* In later years, she was also convicted of theft and fraud. She also made the infamous speech about "liberating South Africa with our matchboxes and necklaces" referring to the horrific ANC practice of placing diesel-filled, rubber tires around the necks of people and burning them to death. "Seer" Michel de Nostradamus (1503-1566) also wrote of *Le Clercq* (F.W. De Klerk?) and the "land of the elephant" (South Africa?).

[De Klerk is a French Huguenot name; originally, *Le Clercq.*]

[footnote continued on next page...]

a federation of states, wherein they could exercise a degree of self-determination. But the De Klerk team suddenly capitulated to the black "negotiators" and agreed to a universal franchise vote. This basically *guaranteed* that the ANC would easily and overwhelmingly win the election and then wield *absolute power*. The ANC swiftly began bussing-in tens of thousands of Xhosas from their Transkei homeland, to the cities, and especially to Cape Town; establishing sprawling squatter-camps there to ensure that they would have sufficient "loyal voters" ready to swing the elections their way.

It is a *common misconception* that the ANC's leader in these early elections, Nelson Mandela, had been jailed for his "political beliefs." He was in fact *acquitted of treason* after a 4-year trial, but re-arrested a few years later, and sentenced to 5 years imprisonment for launching an armed insurrection (as founder and commander-in-chief of Mkhonto weSizwe, the ANC's

---

[159] [...continued.]

The Boer prophet Siener "Seer" van Rensburg apparently predicted a "Night of the Long Knives" wherein blacks would attack whites in the aftermath of the demise of Mandela. He also "saw" a "great black leader" lying in state in a "glass coffin" viewed by the leaders of the world. Some believe that this "glass coffin" had already been manufactured well in advance of that event. Siener predicted that the Boers would then "take back their land" from the blacks. Efforts have been made by the ANC government to suppress this "propaganda." A popular Afrikaans song called "De la Rey" (honoring the legacy of long-deceased Boer General Koos De la Rey), by singer Bok van Blerk, was also recently censured by some within the black government—they claimed that the song was "engendering a new Afrikaner nationalism." However, there was no such outcry in response to the ANC's new president-elect, Jacob Zuma, when he gave stirring song-and-dance renditions on national TV of the old ANC "armed struggle" favorite *Mashini Wami* ("Pass Me My Machine-gun"); nor to Nelson Mandela giving the "Black Power" salute while *singing along* to "Bulala AmaBuhnu" (Kill the Boers) at the funeral of a comrade, who was himself known to publicly lead the ANC in chants of "Kill the Farmer, Kill the Boer" and "One Settler, One Bullet." A "human rights" commission turned down a civil complaint against this for being "hate speech" and instead, declared it to be "traditional"!

militant wing). He was then later charged with 193 counts of *terrorism:* for sabotage and for trying to smuggle, prepare, or manufacture (mostly Soviet-bloc) munitions, including: 210,000 hand-grenades, 48,000 anti-personnel mines, 144 *tons* of ammonium-nitrate, 21.6 *tons* of aluminum powder, 1,500 timing devices, and 2,000 lbs. of black gunpowder. Among his many alleged co-conspirators were 3 communist Jews: Denis Goldberg, Arthur Goldreich, and Lionel "Rusty" Bernstein. Nelson Mandela's personal Makarov pistol ("for killing white policemen") which he buried in Rivonia before his arrest during the ANC's "armed struggle," was never recovered. These were clearly not "trumped-up" political charges. In his eloquent closing statement to the court, Mandela candidly *admitted* his guilt on the charge of sabotage, adding that he was, if needs be, prepared to die for his ideals. It was apparent from the huge amount of smuggled explosives that he was not planning to die *alone.*

Nelson Mandela was sentenced to life imprisonment; not summarily executed, as he undoubtedly *would* have been, in any *black* African country at that time, for the same offenses. Some made fanciful comparisons with the fate of plotter Guy Fawkes, who was *burned at the stake* for his *failed* attempt to blow up the British parliament in 1605. However Mandela conspired not just to bring down the government—he was planning on killing *tens of thousands* of innocent civilians in his quest for power. The judge at his trial did in fact comment that "personal ambition" may well have played a role in his plans. Mandela boldly admitted his guilt. He was never tortured during either his interrogation or incarceration (as he undoubtedly would have been in a black nation). In fact, he was generally treated humanely by his white captors; eventually being transferred from Robben Island, to the mainland, and living comfortably in a cottage in the grounds of the prison for the latter part of his incarceration.

Although he was approached and offered an early release by then-president Pieter Willem (P.W.) Botha (1916-2006), in the mid 1980's, Mandela still steadfastly *refused* to renounced his commitment to violence. Likewise, *even when* he eventually gained an early release (by F.W. De Klerk), about 6 years later, on the condition that he commit his party to peaceful negotiations, he still *refused* to renounce violence. As he walked free from the prison, accompanied by his second wife Nomzamo "Winnie" Madikizela-Mandela (born 1936) he raised his fist in a "Black Power" salute. Further, in the first speech that he made as a "free man," he brazenly announced that the armed struggle would continue. "The rest," as they say, "is history." Nelson Mandela subsequently led his communist-aligned ANC to an overwhelming victory in the first "fully democratic" South African elections in 1994.

One of their favorite chants at political rallies *to this day* is: **"Bulala AmaBuhnu" (Kill the Boers).**[160]

---

[160] Mandela became the first black President of the "new" South Africa, in 1994. De Klerk was also well rewarded, in advance, for his role in this arrangement: He and Mandela shared the NOBEL PEACE PRIZE (with its million-dollar purse) of 1993. Affadavits later alluded to Mandela having foreign bank accounts, on which he paid no tax (according to *Business Day,* March 10, 2007). De Klerk was subsequently divorced from his wife of 39 years (who had been his "college sweetheart" at POTCHEFSTROOM UNIVERSITY), in 1998, after the discovery of his affair (according to *BBC News,* Wed., December 5, 2001) with his long-time mistress, Elita Georgiades (wife of a Greek shipping billionaire, supporter, and family friend)—whom he married a week later. The former Mrs. Marike de Klerk (1938-2001), who reputedly did not share her husband's liberal views, was brutally murdered (strangled and stabbed; found with the knife still embedded in her back) in her own home, on the "safe" side of town—killed by her own black "security guard!" She was murdered while her ex-husband, F.W. De Klerk, was in Stockholm, Sweden attending a NOBEL PRIZE COMMITTEE function. Her high-profile murder drew sympathy from many circles, even the most unlikely: The 2nd President of the "new" South Africa, Thabo Mvuyelwa Mbeki (born 1942), graciously stated that she was a "strong, charming and dignified woman."

Belatedly, her ex-husband, former-president F.W. de Klerk (who oversaw his own peoples' political euthanasia) began protesting against the ANC government's (blatantly racist) economic policies. Agronomists warn that their "expropriation" of thousands of white-owned farms could lead the country towards agricultural collapse. The devastated neighboring country of Zimbabwe is quoted as the one most glaringly obvious example of the spectacular failure of such short-sighted, virulently anti-white, self-destructive government ideologies.

APPENDICES
Appendix A

These principles of segregation in both society and government were also practiced in the early United States republic. God had mandated to His people: "—thou mayest not set a stranger over thee, which *is* not thy brother." (Deuteronomy 17:15) The early American Pilgrims and the Boers both believed that they were God's very Israel people, and thus they obeyed God's command. In order to hold political office in the early U.S., a man had to be a white Christian.

In a number of places in His Word, the Lord forbids His people to intermarry with other peoples, polluting their bloodlines (corrupting their racial heritage, as well as their spiritual heritage). These commands were accompanied by dire warnings of the consequences of such disobedience to His Law (Genesis 24:3, 4, 37, 38; Exodus 34:10-16; Numbers 36:5-13; Isaiah 52:11; 2 Corinthians 6:17, 18; Ezra 9, etc.). Sadly, the Bible is filled with narratives of the calamities that befell God's people when they disobeyed. It follows, then, that the Boers, as "People of the Book" (who they believed themselves to be), *"lived* by the Book." As they answered to God and not to men, the Boers, considered themselves dutibound to keep themselves separate from other races (and believed themselves to be justified in so doing).

Racial exclusiveness within a nation is also nothing unusual and it is not a phenomenon found merely among white nations. No other people on the face of the earth (except European peoples) automatically grants to dissimilar foreigners the status of equality and a voice in the government. *Even today,* in China, Arab nations, Israel, India, and black African nations, *white Christians* are never automatically extended "equality" or any "right" to have a say in how those nations are governed. It *is* only natural and proper that all nations retain their own sovereignty and preserve the integrity of their people. However, hypocritically, these principles of "equality" are not applied consistently. In only one generation, a black-African immigrant to a white nation is considered a full citizen of that country—but even after *350 years* and *10 generations* in South Africa, the whites are still regarded by most nonwhites as "foreigners," in a country they themselves built from "scratch."

It also should be remembered that the Afrikaners did *not* invade established metropolises of black Africa and then "take over." The Afrikaners themselves *built* those cities out of uninhabited wastelands and developed them; to which the blacks later flocked, to partake of the benefits of civilization. All the Afrikaners have ever *really* wanted, was to rule *themselves*, in their own land. The blacks living within the early Boer Republics were initially, apparently quite content—until interlopers stirred up discontent by convincing them that they had the right to *sit at the table itself* and even *be the* master: Michael Davitt, M.P. (who resigned from Parliament in protest over Britain's actions in the SECOND ANGLO-BOER WAR, which he witnessed first hand) in his The Boer Fight For Freedom,* recorded:

"Its objects were obvious to the Transvaal government and to all who followed with any attention the movement for 'the redress of the intolerable grievances' of the German Jews and the cosmopolitan adventurers which was carried on by the paid agents of Messrs. Rhodes, Beit, Echstein and Company in Johannesburg. One comment upon the "grievances" thus manufactured by a subsidized press—the honest and manly view of an upright British soldier who had been conversant with the whole situation in Johannesburg—will be enough to lay bare the hollow mockery, and the mercenary and mendacious character, of the movement upon the existence of which Mr. Chamberlain and Sir Alfred Milner grounded their pretext for a policy of war.

"Captain March Phillips, in his book "With Rimington," (London, Edward Arnold, publisher, 1901, pp. 105, 106) writing, both as a Uitlander and an English officer who had fought in the war, says:

'As for the Uitlanders and their grievances, I would not ride a yard or fire a shot to right all the grievances that were ever invented. The mass of Uitlanders (i.e. the

miners and working men of the Rand) had no grievances. I know what I am talking about, for I have lived
and worked among them. I have seen English newspapers passed from one to another, and roars of laughter
roused by the *Times* telegrams about these precious grievances. We used to read the London papers *to find out
what our grievances were;* and very frequently they would
be due to causes of which we had never even heard. I
never met one miner or working man who would have
walked a mile to pick the vote up off the road, and I have
known and talked with scores and hundreds. And no
man who knows the [Witwaters-] Rand will deny the
truth of what I tell you. [Emphasis mine.]

'No; the Uitlanders the world has heard of were not
these, but the Stock Exchange operators, manipulators
of the money market, company floaters, and gamblers
generally, a large percentage of them Jews. They voiced
Johannesburg, had the press in their hands, worked
the wires, and controlled and arranged what sort of information should reach England. As for the grievances,
they were a most useful invention, and have had a hand
in the making of many fortunes. It was by these that a
feeling of insecurity was introduced into the market which
would otherwise have remained always steady; it was by
these that the necessary and periodic slump was brought
about. When the proper time came, "grievances," such
as would arrest England's attention and catch the ear
of the people, were *deliberately invented.'* (pp.41,42)

[* See p.388 for information on Davitt's book.]

Scripture tells us:

"When the righteous are in authority, the people rejoice:
but when the wicked beareth rule, the people mourn."
(Proverbs 29:2)

"For three *things* the earth is disquieted, and for four
which it cannot bear: For a servant when he reigneth..."
(Proverbs 30:21,22)

"Righteousness exalteth a nation: but sin *is* a reproach to
any people." (Proverbs 14:34)

Appendix B

There is much controversy and confusion surrounding how Johannesburg received its name. President Kruger and the executive council of the ZUID-AFRIKAANSCHE REPUBLIEK (ZAR) had named a two-man commission to find a suitable location to establish a town in the Witwatersrand: *Johann* Friedrich Bernhard Rissik (1857-1925), a surveyor and General Petrus Jacobus Joubert (1831-1900), vice-president of the ZAR. *Johann* Rissik, as surveyor, was assisted by *Veldkornet*[161] *Johannes* Petrus Meyer. The "official" version was that Johannesburg was named after the common name of this surveyor, and a shortened version of the name of his assistant, Johann.

[A second surveyor was also employed, Josias Eduard de Villiers (1843-1898). The two surveyors laid out their plans, in a grid pattern, from opposite ends of the town, with de Villiers apparently often ignoring such "minor irritations" as *natural contours,* and when the roadways finally met, they were found to be almost 20 yards out of alignment. Johannesburg was thus established with a distinct "kink" in almost every one of the main streets in the center of the town!]

A more modern legend explains that after surveying the town, they reported to President Stephanus *Johannes* Paulus ("Oom Paul") Kruger and said, "We thought of naming it after you, Mr President. Since your name is Johannes, we suggest Johannesburg."[162] Kruger, in reply, apparently quipped, "Well, as we are *all Johanneses,* we'll name it as you say."

However, that is the "official" version. An interesting theory[163] is that Johannesburg was actually named after the dynasty of Portuguese kings, *João* (Johan, Johannes or John). Support for this theory is substantial. It is unlikely that the town would have been named after Rissik, who was a relatively obscure *Dutchman* (not a Boer) and because it was *5 years* after the town's founding that its inhabitants were first informed that their city was named

---

[161] "Field Colonel."

[162] "John's Town."

[163] —proposed by Niel Hirschson in his book, The Naming of Johannesburg (1974).

after Rissik and the low-ranking Meyer (while the far more important Kruger was overlooked entirely). South Africa was on good terms with Portugal and was even trying to secretly establish stronger ties.[164] Portugal wanted to develop one large *transcontinental territory* from their colony in Angola (on the west coast of Africa) all the way to Delagoa Bay (now Maputo) in their colony of *Moçambique* (on the east coast of Africa). Kruger had no objections to this, since he wanted to garner greater support from other European powers for possible solidarity against the growing British menace. In 1884, two years before Johannesburg was *allegedly* "officially" named *(post-facto)*, Kruger had even traveled to Portugal where he was bestowed with a rare, high, military honor: the PORTUGUESE GRAND CROSS OF THE ORDER OF THE IMMACULATE CONCEPTION (a.k.a. the KING JOÃO KNIGHTLY ORDER OF THE IMMACULATE CONCEPTION).

One of Kruger's fondest wishes was the creation of a Pretoria-Delagoa railway link; which was finally completed in 1895 and which Kruger himself used in making his escape during the Anglo-Boer War, eventually reaching Europe, where he tried to gather support for the beleaguered Republic. Portugal further honored President Kruger by naming one of the locomotives on this railway after him. However, long before this was possible Britain had ruled in the LONDON CONVENTION of 1884:

"The SOUTH AFRICAN REPUBLIC will conclude no treaty or engagement with any state or nation other than the ORANGE FREE STATE, nor with any native tribe to the eastward or westward of the republic, until the same has been approved by Her Majesty the Queen." (Article 4).

At this time, Britain was not on good terms with Portugal, and to avoid stirring up British resentment, the true origin of the naming of Johannesburg was kept secret and the "cover story" of it being named after the surveyor Rissik or others was thus circulated.

---

[164] —since they were "neighbors," due to the proximity of the Portuguese colony of *Moçambique* (Mozambique).

It is thought that Kruger wished to repay the honor to Portugal, for the honors they bestowed on him, by so naming Johannesburg after Portugal's kings. Further testimony to this is the fact that in the CAPE COLONY, in the early 1800's, there was a stable form of currency in circulation, which was a gold coin called the "Johannes"—which honored several Portuguese monarchs (who were portrayed on the coins). These popular and trusted coins, of course, made their way north into the Boer Republics. The nickname of these coins was the "Jo." It is suggested that this itself is the origin of Johannesburg's nickname—*Jo'burg*—as opposed to the common notion that the name is merely a shortened form of the name Johannesburg.

[Oddly, as late as the mid-1960's South African gold *shares* were still known in England as "Kaffirs" and were traded in the section of the LONDON STOCK EXCHANGE known as the "Kaffir Circus." Gold coins minted during the Boer War were sometimes called "Kruger's Coins" but the name "Krugerrands" became official in 1967. Of course, Krugerrands became outlawed in the U.S. and other liberal nations (even as were Cuban cigars), out of an international boycott of South Africa's policy of Apartheid.]

Appendix C

Poems by Rudyard Kipling

THE WHITE MAN'S BURDEN
(1899)

Take up the White Man's burden—Send forth the best ye breed—Go bind your sons to exile, To serve your captives' need; To wait in heavy harness, On fluttered folk and wild— Your new-caught, sullen peoples, Half-devil and half-child.

Take up the White Man's burden—In patience to abide, To veil the threat of terror, And check the show of pride; By open speech and simple, An hundred times made plain, To seek another's profit, And work another's gain.

Take up the White Man's burden—The savage wars of peace— Fill full the mouth of Famine, And bid the sickness cease; And when your goal is nearest, The end for others sought, Watch sloth and heathen Folly, Bring all your hopes to naught.

Take up the White Man's burden—No tawdry rule of kings, But toil of serf and sweeper—The tale of common things. The ports ye shall not enter, The roads ye shall not tread, Go mark them with your living, And mark them with your dead.

Take up the White Man's burden—And reap his old reward: The blame of those ye better, The hate of those ye guard—The cry of hosts ye humor, (Ah, slowly!) toward the light, "Why brought he us from bondage, Our loved Egyptian night?"

Take up the White Man's burden—Ye dare not stoop to less—Nor call too loud on Freedom, To cloak your weariness; By all ye cry or whisper, By all ye leave or do, The silent, sullen feebles, Shall weigh your gods and you.

Take up the White Man's burden—Have done with childish days—The lightly proferred laurel, The easy, ungrudged praise. Comes now, to search your manhood, Through all the thankless years, Cold, edged with dear-bought wisdom, The judgment of your peers.

The Wrath of the Awakened Saxon

It was not part of their blood, It came to them very late, With long arrears to make good, When the Saxon began to hate.

They were not easily moved, They were icy—willing to wait, Till every count should be proved, Ere the Saxon began to hate.

Their voices were even and low. Their eyes were level and straight. There was neither sign nor show, When the Saxon began to hate.

It was not preached to the crowd. It was not taught by the state. No man spoke it aloud, When the Saxon began to hate.

It was not suddenly bred. It will not swiftly abate. Through the chilled years ahead, When Time shall count from the date, That the Saxon began to hate.

The Stranger

The Stranger within my gate, He may be true or kind, But he does not talk my talk—I cannot feel his mind. I see the face and the eyes and the mouth, But not the soul behind.

The men of my own stock, They may do ill or well, But they tell the lies I am wonted to. They are used to the lies I tell, And we do not need interpreters, When we go to buy and sell.

The Stranger within my gates, He may be evil or good, But I cannot tell what powers control, What reasons sway his mood; Nor when the Gods of his far-off land, Shall repossess his blood.

The men of my own stock, Bitter bad they may be, But, at least, they hear the things I hear, And see the things I see; And whatever I think of them and their likes, They think of the likes of me.

This was my father's belief, And this is also mine: Let the corn be all one sheaf—And the grapes be all one vine, Ere our children's teeth are set on edge, By bitter bread and wine.

THE CHILDREN'S SONG
(first 2 stanzas)

Land of our Birth, we pledge to thee, Our love and toil in the years to be; When we are grown and take our place, As men and women with our race.

Father in Heaven who lovest all, Oh help Thy children when they call; That they may build from age to age, An undefiled heritage.

RECESSIONAL
(1897)
[Composed for Queen Victoria's Diamond Jubilee; needless to say, it received a cool reception.]

God of our fathers, known of old, Lord of our far-flung battle-line, Beneath whose awful Hand we hold, Dominion over palm and pine, Lord God of Hosts, be with us yet, Lest we forget lest we forget!

The tumult and the shouting dies; The Captains and the Kings depart: Still stands Thine ancient sacrifice, An humble and a contrite heart. Lord God of Hosts, be with us yet, Lest we forget lest we forget!

Far-called, our navies melt away; On dune and headland sinks the fire: Lo, all our pomp of yesterday, Is one with Nineveh and Tyre! Judge of the Nations, spare us yet, Lest we forget lest we forget!

If, drunk with sight of power, we loose, Wild tongues that have not Thee in awe, Such boastings as the Gentiles use, Or lesser breeds without the Law, Lord God of Hosts, be with us yet, Lest we forget lest we forget!

For heathen heart that puts her trust, In reeking tube and iron shard, All valiant dust that builds on dust, And guarding, calls not Thee to guard, For frantic boast and foolish word, Thy mercy on Thy People, Lord!

Tommy (Atkins)
1892

I went into a public-'ouse to get a pint o'beer, The publican 'e up an' sez, "We serve no red-coats here." The girls be'ind the bar they laughed an' giggled fit to die, I outs into the street again an' to myself sez I: O it's Tommy this, an' Tommy that, an' "Tommy, go away"; But it's "Thank you, Mister Atkins," when the band begins to play, The band begins to play, my boys, the band begins to play, O it's "Thank you, Mr. Atkins," when the band begins to play.

I went into a theatre as sober as could be, They gave a drunk civilian room, but 'adn't none for me; They sent me to the gallery or round the music-'alls, But when it comes to fightin', Lord! they'll shove me in the stalls! For it's Tommy this, an' Tommy that, an' "Tommy, wait outside"; But it's "Special train for Atkins" when the trooper's on the tide, The troopship's on the tide, my boys, the troopship's on the tide, O it's "Special train for Atkins" when the trooper's on the tide.

Yes, makin' mock o' uniforms that guard you while you sleep, Is cheaper than them uniforms, an' they're starvation cheap; An' hustlin' drunken soldiers when they're goin' large a bit, Is five times better business than paradin' in full kit. Then it's Tommy this, an' Tommy that, an' "Tommy how's yer soul?" But it's "Thin red line of 'eroes" when the drums begin to roll, The drums begin to roll, my boys, the drums begin to roll, O it's "Thin red line of 'eroes" when the drums begin to roll.

We aren't no thin red 'eroes, nor we aren't no blackguards too, But single men in barricks, most remarkable like you; An' if sometimes our conduck isn't all your fancy paints: Why, single men in barricks don't grow into plaster saints; While it's Tommy this, an' Tommy that, an' "Tommy, fall be'ind," But it's "Please to walk in front, sir," when there's trouble in the wind, There's trouble in the wind, my boys, there's trouble in the wind, O it's "Please to walk in front, sir," when there's trouble in the wind.

You talk o' better food for us, an' schools, an' fires an' all:
We'll wait for extry rations if you treat us rational. Don't
mess about the cook-room slops, but prove it to our face.
The Widow's Uniform is not the soldier-man's disgrace. For
it's Tommy this, an' Tommy that, an' "Chuck him out, the
brute!" But it's "Saviour of 'is country," when the guns
begin to shoot; An' it's Tommy this, an' Tommy that, an'
anything you please; But Tommy ain't a bloomin' fool -
you bet that Tommy sees!

Appendix D

"The Boer"

"Take a community of Dutchmen of the type of those who defended themselves for fifty years against all the power of Spain at a time when Spain was the greatest power in the world.

"Intermix them with a strain of those inflexible French Huguenots, who gave up their name and fortune and left their country forever at the time of the revocation of the Edict of Nantes.

"The product must obviously be one of the most rugged, versatile, unconquerable races ever seen upon Earth.

"Take these formidable people and train them for seven generations in constant warfare against savage men and ferocious beasts in circumstances in which no weakling could survive: place them so that they acquire skill with weapons and in horsemanship, give them a country which is imminently suited to the tactics of the huntsman, the marksman and the rider.

"Then, finally put a fine temper upon their military qualities by a dour fatalistic Old Testament religion and an ardent and consuming patriotism.

"Combine all these qualities and all these impulses in one individual and you have the modern Boer."

—Sir Arthur Conan Doyle
[from Chapter 1 of Doyle's book
The Great Boer War (1900)]

[Doyle, the famous author (creator of Sherlock Holmes), was also a physician who served as a medic in the Boer War. He also, interestingly, was the "creator" of "Piltdown Man"—a hoax he fabricated and pawned off on the evolutionists to show their gullibility.]

Appendix E

Since the British could not find any incentive to successfully encourage enough blacks to work the mines, the British resorted to importing hard-working Chinese "coolies." The Chinese were prepared to travel halfway across the world to work for the same, low wages that the local blacks spurned. These indentured Chinese laborers were mostly returned to their homeland after their stint of work had expired (which was generally about 5 years in length). However, some stayed on permanently and prospered, making South Africa their home. Ironically, although blacks found it offensive when Orientals were declared "honorary whites" by the Apartheid government for trade purposes, modernly, the new black government has declared them "honorary blacks," and therefore entitled to racially discriminatory employment opportunities and privileges!

Similarly, hard-working Indian labor was imported to cut the sugar-cane fields in NATAL, because the local Zulu men refused that work. The British then devised a method of *forcing* the blacks into the labor market. The British imposed a "Hut Tax," on black men as an incentive to make them work. This "Hut Tax" was payable only in "cash"—not in cows, goats, snared antelope, chickens or pumpkins.[165] The British may also have levied the tax to encourage black men to have fewer wives: since each wife had her own hut and each hut was taxed separately.

However, the blacks blamed the "unfair white man," in general, for the imposition of this oppressive "Hut Tax,"—rather than blaming the British, who were the only ones actually responsible for it. The imposition of this harsh measure eventually led to a violent black rebellion.

---

[165] This method of "forcing" the blacks to work against their will (through the "Hut Tax"), for wages the British themselves determined—though creative—was tantamount to "slavery." Thus, the British were guilty, immediately after the war, of the very same thing for which the British claimed the war was waged: to deliver the blacks (and "foreigners") from oppression. Corrupt politicians of all nations have implemented similar taxation measures to enslave the formerly free peoples of such nations.

However, the hard-working Chinese and Indians *prospered,* under the same "oppressive" Apartheid that the blacks resented. Further, the Chinese and Indians actually imposed *their own* "Apartheid"—by their own choice, they remained socially segregated from the blacks. The Indians, even under Apartheid, developed some of the plushest neighborhoods in Durban and other cities. Yet, while seemingly unwilling to wholeheartedly contribute to their own economic betterment, the blacks still demanded the "benefits of civilization" ("government hand-outs," free education, health care, housing, etc.)—while also apparently "reserving the right" to continue their apparently "traditional, preferred method" of self-improvement: *stealing from the whites!* Some claim that this was one of the real reasons that the blacks resented Apartheid: because with the imposition of curfews, after which time blacks could not legally be in white neighborhoods, the blacks then had limited access to the white households, and thus stealing from the whites was greatly curtailed.

Further, Apartheid was not a "one-way" street: Whites were also thus prevented from opening shops and businesses in many "black" areas, leaving the field open to *black* entrepreneurs to succeed in those neighborhoods without *any* white competition. A few did. However when rioting broke out in Soweto in 1976, those black enterprises were among the *first* to get looted and torched by other blacks.

Nonetheless, Apartheid *did* keep crime rates amazingly low— even in the *black* neighborhoods. Once "Separate Development" was abolished, *all* of society suffered as crime skyrocketed; while most of the blacks (with the exception of the new "cleptocracy" and those "connected few" who benefitted from affirmative postings and contracts) lived little different than before—other than the fact they were now unrestrained in their criminal conduct. Apartheid, it is argued, didn't "*keep all blacks down*;" many blacks *have chosen* to live and behave the way they do, all over the world— even in their own homelands under their sole control and in lands where no whites have had any significant influence.

[In a sense, the BRITISH EMPIRE functioned similarly to the ROMAN EMPIRE, which transported its "slaves/labor" from one conquered nation to another, creating further racial tensions and mixture, thereby further *weakening* the vanquished nation. The fact that the priority after the war was getting the gold mines operating, seemed to dispel any notion that the "official" reason the Brits invaded South Africa was to "liberate" the *Uitlanders* and the poor "oppressed" blacks—especially since after the war, hardly any political changes were made in favor of the blacks (and since the British then imposed the new oppressive "Hut Tax"); things went back to the way they were—with the exception that the British now controlled the diamond and gold mines (or rather, Rothschild agents now controlled the mines[166]). Britain was apparently fi-nagled into the war by subversive, foreign elements within their own government. Their real reason for vanquishing the Boers was to steal the *gold* (and diamond) mines—and one of the first orders of business was to get those mines up and running imme-diately. Ironically, the British, who were allegedly so "conscien-tious" about the Boers "oppressing" the *blacks* by paying them "low wages"—then resorted to importing *Chinese* to exploit and oppress, *at those same low* wages (since the blacks still refused to work the mines in sufficient numbers).]

---

[166] Milner and Rhodes were also reportedly Rothschild agents. Rhodes obtained a £1,000,000 loan from the Rothschild's of London in 1887, and acquired the claims of COMPAGNIE FRANCAISE DES MINES DE DIAMANTS DU CAP ("FRENCH COMPANY OF CAPE DIAMOND MINES") next to KIMBERLEY CENTRAL. DE BEERS CONSOLIDATED MINES was founded in 1888 (merg-ing with controlling shares of the mines in KIMBERLEY CENTRAL, DUTOITSPAN, and BULTFONTEIN) and controls 90% of the world's dia-monds. Ernest Oppenheimer arrived in South Africa in 1902—the year Rhodes died—as an agent for diamond brokers A. DUNKELSBUHLER & CO. However, Oppenheimer then founded his own, ANGLO AMERICAN CORPORATION OF SOUTH AFRICA (AACSA) in 1917, which is closely associated with De Beers; the two companies, since 1929, have almost always shared the same chairman. Ini-tially, the primary goal of the AACSA was to mine gold on the eastern Witwatersrand. However, in 1919 (5 years after the South African Union Army "invaded" SOUTH WEST AFRICA to "drive out" their former allies, the Germans) the AACSA began acquiring diamond interests (which had belonged to members of the German DIAMOND REGIE) there, in what is now Namibia. The next year these diamond interests were transferred to a specially formed corporation, CON-SOLIDATED DIAMOND MINES OF SOUTH WEST AFRICA, Ltd. (the very year in which the League of Nations placed South West Africa under South African administration: 1920). Many Afrikaners rebelled against Union support for Imperialists.

Bibliography, Reference & Recommended Reading

[Those titles below with prices are available from Sacred Truth Publishing.]

P.O. Box 18 Mountain City, Tennessee, 37683

[For overseas shipping info contact: stm@mounet.com]

Bird, John. The Annals of Natal 1495-1845. Cape Town: Struik, 1965. [Containing The Personal Diary of William Wood. Copyright held by Robert Dean Wood, U.S.A.]

Blessynski, Nick. Shoot Straight, You Bastards. New York: Random House, 2002. [Sympathetic account of "Breaker" Morant's role in the Boer War/ Bushveldt Carbineers; 650pp.]

Bulpin, T.V., ed. Illustrated Guide to Southern Africa. Cape Town: Readers Digest Association, 1980. [544pp.]

Cassidy, Martin. The Inniskilling Diaries (1899-1903). U.K.: Leo Cooper, 2001. [252pp.]

Cloete, Stuart. Turning Wheels. Glasgow: Fontana/ Collins, 1937. [A novel of the Great Trek; 380pp.]

Giliomee, Herman. The Afrikaners: Biography of a People. Cape Town: Tafelberg, 2003. [560pp., pb., 9^{00} + P&H.]

Greaves, Adrian. Isandlwana. Johannesburg: Johnathan Ball, 2001. [217pp.]

Greaves, Adrian. Rorke's Drift. Johannesburg: Johnathan Ball, 2002. [446pp., pb., 10^{00} + P&H.]

Joyce, Peter. The South African Family Encyclopaedia. Cape Town: Struik, 1989. [432pp.]

Leach, Charles. Zoutpansberg Skirmishes Route Guide. Various personal communications, 2008.

Meredith, Martin. The Fate of Africa: From the Hopes of Freedom to the Heart of Despair; A History of Fifty Years of Independence. American edition. New York: PublicAffairs, 2006. [752pp., pb., 22^{00} + P&H. English edition titled, The State of Africa.]

Menzies, Gavin. 1421: The Year China Discovered the Americas. American edition. New York: William Morrow, 2004. [672pp., pb., 16^{00} + P&H; 576pp., Hb., 24^{00} (reg. 28^{00}) + P&H. English edition titled, 1421: The Year China Discovered the World.]

Michener, James A. The Covenant. New York: Random House, 1980. [A novel; 1243pp., mass-market pb., 9^{00} + P&H.]

Morris, Donald R. The Washing of the Spears: Rise and Fall of the Zulu Nation. London: Pimlico/Random House, 1965. [655pp.]

Orford, J.G., ed. "The Verdict of History." Military History Journal. Vol. 2, No. 2 (1971). [Information on General Koos De la Rey and Siener van Rensburg; and various other journals of the SOUTH AFRICAN MILITARY HISTORY SOCIETY.]

Pakenham, Thomas. The Boer War. Johannesburg: Johnathan Ball, 1979. [659pp.]

Pakenham, Thomas. The Scramble for Africa. New York: Harper, 1992. [800pp., pb., 24^{00} + P&H.]

Preston, Antony. Pictorial History of South Africa. Johannesburg: C.N.A., 1989. [192pp.]

Pretorius, Fransjohan. Life on Commando during the Anglo-Boer War (1899-1902). Cape Town: Human & Rousseau, 1999. [479pp.]

Radcliffe-Brown, A.R., and Forde, Darryl. African Systems of Kinship and Marriage. London: Oxford, 1975. [339pp.]

Radcliffe-Brown, A.R. Structure & Function in Primitive Society. London: Routledge, 1976. [219pp.]

Readers Digest Association. Illustrated History of South Africa. Cape Town: Readers Digest Association, 1992. [554pp.]

Reitz, Deneys. Commando. Johannesburg: Johnathan Ball, 1990. [A Boer journal of the Boer War; 320pp., pb., 28^{00} (reg. 31^{00}) + P&H; Hb., 41^{00} (reg. 46^{00}) + P&H.]

Rosenthal, Eric. Encyclopaedia of Southern Africa. London: Frederick Warne & Co., 1967. [638pp.]

Snyman, Adriaan. Words of a Prophet: Visions of Seer van Rensburg. Mossel Bay: Vaandel, 2005. [344pp.]

Supreme Court of South Africa. The State v. Nelson Mandela et al. Transvaal Provincial Division, 1963-64, Indictment.

Todd, Pamela and Fordham, David. Private Tucker's Boer War Diary. London: Elm Tree London, 1980. [192pp.]

Young, Francis Brett. The City of Gold. London: Mayflower, 1971. [A novel of Johannesburg; 539pp.]

Wilcox, John. The Horns of the Buffalo. London: Headline, 2004. [A novel; 406pp., pb., 10^{00} + P&H.]

Witton, Lt. George. Bushveldt Carbineers: The War Against the Boers in South Africa and the 'Breaker' Morant Incident. 2008 Edition. U.K.: Leonaur LTD. [228pp., Hb., 29^{00} + P&H; pb., 18^{00} + P&H; originally, Scapegoats of the Empire. Melbourne: D.W. Paterson, 1907. Also available free online at "Project Gutenberg."] ["The Breaker" Morant/"Bulala" Taylor affair, written by one of the accused in their trial.]

Wright, Esmond. An Illustrated History of the Modern World. London: Chancellor Press, 1984. [494pp.]

Leigh, Maxwell. Touring in South Africa. Cape Town: Struik, 1995. [A field guide; 192pp.]

Further Recommended Reading

- Battle For Rhodesia (1967), Douglas Reed (1967), 150pp. Hb., 20^{00} + P&H.
- The Boer Fight For Freedom (1902), Michael Davitt, M.P. 600+pp., plastic comb-bound; 35^{00} + P&H. (Witnessed war first hand, wrote this book & resigned from Parliament in protest.)
- Cecil Rhodes: Man and Empire-Maker (1918), Princess Catherine Radziwill, 176pp., pb., 17^{00} + P&H.
- Gentile Folly: The Rothschilds (1940), Arnold Leese, 68pp., 5^{00} + P&H.
- The Great Boer War (1900), Sir A.C. Doyle, 524pp., pb., 28^{00} (reg. 33^{00}) + P&H. (From a British perspective)
- The Hapless Boers (1940), Eugene Vroom, 51pp., 5^{00} + P&H.
- History of Great Boer Trek and Origin of South African Republics (1899), Hon. Henry Cloete, LL.D., (SBS), xxiv/196pp., plastic comb-bound, computer-enhanced edition; 20^{00} + P&H.
- A Martyr Speaks: Journal of Late Corporal John Alan Coley [of the Rhodesian Light Infantry, died 1975, age of 25} (His journal of experiences in Rhodesia and South Africa.) 246pp., pb., 8^{00} + P&H.
- A Policeman's Narrative of Witchcraft and Murder in Zimbabwe, Henry Alfred Clark, 163pp., pb., (Out of print; used copies possibly available)
- The Story of the Nations: South Africa (1894), George McCall Theal, D.Litt., LL.D., 452pp., 8.5x11 (2x2 xerox), plastic comb-bound; 22^{50} + P&H.
- Uncovering the Mysteries of Your Hidden Inheritance, Robert Alan Balaicius, 197pp., well illustrated; pb., 16^{00} + P&H; Hb., 26^{00} + P&H; [Shows the common origin,

history, and ancient Biblical roots of the European peoples (which has been kept hidden from them) in great detail from earliest times (Scythians, Saxons, Germans, Netherlanders, Celts, Franks, Scandinavians, Brythons, Balts, Slavs, etc.)] This book is highly recommended to those scholars and readers seeking the true origins and hidden heritage of our people.

(Available also in Afrikaans and Danish; inquire for more information).

- For STP's complete catalog of 6,000+ titles (including hundreds of rare reprinted titles, many of which are available nowhere else), send USD5^{00} + P&H.

MAP 1
The Great Trek
c.1830-1850

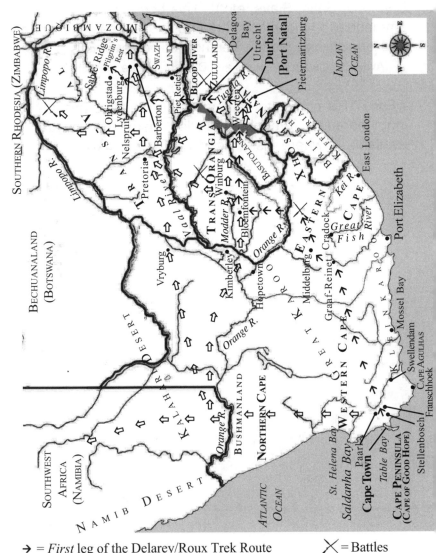

→ = *First* leg of the Delarey/Roux Trek Route
⇢ = *Second* leg of the Roux Trek Route
⇨ = Routes taken by other Voortrekkers
▲▲▲ = Drakensberg ("Dragon Mountains")

✕ = Battles

[Note: Geographic places on this map are approximations, not exact.]

MAP 2

BATTLES IN NATAL

✕ = Anglo or Boer vs. Zulu battles

✕ = Anglo vs. Boer battles

[Note: Geographic places on this map are approximations, not exact.]

MAP 3
Newer Settlements and Infrastructure in South Africa
c.1850-1903

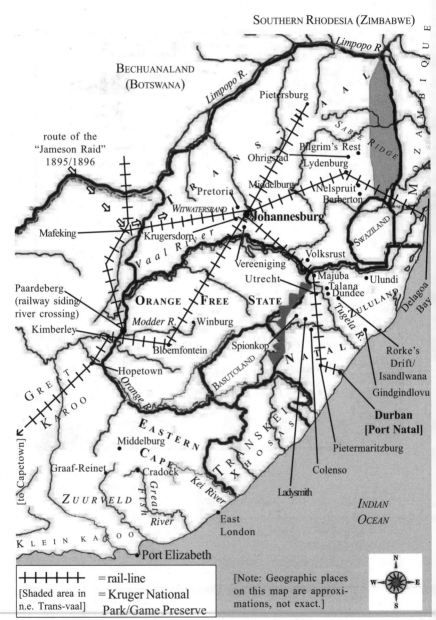

SOUTHERN RHODESIA (ZIMBABWE)

Limpopo R.

BECHUANALAND
(BOTSWANA)

Limpopo R.

Pietersburg

SABIE RIDGE

route of the
"Jameson Raid"
1895/1896

Pilgrim's Rest

Ohrigstad
Lydenburg

TRANSVAAL

Pretoria

Middelburg

Nelspruit
Barberton

MOZAMBIQUE

WITWATERSRAND

Johannesburg

Mafeking

Krugersdorp

SWAZILAND

Vaal River

Vereeniging

Volksrust

Utrecht

Majuba
Talana
Dundee

Ulundi

Delagoa Bay

Paardeberg
(railway siding/
river crossing)

ORANGE FREE STATE

Modder R. Winburg

Kimberley

Bloemfontein

Spionkop

ZULULAND

Tugela R.

NATAL

Rorke's
Drift/
Isandlwana

Gindgindlovu

Hopetown

Orange R.

BASUTOLAND

GREAT KAROO

[to Capetown]

Durban
[Port Natal]

TRANSKEI XHOSAS

Pietermaritzburg

EASTERN CAPE

Middelburg

Graaf-Reinet Cradock

Great Fish River

Kei River

Colenso

Ladysmith

ZUURVELD

KLEIN KAROO

East
London

INDIAN
OCEAN

Port Elizabeth

┼┼┼┼┼┼ = rail-line
[Shaded area in   = Kruger National
n.e. Trans-vaal]   Park/Game Preserve

[Note: Geographic places
on this map are approxi-
mations, not exact.]

N
W · E
S